KINGS CROSS

Louis Nowra is a playwright, novelist,
screenwriter and non-fiction writer.

TO MANDY

A BIOGRAPHY

LOUIS NOWRA

NEWSOUTH

A NewSouth book

Published by
NewSouth Publishing
University of New South Wales Press Ltd
University of New South Wales
Sydney NSW 2052
AUSTRALIA
newsouthpublishing.com

National Library of Australia Cataloguing-in-Publication entry
    Author: Nowra, Louis, 1950–
    Title: Kings Cross: a biography / Louis Nowra.
    ISBN: 9781742233260 (pbk)
    ISBN: 9781742241562 (ePub/Kindle)
    ISBN: 9781742246550 (ePDF)
    Notes: Includes bibliographical references.
    Subjects: Kings Cross (N.S.W.) – Social life and customs – Anecdotes.
    Kings Cross (N.S.W.) – History.
    Sydney (N.S.W.) – Social life and customs.
Dewey Number: 994.41

Design Sandy Cull, gogoGingko
Printer Griffin Press
Cover image Shutterstock
This book is printed on paper using fibre supplied from plantation or sustainably managed forests.

Extracts from 'Five Bells', 'Gardens in the Sky', 'Life at the Cross' and 'William Street' reproduced
courtesy of Paul Slessor and the publisher Tom Thompson, ETT Imprint.

Australian Government

This project has been assisted by the Australian Government through the Australia Council for the
Arts, its arts funding and advisory body.

CONTENTS

In the building you live in: notice how unfamiliar things may come to seem as a result of taking staircase B instead of staircase A, or of going up to the fifth floor when you live on the second ... In apartment buildings in general: look closely at them; look upwards; look for the name of the architect, the name of the contractor, the date when it was built ... in the case of a new building, try to remember what was there before.

GEORGES PEREC:

Species of Spaces/Especes d'espaces

The third, and most intriguing ... is the interzone – which is neither office nor street. The zone where everything is permitted that is not forbidden.

IAIN SINCLAIR:

Lights Out for the Territory

AUTHOR'S NOTE

ONE OF THE FEATURES OF KINGS CROSS is how many name changes it has undergone. Once the area was known as Woolloomooloo Heights, Mill Hill, Darlinghurst, Queen's Cross, then King's Cross, and by the middle 1930s the apostrophe was being left out.

Kings Cross Road was formerly Woolcott Street, and before that Upper William Street South. Other roads have vanished during the building of the railway station and the tunnel. Nightclubs and hotels have changed their names. Even recently locals would call the Mansions Hotel by its old name, the Hotel Mansions. Clubs and nightspots frequently changed addresses. The Pink Pussycat shifted from 86 Darlinghurst Road down to 38a after the building was demolished in 1970s to make way for the Hyatt Kingsgate. A striptease club like the Staccato had several different addresses. As for the addresses of illegal casinos, they changed constantly, even if the name stayed the same. Because of all these variables I have tried to stick to the most well-known addresses and names. I have on occasion changed the names of people to protect their privacy or reputation.

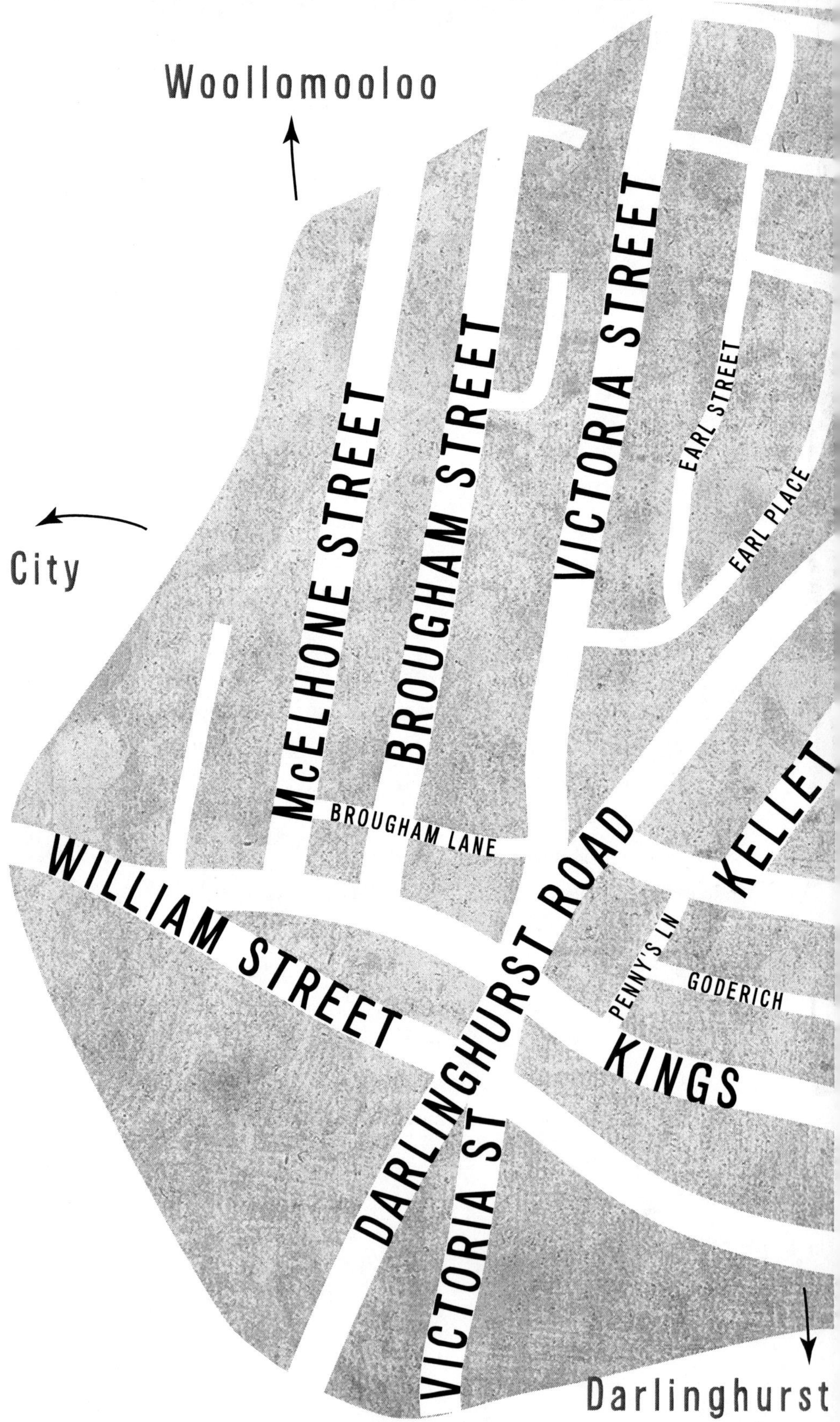
Woolloomooloo
City
McELHONE STREET
BROUGHAM STREET
VICTORIA STREET
EARL STREET
EARL PLACE
BROUGHAM LANE
WILLIAM STREET
DARLINGHURST ROAD
KELLET
PENNY'S LN
GODERICH
KINGS
DARLINGHURST
VICTORIA ST
Darlinghurst

Rushcutters Bay
HUGHES STREET
GREENKNOWE AVENUE
ORWELL STREET
MACLEAY ST
ROSLYN STREET
AVENUE
KELLETT LANE
STREET
WARD
ROSLYN GARDENS
BAYSWATER RD
LANE
CROSS ROAD
CRAIGEND STREET

I WAS ON A BUS VISITING KINGS CROSS for the first time when a woman pulled a knife on me. It was the late 1970s and I had just shifted to Sydney from Melbourne and was going to see my agent, whose offices were on Darlinghurst Road. As the bus was labouring up William Street through the stultifying humidity of a summer's morning, I was excited to be going to a place I only knew from newspaper reports and television which emphasised its danger and moral baseness, always prefacing its name with adjectives like *notorious, red light district, squalid, the dirty half mile, sleazy* and *sinful*. If I knew anything about Kings Cross it was that its name was shorthand for brothels, street walkers, junkies, gangsters, strippers, police corruption, the desperate and a neon jungle of depravity.

I had been gazing out the window at dreary William Street, with its bland office buildings, tacky take-away shops and car showrooms shimmering in the heat when, out of the corner of my eye, I glimpsed an old woman in a heavy coat with a sheen of perspiration on her forehead muttering to herself a few seats from mine. At the stop halfway up the street the handful of passengers, except for the old lady, hurried off the bus. As it started off again I noticed she was now standing in the aisle, a handbag draped over one arm and brandishing a carving knife in the other hand. She was talking to herself, saying repeatedly, in a quiet determined mantra, 'I'm going to kill you.'

My body stiffened and I felt a prickle of fear course through me. I thought of jumping up and pulling the cord to warn the driver what was happening, but I was afraid that any sudden action would direct her attention to me.

She snapped out of her self-absorption and turned to the front of the bus and yelled out to the driver, 'I'm going to kill you!' He didn't seem to hear and, as she advanced down the aisle, she continued to shout her threat. This time he heard her because I saw his eyes widen in his rear-vision mirror. They registered confusion and then terror. The bus began to gather speed, as much as it could, and it lumbered asthmatically towards the top of the hill.

Then the old woman slowly turned, as if she sensed my presence for the first time. She stared at me as if trying to decide whether I were real or not and started down the aisle towards me. There was nowhere for me to run or hide. She stopped two metres away and pointed the blade at me, saying nothing.

I heard the bus gears clank loudly, the horn beeping and, as it rounded sharply to the left, the old woman, put off balance by the sudden turn into Darlinghurst Road, toppled over into one of the seats. The horn was now blasting constantly as the driver weaved his way in and out of the traffic. The woman pulled herself up into a sitting position with considerable effort. She was now furious with the driver, shouting at him to slow down. When he took no notice she stood up again and waved the knife at me.

'I'm going to kill you and then that idiot driver,' she threatened.

The bus swerved to avoid an oncoming car and the woman keeled over again. It picked up pace along flat Darlinghurst Road, the driver thumping the horn. Then it turned a hard right and suddenly braked to a stop. I was jolted backwards. The front door hissed open and the driver jumped out, shouting for the police.

In his hurry to flee he hadn't released the rear door. The old woman stood up and I realised it would be impossible to get past her to the front. I sat still, hoping not to be noticed. I could hear the driver yelling out, *'She's in there! She's got a knife!'*

The old woman peered out the window and then hurriedly stuffed the weapon into her handbag. A policeman stepped into the bus. He glanced at me at the back and then at the old woman sitting halfway down.

'Not again, Shirley,' he sighed. 'Come on, out you come,' he said with the smile of someone who had been through this many times before, and held out his hand. She got up and, looking like a mild-mannered grandmother, meekly handed over her handbag. He stepped aside to allow her to pass and opened the handbag. He shook his head on seeing the knife and looked across at me. 'She's actually harmless,' he said, amused by my predicament and no doubt my shocked expression.

The driver had stopped the bus outside Fitzroy Gardens. I stepped out, wobbly from the tension, and walked back along Darlinghurst Road to my agent's office. The entrance to number 49 was a narrow doorway. Standing beside it, as if guarding the entrance, was a mini-skirted woman in her thirties with a hard face that her heavy make-up and vivid pink lipstick couldn't hide.

'Would you like a lady?' she asked. I didn't reply and attempted to get past her. 'You'll get a good time for your money,' she added, with a touch of desperation.

'Look,' I said helplessly, 'I'm here to see my agent. I'm a writer.' She took a step back.

'A writer …' she said, shaking her head, irritated she had wasted her time on someone who obviously had no money. I squeezed past her and walked up the dark narrow steps with their frayed dank carpet and into the reception.

It was only later when I was on a bus heading back down William Street that I realised I was exhilarated by what had happened with the crazed woman and being importuned by a prostitute because the incidents confirmed what I had heard and read about Kings Cross. It was a dangerous place, physically and morally.

My agent shifted offices to Surry Hills soon afterwards and I seldom went to the Cross and when I did I found it tawdry of a daytime and aggressive of a night, with menacing bouncers, insistent spruikers, persistent hookers and drug overdoses, one of which I remember vividly because a man and a woman collapsed into a coma in front of me outside a take-away shop. It was only in 1990 that I shifted into the Cross after a relationship broke down (a not uncommon reason for men and women to come and live in the area). I rented a room in a house in Brougham Street near the Butler Stairs, then later an apartment in Ithaca Road. I was to buy an apartment in Oceana, at the end of Elizabeth Bay Road, then at the turn of the millennium I rented a flat in Kellett Street and finally I bought an apartment near the top of William Street a decade ago, where I am writing this.

Gradually I began to appreciate the complexity of Kings Cross's human interactions and streetscapes, the stunning juxtapositions of beauty and ugliness, its tolerance and its almost arrogant sense that it is markedly different from the rest of the community. At times it has been dangerous (ice addicts can be irrationally violent) but that's unusual. I have watched it undergo several transformations, as it in turn changed me, making me less judgmental, more fascinated by the almost Dickensian range of characters and ways of living.

Over time the Cross has become a giant palimpsest for me. I'm conscious that every house, apartment block or shop has a history of reinvention and change. Streets, roads and lanes have vanished to be replaced by tunnels, malls or new thoroughfares; cafés have become sex shops, strip clubs have been transformed into internet hubs, a pinball parlour has become an injecting centre, dim perilous lanes have been turned into gaudy restaurant precincts, nightclubs have segued into newsagents, hotels have been converted into swish apartments and bordellos into cafés.

It is the most densely populated area in Australia, with residents who range from the wealthy to the underclass, people who live in some of the most exquisite examples of art deco buildings or sleep on the streets. Famous people have lived in the Cross and others have become famous by living there. Backpackers, junkies, whores, strippers, chefs, mad men, beggars, booksellers, doctors, musicians, writers, gangsters, druggies, dealers, eccentrics, judges and artists live side by side. It has one of the most diverse and tolerant communities in Australia.

For decades it was the safety valve for our society and at the forefront of Australian social and cultural change. Its name has become shorthand for any vice you care to mention.

But how to tell its extraordinary story? I've taken what I call a prismatic approach, believing that a biography of the Cross cannot be aptly undertaken just through a chronological history. The area is not one for cars, so unconsciously or consciously long-term residents have become flâneurs, with an intimate knowledge of its streets and people. And it seems to me that the history of the place is also one of how flâneurs experienced it. So I have written chapters on the various routes to provide a street-level history of the area.

I am also making a claim that the history of Australia is impossible to imagine without acknowledging the contribution of Kings Cross to modernity, the art of living in high rise apartments, and how it provided a refuge for those whose behaviour, ideas, ethnicity and sense of morality was, for many decades, at odds with mainstream Australian society and culture. The third strand of the book is based on a series of themes and subjects that add an extra resonance and understanding of the Cross.

Kings Cross's history has been one of reinvention and transformations and, at times, the cataclysmic demolition of whole streets, but it has always managed to maintain its own singular identity; that is, up until now. The social changes of the past decade are permanently altering the Cross. This book is driven by a sense of urgency to record its history, to illustrate its importance and how it has affected my own life.

THEY'VE COME
TO STAY

WHEN I WALK UP TO KINGS CROSS from the city I am conscious that my route down Market Street, through Hyde Park, past St Mary's Cathedral and then up the hill to the top of the ridge, was originally a path made by the Cadigal people, whose territory ranged from South Head to the Petersham area. They used what was just a track through the woods to cross over the ridge and head towards the eastern beaches.

The Cadigal were one of a number of bands that are loosely referred to as the Eora. They inhabited the land around what was to be called Port Jackson and lived primarily on the catch from the harbour. Men speared fish from rocks and women fished using a hook and line from a simple bark canoe. Their dwellings were caves and sandstone overhangs.

Before 1788 the harbour foreshores were galleries of paintings and engravings. Rock paintings were on the walls and ceilings of overhangs in and around Sydney. Among the prominent subjects were fish, whales and sharks. The importance of fish to the lives of the Eora is plain to see. There are few carvings of birds, but fish represent about a quarter of the petroglyphs around the harbour. There were probably about 1500 Aborigines in the Port Jackson area when the First Fleet landed at Sydney Cove; of these there were about fifty to sixty Cadigals, but after a smallpox epidemic in

1789, only a handful were thought to have remained alive (there is some evidence that a number of Cadigals may have escaped the epidemic and settled in Concord).

For the first three years of white settlement the Aborigines kept their distance from the invaders, believing they were ghosts or reincarnations of their dead. But by late 1790 the Eora had come to the conclusion that the British had come to stay. Attracted by free food, especially bread and tea, alcohol and blankets, Aborigines from the far north shore and the south poured into the colony. As one colonist remarked of their numbers, 'The people can scarcely keep them out of their houses in daytime.' Of the remaining three Cadigals, David Collins, the Judge-Advocate of the First Fleet, wrote that they 'found themselves compelled to unite with some other tribe, not only for their personal protection, but to prevent the extinction of their tribe'.

There is a lack of information to determine what relationship the Cadigal had with the ridge that threads its way from Potts Point right through Darlinghurst to Waverley, though it's thought that the word *Carrajeen* (or *Carragin*) was Elizabeth Bay, *Derawun* was Potts Point, and Garden Island, *Ba-ing-hoe*. Given that the Eora seldom wore clothing, it's hard to imagine them living on the peninsula outcrop because, as everyone who lives in Kings Cross knows, the strong late afternoon winds can be bitterly cold and decidedly unpleasant even when one is rugged up. There is little evidence of rock carvings or occupation of the area. There are reports of rock engravings in Potts Point but, of course, they've been built over.

In 2000 two Aborigines protested against the Kings Cross injecting centre on the grounds it was an Aboriginal burial ground. They presented no evidence but I think this belief can be traced back to the early attempts to discover the original meaning of Woolloomooloo. In *Our Antipodes* (1846) Lieutenant-Colonel

Mundy suggested that Woolloomooloo 'is merely a corruption of *wala mala*, the Aboriginal term for *the place of tombs* and that it was an old burial place of the blacks.' This may have been true but it would apply more to the present area of Woolloomooloo Bay than the sandstone escarpment, where digging graves would have been much more demanding.

But the meaning and pronunciation of Woolloomooloo has many theories and spellings. At the time of Governor Phillip, the Eora called the area 'Walla-bah-mullah' which may have meant a black male kangaroo; others thought it described a good place to fish. There were many variations on the way to spell it, from Walloomoola to Wallamullah. There was also the theory that the place the Aborigines called 'Woollooh-moolloh' was the name of a whirlpool, whirlwind or anything whirling around, and was used to denote the sounds of windmills along what became Woolloomooloo Hill. By 1864 a reporter for the *Sydney Morning Herald* could come to no firm conclusion how the name came about, writing that, 'Some future topographer may, perhaps, unravel the knotty question.'

One of the fascinating aspects of the social and cultural interactions between the natives and the British was how the Aborigines came from afar to display their fighting prowess to the whites. These battles and duels were attended by hundreds of spectators, who appreciated the skill, daring and bravery of the warriors. One memorable event was held in March 1804 when four men from south of Jervis Bay who, the *Sydney Gazette* reported, 'were of hideous Aspect, wore frightful beards, and hitherto were estranged to every race but their own' staged a grand battle at 'Wooloomoola' (Woolloomooloo).

Whether this was on the 100 acres granted to Mr Commissary John Palmer in 1793 is unknown, but Palmer's land began at Woolloomooloo Bay (for years called Palmer's Cove) and stretched as far as present day Albion Street, Surry Hills, and from Hyde Park to the present Forbes Street, Darlinghurst. He established a model farm of five acres (which included a vineyard) and built a fine house.

Lachlan Macquarie was sworn in as Governor in 1810, intending to stay for only three or four years but continuing until replaced by Governor Brisbane in 1821. When he arrived he found the colony 'barely emerging from an infantile imbecility', the public buildings in ruins, the town devastated by rum, the educational system practically non-existent and the people morally debased. In transforming Sydney he paid particular attention to the Eora, believing that the way for them to survive was to adjust to European ways. As part of this process he opened the first school for Aborigines.

In 1820 Macquarie chanced on the inlet next to Woolloomooloo Bay and christened it Elizabeth Bay in honour of his wife (like a narcissistic Adam he set about naming roads, rivers, islands and harbours after himself and his spouse). He thought the bay was perfect for his experiment in establishing a native village. Two years later he visited 'the native town' with his wife and son. By this stage his plan of 'civilising the adult natives' was in earnest. He had built for them a neat row of huts in the European style erected on high ground on a sheltered beach. Each hut had a small garden and there was also an orchard. There was a special fishing boat and salt and casks to preserve the fish. A convict servant lived on site to teach the Aborigines how to cultivate the soil. A month later Macquarie and his family returned for a breakfast with a 'few select Friends at Elizabeth Town, the Native Village, where we have established the Sydney Tribe ... We also treated 42 Natives to Breakfast and Tobacco.'

It all seemed to be going well. A road was built to Elizabeth Bay and on Sunday afternoons locals would drive out to gawk at the natives. Governor Macquarie believed he could make farmers or mechanics out of them but it didn't happen. Not long after Macquarie's visit the Aborigines demolished the huts to use as fuel or the sheets of bark were taken to Sydney to be exchanged for bread and drink. The gardener's position was abolished. The remaining Eora, who had borne the initial brunt of the arrival of the first Europeans, survived by fishing, bartering their catch for cast-off clothes, tobacco and, the most pernicious product of all, rum.

In 1825 Mr Justice Field wrote that it was useless to force and cajole Aborigines into European ways: 'They will not serve, and they are too indolent and poor in spirit to become masters ... They bear themselves erect, and address you with confidence, always with good humour, and often with grace. They are not common beggars, although they accept of our carnal things in return for the fish and oysters, which are almost all we have left them for their support ... They are carriers of news and fish; the gossips of the town, the loungers on the quay. They know everybody; and understand the nature of everybody's business, although they have none of their own – but this.'

The Eora gradually disappeared from around Sydney. Up along the ridge the Aboriginal presence was stronger on the southern side of what is now William Street, especially on Barcom Glen, the huge 75-acre estate of Thomas West, an emancipist carpenter who was the first European to settle between Oxford Street and Rushcutters Bay, utilising the water that ran through the valleys into the bay to power a watermill for milling grain. West's land extended from around the present site of St Vincent's Hospital to Rushcutters Bay. According to West's son, Obed, the land running down to Rushcutters Bay was a camping place for the blacks, particularly the slope on the Darlinghurst side. In the 1830s and 1840s West's estate was covered with bush and large gum trees. In Arthur Dowling's reminiscences, the bush was 'The resort of semi-civilised aboriginals, chiefly half-caste, where they formed a large camp, which was a nuisance to the neighbourhood.'

In *On Darlinghurst Hill*, John O'Brien, writing about the mid-nineteenth century, contends that, 'Along the ridge towards Kings Cross blacks were camped ... the Aborigines were numerous enough then, and continued so in places further out for some years.' If it's true, then this was not so much the Eora reclaiming their traditional ground as confirming their existence as fringe dwellers and drifters. This was a way of life forced on them, as the explorer and surveyor Thomas Mitchell realised very soon after arriving in Sydney in 1827. He pointed out there was scarcely a spot near Sydney or on the shores of Port Jackson where an Aborigine could camp without intruding on private property. But like many Europeans of the time, Mitchell believed that the relentless approach of civilisation meant the gradual extinction of the Aborigines and the only way they could survive was by assimilation.

Gwara was the Cadigal word for wind and it was one of the few sources of energy during the first years of the settlement. An early problem for the settlers was the grinding of wheat into flour. The answer was the humble windmill. The first one was erected on York Street in 1797 and a decade later there were seven windmills operating around Sydney. As anybody who has lived in Kings Cross knows, the early morning and late afternoon winds that rush up from the harbour can be robust enough to push you over, as I have seen happen to old people and toddlers (I witnessed one old woman's fall under the Coca-Cola sign turn into an undignified cartwheel). It was obvious then that the ridge was a logical site for windmills as the settlement gradually expanded eastwards.

Eventually out of the nineteen windmills in Sydney, six were in the Kings Cross and Darlinghurst areas. There were two windmills close together where Roslyn Street joins Darlinghurst Road.

Thomas Barker built the first one in 1826, which was soon followed by one constructed and owned by a French-born convict, Francois Girard, who had arrived in 1820. Both Barker and Girard became wealthy from their flour milling. The two windmills were such prominent fixtures in the landscape that Macleay Street, formerly Woolloomooloo Road, was commonly known as Mill Hill Road.

Another mill was erected near Craigend Street and a couple more along the ridge. A Joseph Fowles painting of the late 1840s shows a half a dozen windmills along the ridge like a bucolic scene in the English countryside. Just before he died in 1902, Judge James Dowling, whose father built the splendid mansion Brougham Lodge in the 1830s, reminisced about the mills: 'They were picturesque features of the district, and equally so whether the sails were in a quiescent state or yielding to favouring winds.' The last of the windmills were demolished in the late 1860s, but by then Woolloomooloo Hill had changed beyond recognition.

DONCASTER HALL

DONCASTER HALL IS NEAR THE TOP of William Street. I've lived for over a decade in this seven-storey building constructed in 1922, when it was one of the tallest in Kings Cross. Its facade is topped by two A-shaped turrets which have wrought-iron Juliet balconies. Joining the turrets together is a roof of ochre-coloured terracotta tiles in the Spanish Mission style, hinting that the interior has a similar romantic Spanish influence, but the reality is that the building is a basic box structure with two flats on the ground and top floors and four per storey, making a total of twenty-four apartments. The mortar between the bricks that make up the facade is host to ferns and grasses. The rooftop has glorious 360-degree views far across to the North Shore and south to the airport.

The long foyer has faux stucco yellowish-white walls and a polished terrazzo floor that is cold and uninviting. It's so narrow that it's barely wide enough for two people to walk side by side. You can tell that there is a considerable turnover of tenants by the always full return-to-sender box, which is bigger than the residents' mailboxes. The lift is the original Otis, featuring a clattering concertina gate and an outer half-door you have to slam to make sure that the lock is firmly in place. It's so temperamental that residents like me take the bare concrete stairs, having been stranded in it once too often when it's broken down. There have been numerous cases of our geriatric tenants being stuck for up to half a day waiting to be freed. Sometimes the capricious lift stops temptingly near a landing and many of us, especially in the early hours of the morning, when a lack of sobriety has made us reckless and impatient, have pulled open the door and squeezed out through a small gap onto the landing, risking decapitation if the lift had suddenly started up again.

I don't use the lift ever since one early Sunday morning I was stuck in it. Realising that a repairer would not be available for hours I had no way of escaping except to smash the lift window. The problem was that it was only the size of a tabloid newspaper. But, given I had had many glasses of wine at the annual Kings Cross ball, it seemed possible. I grabbed hold of two bars on the ceiling and swung myself at the window, smashing it with my boots. I gingerly plucked the rest of the broken glass from its frame and, grabbing the bars again, swung myself out, managing in one miraculous (i.e. accidental) movement to pass through the small rectangle and land on my feet on the landing, spooking a jittery ice-addled Ted, a hulking barman who had just come up the stairs because the lift didn't work.

The creaking of the lift door opening and the echoing bang of it closing can easily be heard inside the apartments, so you always know when someone is arriving on your landing. However, I can barely hear it from my desk, which is in a small enclosed balcony out at the front of my third-storey flat. The wooden window frames of my study are rotting and the sulphur-crested cockatoos have taken so much of the grouting that when it rains water leaks onto my desk and papers. Although it has to be said the cockatoos haven't caused as much damage as they have in the nearby art deco buildings of Elizabeth Bay, where residents have tried to get rid of them using flashing lights, rubber snakes, spikes on sills, mirrors on windows, water pistols and hoses.

A whisper of a woman in her eighties, with cheaply dyed red hair the airy texture of fairy floss, took delight in feeding the cockatoos, but if she was late the manic birds would fill in the time by knocking their beaks on the front windows of the other apartments to get attention and food, and if it didn't eventuate they'd revenge themselves by ripping out the grouting keeping the glass in the window frames. The bird-woman's eccentricities developed into the daffiness of senility, and when she was found wandering the streets of the Cross in her dressing gown once too often, she was placed in a nursing home, the cockatoos lingering around our windows noisily demanding to be fed before thankfully vanishing for good.

In my years residing in Doncaster Hall – its name proudly displayed on the glass above the front doors in black 1920s typeface – I have seen many people come and go. It's an apartment block that has gradually declined from being one of the most glamorous in the 1920s and 1930s to something decrepit or even seedy. The electrical wiring is the original and is badly frayed and dangerously shrunken. The plumbing and pipes are so arduous to get to and fix that plumbers refuse to work here. The levies are so low that it is too expensive to incorporate new wiring, pipes and tubes into the structure of the building and so they are simply attached to the walls, the worst example being a large heavy metal pipe, the diameter of a dinner plate, running the length of the foyer. The variously coloured wiring, tubes and metal pipes seem like a primitive artist's attempt to pay homage to the Pompidou Centre. And each new cable, pipe, tube or piece of plumbing added to the walls only devalues the building even more.

The building has an abjectness, a sense of irrevocable decline, as if it is exhausted and patiently waiting to be demolished. This is not a place to aspire to any more, which is probably why most of its tenants are transients who will go on either to fulfil their aspirations or become life's losers. In other words, Doncaster Hall is not the new Cross with its brand new apartments peopled with young professionals, but a reminder of the old Cross that was also home to the bohemian, the desperate, the resigned, the transient and the weird.

When I first shifted in I lived on the fourth floor directly above my partner's apartment (Mandy and I married later). It was at the rear of Doncaster Hall, which meant I had spectacular views from my balcony overlooking the harbour, its majestic bridge, the curvaceous Opera House and the soft green napkin of the Domain, a stark contrast to the spiky horizon of Sydney's CBD rising behind it.

Down below the rear of the building is Brougham Lane, a conduit connecting Woolloomooloo to the Cross. It's a popular thoroughfare. Its narrow pathway between two high buildings creates a natural amphitheatre so you can hear the most intimate conversations and the most violent, the sounds of slurred curses and vomiting, the agony and ecstasy of drug-addled minds and, of a day, mothers chatting to their children as they wheel their prams up the lane.

Brougham Lane leads up from the dimly lit McElhone Street, through the shadows and pale light cast by a couple of street lamps, into dazzling, neon-drenched Darlinghurst Road. The lane reeks of urine and is a favourite place for police to catch drug dealers, because they can easily block off both ends. It's also an artery for the Housing Commission tenants of Woolloomooloo to come up to the Cross. You can tell they're from the 'Loo by their vocabulary, which is not only limited, but which makes use of 'fuck' as a verb, noun and adjective. The word 'cunt' is used as a modifier and for emphasis. The squalid reputation of the lane has been a feature of the Cross for over seventy years.

From the beginning it has been a perfect lonely place to seek revenge. In the 1920s there was a shoot-out in the lane that left one man dead. H.C. Brewster, author of *Kings Cross Calling*, first published in 1945, recounts an incident one night a few years before in Brougham Lane when a gangster was found dead, 'victim of a vengeance perhaps expected and long dreaded'. I had been living in the flat for only a couple of months when I heard several shots, followed by screams of agony and groaning. Two men had been kneecapped. Before they were put in an ambulance, a detective asked them who had shot them. 'We didn't see nothink,' said one wounded oaf, conforming to the perverse honour code of the habitual criminal.

One night I heard a furious man turn on his girlfriend, yelling at her, 'All right, if you think he's so fucking hot, why don't you go back to the pub then?' There was a pause and she answered defiantly, 'I will then.' I heard her hurry off, her high heels clicking and clacking on the asphalt like badly played castanets. He must have been surprised his brinkmanship didn't work because I heard him chasing after her: 'Hey, wait! Where do you think you're going?'

Sometimes there are the ghastly sounds of a woman's uncontrollable weeping and a male voice shouting, 'Shut up, bitch!'

The language can be obscene and shrill and very different from the conversations Brewster overheard in 1940s, such as this one between an Australian girl and an American sailor: 'It's marriage I want and nothing less ... and I've got a right to expect it. You can't play fast and loose with every girl you meet.'

The lane is also a testimony to the mercurial effects of alcohol. Early in the evening couples are jolly, near midnight the drink makes the girls giggly and loud, the men boisterous, but in the early hours of the morning comes the crying of women (*You fucking bastard!*), the shouts of the men (*You fucking cunt!*) and shrieks of despair as the drunken men thump drunken women. Near dawn are the more urgent and desperate cries of both sexes when drug deals have gone wrong: *Where is the fucking money, cunt! Where's the stuff, fucker!* At times like this the voices become a Dantean Hell of hysteria, befuddlement and anger.

Mandy moved out of Doncaster Hall, because we bought an apartment for her on the other side of William Street (from where I write now I can see the rear of her apartment in winter when the liquidambar tree outside her window loses its leaves). I shifted into my present apartment in the front of the building not long afterwards. The panoramic view I once had in the rear is now reduced to a glimpse of the harbour from my living room window.

Some apartments peer into the rear of the Irish-themed pub next door. O'Malley's customers are Irish and British backpackers whose main aim seems to be to drink to excess. As an added incentive the hotel offers topless waitresses on Thursday nights, 'Sex Bomb', a dance group of six girls in bikinis, and on Friday night the barmaids wear only lingerie. One afternoon I glanced out my window and saw a naked man in his early twenties casually leaning out of the window of his hotel room wistfully smoking a cigarette, while behind him his naked mate was having sex with a dutifully moaning blonde, whom I recognised as a favourite working girl of a plump accountant who lived below me. She was in a minority of prostitutes who took on more than one man. Many times I've heard prostitutes in Darlinghurst Road say no to two men at a time. Quite simply it's too dangerous for the girls because, for some inexplicable reason, the mates egg one another on and, as one whore told me, 'Things can get out of hand.'

There have been prostitutes in the building, including two who worked to pay for their crack addictions, and a transvestite who was always accompanied by her surly pimp because she was frequently beaten up by her clients. There was also Star Delaney, another transvestite, who rented upstairs. Last year David, who lives across the landing from her, began to worry because he hadn't seen her for ten days. After knocking on her door and getting no answer, he had the police to break in. There was a suicide note, but no body. She had neatly stacked up everything in her apartment as if ready for the removalists. A policewoman asked David if Star had any identifying marks. He told her she had a tattoo of the symbol for infinity on her wrist. It didn't take long for the symbol to be matched to a body that had been plucked out of the harbour ten days before. For David that was the awful thing – no-one had come forward to say that she was missing, except for him.

'She was unhappy a lot of the time,' a devastated David told me a few days later as we passed from the foyer into William Street.

There were also examples of just how Kings Cross can, in a short time, destroy your life. A 22-year-old girl rented a room across the landing from me. When she came to live in Doncaster Hall she was a vivacious attractive blonde who worked as a barrister's personal assistant in the city. In a few short months she began to lose weight until there was no mistaking her anorexia. Her face, once clear and fresh, became splotchy and pinched. Her ice addition made her unreliable. She was fired from her job. In the early hours of the morning I'd hear her vacuuming in a frenzy of cleaning. One night I smelt smoke and rushed out to find that she was burning her mattress on the landing. I stamped it out while she watched with complete indifference. When I asked her why she had set fire to her mattress, she grinned and said, with some satisfaction, 'Because it was dirty.' She didn't stay long after that. I saw her once more and that was in Bayswater Road. She was gaunt and sick-looking with scarlet lipstick that was smeared over her lips and bleeding down the sides of her mouth. It was obvious she was on the game. It was also clear that she didn't have long to live.

Although there are many transient tenants, those of the older generation who own their apartments have lived here for years. Gladys, who was in the apartment directly above me, was in her late seventies when I shifted in. She had been there since 1944. She had a walking frame and her bent back made her look like a dwarf hunchback. Once when I was holding the front door open for her as she made her laborious exit into William Street, her handbag securely tied to her Zimmer frame for fear of it being snatched (even that precaution did not stop it from being stolen by a junkie one day just outside the building), I asked her if she were a widow. She shook her head and looked up at me with some effort: 'I went out with a Pommy during the war. He did the dirty on me. That was enough of Pommies and men for me.'

She began to hear noises and thought I was causing them. She'd thump her walking frame against my door and when I'd open it she'd accuse me of making her life a misery. I'd allow her to come in and inspect my apartment to see that I wasn't making the noise, but she didn't believe me. One morning she demanded I come up to her flat and experience what she was hearing. I expected her apartment to be cluttered and smelly with old age, but it was neat and clean, with many framed photographs of relatives proudly displayed on the mantelpiece. I stood in the middle of the living room but heard nothing from underneath. She asked me to take my shoes off so I could feel the noise. When I said I felt nothing she ordered me to lie on one of two single beds in her bedroom. I lay on one but still could hear nothing. She was furious with me, certain of my mendacity.

Her anger towards me continued to grow and then one day she disappeared. I thought she had died, but I met her in the foyer several weeks later. She had been in hospital and was weaker and had shrunk even more. She lifted her head up with difficulty to face me and said sorrowfully, 'I'm sorry, Louis, those noises were in my head. You're not to blame.' She died not long afterwards. She was part of a trend of old people, once a feature of the Cross, dying and not being replaced because aged people can no longer afford to live in the area. Her apartment was later bought for a high price by a gay professional who renovated it (listening to the cacophony of his extensive renovations I felt an empathy with the deceased Gladys).

Another resident has lived here for over forty years. Theo is portly and short like his wife, who recently died of cancer. He has a choleric face, is permanently surly, a miser, humourless, and wears pyjamas of a daytime. Her personality was his direct opposite; she was charming, happy and wore brightly coloured gypsy-like dresses and never the same one twice. They owned two units in the building. I often saw them going into one of them but not the second one on the floor below, which didn't seem to have a tenant. After she died I was walking up the stairs and saw the widower open the door of the second apartment. What was inside amazed me. There were hundreds of his wife's dazzlingly coloured dresses, hanging from the ceiling, from the walls and laid out on the floor. The whole apartment was both a colossal wardrobe and a shrine to her clothes. He saw me and made his irritation clear, as if my prying eyes had desecrated his secret world. To let me know how he felt he went in, slamming the door loudly behind him.

Other tenants live secret lives that one only becomes aware of by accident. I served a time on the strata board and one day, as part of my duties on the board, I had to inspect a flat downstairs for water problems. When I knocked on the door an overweight woman in her mid-thirties wearing a semi-transparent black chiffon nightdress with black bra and panties greeted me. It seemed as if she were expecting someone else, but she invited me in. As I passed through the living room heading into the bathroom I saw that one wall was completely covered with about fifty to sixty crucifixes of all shapes and forms. A neighbour later told me that she was a dominatrix. She lives two storeys below me but I can tell when she's finished seeing a client because I can hear her vacuuming at odd hours of the night – just what she's cleaning up I don't want to imagine.

Of all the thousands of people who have passed through Doncaster Hall perhaps George Sprod was the one who cherished Kings Cross the most. He had lived in apartment one on the ground floor since 1973. He was short, stocky and wore a workingman's cloth cap. He would leave his apartment near noon. If you were in the foyer when he opened his door the stink of nicotine and stale beer violently assailed your senses. A peek inside his dark flat was enough to make one shiver. He smoked so much the original white walls had turned a grimy yellow. With tiny deliberate steps, almost as if he were telling himself to put one foot in front of the other, the eighty year old would make his way up William Street with slow methodical steps and then shuffle along Darlinghurst Road to the Sports Bar in the Crest Hotel complex where he would steadily work his way through four schooners of beer, then retrace his methodical steps back to his apartment, where he'd have a nap before venturing up the hill again to drink late into the night.

He wasn't much of a talker but he'd listen with a bemused expression as if he had seen too much in his life and nothing he heard could match what he had experienced. The residents liked him despite his occasional feral behaviour. When he was drinking at home with his best mate, Sticky, he'd keep the front door open and when they'd finish a bottle of beer they'd throw it out onto the landing, cheering when it smashed. The reason why we all cut George a lot of slack was that everyone knew he had survived the vicious brutality of the Japanese during the Second World War. He had put his age up a year so he could join the Army in 1940. A gunner in the 29th Battery, he was stationed in Singapore when the Allies surrendered to the Japanese in February 1942. Imprisonment in the POW camp at Changi was bad enough, but worse was to come when he was shipped to Thailand to work on the infamous Thailand–Burma Railway. So hideous were his experiences and those of every other Allied soldier that he thought it was a man-made catastrophe ranking only with the destruction of the Jews by the Nazis.

He remained a prisoner-of-war for three and a half years. He had lived in Woolloomooloo and was a cleaner and street photographer before joining up. In Changi he became friends with the English cartoonist Ronald Searle (creator of *St Trinian's*), and he took to cartooning. He was repatriated back in Australia late in 1945 but there was little work so he set sail for London in 1949. He soon became a regular contributor to *Punch* magazine. Malcolm Muggeridge, the editor of *Punch* at the time, wrote of Sprod's cartoons that they were 'very funny indeed ... The inherent absurdity of human life positively pleases him, and his bold line and uproarious situations convey that pleasure.' Muggeridge thought him 'enigmatic' and observed, from weekly editorial conferences at *Punch*, '[He] sits mostly silent and wearing a slightly quizzical half-smile which is very characteristic of him.'

George married once – disastrously – then in 1969 he returned alone to live in Australia, where he illustrated for the *Australian Women's Weekly* and drew cartoons for newspapers such as the *Sydney Morning Herald* and the *Sun-Herald*. He and his mate Sticky were regulars at local pubs like the Crest in Darlinghurst Road, the Hampton Court and the Kings Cross Hotel. He could be obstreperous when drunk and was banned from several hotels. One late morning I found him outside the Sports Bar pushing at the closed glass doors in total bewilderment. I told him it wasn't open because it was Good Friday. 'How come the Christians tell us when to drink?' he asked me, rubbing his stubble, coldly furious at this disruption of his daily routine.

He wrote a quirky autobiography, *Life on a Square-Wheeled Bike: the Saga of a Cartoonist*, and a volume called *Bamboo Round My Shoulder: Changi, the Lighter Side*. This is one of the most curious books to come out of the horrors of Changi and the Burma Railroad. There is no obvious bitterness towards the cruel Japanese guards. His is a gentle mockery of their toothy grins, slant eyes and bottle-thick glasses. The book is a whimsical series of skits of Australian POWs putting one over on their guards or trying to make do with the lousy food. It was typical of George, however, because unlike many others he had little room for hatred. He had seen human beings at their best and beastly worst and had come to the conclusion we are an absurd species.

His fifth and last book, self-published, was *When I Survey the Wondrous Cross: Sydney's King Cross, Ancient and Modern*. It's a genial, slim book mixing illustrations and short essays on the Cross. He quotes the poet Kenneth Slessor in order to explain his close attachment to Kings Cross, which 'will always be a tract apart from the rest of Sydney, still contemptuous of the rules, still defiantly unlike any other part of any other city in Australia'.

He was not a subtle draughtsman and his caricatures have a limited range of subject matter. His prostitutes are generally buxom, blowsy and thickly made-up and the clients are hesitant bumbling men who all look suspiciously like George. There is no doubting his fascination with the girls on the game, best summed up by a cartoon of two prostitutes waiting for customers under a sign saying *You are now entering the erogenous zone*. His Kings Cross is one of tuneless buskers, whores flaunting themselves on the balcony of the Bayswater Road terrace, the Nevada, that advertised 'Australia's Largest Bed', sailors cruising for hookers, grifters selling gaudily dressed Americans fake Swiss watches, packs of leering Japanese tourists wanting to share a whore, effeminate gay men at a hysterical loss after their handbags are stolen, butch lesbians and the ubiquitous sacred ibises fossicking through rubbish bins.

Like all writers on the Cross he was intrigued by the larger-than-life characters who defined the unique aura of the area: Beatrice 'Bea' Miles ('For sixpence she would recite you the whole of Lady Macbeth's ramblings and throw in Hamlet's soliloquy for good measure'), Rosaleen Norton ('A skilled artist, in a perversely demoniac way'), the painter William 'Our Bill' Dobell ('He was as famous as any racehorse or footy player'), Kenneth Slessor ('To him the neon lights at the top of William Street were as exciting as the Aurora Australis'), Dame Mary Gilmore ('An ornament to Kings Cross ... in view of her sterling services to education, the arts and humanity'), Ada Green ('Sydney's most indefatigable evangelist ... During the week she was to be found outside the Bank of New South Wales in Darlinghurst Road, where she needed every ounce of her rhetorical powers to cope with the crowds of yahoos, drunks, idlers and fallen women who treated with such derision her exposition of the Word of the Lord') and the actor Chips Rafferty ('... he was strolling with his wife down Macleay Street ... having enjoyed a convivial lunch ... with Hollywood film-actor Jerry Lewis, he was feeling great. Then he suddenly dropped down dead. Heart attack').

He may have been a man who kept his emotions to himself but he could be openly romantic and nostalgic about the Cross's effect on him when he was impressionable and young:

> The coffee shops where the Bohemia of Sydney sat ... The night-birds, the artists, would-be artists, actors 'resting', ex-chorus girls from the Tivoli, students from the Uni, arty-crafties ... dilating at length upon Art, Life and Love and how to get a quid without working ... swapping exotic brands of cigarettes – Turf, Craven A, Capstan – boasting of the plays they would write, symphonies they would compose, masterpieces they would paint, worlds they would conquer ...

One afternoon Mandy and I joined him and his mates for drinks in the Sports Bar. I asked him if he had seen the TV series *Changi*. He nodded severely, indicating his displeasure and then said quietly, 'We were not fat like those actors. We were skin and bones.' He remained silent for some time as if musing about it and then said quietly but firmly, 'Changi was no holiday camp.' Later that evening we walked home with him. I didn't think he was that drunk but when we guided him to his front door he looked bewildered.

'Where are you taking me?' he asked, glancing at me as if I were tricking him.

'We're taking you home. This is your front door,' said Mandy.

He thought about this for a time and, deciding she was telling the truth, put the key into the lock and opened the door. The stink of nicotine and stale beer poured out of his apartment like a deadly cloud of halitosis. He shuffled inside and closed the door. It was the last time we saw him.

A few days later he came home drunk and fell onto the two steps that led to his door. The fall caused bleeding to his brain. He was put in an aged care facility where he never regained full possession of his faculties and died seven months later in 2003. His apartment was bought and renovated into a trendy minimalist space, totally unrecognisable from George's rank den. He was not around to see that the historical plaques embedded in the footpaths of Darlinghurst Road quote him the most. His abiding affection for the area is shown in one plaque in his quiet glee in quoting the horrified reactions of suburbanites: *All I can say is she's got a nerve getting around like that. Why she's practically naked. I've got a good mind to call the police.* All four plaques are testimony to the great love of his life – the Cross.

THE QUARREL

KINGS CROSS IS THE RESULT of one man's petty act of revenge. It's also the story of an old man's dull pragmatism destroying a younger man's vision. Both were Scotsmen, intelligent, widely read and single-minded. The older man, 59-year-old Alexander Macleay, arrived in Sydney in January 1826 to take up the position of Colonial Secretary; Thomas Mitchell, twenty-five years younger, came a year later to begin his job as Assistant Surveyor-General of New South Wales.

Both arrived at a time when Sydney's population was hovering between 12,000 and 13,000 people. More than half its population were ex-convicts or convicts still serving their sentences; of these, many of the men worked on road gangs, and women were assigned as servants. Executions were performed in public in the gaol yard in lower George Street. There was also a small minority of civil and military officers, merchants and wealthy settlers who tried to reproduce the high society of the Mother Country with refined soirées, dinner parties, regattas and exclusive balls. Overseas visitors remarked on how elegant parts of Sydney were and how the rich flaunted their wealth with handsome coaches, cabriolets and gigs, horses superior to any in Britain, and women wearing the latest English fashions.

But after dark the city became a noisy amphitheatre of troublemaking drunks and thugs. If there was one thing that bound together all strata of Sydney society it was the pleasures and dangers of alcohol. Between December 1831 and December 1832, 352,549 gallons of spirits and 104,406 gallons of wine were imported and at least another 11,000 gallons of gin were distilled locally, this at a time when the population was barely 15,000. By 1834 there were 197 licensed public houses in Sydney and as many sly grog shops. Bordellos proliferated throughout Sydney, from the Rocks to Elizabeth Street, where one newspaper reckoned there were fifteen to twenty houses in a row used as brothels. This reflected the masculine character of the town where there were four men to every woman; the result, as newspaper editorials were never tired of pointing out, was 'Female depravity and poverty'.

As for other entertainments, cockfighting was popular, as was bulldog fighting and, near present-day Old South Head Road, hundreds of men and women watched boxing, with some fights lasting fifty rounds. At nights Sydney could be lawless. One January evening the year Mitchell disembarked in Sydney, an Aboriginal woman was brazenly gang raped by seven or eight thugs in Castlereagh Street.

The violence, drunkenness and mayhem that ruled the night would come before the courts the next day in a monotonous parade of abject, defiant, hungover or resigned offenders, an astonishing number of them women. The *Sydney Gazette* reported on this miserable parade over the years; one journalist in 1841 commented sarcastically on one morning's line up: 'There were only fifty-nine cases before the Police Courts, of which twenty-four were drunken charges, sixteen of various charges, mostly originating in drunkenness and nineteen charges were against convicts.'

The distinction between the settlers and convicts became

pronounced during the governorship of Lieutenant-General Ralph Darling (1825–1831), whose administration became involved in an ongoing tussle between the freed convicts ('the emancipists'), and the rich free settlers ('the exclusives'). Darling was a military officer, industrious, humourless and a man who mistook cold emotional distance for dignity. He was ultra-conservative, sensitive to criticism, and self-righteous. His previous position had been head of a military government in Mauritius. When he disembarked in Sydney he was fifty-three years old and set in his ways. He saw his role as the governor as bringing a military and moral discipline to an unruly, rapidly expanding town. As he wrote in 1826 to the Colonial Office:

> *Surely there is no colony under His Majesty's Government where attention to the selection of Individuals is so important ... not only the character of the Government, but the moral improvement of the people mainly dependent on it.*

One of the men who fulfilled his requirements was his newly arrived Colonial Secretary, Alexander Macleay. On the surface it seemed that the two men had little in common. Macleay was classically educated. He had been a public servant for most of his working life and was also an entomologist of considerable accomplishment. He had been elected Fellow and later Secretary of the Linnean Society and made a start on a monograph on the *Paussus* (a genus of beetles), of which he had a rich collection. By the time he came to Australia he had one of the most extensive insect collections of any private individual in the world.

Although some considered him too old, he worked up to twelve hours a day, six days a week, in a close personal relationship with the Governor, where he was able to use his diplomatic and administrative skills to provide a human face to Darling's stiff and forbidding regime and carry out the Governor's wishes, which were at times decidedly unpopular. Macleay himself divided the colony and he was accused of always being 'engaged in scores of petty quarrels'. Fun was made of his grotesque body. He was stout, squat, grumpy, going deaf, suffering from painful gout and dropsy, which gave his legs the appearance of tree trunks. His infirmities no doubt contributed to his reputation as 'testy'.

Besides his arduous work, he continued to collect insects, headed many public committees and was an active supporter and contributor to such fledgling cultural institutions as the Australian Museum and the Public Library. He encouraged exploration and still had time to father seventeen children. Like Darling, he was a Tory, loathed the free press and had no time for the emancipists, believing they were 'absolutely unfit to sit on any Jury on account of their ignorance and their drunken and immoral habits'.

He was revered by friends and work colleagues but he had his enemies and critics. One was Justice Sir James Dowling, who had come to Sydney in 1828 and quickly established a reputation for hard work, brilliantly discharging his judicial duties and earning plaudits for his liberal views, kindness and role as an adored father. It's therefore interesting in light of what was to happen between Macleay and Mitchell that Dowling, who rarely spoke ill of anyone, had a distinctly jaundiced opinion of the Colonial Secretary:

The first appearance of Mr Macleay struck me very forcibly. He appeared to be a man of about 60 years of age, bald headed and what hair he had was grey. He was short, thickset, square-built and although not absolutely vulgar, he impressed me with the idea of a decent keeper of a Scotch Royal Burg. He had two quick intelligent eyes but his carriage and look were altogether ungentlemanly and discouraging. I thought he examined me with

a prying curiosity of aspect, which by no means impressed me
favourably with his manners. I soon found that he had a vulgar
Scotch dialect, neither highland or lowland. Altogether he was a
sort of body I took a dislike to.'

If attitudes to Macleay were divided, there seemed a general con-
sensus in the colony that Thomas Mitchell, the Surveyor-General
(he had assumed the top position the year after he arrived), was a
particularly arrogant, ambitious man with a volatile nature – or,
as the merchant Alexander Berry once said of him:

He is one of the most vain, querulous, ill-tempered men in
existence. He is a tyrant to all the surveyors under him and keeps
them at an awful distance. He calls them into his presence with
a boatswain's whistle and receives and dismisses them with more
hauteur than I have seen any other person treat their convict
servants.

Born in Scotland in 1792, Mitchell joined the Army and fought
under Wellington in several major battles. He had a natural
ability as a surveyor and map-maker and, as he rose up in the
ranks, he published works on military plans and surveys of bat-
tlefields. His draughtsmanship was superb and he had a sound
knowledge of mathematics. He had studied chemistry, geology,
astronomy and learnt Greek and Latin so he could read Virgil
in the original. He translated the *Lusiad of Luis de Camoens* from
the Portuguese and wrote one of the first treatises on the culti-
vation of wine in Australia. He was physically fit, had a partial-
ity to witnessing executions, and liked a drink. He loathed the
French and this, coupled with his notorious temper, resulted in
an incident when he was in Paris. While travelling in a coach
he thought it was stuffy so he opened a window. A French-

man sitting opposite shut it. This was too much for a choleric Mitchell, who simply smashed the window with his elbow.

From the time he started his job to 1834 Mitchell worked onerous hours to produce his seminal 'Map of the Colony of New South Wales' of what had previously been wild uncharted mountains, valleys and bushland. What made this feat astonishing was that he and his staff had accomplished this immense undertaking using primitive theodolites, limited manpower, and a handful of bullocks and horses. Through several gruelling explorations, using both male and female Aboriginal guides, Mitchell explored and mapped eastern Australia and laid out towns, roads and public reserves. In 1829 he was given control of the construction and maintenance of the roads and bridges.

Mitchell knew what he was doing when he plotted and constructed a new western descent from the Blue Mountains on to Bathurst, but Darling was convinced that his Surveyor-General had made a mistake and that the routes would be quickly and expensively superseded. An angry Mitchell thought the Governor was wrong (correctly; these roads remain the template for those used today) and told him so in his usual irascible fashion. The disagreement permanently soured relations between the two and would have repercussions for the Cross for more than 140 years.

Unlike the era of Macquarie, whose governorship was a frantic period of constructing houses, government buildings, hospitals and churches, Darling had no such grandiose plans, blaming the dearth of such projects on the poor quality of architects and craftsmen.

It therefore must have come as a surprise when, a year after complaining about the lack of qualified architects and builders, he came up with a unique concept. He ordered that land extending from Woolloomooloo Bay, through Potts Point, Elizabeth Bay and southwards towards where Darlinghurst Gaol would eventually be built, to be divided into seventeen allotments, with a minimum lot size of eight acres (3.2 hectares). (Although the Colonial Secretary was granted fifty-four acres by his close friend the Governor in a dubious deal.) He directed that not only must the houses be built within three years but that he had final approval of the designs. It was also stipulated that they must cost at least £1000, an extraordinary sum at that time (the equivalent of a year's salary for a noteworthy few). Finally he insisted that all the houses should face the city. The first seven land grants were made on 26 March 1828, with further allotments approved on 19 March 1831. Most of the grants went to senior public servants.

Darling's concept accorded with his belief that Sydney was rapidly transforming itself from a penal settlement into a free colony, and from military to civilian control. The mansions, built on the ridge called Woolloomooloo Hill, would hover above the stink, dirt and crime of the town. The villas looking down on the town would be a visual statement of Sydney's grandeur and a constant reminder of the gulf between the elites on the ridge and the convicts and emancipists below in Sydney Cove.

The windmills on the sandstone peninsula may have been necessary to the colony's grain needs, but Woolloomooloo Hill was for many an eyesore. The soil was poor but conducive to native fruit like five-corners, geebungs and ground berries. There were sand hills, low-lying shrubbery, waterholes, a few melancholic clumps of trees and desolate areas where snakes thrived. Newspapers often referred to the ridge as 'sterile'. The steep ascent up Woolloomooloo Hill, now William Street, was a track of treacherous sand dunes, 'a trap to carriage, chariot and horsemen'. The area was prone to bushfires, and one time the whole of what is now Potts Point was in flames. Two contemporary paintings, *Early view of a bushfire at Potts Point, Sydney* painted by Thomas Wingate and *Bush Fire, Potts Point (1840),* show the ferocity of the fires consuming the vacant land to the east; one time a bushfire came close enough to threaten the villa Roslyn Hall. The *Sydney Gazette* summed up what many thought: that the heights of Woolloomooloo Hill were 'a frightful picture for the eye to rest upon' and its bushland a dismal and 'sombre covering'.

Amongst the first people to be given land were Macleay and Mitchell. Macleay's allotment stretched from the ridge down to Elizabeth Bay. In October 1831 Mitchell was given allotment number 12, a grant of nine acres, perched on the highest point of the ridge. His Craigend, named after his birthplace, was one the first of the great houses to be built, an elegant Italianate two-storey mansion. Mitchell designed the villa himself and, discovering that there were no masons sufficiently skilled to carve the Ionic pillars, did a great deal of the carving himself. Craigend and its Parthenon-style portico and elevated position on the hill led to its being nicknamed 'the Acropolis of Sydney'.

Another surveyor to receive a grant was Samuel Augustus Perry, the Deputy Surveyor-General (and eternal critic of his boss), who was given an allotment of about three acres on the eastern slope leading down to Rushcutters Bay (the Hotel Mansions was built on the site in 1885, later becoming the Mansions Hotel). Other land grants were given to Captain Samuel Perry, who built Kellett House; the New South Wales Solicitor General, Orwell House; and Judge James Dowling, Brougham Lodge. Springfield Avenue stands on the site of Springfield, built by Alexander MacDuff. In 1832 Colonel Thomas Shadforth, soldier and successful company director, built Adelaide Cottage, situated between the present Rockwell Crescent and Challis Avenue, incorporating into its design a bathing house and an entrance gate. The land where the bathing house stood was later reclaimed and the McElhone Stairs now stand on the location.

These villas were impressive and imposing, with standards

of luxury not seen before in the colony. The Hallen brothers, Edward and Ambrose, designed several of them, including Roslyn Hall for the wealthy miller Thomas Barker. It had fretted roofs, Turkish carpets, crystal door handles and woodwork of the finest polished cedar. Its staircase was reputed to have been a spiral design 'wide enough for a coach and pair'. The bedrooms were large and had a remarkable feature: each contained a bath flush with the floor, so that one stepped down, rather than up, into it. Visitors thought it was more like a palace than a home.

But there was one man who gave what was now becoming known as Darlinghurst its architectural style, so distinctive a feature of the 1830s that it has been dubbed 'the Golden Decade of Australian Architecture'. It was almost by chance that he became involved at all. John Verge was born in 1782 and worked at the building trade in London where he became quite successful, but ill health forced him to turn to farming. After his marriage failed he sailed to Sydney, arriving in 1828 with his son, a flock of sheep plus shepherd, and agricultural supplies. He took up farming but didn't prosper as he hoped, so he returned to Sydney and to the building industry, which was flourishing in good economic times. He must have had talent because Darling, despairing of the paucity of skilled architects, personally invited Verge to tender for some of the villas.

He was prolific. In 1830 he designed a stone mansion, Goderich Lodge, for Thomas Hyacinth Macquoid, on an allotment of four acres. Described as 'a simple, two-storied, verandahed villa with eaves, shuttered double hung sash windows, and French doors into the verandah', it was also known for its exquisite cedar fittings. Macquoid had arrived in 1829 and named the villa after his patron, Viscount Goderich, who had arranged for Macquoid's appointment as Governor's Sheriff. The social climbing, spendthrift and shifty Sheriff earned £1000 a year, yet it didn't seem enough to have not only constructed Goderich Lodge but also paid for the cedar fittings and furniture which were stunning features of the house. (The site is now occupied by the Hampton, an apartment block which was formerly the Hampton Court Hotel.)

A better example of Verge's work is Tusculum in Manning Street. Built in 1831 for the Scotsman Alexander Spark, a wealthy merchant, land speculator and company director, Tusculum is rectangular in plan, with verandahs supported by delicate cast-iron Ionic colonnades at their edges right round two floors. The ornate verandah ceilings are of panelled cedar that deftly complement the finely dressed stone walls. Nearby in Rockwall Crescent was another Verge villa, Rockwall, designed in his familiar Regency style. It has restrained and sober lines, although some architectural critics believe the columned porch seems to overpower the flanking verandahs in scale.

Macleay's mansion is where Verge's architecture is at its most sensuous and dramatic. Constructed between 1835 and 1839, Elizabeth Bay House has a simple Regency front, which was designed to have a patio and colonnade but, due to a lack of money in the 1840s depression, it was never built. Conrad Martens' optimistic 1828 version of the mansion, painted years before the Macleay family shifted in, shows what might have been. The interior has some splendid rooms and a superlative oval saloon. The stairs and its upper landings sweep round the curved walls. The rear of the villa is basic, the cramped servants' quarters typical of the period and of the low esteem servants were held in. As is usual in buildings of the time, the kitchen was out the back of the house.

But it's the giddy elegance of the spiral staircase that thrills as the eye traces the stairs upwards until they seem to vanish into the golden light of the dome. It is an extremely theatrical work and a superb example of the best of colonial architecture. Coupled with the original 54-acre garden filled with rare and exotic plants, it was easy to see why it was called, without contradiction, 'the finest house in the colony'.

Verge's brilliance – which could be erratic at times, especially when he struggled to reconcile the exterior of a house with its interior design – was obvious to many and by 1832 he was a celebrated name and honoured by a leading article in the *Sydney Gazette*, which reported proudly that:

> *To his judicious taste we are indebted for the elegance of most of the villas on Woolloomooloo Hill, some of which are worthy of the suburbs of London.*

While this frenetic building continued, Mitchell pondered the future of the area. He knew that the city would expand beyond the ridge to the east and realised that the Aboriginal track that led up the hill – the present William Street – could become a glorious broad avenue. It would be a practical yet a handsome route over the hill and into the eastern regions. On 10 December 1830 he sent a letter to Macleay detailing his plans to extend Park Street to run in a straight line until it reached the base of William Street, which was primarily a sand hill. In order to avoid its steep gradient, Mitchell's road would follow the continuation of the Aboriginal track and make a wide detour with an easy grade down into Rushcutters Bay. The route would have to pass through an insignificant section of Thomas Barker's Roslyn Hall estate and would cut off Barker's gardener's cottage from the main property. Although offered an acre of land in compensation, the wealthy miller refused to agree to the proposal. Macleay, who had yet to build his house on his immense property – and who was a very close friend of Thomas Barker – was also a fierce opponent of the scheme.

Frustrated by such petty-minded intransigence, Mitchell, meticulous in his preparation as always, constructed a model of the sand hill with the proposed deviation of the route to the east to show to his critics in the government. He was about to embark on an exploration inland and before he left he wanted a decision on his proposal. But none was made and he set off in 1831 no doubt believing that the government would see sense and follow his plans. After he left, work started on William Street.

Macleay, who knew more about beetles than surveying, took the opportunity of Mitchell's absence to walk onto the site one day and ordered the Deputy Surveyor-General to run the street straight up the sand hill and stop at the top of the ridge without crossing the brow of the hill and extending the route down into Rushcutters Bay. Instead of the wide thoroughfare imagined by Mitchell, Macleay narrowed it. There is no doubt that Macleay's close friendship with Darling meant that he had discussed it with the Governor and that Darling would have given his blessing to ignore Mitchell's grandiose plan. Given the Surveyor's fractious dealings with the Governor and Macleay, plus his temper tantrums, rudeness, and intellectual arrogance, it's easy to imagine that the abrupt derailing of the Surveyor-General's plan was a moment of immense satisfaction for the Governor and the Colonial Secretary.

Macleay's interference meant that William Street stopped at the rear end of Macquoid's estate and his Goderich House. When Mitchell returned eight months later in 1832 he was appalled and angry at what had been done. He abused everyone involved in the fateful decision. Although he continued to argue for his plan, it was never implemented. The result of Macleay's self-serving interference was that Kings Cross would become Australia's worst traffic bottleneck, a Gordian knot of seven streets running into one another at the top of William Street, creating such a tangled havoc that the intersection became infamous for its traffic problems and accidents. The solution only arrived in 1975 when the Kings Cross Tunnel was opened. Earlier in the twentieth century William Street had to be widened at great economic and social cost. All this could have been avoided but, as the creation of Kings Cross proved, in Australia it seems self-interest nearly always defeats the visionaries.

Falling

WHILE WE WERE PLAYING SCRABBLE out on the balcony of the third floor of Doncaster Hall, Mandy and I heard a loud, urgent knocking at the front door. It was the woman who rented the adjoining apartment.

'Please,' she said, 'can I use your balcony to climb into my flat?'

She wanted to clamber from Mandy's balcony into her own. Because her balcony door was unlocked, and she had lost her front door key, it was the quickest way for her to get inside without calling the locksmiths. The only way to get across into her apartment was to stretch out one's left arm to clutch the side of her balcony while clinging to the edge of Mandy's balcony and then pull oneself a metre across an empty space over a drop of twenty metres. I told her it was too dangerous and if she fell into Brougham Lane she would probably kill herself.

'You don't understand,' she insisted, 'I have to get my two Bledisloe Cup tickets because the match is on tonight. If I don't get them,' she added, 'then my boyfriend will kill me.'

My refusal made her furious. When I could get a word in I told her that over the years two people in Doncaster Hall had fallen to their deaths attempting to do the same thing.

If the Cross meant high-rise buildings it also meant the hazards of height. People accidentally fell through skylights and down lift chutes to their deaths; others, drunk, tumbled off roofs. In the late 1940s a young seaman tried to climb around a partition on a balcony which divided two flats when he slipped and fell to his death from the Goderich Private Hotel. Police photographs showed finger marks and scratches where he had clutched frantically at the parapet before falling.

Over the years people found ingenious ways of falling. In the 1980s a 24-year-old woman plunged five storeys from the roof of a Kings Cross carpark in Ward Avenue while making love to her boyfriend. The couple had been drinking on the roof around 11 pm when they decided to have sex. They climbed a fence around the rooftop area, hid behind the bushes and, as they grew more amorous, she turned one way and he the other. The bushes were close to the edge and she rolled through them and into thin air, her descent fortunately broken by the branches of a tree. She was unconscious when she hit the ground. The police said it was a miracle she was still alive.

Some people fall deliberately. We have a friend who came home to his apartment after shopping, taking a bag of groceries up to his flat before returning to his car for the rest. While he was unpacking he heard a ferocious argument between the gay couple on the floor above. There was a piercing cry of 'You fucking bastard!', a sudden silence and then the sound of a heavy object crashing into metal. John peered over his balcony and saw that one of the men was lying on the crushed roof of his car, having jumped to his death.

Sometimes these deaths are reported in the newspapers as simple statements of fact, leaving readers to make their own judgments. During the Second World War a soldier booked into the Mayfair Hotel and almost immediately plunged to his death. Because he was a soldier the police insisted he fell because he was trying to take a photograph from his open window, but he fell from such an extreme angle that the only conclusion was that he jumped.

Sometimes there was no mistaking the reason for falling. In 1949 Harold Duff, twenty-six years old and married for just three months, was said to be suffering from 'acute neurosis' and had an appointment to see a 'nerve specialist' the following day. Instead he slashed his throat and jumped out of the third-storey window of his flat. His screams as he fell startled the residents and his wife in their living room, who rushed to the window and saw his inert body spreadeagled in the laneway below.

Hampton Court seems to have been a popular place to launch yourself into oblivion. In 1953 Frederick Williams, a man in his early seventies, lived in the luxury suite of the hotel, of which he was also a director. He was a well-known former jockey, horse trainer and wealthy property owner. He had been ill for years, confined to his suite and cared for by a nurse. One day he decided he'd had enough and he leapt fifty feet to his death into the parking lot on the hotel grounds. Another man, a member of the RAAF, plunged fifty feet from the Hampton Court Hotel. He had been ill for some time and despaired of a cure. He left £15,700 – an extraordinary sum for the time.

There were also people who came into Kings Cross for the express purpose of killing themselves. In 1947 a suburban housewife in her middle fifties, Mrs Ideal Greenwood, left her Strathfield home to shop in the city. While there she resolved to end her life and went looking for a high building. She took a tram to Kings Cross and chose Kaindi flats, a seven-storey building behind the Hampton Court Hotel. She had never been to the flats before and it was thought she either climbed the stairs or went up in the lift to the rooftop garden. The owner of the penthouse saw Greenwood around 2 pm peering over the iron rails down the sheer drop between the stairs. Not long afterwards Greenwood carefully placed her hat, an attaché case full of fruit she had bought in the city and her handbag on the roof, and jumped. Another woman in a first-floor apartment saw Greenwood's body silently hurtle past her window onto the brick path near the side entrance of the flats.

It's been said, though it's hard to find precise figures, that the Cross is the suicide capital of Australia. Given its high density it stands to reason that there would be more people doing away with themselves than in more sparsely populated areas, but there are additional factors at work. There is no doubt that there are friendless souls living solitary and dismal lives despite being amongst thousands of people. One of the most telling signs of loneliness is that a body is not discovered until its putrid smell offends others in neighbouring apartments. I know of two men this happened to. One was a publisher who lived in a Victoria Street apartment. He hanged himself, and his body was not found for a week. The other, Peter, a 50-year-old New Zealand friend, was head waiter at the exclusive Aria restaurant in the city; he had finicky epicurean tastes, gracious manners and loved his job. I had once shared a house with him in Brougham Street and an apartment in the Oceana in Elizabeth Bay. He was living by himself when he died of natural causes. His body rotted away for five days, the posh restaurant seeming to ignore his continuing absence, until his closest friend, alarmed at his silence, called the police, who had to break into his flat.

Others use the privacy of their flats or rented rooms to end their lives. The most popular method for decades was gas. In 1939 the owner of a residential hotel in Hughes Street, Ada Maria Broome Witts, aged sixty-four, was found dead with a tube from a gas jet in her mouth. Born in rural New South Wales, she was the wife of a baronet and had lived in South Africa and Melbourne. Her brother George said his sister had no financial problems but was very highly strung and always discontented. If the reason for her suicide seemed vague, John Morelli's wasn't. The small-time gangster's body was discovered in his Kings Cross flat in May 1947, two days after he gassed himself. He left a note saying he was ending his life because of a woman.

There are those who had no intention of gassing themselves. In one horrific incident two 14-year-old boys were found dead in a flat. They had been suffocated by gas escaping from a bath heater which had exploded. One of the boys' mothers came home near midnight and found the bodies naked on the floor, one near the door and the other near a window which he had tried to open. The other boy apparently had struggled vainly to open the door, as the door knob was found broken on the floor.

Then there are the falling objects. One time I was returning to my apartment only to find the building cordoned off – someone on the top floor was throwing chairs, vases and glasses out of the window onto William Street. 'It's some drag queen on drugs,' said one cop to me as his partners organised for the door to be smashed down. One sunny afternoon I heard a woman screaming on the balcony of her Zenith apartment, overlooking the Coca-Cola sign. She threw the balcony table and chairs onto the road below, disappeared inside a few times and returned with objects, including a television, and hurled them over the balcony in a fit of nihilistic wrath, caused, as the police were later to report, by a three-day ice binge. During her rage she managed to smash a car window and nearly kill a pedestrian with the television.

On Christmas morning 2011 I heard a wail of sirens that stopped not far from my apartment. I looked out my window and saw a dozen police cars, trucks and ambulances parked next to the Kings Cross Tunnel underpass. A fire brigade truck was parked in the underpass just under the walkway. Television crews began to arrive. It was then I saw the reason for all this activity. An Aboriginal woman, dressed in a blue top and black pants, was hanging backwards, clinging on to the overpass railing like a diver about to do a back flip into the water.

Traffic on either side of the underpass was stopped. Every time the female negotiator came near her, the woman threatened to let go. It didn't surprise me. I had seen her the past two days high on ice, walking and talking ceaselessly, screaming at the world and throwing soft drink bottles onto the footpaths and streets. For an hour she kept threatening to jump until a male negotiator turned up. He managed to surreptitiously step closer while she wailed at the sky, and grabbed her. Immediately another half a dozen cops pulled her up and onto the overpass and, as she thrashed and screamed, they strapped her to a gurney. Just then, like something out of a sentimental Hollywood movie, the Christmas bells of St Mary's began to toll as if celebrating her deliverance.

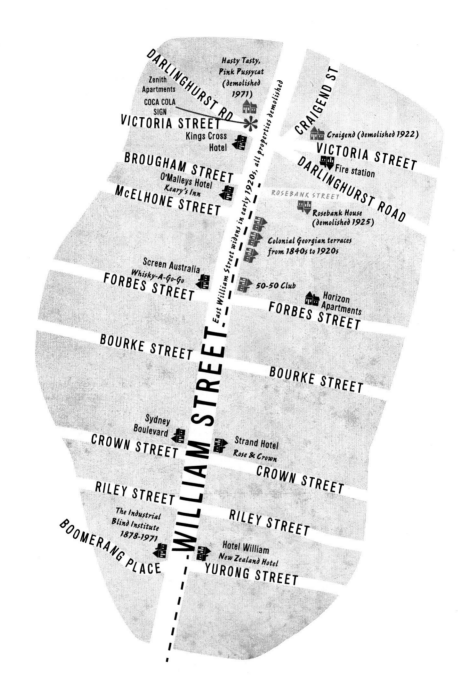

DARLINGHURST RD

Hasty Tasty,
Pink Pussycat
(demolished 1971)

Zenith
Apartments
COCA COLA SIGN

VICTORIA STREET

Kings Cross Hotel

BROUGHAM STREET
O'Malleys Hotel
Keary's Inn

McELHONE STREET

East William Street widens in early 1920s, all properties demolished

CRAIGEND ST

Craigend (demolished 1922)

VICTORIA STREET
Fire station

DARLINGHURST ROAD

ROSEBANK STREET

Rosebank House
(demolished 1925)

Colonial Georgian terraces
from 1840s to 1920s

Screen Australia
Whisky-A-Go-Go

FORBES STREET

50-50 Club

Horizon
Apartments

FORBES STREET

BOURKE STREET

WILLIAM STREET

BOURKE STREET

Sydney
Boulevard

CROWN STREET

Strand Hotel
Rose & Crown

CROWN STREET

RILEY STREET

The Industrial
Blind Institute
1878-1971

RILEY STREET

BOOMERANG PLACE

Hotel William
New Zealand Hotel

YURONG STREET

WHEN I VENTURE OUT OF the foyer of Doncaster Hall, on my
immediate right is a shop which is part of my building. It sells insipid
Aboriginal art and offers boomerang throwing lessons for foreigners,
most of whom are Scandinavian backpackers looking for cheap
souvenirs to take home. Next to it is an empty shop with two large *For
Lease* signs plastered on its dusty graffiti-marked windows.

It was once one of the most glamorous and renowned menswear
shops in Sydney. De Ferrari Moda (the Ferrari of Fashion) opened
in the early 1970s and only closed with the owner's death in 2006.
Giuseppe Simonella was born in Italy and, before migrating to
Australia, worked in Rome cutting and stitching for the Hollywood
actors Tyrone Power, John Wayne and Henry Fonda, as well as for
leading Italian actors and directors. The actors' influence was evident
in the matinee idol moustache he cultivated.

The customers of De Ferrari Moda were a varied bunch. There
was former premier Neville Wran (who spoke at Simonella's funeral),
the famous horse trainer Bart Cummings (whose twelve Melbourne
Cups gave him ample opportunity to show off his De Ferrari Moda
suits in the winner's circle), visiting celebrities such as Bob Dylan and
Ginger Rogers, and many euphemistically called 'colourful Sydney
identities'. Simonella had a passion for food (his wife ran a local
Italian restaurant) and for horse racing, although he seldom made
bets bigger than five dollars. Many suits were especially tailored for
customers to wear to the races; they were easy to spot, with their
shiny slip-on shoes, pastel colours, bright ties and sharp creases. It
was a very dapper and Italian look.

A reserved man, Simonella addressed all his customers as
'mister'. His health was always fragile and he never recovered from
the sudden death of his eldest son, Roberto, in 2000. So important was
his memory that when Mandy wanted to buy the apartment she was
renting in Doncaster Hall, which was where Roberto had lived and
was still in his name, the Simonella family refused to part with it, even

though the offer was above the apartment's actual value.

As bon vivant and arts festival director Leo Schofield, a regular client, put it, during the last six years before a grief-stricken Giuseppe died at seventy, the shop 'was never the same as in its glory years, when the great and the good rubbed shoulders with dubious-looking characters from the Cross'.

When the door finally closed the interior was left untouched. His loyal staff allowed privileged customers like Bart Cummings to come and buy any of the remaining clothes. But De Ferrari Moda seemed more a dwelling place of ghosts than a menswear shop and a few years after Simonella's death the stock and fittings were sold. Peek inside and the dusty interior is desolate except for four wooden Doric-style columns, three wooden archways leading into a backroom, and a back wall covered in dull gold peeling wallpaper. It looks like the ruins of a B-grade movie set.

If I turn to the left when I exit Doncaster Hall, there is Bell's the locksmiths, who use one of the flats in the building as their office. There is a staff of twenty to service the area. They have an average of four to five calls a day to help people in the Cross who have lost their keys or accidentally locked themselves out. But as one assistant told me, 'Weekends are the worst, especially Friday and Saturday nights. Sometimes we're run off our feet.'

It's at night that, even in the coldest weather, William Street hosts flimsily dressed trannies, who artfully arrange themselves in the shadows and street lights, showing off their tall, gorgeous bodies and confirming the opinion of locals that these faux women are more attractive than the actual women prostitutes. For over a hundred years William Street has been a thoroughfare of flesh for sale. Street walkers used to work openly and when new laws were passed after the First World War, the prostitutes retreated to brothels which nestled among the boarding houses, shops and hovels. Even so, there were women who preferred street walking to paying a

huge percentage of their earnings to a brothel keeper. In his poem
'Cannibal Street', Kenneth Slessor summed up the brutal reality and
seediness of the trade, describing women on the game being seen by
men as nothing more than pieces of meat.

It's still a street for selling flesh but now it is 'crossies' and
'trannies' who display themselves on the windswept street in short
dresses and towering high heels. Generally the trannie or crossie will
motion the client to park his car down one of the dark side streets
where the action will take place. During the 1990s the northern side
of the street was a fiercely contested site between the crossies and
trannies, with the crossies (more highly sought after because they
still had a penis) demanding to work under the streetlamps so they
could show themselves off, while the trannies were relegated to the
shadows.

When the William Street upgrade started in 2005, landscape
architect Adam Fowler, who helped with the design, was practical
about the prostitution:

'It may well be that the gentrification of William Street displaces
some of that activity into the back streets, but it's not going to get rid
of it. It's got to be somewhere in the Cross.'

Once the office workers go home, the street can seem deserted
and forlorn and nothing like the bustling community of shops,
businesses and boarding houses that once made it one of the most
popular shopping boulevards in Sydney. One night Mandy and I
were walking back from the city and, as we passed Forbes Street, I
noticed out of the corner of my eye two policemen about to emerge
onto William Street. Just then a young man, probably about nineteen
or twenty, came striding down the footpath towards us, his body
twitching, his face contorted with rage at the world. I had seen this
look many times. He was on ice and, as I knew, it was when the
sleepless addict has been up for a couple of days and nights that
he is most prone to violence. One user loomed up at me near the

pedestrian crossing next to the Kings Cross Hotel and, like a kick boxer, started to throw kicks at my head, spitting wildly and laughing as his boot got closer to my face with every kick. Another ice addict was so demented that he would sit outside the newsagency next to the railway station picking at imaginary insects living under his skin until his legs resembled pieces of bloody raw meat.

As the young guy came closer he looked over at me, his eyes sparking with hatred. By this stage I was tired of being menaced by ice addicts and realised that, if my timing was right, I could get this fellow. He glared at me and when I kept staring back at him, he came straight at me, screaming, 'What are you staring at, fucker?' Mandy was scared but I was focused on what was going to happen next. 'You stupid fucker!' he yelled as he was about to hit me. But, as I had hoped, the two policemen had turned the corner and were only a few steps away from the drugged maniac. Immediately sensing he was on ice, they threw him to the ground and wrestled him into submission while he squirmed in a paroxysm of obscene language and incoherent fury. *Who's the stupid fucker now?* I thought. I had no sympathy for him. He was no longer a rational creature but a human vessel of primal and atavistic fury driven by a chemical cocktail, who had not the slightest empathy for any other human.

Night softens the brutal architecture of the street. The ugliness of the northern side is obvious in the daylight. Slessor's William Street no longer has pawn shops and cheap restaurants with 'smells rich and rasping'. There are a couple of restaurants down near the bottom but the street is mostly commercial office buildings of no distinction, showrooms with shiny bright cars gleaming in the specially arranged lights, ten backpacker campervan businesses and Bugden's, a second-hand bookshop, its window filled with pristine books sold to the owner, Paul Bugden, by insolvent book reviewers.

William Street has become simply a featureless conduit to the city or the Cross. In the early hours of the morning cleaners, most of whom are Asian, go about their business in the sleeping city and the hotels and apartment buildings of the Cross, working hard, knowing little English but determined to make it in their adopted country. After them comes a trickle of men and women, generally badly dressed, slouching into town to their lowly jobs. By half-past seven William Street is packed with young professionals in suits and smart dresses striding to their offices, the women wearing sandshoes and carrying their high heels, some of them sipping coffee from paper cups, all of them ignoring the street itself, immersed in their own preoccupations or inuring themselves to the auditory reality of the world by listening to music on their headphones. The girls going to the exclusive Protestant private girls' school, SCEGGS, walk down to Forbes Street in a sudden stream which emerges from the railway station, generally in pairs, some with bouquets for their girlfriends or a favourite teacher and decorously clutching their dresses if the wind is blowing. Between half-past eight and nine the highest paid professionals saunter into the CBD knowing they don't have to be on time. None of them stop because there's nothing of interest to see.

Walking along the southern side of the street is to notice a peculiar thing: most of the buildings (hotels, residences and office blocks) have 1924 inscribed on their facades. This can be traced back to 1916, when the Sydney City Council decided that ninety-four properties on the south side of William Street would be demolished, including five hotels: the Prince Albert, the Gladstone, the Royal, the New Zealand and the Cosy Parlour, a popular bar. The razing of all these properties, the dislocation of people and the destruction of a dynamic working-class community was because of one man, the myopic and recalcitrant Alexander Macleay, who had tampered with Thomas Mitchell's plan to make William Street a wide thoroughfare to the east.

The Sydney City Council had come to the conclusion that the narrow street had to be widened from 41 feet to the original plan of

100 feet. Mitchell had also wanted to find an easier gradient for the route, but Macleay and the wealthy miller Thomas Barker had put a stop to that. The gradient was so steep that William Street trams were considered the slowest in Sydney and heavily laden vehicles found it hard going, with the gradient 1 in 11½ at the top and 1 in 14 near College Street. William Street had also become the main outlet for traffic to the eastern suburbs, and as the population increased so the traffic situation grew worse.

Besides the hotels, fifty-five shops, a post office, bank, school, factories, stables and twenty-eight boarding houses were demolished over a period of six years. At the time William Street was a major shopping strip for Sydneysiders, with butchers, chemists, cake shops, bakers, grocers, dress makers, oyster saloons, dyers, pet shops, tailors, printers, wig makers, cigarette and cigar shops, and, of course, pawnshops run by Jews, who were a significant presence. The huge variety of shops was matched by the lively and eclectic mix of nationalities: Chinese, Jews, Italians, Greeks, Maltese, British and native-born Australians.

The architecture was also a delirious mix of styles, as Max Kelly depicts in his meticulous *Faces of the Street: William Street Sydney 1916*:

> *Colonial cottages, Georgian in detail, exist alongside fanciful and grand Victorian terraces built for the middle classes. Italianate terraces ... a beautiful Regency terrace of three houses.*

The Italianate style became extremely popular. It was a mash-up of classical Rome, Renaissance Italy, asymmetrical design, ornate detailing in stone or rendered brick, decorative wrought-iron verandahs with cast iron columns, coloured glass in doors and windows, and interiors of finicky and elaborate plaster designs hidden behind a clutter of Victorian furnishings and bric-à-brac – a bastard mix of influences that reflected Australia's breathless desire to emulate European styles of architecture. For many, William Street offered 'a virtually intact, open-air museum of nineteenth-century building practices and decoration'. It was also a place for the poor and working class, with cheap and shoddy shops and modest cafés and dining rooms run by women.

One of the features of the area was the ubiquitous boarding house. It is estimated that between fifteen to twenty per cent of Sydney's adult population lived either as boarders or lodgers in the early twentieth century. In East Sydney and Kings Cross there were 182 boarding houses and 148 were run by women; home to about a thousand adults. Nearly all these women were married but ran the houses on their own. Many of the establishments were on Crown, Palmer, Dowling and Brougham Streets; even the formerly posh Victoria Street had boarding houses, a situation that was not only due to the depression of the 1890s but a change in the middle classes' attitude to terraces. They now sought the pleasures of a house and garden of their own in suburbia, especially the North Shore.

The indignant Kelly writes that the extraordinarily costly widening of the street and razing of so many properties between 1916 and 1923 'succeeded in removing a vibrant and independent working class community'. The result was that many of the poor retreated further into the grubby lanes, narrow streets and cockroach and rat-infested slums of East Sydney and Surry Hills.

After the rebuilding of William Street there were hopes that it could be Australia's Champs Élysées, and in 1969 the City of Sydney decided it would create a great boulevard lined with trees, shops and modern residential buildings. Nothing happened, of course. But in 2003 the Council set about trying to improve the street. It wanted a colourful tree-lined pedestrian boulevard, with footpaths widened and replaced with black granite, and more than eighty London plane trees planted to take advantage of the drop in traffic the Cross City tunnel was expected to provide. There would be more street furniture and 'smart poles', which carry traffic signals, electronic street signs and lighting.

The dramatic drop in traffic didn't happen. The pavements were widened, plane trees planted and smart poles erected but there was no transformation that created Sydney's version of the Champs Élysées. There is a green bicycle path that is seldom used because, as people have discovered since the street came into existence, the gradient is daunting. The exhausting heave up William Street was awful for horses and a taxing climb for tramcars.

There are others who view the hill as a supreme challenge. Don Athaldo was reputed to be the strongest man in the world. Born Frederick George Lyons in Sydney in 1894, he extolled the virtues of physical fitness in books like *Health, Strength & Muscular Power* and *Meet Don Athaldo*. He thought that weight-lifting, diet and fresh air could overcome many illnesses, including cancer and bad breath. He attempted spectacular feats of strength like lifting a horse, but needing to outdo himself, he picked William Street for the greatest and most outlandish feat of his career. He demonstrated his fabulous strength by pulling a touring car with six passengers more than half a mile (805 metres) up the hill to Kings Cross. He would be pleased, if not a little astonished, that his one-man crusade for the importance of fitness is now an obsession for the young professionals who crowd the gyms at the top of William Street all day and night.

If you're walking from the city and pay attention to the streetscape, something begins to nag. A glance at pre-2000 photographs of William Street reveals a picturesque conformity of height and scale, but looking up William Street now, three enormous buildings dominate: Horizon Tower, Zenith and the Elan.

From the mid 1990s councils and government allowed undisciplined development of the area and these enormous apartment towers contributed to a loss of scale. Zenith was formerly

the Millennium Hotel above the Kingsgate Shopping centre, a grey
bunker-like building which had a reputation for ghost sightings. One
guest woke up in a room on the twelfth floor to find 'a female spirit
overpowering him, hovering about eight inches in front of his face'.
He said it was terrifying, with bright-red eyes and a glowing aura
all around it. Tennis champion Pat Cash reported that something
invisible was hanging around his room. By 2000 the hotel had closed
down because tourist numbers in the Cross were dwindling, and it
was converted into an apartment complex called Zenith. The Elan
was built over the Cross City Tunnel and at forty storeys high it is
one of the top ten tallest residential apartments in Sydney. Harry
Seidler's Horizon Tower is forty-three storeys and casts its pompous
shadow over the surrounding landscape like an alpha dog marking his
territory. All three buildings are classic examples of male architects'
phallic competitiveness.

On Friday and Saturday nights William Street is a gridlock as
hundreds of cars snake their way into the Cross, their loud doof-doof
music joining the ear-splitting cacophony of noisy motor bikes and car
horns as drivers become impatient at the glacial pace of the traffic
turning left into Darlinghurst Road, their blazing headlights like white
phosphorescent fish in the black waters of a river. The noise of the
music, sirens, shouting and horns will swell until it fades early in the
morning as the traffic dwindles and revellers return to their suburbs,
leaving the daylight to the locals.

Walking up William Street, one neon sign rules over the Cross.
The Coke sign is symbolic of the supremacy of global brands.
From the late 1940s onwards the top of William Street had been
an incandescent stew of neon, advertising dozens of brands, from
electrical firms, wine, paints and restaurants as each firm tried to
outdo the other, with pulsating colours of yellow, red, blue, green and
white jostling to attract attention. One of the most famous was a large
throbbing arrow continuously penetrating the centre of a pulsating

Goodyear car tyre, an obvious subliminal paean to the sexual vibrancy of what awaited the visitor just off to the left. By the 1960s the top of William Street became even more alluring when a huge cut-out figure of a voluptuous, scantily clad woman graced the facade of the notorious Pink Pussycat club, her image a siren call to men to experience the carnal delights of watching strippers tease their audiences with glimpses of female flesh.

There must have been thousands of young, desperate people over the years who were drawn towards the cauldron of effervescent lights like insects mesmerised by a ultraviolet fly zapper. Now there's only one neon sign consisting of a mere two colours, red and white. The sign not so much astounds your senses but dominates like a visual megaphone.

THE SWELLS OF
WOOLLOOMOOLOO HILL

ON A MONDAY IN LATE April 1834, four convicts, named Smith, Herring, Lahy and Lawless, belonging to the hulk *Phoenix*, were given permission to row across to Lane Cove to cut wood. Instead of gathering firewood, Smith convinced the other three that they should become bushrangers. But before heading off into the countryside to pursue their new career, they needed food, clothes and guns. It was the beginning of a six-day crime spree as they terrorised householders from Concord to the North Shore. The victims were threatened with axes and guns and forced to feed and arm the criminals, who also stole money and clothes to disguise themselves.

On a Friday night they turned up on South Head Road where, probably drunk, they confided in the overseer of a road gang that they would remain in the area until they had attended the races, but before then they intended to rob all of the 'swells' on the Woolloomooloo Hill, starting with James Laidley, the owner of the mansion Rosebank.

They never got around to it, instead resorting to plundering isolated houses and threatening to kill the occupants. Eventually the police tracked them down to a bridge on Botany Road around 9 o'clock on Saturday night. There was a shoot out. Smith, the leader of the gang, was killed, Herring and Lahy were captured and Lawless (remaining true to his surname) escaped into the night.

What is intriguing is how quickly Woolloomooloo Hill had become synonymous with wealth and luxury; a lofty enclave where the toffs and 'swells' lived. Governor Darling, who departed for England in 1831, would have been pleased. The ridge was an island of privilege and the envy of neck-craning hoi polloi living down below in the unsanitary city. Once it had been considered sterile bushland but by 1831 Woolloomooloo Hill was, as one visitor said, 'traversed by an elegant carriage road and picturesque walks, decked with respectable mansions, clothed with gardens, and bidding to become the Richmond or the Kensington of the Australian metropolis'. For many tourists and settlers their first view of Sydney was of Woolloomooloo Hill (including an impressed Charles Darwin in 1836), and all were entranced by the beauty of the mansions, the windmills, and the botanical richness of the gardens. A lecture on beauty and taste by John Rae (artist, writer and the first Town Clerk of Sydney) at the School of Arts in July 1841, saw the Hill, where he lived, as an ideal of aesthetic beauty:

> No-one can look on the harbour of Port Jackson without pleasure ... its romantic wooded borders, presenting the appearance of promontories, creeks and bays, and spotted with white cottages, rising gracefully among the trees – the picturesque windmills, the splendid villas, and the castellated and baronial looking buildings that crown the heights of Woolloomooloo.

The *Sydney Gazette* proudly announced that the barren land had been transformed 'into an epitome of the far-famed Eden'.

For many owners of the great houses, commissioning a painting was a favourite way to show off the estate. One of the most popular artists was Conrad Martens, who came to Sydney in 1835 after sailing on the HMS *Beagle* with Charles Darwin. He became obsessed by Sydney Harbour and its changing moods of light and shadows, but in order to earn quick money he painted watercolours of some of the mansions in his typically lyrical and romantic style. But it was a lesser-known artist by the name of George Edwards Peacock who was probably the most prolific painter of the estates. Slight and short, Peacock had arrived in Port Jackson in 1837 as a convict after embezzling the huge amount of £7814 from his brother, a Reverend. He had been tried at the Old Bailey and sentenced to death, but the sentence was commuted to transportation. His marriage didn't survive and he became a meteorological observer at the government weather station on South Head, living alone in an adjacent cottage. He took up painting in the early 1840s, strongly influenced by Martens. His earliest dated work is from 1843 when the new owner of Craigend, Colonel Rogers, commissioned Peacock to paint six views of, and from, the house. He went on to paint many Woolloomooloo Hill estates, creating an enchanting, even hermetic, world reminiscent of English mansions and gardens, but at the same time never sacrificing topographical fidelity. Peacock, a true recidivist, seems to have stopped painting in 1856 when he scurried back to England just ahead of the police, who were ready to arrest him for embezzling money in his most recent job as a clerk.

One of the pleasures of the mansions and the lifestyles of their owners was the way it mimicked the world back home. Many visitors commented how the colonists had recreated an 'Albion Arcadia'. Lieutenant Colonel Godfrey Mundy stayed for a time in Tarmons, which had been built in 1838 for Major General Sir Maurice O'Connell, and was lent to Mundy by the new owner, Sir Charles Nicholson. It was not only the beauty of the villa that appealed to the discerning soldier but how much it reminded him of the Mother Country:

> ... *There were brisk coal fires burning in both dining and drawing-room and the general appliances of the household, the dress of guests and servants, were entirely English as they could have been in London.*

What was naturally Australian was the food: wallaby tail soup, kangaroo and wonga wonga pigeon.

The interiors of these villas were also remarkable, as one can see from this 1837 advertisement for Craigend and its contents, which included:

> *Splendid household furniture, mirrors, plate, grand piano, carriage and horses, large sized Brussels carpets, Grecian couches (very fashionable), antique lamps in bronze, pair molu candelabras, chintz curtains, plate chest, salvers, rich double-plated wine filters, silver tea service suitable to a first-rate establishment ... The house and offices will ... be offered for sale with about three acres of land, including the lawn, vineyard, shrubbery, sufficient kitchen garden etc.*

The number of staff varied from villa to villa; in 1841 Elizabeth Bay House had eight domestic servants, in addition to labourers and those who worked in the stables and gardens. These servants were convicts and were the cause of much angst. The Macleay women fretted daily over the constant thievery, with the domestic servants stealing clothing, silver or anything that was worth money. To counter burglary, every window in Tusculum had a hanging bell fixed to a slot, so that should an intruder attempt to open one the bell would at once wake the family. Also by every bed was a policeman's rattle. Sometimes the problems with the servants were that they were lazy and only performed their chores reluctantly. Mitchell was forever complaining about his female convicts. Sometimes the feeling was mutual. Honora Cranley was found drunk in Market Street, lost and confused, and said she would rather be sentenced to two months in the third class of the dreaded Female Factory than continue to work as a domestic servant on the hill.

Many convicts lived in huts and their extreme behaviour and outbursts would occasionally disturb the tranquil running of the estates. Sometimes the violence seeped into the mansions themselves. The Long family of Tusculum were having lunch one day when a commotion was heard in the entrance hall. It was followed by shrieks from the drawing room, then the sound of heavy blows and groans. The family rushed into the drawing room where a terrible sight greeted them. A blood splattered convict was using a heavy iron bar to brutally beat a woman who was huddled up on the floor. He was overpowered, with difficulty, but she was already dead. The argument had developed in the huts at the rear of the garden and the wife had fled to seek refuge in the house. If she had turned left on reaching the hall instead of to the right, she would have run right into the family at lunch and probably have been saved.

As if to emphasise how it was almost impossible to separate the reality of crime from the world of privilege, the Darlinghurst Gaol was opened in 1841 just half a mile away from the elites of Woolloomooloo Hill. The juxtaposition was all too apparent when, one afternoon in 1860, boys playing cricket on Darlinghurst Road were startled to see up to twenty convicts in prison garb who had escaped from the gaol hightailing it across their pitch. The fugitives ended hiding in the trees of the Rosebank estate, near the top of William Street, where the police found them perched up high in the branches.

There were other dangers in the 1840s, one of them being the attraction of the main road along the ridge, where drunk or angry cabmen were a menace. Thomas Baxter was fined £4 for 'furiously driving' on the Woolloomooloo Road one evening. Inside the cab were a man and a woman; the woman, perhaps fearing she was going to die, leapt from the speeding vehicle before it stopped. Once the cab came to rest, the man inexplicably bolted off in the opposite direction. Another cabman, named Bussey, was convicted of 'furiously driving' down Woolloomooloo Road with panicked passengers inside his cab; pedestrians afraid of being killed by the galloping horses had to jump out of the way.

As for Aborigines, there are few mentions by residents except for a curt reference to them in James Dowling's son's memories of his youth living in Brougham Lodge, where he relates that the land in front of the house was a favourite camping ground for the blacks, 'who used to assemble at times in great numbers and were guilty of all sorts of orgies'.

Crime and violence were minor inconveniences compared to the drought and severe depression of the early 1840s. The wealthy merchant Alexander Spark had to mortgage his property Tusculum for £6000; then, when he faced financial ruin, it was bought by William Long, the wine and spirit merchant. Justice Dowling announced he couldn't keep out of debt 'even with my frugal habits' (he walked from Brougham Lodge into the city each morning instead of taking a cab, a route still followed by office workers today). Sheriff Macquoid was in even more serious trouble. On 12 October 1841 he retired to one of his rooms in Goderich Lodge and blew out his brains. The Coroner decided that he had 'destroyed himself in a fit of temporary insanity' but, really, it was the last act of a desperate man. He had spent monies to the value of about £2400 belonging to suitors of the court, that is to say, monies levied on petitioners of the court as directed by the judges.

Further investigations revealed that his slippery way with money had been evident way back in 1824, when he was required to give security in the Supreme Court of £1000 for the estate he had bought – something he avoided doing. The Colonial Secretary Macleay had been so concerned about Macquoid's failure to lodge the security money that he wrote to him in 1829 demanding it be paid, but strangely nothing more was done about it.

Macleay himself had always spent beyond his means (he even had a Venetian gondola built to sail around the harbour). In order to avoid bankruptcy, his eldest son, William, took over the finances. He sold his father's precious library of 4000 books, then the exquisite furniture, and in 1841 subdivided the estate into forty-four allotments, of which only eight sold. William's ceaseless attempts to save Elizabeth Bay House were met not with praise but his father's Lear-like wrath.

Craigend was sold in 1841 and was eventually broken up. The sub-divisions would transform the isolated bucolic world of the ridge.

ON THE CORNER OF WILLIAM Street and Brougham Street, one shop up from Doncaster Hall, is O'Malley's Hotel, which was once Keary's Woolloomooloo Hotel. It was more than a boozer. From the late 1860s through to the beginning of the twentieth century it was a community hub and a meeting place for all sorts of political, cultural and sporting groups (including the Woolloomooloo Bay Rowing Club). Edmund Barton, soon to become our first Prime Minister, delivered his election speeches from the hotel balcony to up to five hundred people. Coronial inquests were held inside and ranged from an investigation into the road death of the four-year-old son of the Reverend George Martin, who lived in Upper William Street North (now Bayswater Road), to a drunken husband who bludgeoned to death his wife of forty-six years in a Rushcutters Bay hotel.

The hotel saw drunkenness, carousing, murder and suicide. Perhaps the suicide that affected the Keary family most was the death of James Keary, a relative of the owner, Thomas Keary. James was about thirty years old and living and working at the hotel as a barman when in late 1904 he drowned himself at Manly near the ladies' baths. He left a note full of self-disgust:

> *I am going to do away with myself and if my body is found have a*
> *look at it and go to my funeral. I have done wrong and disgraced*
> *you all.*

Its present incarnation as an Irish-themed pub filled with backpackers and newly arrived Irish immigrants is far removed from the sense of community that the original Keary's Hotel cultivated. The patrons imbibe at prodigious levels, smoke furiously on the footpath, spew on the steps of my building or leave bloodstains in the doorway after a drunken brawl.

The Chinese-themed entrance to O'Malley's poker machine rooms is around in Brougham Street, once known as one of the most dangerous streets in the Cross. Badly lit, lined with cheaply built cottages, decrepit terraces and hovels, its poverty and criminals were infamous as was typified by the vicious Brougham Street gang in the 1930s. Its seedy, violent reputation was such that policemen seldom ventured down it, unless armed and in groups.

Opposite O'Malley's in Brougham Street is the former El Rocco nightclub, once the seminal venue for modern jazz in the 1950s and early 60s. It closed down in 1969, briefly re-opened as a jazz club in the 1980s, but has never regained its former cachet. Since the late 1970s it has undergone many transformations, from a forgotten closed-up space to pizza bar, cabaret club and now a venue for stand-up comedy called Happy Endings (a name that doesn't bode well for its eventual and certain demise).

Across Brougham Lane is the rear of the Holiday Inn, built on the site of the Oriental Hotel, which in turn was erected on the site of James Dowling's gorgeous Brougham Lodge.

Facing the hotel across the street are two terraces that form the Asylum Backpackers. The noisy behaviour at night drives Ted, who lives in a rear apartment of my building, to distraction. An enormous hulk of a man, he sits drinking beer into the night, sitting at his open window and shouting at the backpackers to shut up. Not far along from the backpackers are the Windsor Flats. Although built recently they are squat, ugly and forgettable, with most of the residents probably not suspecting that where they live was once a hovel. At number 179, Rosaleen Norton, the Witch of Kings Cross, lived in a cluttered, decrepit terrace with her lover Gavin Greenlees. Down in the basement was where they held black masses, engaged in sadomasochist sex and produced pornographic photographs that can still shock.

A little further on is probably one of the most drab one-storey houses in the street. It has green shutters and a cream façade, but otherwise is an example of a simple Georgian style. This is Telford

Lodge, build in 1831 and therefore one of the oldest buildings in the Cross, its historical value far outweighing its architectural significance.

It's a different Brougham Street now from the perilous thoroughfare of previous decades. Still there are the druggies who haunt its dimly lit footpaths of a night, eyeing any parked car that may have something inside it worth selling. Some mornings it's difficult to negotiate the footpaths because they're littered with the shattered glass of car windows, a junkie's version of *Kristallnacht*. Yet there are many signs that the street is changing its character. Terraces have been converted into offices and many old slum houses have been replaced by rows of uniform terraces for naval personnel.

When I first shifted into the area I lived at number 60, a two-storey terrace with a deceptively narrow frontage which belied its four spacious bedrooms, high ceilings and a backyard. The first floor balcony had a panoramic view across to the city. At night, especially when there was a misty rain, the city seemed to float in a sea of soft neon colours and muted lights.

What became quickly apparent when I lived there in the early 1990s was that Brougham Street may have been in the process of losing its notorious reputation but it was – and still is – one of the most unsafe streets in the Cross. Because it's a one-way, and can only be entered from Cowper Wharf Road, down in Woolloomooloo, impatient people find it easier to enter at the top of William Street and drive backwards – especially when drunk. I grew used to the sounds of cars crashing into parked vehicles. One night I heard a car crash several times in succession. I looked down from the balcony and saw the drunken driver standing under the street light leaning on his damaged car, surveying the wreckage of four other cars. His right hand was clutching his forehead, and he had the dumbstruck expression of someone who is hoping to wake up from a nightmare.

A few doors down are the Butler Stairs, which rise up into Victoria Street, testing the fitness of the unhealthy and the old. As you progress north there is a sense you are leaving the Cross behind, and this is especially so in Rowena Place, a stubby lane on the right-hand side which features six petite workers' cottages built in 1860. They have been restored in vivid colours, reminding me of a storybook village. At the end of the truncated lane are gigantic brick archways, covered in anti-pigeon netting. You have to crane your neck to see the backs of the large mansions far above on Victoria Street, so high that they seem to be floating heavenwards. How great the contrast must have been in the nineteenth century between the hovels and workers' cottages of Brougham Street and the haughty mansions high up on the ridge.

Behind the bland, even ugly facades of the terraces and the public housing estate on the western side, there is still a lawless component to the street. There are several dealers, mostly selling marijuana. One of the most popular is Hugh, a skinny, tousle-haired guy who walks with a pronounced limp because he once broke his back falling down his stairs trying to escape a drunken – and armed – Serbian criminal who wanted a slice of Hugh's business. Most dealers want their customers in and out as quickly as possible – not Hugh. He holds open house and clients often stay to smoke their dope and watch music video clips on the enormous plasma screen. One time I visited Hugh with Coco, my chihuahua. Hugh was in the living room playing poker with some mates and snorting copious quantities of cocaine. There was also a Great Dane resting on the couch, which apparently belonged to one of the card players. While I was waiting for Hugh to sell me some dope I noticed that Coco, who studiously ignored other dogs, was becoming almost feverish in her flirtatious behaviour with the Great Dane which, in turn, was showing an intense amorous interest in her, only he had had the chop and was whimpering with frustration. Their eyes sparkled and they were highly energetic, chasing one another and playing. It was only when I saw them sniffing the carpet that I realised both dogs had been snorting the cocaine that spilled off the table. It took hours for Coco to calm down.

There are also purveyors of illegal powders and prescription drugs. Chemical Bob, as he is known, looks like a hungry ferret and will not answer knocking at his door. You have to yell through the mail slot in the front door because he finds it easier to recognise voices rather than faces. He has plastic buckets filled with a cornucopia of all sorts of mind-altering substances. One time a woman I know, feeling depressed, bought ketamine from him. A quarter of an hour later, Chemical Bob and several of his middle-aged mates were chasing her down the streets into Woolloomooloo as she ran as fast as she ever had, despite high heels. Was she heading away from some horror or heading towards an imagined paradise? When I asked her later she didn't remember. All she knew was that she would never take the drug again.

There's a fellow I drink with who deals with goods that my father would have said *have fallen from the back of a truck*. I often wear suits and he asked me once if I needed a new one as he had a range of them in his flat. When I entered his living room I was stunned. It was like a department store, with racks of top brand-name suits, frocks, boxes of watches and expensive spectacle frames. The clothes still had their price tags and I bought a suit at a quarter of the original cost. From then on there has always been the standing offer of, *Just put in an order if you want a new suit or a Rolex watch, Louis.*

As Brougham Street slopes more steeply, the feeling of being cut off from Kings Cross is further reinforced down the street where there are no houses, only a massive sandstone cliff face, a cutting that rises sharply for thirty metres or so, dramatically isolating the flâneur from the peninsula of the Cross. The stained sandstone cliff face constantly seeps water and is smudged with moss, thistles and hardy grass. The cliff face is so friable that there is a permanent sign attached: *Rock fall hazard.* It's as if the very geology of the street further reinforces separation from the ethereal heights of the ridge.

By the time you reach the Hordern Steps (named after Edward Hordern, a local who worked for Sydney Council) you have descended into the trough of Woolloomooloo. The stairs were built in 1882 and were one of the few access points up into Potts Point. The artist Julian Ashton made a painting of the steps around 1885. In it a fashionable lady with a long white dress and her face shaded by a red umbrella takes a late morning stroll through the summer haze down the stairs. Beyond the Steps is Woolloomooloo Bay, once a busy port, but now home to the trendy Cowper Wharf Hotel, expensive apartments and restaurants. The Navy docks are still there, almost within touching distance, an unmistakable reminder that all main roads of the Cross lead down to the harbour, and that the Cross is, indeed, a port town.

The feeling I've always had about this street is that it is not really part of Kings Cross. It's as if the street doesn't have its own identity but is merely a thoroughfare between the Cross and the public housing estates of Woolloomooloo. Trees have been planted to bring shade and perhaps some character, but really it is an inoffensive, forgettable route.

The quickest way to ascend into the Cross from lower Brougham Street is by way of the steep Hordern Stairs. These seventy steps are made from tessellated bricks which lead up to the top landing where a metal disposal bin is strategically positioned for the junkies of Woolloomooloo as a last chance to get rid of needles. It's a glaring antithesis of Ashton's sunny and romantic vision. Past the needle bin there is a path that turns at a right angle and continues another thirty paces along a pathway between the backs of cheerless apartment buildings into verdant Victoria Street. The contrast with lacklustre Brougham Street couldn't be starker. It's as if you have left a sterile world and suddenly found yourself in a verdant arbour.

A tap on the car window

THAT KINGS CROSS CAN BE a dangerous place is a given but it can also be enticing for all the wrong reasons. It can be sinister in a subtle way, when its louche charm and cavalier attitude to society's moral code seduce the unwary by cultivating an aspect of your personality no-one, not even you, suspected was curled up inside the darker recesses of your mind. Rene Rivkin was to discover this when Kings Cross came knocking on his car window in Victoria Street.

A brassy multi-millionaire, he was always seen with a huge cigar clamped between his teeth and gold worry beads constantly clattering in his hands. With a fondness for the limelight, Rivkin had made his money in stockbroking and ran a successful business newsletter. Born in pre-Communist China, when he was about four he contracted a mysterious illness for which the cure was equally mysterious – an all-cream diet. The consequences were drastic. By the time he was fourteen and living in Australia he was 122 kilos and teased and ostracised because of his weight.

At the age of forty-seven he was a plump man with greying stubble that could not hide his descending staircase of chins. He had five children, a beautiful wife and a magnificent mansion, Carrara, in the exclusive eastern suburb of Bellevue Hill; his friends included fellow millionaires, popular radio jocks like

John Laws and politicians such as Graham ('Whatever it Takes') Richardson, the former Labor senator and ruthless power broker. Richardson, who was even more physically unappetising than Rivkin, had a hint of the hunchback to him and no neck to speak of. His cynicism was so ingrained that it was an inherent strand of his DNA.

By 1991 Rivkin was at a loose end. He had sold his business and was contemplating what to do next. The problem was that his wife, Gayle, didn't want him around the house all day. He was sitting in his Bentley near the southern end of Victoria Street, waiting for his driver to pick up some medication for him from the chemist, when there was a knock on his car window. Staring in at him was a swarthy, bearded Lebanese man who indicated he wanted to talk to him. Rivkin cautiously pressed the window button and it opened just enough for him to hear what the man wanted. He said he was Joe Elcham and was a fan of Rivkin's. He had just opened a café across the street with the imaginative moniker of Joe's Café. The more the café owner praised Rivkin, the more intrigued the man sitting in the back of the Bentley became. Elcham said if he wanted good coffee, then he should come and try one for free. Rivkin surprised Joe by turning up the following morning. Who knows what he thought of the coffee, but he was charmed by the place, even though the décor was prosaic and the furniture functional. He decided that Joe's Café was where he could escape the confines of home and avoid his usual upmarket haunts, where his fellow businessmen were beginning to bore him. The raffish ambience satisfied something deep within, as did the young men who began to congregate around him. That tap on his car window was to transform his life.

The word quickly spread that Rivkin adored being surrounded by men in their twenties. These were different from his usual high rollers and successful professionals; they were car washers, gym junkies, motorbike aficionados, plumbers, cocaine users, tilers and handsome unemployed hustlers.

Every weekday morning he held court at Joe's. The young men fought over the privilege of buckling a seat belt around his enormous girth and being the first one to pull out his chair on his arrival of a morning or his return from the toilet. The inner circle of this bargain basement salon was nicknamed the 'performing seals' and 'ship of fools' by those amused by the daily spectacle. In return for their adulation, Rivkin showered his sycophants with money and gifts. He took them on all-expenses-paid holidays, joy rides in his helicopter, trips on his luxurious yacht, and handed out Rolex watches and Hugo Boss suits like an Eastern potentate doling out gifts to his servants. He set up one lad with a tattoo parlour called Skins 'n' Needles in Darlinghurst. It quickly went broke. When a car washer wanted a loan of $20,000 to buy a Harley Davidson, Rivkin said he would give him the money if he kissed his feet. The grateful young man duly bent down and planted his lips on his benefactor's shoes. Rivkin had been used to talk about intricate financial matters and the vicissitudes of share markets, but most of his new friends were not well-educated nor great conversationalists. A favourite game at the café was to speculate on what sort of sexual favours you'd do for money. As the price rose from $1000 to $1 million the sexual favours became more revolting.

For Rivkin, Joe's Café was a piece of theatre. He sat at an outside table where, sucking on a cigar and smirking at the world, he showed off the handsome men who fluttered around him. It was as if he were putting on a show that publicly and deliberately disassociated him from his former life.

It wasn't long before family and friends noticed that he had changed alarmingly. His wife hated what Kings Cross had done to him:

'He became definitely narcissistic, extremely selfish, quite cruel, insensitive, erratic, buying into nightclubs, fashion, cars ... areas he had little or no knowledge of.'

Rumours began to spread that Rivkin was in homosexual relationships with some of the men. But as far as the businessman was concerned he liked his young coterie:

'... because I can do whatever I want in front of them, and I can't do whatever I want in front of my contemporaries. Whereas they [the young men] will take anything I dish out. When I say dish out, I don't do anything to hurt them ... They just take me as I am ... of course I have young interests. I love motor cars, fast motor cars, fast boats.'

One man who watched this daily exhibition was Gordon Wood. He was in his early thirties, older than Rivkin's boys, with a gym-toned body, blond hair, chiselled features and a 'cultured voice'. He had an economics degree but was more interested in acting. He had worked in a theatre restaurant as a singing wait-er but had little money and few job prospects. He lived above a laundry in Victoria Street with his 23-year-old model girlfriend, Caroline Byrne, who complained about his laziness and how he'd just lie in bed all morning doing nothing. Wood was a man who struck people as insincere, vain and with a grating oleaginous manner. He liked to greet women with the practised line, 'Hi, I'm Gordon; I feel like I've known you forever.'

Wood hatched a plan: he had seen the presents that the young men received from the multi-millionaire and set out to become an indispensible member of Rivkin's court. For weeks he hung around the café in his gym gear until Rivkin began to notice his handsome Nordic features, a startling contrast to his circle of swarthy flatterers. Gradually Wood wheedled his way into Rivkin's presence and in October 1993 became his chauffeur and personal assistant. He had to be on call twenty-four hours a day on both his mobile and pager. A delicate aspect of his job was to manage Rivkin's mood swings, which ranged from elation to melancholic sulkiness.

Wood, who found it difficult to separate fantasy from reality, talked up his role with Rivkin, insinuating to Byrne and friends that he was more than a chauffeur, that he was his boss's confidant and that Rivkin often sought his sage financial advice. Rivkin did seem to trust him, because he told Wood to buy shares in a printing firm called Offset Alpine, owned by Rivkin, Trevor Kennedy (a former director of Qantas) and Graham Richardson. Wood told friends and relatives to buy the shares. Not long afterwards, on Christmas Eve 1993, the printing factory mysteriously caught fire and burnt to the ground. The strange thing was that the assets were worth just $3 million, yet there was a $53 million insurance payout. It was one of the largest insured property losses in Sydney's history. There were rumours that the fire was deliberately lit and even loose-lipped Wood told friends it was 'a set-up'. Despite this, Rivkin took Wood with him to Zurich to meet with Swiss bankers to make certain his secret accounts, which he used illegally in his share-trading, were never revealed to Australian authorities.

Wood was so often in Rivkin's company that Byrne began to suspect that her boyfriend and his boss were having an affair. He was to claim later that his employer wanted to have sex with him but he had rejected his approaches. It is doubtful that this happened. Rivkin may have had a secret erotic attraction to his boys but he probably never acted on it. He got his rocks off from being adored and fussed over by his obsequious group of misfits. It was a long way from the schoolyard where he had been despised and shunned. He was now king of the kids and he wanted the world to know it. His court jesters and sidekicks were such an unintelligent, tattooed, greedy bunch that Rivkin was openly mocked, but he didn't care; Kings Cross supplied what he had always craved – unconditional devotion and respect.

He had frequently advised clients, 'Never do business with people with a shady past – no exceptions!' but he broke his own rule when he hired a 207-centimetre monster of a man, Nathan Jones, a convicted armed robber. Rivkin had no need of a bodyguard, Jones was just there as another cast member of Rivkin's Victoria Street theatre, which was disintegrating into a carnivalesque sideshow. Rivkin was noticed having coffee at Joe's with the infamous drug trafficker Bruce 'Snapper' Cornwell. It was one more example of how he was allowing himself to slide into a murky, morally dubious world. Police were so concerned that in 1995 they installed themselves in a flat opposite Joe's, ironically above the very chemist's shop where Rivkin had stopped a couple of years before. They spent a fruitless year spying on the millionaire in the hope of finding out whether he was involved in the drug trade.

On 8 June 1995 Caroline Byrne's body was found at the bottom of the Gap. At first it was thought she committed suicide but Wood's version of events began to unravel as police discovered he had lied about his whereabouts on the day she died. Richardson was caught up in the fibs when Wood used him as an alibi, telling the police he had been chauffeuring Rivkin's business partner around Sydney on the day Caroline went to the Gap. Richardson proved this was not true. The evidence built up suggesting that Wood, probably with an accomplice, threw Caroline over the cliff. His behaviour after the murder was odd. He told friends and relatives an unlikely story that Caroline had died in a car accident. With a callousness that shocked everyone except himself, he made withdrawals from Byrne's ATM account after she died. On visiting the morgue to see her body, the upper section and head smashed to a pulp, he asked the attendant 'Do you mind if I look at her tits?' The coroner gave an open finding but did remark that Wood's evidence was bizarre, with 'glaring inconsistencies'.

One of the reasons alleged for Wood killing his girlfriend was that she was threatening to leave him and tell the police that the Offset Alpine fire was an insurance scam. Whatever the motive, Rivkin fired his chauffeur and refused to return Wood's increasingly desperate phone calls. Knowing he was the object of continuing investigations, Wood fled to England where, despite having no qualifications, he found a job that paid him $400,000 a year.

Back in Australia, in 2003, Rivkin was convicted of insider trading in Qantas shares. He was sentenced to nine months of weekend detention. Before serving his time, he bragged that the prison sentence didn't worry him at all, but he was an anxious man. His supposed fortune was based on paper shuffling rather than real profits. His financial acumen was exposed as conceited nonsense. The humiliation of jail and the desertion of his young cronies and his increasing detachment from his domestic life rattled him. The hubris was long gone. Underneath the bluster he was a coward. He managed to serve only two days in jail before collapsing and being taken off to hospital with a supposed bipolar disorder. The sixty-one year old became increasingly hysterical, self-pitying and maudlin. He tried to commit suicide but failed. Then in May he separated from his wife and went to live with his 87-year-old mother. In June he lay down on the bed in the spare bedroom of his mother's apartment, swallowed barbiturates, taped his mouth shut and placed his head in a plastic bag.

His suicide didn't cleanse his name. Post-death he was linked to insider trading, undeclared bank accounts, arson and the death of a beautiful model. Wood was extradited from England to face trial for the murder of Caroline Byrne. Rivkin's ghost must have squirmed to hear his name mentioned so frequently in the terrible, sleazy details revealed at the trial. Wood didn't go into the witness box; even his flamboyant lawyer must have known that his client wouldn't be able to tell a convincing story. The trial revealed him as a hollow man, a narcissist more in love with the doppelganger in the mirror than any other human being. He was found guilty of his girlfriend's murder in November 2008.

Three and a half years later, Wood was released on appeal because the evidence against him was insufficient. He was then paid $200,000 for a television interview. Rivkin is now known more for his association with the charmless, opportunistic Wood than his share market successes. If only he hadn't answered the knocking on his car window years before, he may not have succumbed to the temptations of Kings Cross, which ended up wrecking his life.

THE REVOLUTIONARY
AND THE BOOK COLLECTOR

FOR THE FIRST FEW DECADES of the nineteenth century William Street was almost a private road for the rich to travel between the city and their mansions on the hill. Given that the estates were private property and there was a ban on trespassing, it meant that people couldn't go around the harbour foreshores but instead had to follow a route up what is now Oxford Street to Taylor Square and then head north along Darlinghurst Road to Potts Point. Because of this, the settlement began to concentrate around the Darlinghurst and Surry Hills area. At the same time, houses and shops sprang up in William Street, and by the mid-1850s there were forty-three buildings on the north side of William Street and nineteen on the south side. The thoroughfare was a quagmire in winter and a dustbowl in summer, made worse by the stink of horse manure and oppressive clouds of flies and mosquitoes.

The depression of the 1840s continued to be felt. Many estates changed hands or were subdivided. Goderich Lodge was bought in 1850 by the wealthy wine and beer merchant Frederick Tooth, and at the other end of the Macquoid estate was the villa Waratah, where Frederick's brother Edwin lived. The two houses became celebrated for their hospitality. William Long, who owned several lucrative hotels, bought Tusculum (both the Tooths and Long were importers of wines, spirits and beer, as colonial beer was not widely drunk until the 1880s).

Sir Charles Nicholson, an obstetrician, landowner, business-man, connoisseur, classical scholar and one of the founders of Sydney University, bought Tarmons. He was one of the most cultivated men in the colony, helping to establish Sydney University and having probably the best collection of books in Sydney, which he held in his Tarmons library, a highly impressive forty-eight feet long and with a thirty-foot-high cedar ceiling. His house held several risqué statues based on classical models. His Scottish servant was so appalled by them that she threatened to cover them up when visitors came.

It's a nice irony that in 1853 Nicholson sold Tarmons and its salacious statues to the Sisters of Charity. The first Sisters had arrived in Sydney over a decade before, carrying with them a vow of service to the poor and a heavy iron crucifix depicting a black Christ, because they had learned that the Aborigines were black. They transformed the old ballroom into their first chapel, retaining the stained-glass window that was a parting gift from Nicholson. Soon they saw a need for a hospital and took the highly unusual step for the time of admitting patients without making any distinction on the grounds of religion. In a rare ecumenical display, Protestants, Jews and Catholics all took part in the fundraising. In 1857 the Sisters treated their first patient and a few months later a women's ward opened, which was followed by a men's ward the following year. The house was renamed St Vincent's after the seventeenth-century priest and charity worker who founded the French Sisters of Charity in 1660. The former Tarmons was an idyllic spot with uninterrupted views overlooking Sydney Harbour.

In the 1860s there was a ribbon development of terrace houses along Macleay and Victoria Streets. For sixty years both streets became fashionable addresses for bankers, lawyers, businessmen and publishers like John Fairfax, the founder of the *Sydney Morning Herald*. The dismantling of the estates continued and in 1864 the Kellett estate was sub-divided. A portion of the land from Kellett Street along Darlinghurst Road, almost to Macleay Street, was sold to the Jewish businessman and property developer Mr John Solomon, who built Alberto Terrace, a very fashionable address on the eastern side of Darlinghurst Road. Many Jewish families lived in Macleay Street for practical reasons – the synagogue down in Elizabeth Street was 'a Sabbath Day's journey' away, or roughly a mile.

Yet it would be a mistake to think that the houses and terraces on the ridge were part of a planned geometric grid. A report in the *Sydney Morning Herald* in 1864 thought the area 'inchoate':

> *In this pretty hamlet, which stands on a rocky eminence ...*
> *anything like a rigid, mathematical regularity in the lines of the*
> *streets has, from the nature of the locality been impossible, so that*
> *sweeping curves, sharp corners and mysteriously obtuse angles,*
> *here appear to be the rule instead of the exception.*

The reporter remarked on how one could walk down a well-kept road only to turn a corner and find it had petered out into a marsh, or one was forced 'to clamber over rocks and hillocks using only a worn track'. Despite this, the area was still impressive:

> *There are several fine mansions with gardens and pleasure*
> *grounds ... where the comfort and privacy of old country*
> *habits appears to have been consulted more than is usual in the*
> *mansions of the wealthy in this part of the world.*

The problem that Thomas Mitchell foresaw thirty years before now became manifest. There was a brash and untidy mixture of shops, boarding houses, schools, houses, brothels, hotels and dressmakers gradually and inexorably moving up the hill. As more people began to live and work in William Street, the pressure grew for a more direct way to the eastern suburbs: William Street finished in an abrupt stop at Goderich Lodge. In the early 1860s tracks on either side of the inconvenient Goderich estate became two routes, Upper William Street South (later Kings Cross Road) and Upper William Street North, which led down to Rushcutters Bay and beyond (later the street became Bayswater Road, hyperventilating with cars and trams). The two streets joined at the far eastern side of the estate in a continuation of William Street. These streets added to the confusing tangle of routes at the top of William Street. Over the years the relationship between Darlinghurst Road and William Street became deeply symbiotic until it was difficult to imagine Kings Cross without the essential artery that leads into its heart.

In the slim book *An Illustrated Guide to Sydney, 1882,* William Street is described as 'the principal thoroughfare of Woolloomooloo boasting many excellent shops'. Its buildings were like a geological strata of six decades of architecture: colonial cottages, Georgian houses, grand Victorian terraces, Italianate and Regency terraces. The steep gradient of the street was reflected in the fact that the newly introduced 24-passenger horse omnibuses, their floors covered with straw and their interiors lit by candles or kerosene lanterns in the evenings, were generally hauled by two horses but for William Street, when four horses were used. The horses frequently stalled because of exhaustion and boys were employed to urge them up and around into Darlinghurst Road.

The economic boom of the 1880s also resulted in an increasing number of sub-divisions of estates and the demolition of some beautiful mansions. Brougham Lodge was pulled down. In 1885 the gold prospector, astute landowner, pastoralist and breeder William Buchanan bought Kellett House and immediately demolished it and built the magnificent and imposing row of houses Bayswater Terrace, which still remain, even some 120 years later, striking examples of Victorian optimism.

If there were two men who were representative of the demographic changes that were happening in Darlinghurst, as it was now called, it was a Frenchman and a native-born Australian who were to play significant roles in the cultural life of the colony.

Lucien Felix Henry was born in the French provinces in 1850 and shifted to Paris to study art when he was sixteen. A few years later he was caught up in the bloody events of the Paris Commune, fighting on the side of the revolutionaries. His comrades thought him courageous, handsome and possessed of the rare gift of grace under pressure. On 18 April 1872 Henry was condemned to death for his 'insurrectory actions' in the Paris Commune. Two months later his sentence was commuted to exile and imprisonment on Ducos Peninsula, New Caledonia. After seven years of imprisonment he arrived in Sydney, aged twenty-nine, at a time of growing prosperity in the colony due to agriculture, gold and English investment. Within six months he had married Madame Rostoul, a professor of French nine years his senior. She was a fellow radical and utopian socialist who had come to Sydney in 1874 with her two children, having been deported from New Caledonia for assisting the escape of communards from the penal colony. She had been widowed when her husband drowned attempting to escape the prison island.

Although Henry had arrived in Sydney without any money, he quickly rose to prominence as an artist, decorator and teacher. The Henrys shifted into a rented apartment at 156 Victoria Street. He had a large faux French republican crest hanging over the living room doorway, the walls featured many of his landscape paintings, and the spacious rooms were filled with ornate cabinets, vases of flowers, cane chairs and a languid clutter of herms.

His paintings showed an intense interest in the Australian landscape. Rather than copying European trends and traditions, he urged his pupils to utilise the imagery of the natural world around them. He had come at the right time. There was a growing tide of republicanism and rigorous public debates about nationhood. The question of what constituted Australian culture assumed great importance as the colony moved towards its centenary. Henry insisted that local artists should choose subjects that were appropriate for Australia. The usual oak and laurel leaves should be replaced by native flora and fauna. In his own paintings, sculptures and stained glass windows he depicted staghorns, sea horses, native water lilies, black swans, giant clams, lyrebirds and the waratah. The large dense flower heads of the crimson waratah with their numerous small flowers fascinated him; he felt it was the quintessential Australian flower.

He was an inspirational teacher and artist whom the *Illustrated News* called 'An extraordinary genius'. In 1884 he was appointed first instructor in the Department of Art at Sydney Technical College in Ultimo, and mixed with artists, architects, engineers, politicians and businessmen. His radical political beliefs were at odds with his bourgeois appearance (trim beard, crisp suits and spats), but it's telling how well he was fitting into the Sydney social scene that he also became a foundation member of an informal social club that included J.F. Archibald, the editor of *The Bulletin*. Years later one of its members, Ernest Wunderlich, wrote that it was a group made up of 'bohemians, struggling journalists, poets and other freelances, with whom we argued, wrangled and disputed on great and small things'.

Henry's work ranged from designing a massive crematorium overlooking the Pacific Ocean based on an inverted firewheel flower, to decorative carvings and electric light fittings in the shape of lyrebirds for the Hotel Australia in the city (its Long Bar famous for its uneasy mix of bohemian and bourgeois patrons). But much of his work has vanished except for two stained glass windows in the Main Hall of the Sydney Town Hall, finished in November 1889. Called the Centennial Windows, one is of Captain Cook, the other of New South Wales personified as a tall, confident woman, whose head is crowned with the horns and wool of the ram that had created boom times for the economy. She holds a trident and a miner's lamp, symbolic of how the maritime and mining industries had also helped create Australia's wealth. Captain Cook stands on the deck of a ship holding a telescope. It's a portrait of Cook not as an imperial adventurer but as a scientist, explorer and cartographer. In one critic's view, the Centennial Windows had fused the medieval craft of stained glass with Australian nationalism.

Over the years Henry had been writing a book: 'Australian Decorative Arts: one hundred studies and designs'. It failed to find a publisher in Australia and he left for Paris in 1891. He arrived with his pregnant mistress, former student Frances ('Fanny') Broadhurst, who died giving birth at the age of twenty-eight. His obsession with the waratah paid off. He wrote a short story about the Australian flower which gained him some money and brief fame, but he was soon broke. The 1890s depression was just as severe in France as in Australia and he could find no publisher for his magnum opus. He died, bankrupt, in 1896 of the consumption he had contracted as a political prisoner in New Caledonia.

Henry wasn't an important artist but his influence on his pupils was profound. It took a Frenchman to compel our artists to appreciate their natural world and use it as a way of developing and inspiring unique Australian imagery, which was also an expression of radical Australian nationalism.

When Henry lived in Victoria Street, another man resided a couple of minutes away in Darlinghurst Road who would have an even more colossal effect on the cultural life of Australia. David Scott Mitchell was born in 1836 and spent his childhood in one of Sydney's grandest mansions, the Francis Greenway designed Cumberland Place in the Rocks. His father made his fortune from a 20,000-hectare coalfield in the Hunter Valley, and Mitchell was brought up in a world of privilege where he could indulge his passion for books from an early age, no doubt influenced by his parents, who also collected books. He was one of the first law graduates from Sydney University, but his wealth meant that he didn't need to practise. Instead his life passed in a pleasant blur of cricket (a game he followed keenly all his life) and whist (he was considered the best player in Sydney) and enjoying dancing (apparently he was excellent), dinner parties and acting in amateur theatricals. Unlike many men of his age and wealth, he felt no need to visit the Mother Country and never left our shores. It seems that as he neared thirty he came to the practical realisation that he should do the conventional thing and marry. His proposal to Emily Manning, the 19-year-old daughter of a wealthy former Supreme Court Judge and Solicitor-General, and its consequences seem to have left him with a queasy case of aftershock. He wrote to his cousin, Rose Scott:

It is now more than three weeks since I became that queer beast an engaged man and even yet I can scarcely realise the position ... It will be a long engagement as I have to make up for good many idle years.

There is a sense that the twenty-nine year old was trying to find a purpose to his life. His light-hearted poems to his fiancée have no emotional urgency and after a few months Mitchell stopped writing and visiting her.

It isn't known who called off the engagement but in the following year Mitchell played the role of Peter Pinkey in John Buckstone's comedy *A Single Life*, a play performed at Government House on 31 August 1866. It was a part that either Mitchell asked to play or the producer thought was made for him, because the character Peter Pinkey is a bashful bachelor who longs to shake off his shyness and propose to his beloved. Mitchell must have seen himself as a man like Pinkey, and it would have confirmed to him, as he performed before Sydney society, that he was indeed disturbingly similar to the man he was impersonating. Still, there was nothing unusual about his decision not to marry, given that forty-three per cent of the population at that time didn't.

He continued to collect books but it was only after his mother Augusta died in 1871 (his father had died two years before) that he found his vocation in life. In that same year he bought number 17 Darlinghurst Road. It was a freestanding, double-fronted Georgian terrace of two storeys, with the small front yard protected by a fence of iron railings and a gate that led to six white marble steps. Its patio columns were wreathed with creepers. Three large shuttered windows greeted the visitor. The stables were at the rear and the house was flanked by simple one-storey cottages. He paid £5000 for the seven-room house and it was certainly modest in size compared to Tusculum or Goderich Lodge. But part of its attraction – which is hard to imagine now – was the tranquillity of the location. He shifted in December 1872, his substantial book collection barely being able to fit in the seven-room house. The bachelor could now engage in full-time book collecting, unhampered by love and marriage; the only woman in his life his live-in housekeeper, his affection reserved for his black cockatoo. He remained in his Darlinghurst Road house until he died.

He had never worked a day in his life but attacked the job of book collecting with a serious single-mindedness. He read voraciously and collected widely, visiting the city's booksellers every Monday morning. He was known to the cab drivers as 'Old Four Hours', which was the time he took to tour the bookstores. In the beginning he had focused his attention on Elizabethan literature and drama, but gradually he developed a taste for Australiana and described his quest as:

> *To gather a copy of every document relating to Australia ... The main thing is to get the records. We're too near to our own past to view it properly.*

He widened his searches to include not only books, but pamphlets, journals, newspapers, engravings, documents and any piece of ephemera that related to Australian history and literature.

The former social butterfly withdrew into the cocoon of his house and gathered a reputation as a recluse, but in fact he had many visitors and was considered to be 'a witty and wise' conversationalist. He was a naturally shy man, with a strong dose of Scottish conservatism running through his veins and, unlike his father or cousins, shied away from public and social life. All his money went on collecting, and in order to finance this obsession, he was frugal in his daily life, eating only two identical meals a day: grilled lamb chops for breakfast at 11 am and for dinner at 8 pm. Besides his many callers (including his dear friend John Rae, an artist and lecturer who lived nearby in the grand three-storey mansion Hilton in Liverpool Street which had a camera obscura at the top to take advantage of the views) there was the constant ringing of the front door bell announcing the arrival of more packages of books from local and overseas booksellers. As the bookseller George Robertson said of Mitchell, unlike many book collectors, he had 'those rare qualities, taste and discrimination'.

One of the few photographs of him was taken when he was thirty-four; he had no moustache, a slightly unkempt beard, a large mouth which conveyed a sense of humour (he adored comedies) and piercing, melancholy eyes. From then on he avoided being painted or photographed. His book collection began to take over the house, including his bedroom; its single bed did not take up much space, which was lucky given that the room held a wire-door bookshelf and five revolving bookcases. One wonders if it was in the bedroom, more specifically in that wire-door bookshelf far from the prying eyes of his housekeeper, Sarah Milligan, that he kept his collection of erotica, the most extensive in the colony.

During the 1890s Mitchell was driven by his quest to collect as many of the original source materials of the early history of the colony as he could buy, knowing so much of it could disappear given the indifference shown to the past by Australians. Even so, as he said to the bookseller Fred Wymark, if he had known what a huge and time-consuming thing the collection would become he would never have started it. There is no doubt he was driven to achieve his aim but there must have been a psychological need for him to surround himself with books. Like many similarly obsessive people, perhaps the collection gave him an emotional succour he couldn't find anywhere else and a sense of personal control over his life that he needed.

His greatest wish was to create a grand library for Sydney, where Australians could understand how the nation came into being and evolved. He amassed the largest purely Australian collection in existence. In 1898 he made it clear that he would bequeath:

... 30,000 volumes, prints, engravings and pictures the
Australasian portion of which I have collected as the main object

of my life, to enable future historians to write the history of
Australia in general, and New South Wales in particular.

He became increasingly housebound, his monotonous and nutri-
tionally poor diet giving his skin the appearance of pale parchment. The house began to crumble around him. One story has it
that part of his patio collapsed into the street. Without even looking up from the book he was reading, the unflustered bibliophile
told Milligan to arrange for the mess to be cleared. Near the end
he was frail, with the stooped, rounded shoulders of the book-
worm. But he continued to collect, even on his death bed. A few
days before he died Wymark presented Mitchell with *First Fruits
of Australian Poetry,* the first book of verse published in Australia,
a volume Mitchell had been searching for in vain for years.

'I did not think we would ever see this,' he gasped. His head
fell back on the pillow and the bookseller thought he was dead,
and was about to call Milligan, when a familiar voice came from
the pillow: 'Now where were we, Fred?'

The proud Australian did not believe in God and remarked
to Wymark, 'If you hear anyone say I was converted, say I died
mad.' He died on 24 July 1907 without seeing the completion of
the public library that housed his astonishing collection.

His legacy is not only the Mitchell Library but the thousands
of rare books, documents and ephemera that are a magnificent
record of the history of a nation from its first settlement. Henry's
nationalism focused on Australian images, Mitchell's centred on
the word, but both men, who for a decade lived a short walk from
each other, played crucial roles in Australia's cultural and social
history and were, in their own way, harbingers of the writers, artists and bohemians who would become a defining feature of the
area, which, it seemed, couldn't decide what to call itself.

It had gone through several official and unofficial names over the years, including Windmill Road, Woolloomooloo Heights, Woolloomooloo and Darlinghurst. Again the name was changed in 1897, this time to Queens Cross to celebrate Queen Victoria's diamond jubilee in 1897. It was thought that the name could be confused with Queens Square in the city, so it was changed again a few years later in 1905 to Kings Cross, honouring King Edward VII. The name Kings Cross wasn't officially gazetted so it was uncertain just what area was covered by it. At first it applied only to the intersection of William Street, Darlinghurst Road and Victoria Street, but it quickly became less a specific geographical location than a fluid definition that could never be pinned down. The name morphed into the colloquial term 'the Cross', not so much a real address as one whose boundaries were left up to the imagination of its inhabitants and the fantasies of those who dreamed of visiting it.

Only when I was first living in the Cross did the name begin to have more associations. This occurred to me when I watched a bank customer fill out the location of his bank as Kings X. The X seemed to give the name a mysterious aura, as if the reduction of the word to a symbol hid meaning, but at the same time gave rise to myriad interpretations.

The Cross itself was given a literal meaning by the poet Wilhelm Hiener who, in the 1960s, as an appendage to his poem 'William Street', made the observation that the thoroughfare:

> *... can be seen to form the upright of a cross, outlined in lights, and sometimes, from a certain height, shadows suggest the hunched shape of a crucified man.*

I find it impossible to see such a shadowy literal suggestion of a cross, but the X symbol is used as the Christian cross, as it is also used to designate a person, thing, agency or factor whose true name is unknown or withheld, as, say, the anonymous witness in a court trial. It also marks the spot where treasure is buried, it can indicate crossroads, an illiterate's personal mark, an unknown variable in mathematics and films classified as for adults only. In other words, the X at one time or another can represent anything you want it to be.

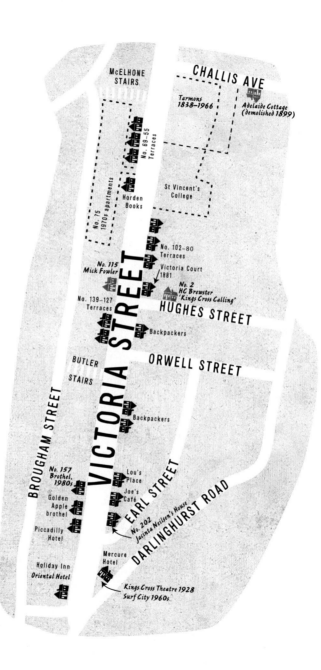

IF YOU WALK UP THE Butler stairs from Brougham Street you
emerge halfway along Victoria Street. If it's summer and you face
north, there are gigantic plane trees on both footpaths that look as if
they're bowing to each other across the street, nearly touching each
other, and forming a green gateway that leads the eye down to a
beckoning patch of sparkling light bouncing off the waters of Sydney
Harbour. In winter the moon peeks through the bare branches like a
white eye trying to peer through outstretched fingers.

But if you walk into Victoria Street at the southern end, next to
the Kings Cross Hotel, you find the milieu not so much beautiful as
utilitarian. Straightaway you are greeted by two of the last remaining
tourist hotels in the Cross, facing each other across the street.
There is the grey concrete convex facade of the Holiday Inn, its name
illuminated by gaudy green neon, and the other, formerly the jaded
Crest, which closed for several years, is now the Mercure, refitted
and relaunched at a cost of $30 million with a black and brown colour
scheme that is stylish but sombre.

The customer mix for the Holiday Inn is typical of the dwindling
number of hotels that remain in the area: ten per cent airline crews,
fifteen per cent local businessmen, thirty per cent tourists from
America, Europe and Japan, thirty-five per cent corporate bookings,
and ten per cent off the street.

The hotel presents itself as a defiantly sober, generically bland
building and has rarely been a subject of scandal, unlike some other
Kings Cross hotels. But not so long ago it was in the newspapers
because of one of its employees, Bill Sitzimis, a 21-year-old reception
supervisor. When he'd finish his shift of a day, Sitzimis would
surreptitiously take the staff lift to the third floor to room 357 and
transform himself into Aaron Boyd, a mysterious big-spending guest.
He lived there for two months and avoided detection by using service
elevators and rear entrances. At the end of two months he had racked
up bills of almost $10,000 on accommodation, room service and

telephones. As his account grew, he accessed a hotel computer to transfer the costs onto the accounts of other hotel guests. He was caught by a suspicious colleague and in court blamed his actions on his father, who he said was angry that he had chosen a career in the hospitality industry instead of working in his family-run milk bar. Sitzimis escaped with a two-year good behaviour bond and was ordered to repay the money. He refused to work for his father, and instead was employed by another hotel as a porter.

This section of Victoria Street is a motley collection of residences, backpacker hostels, cottages, cafés and shops that are so architecturally diverse that the streetscape is visual gibberish. There are bland apartment blocks, an ugly car park, and decrepit narrow houses including number 202, one of three lugubrious 1840s workers' cottages. There is a memorial plaque outside number 202 commemorating 'Juanita Neilsen', who campaigned against the redevelopment of the street and lived there before she was murdered in 1975. The brass plaque misspells her name. The tiled doorstep leads into a room of worn pine floorboards and exposed hand-fired bricks from the 1840s. A maze of small rooms leads to a rear patio of viper green tiles while the upstairs bedrooms are lined with pine. The City of Sydney has put Nielsen's house and the two adjoining properties under a heritage order that, to use its terminology, allows it to be used for 'adaptive reuse' but not demolition.

At night, especially of a Friday and Saturday, the street becomes one of the most beautiful boulevards in the Cross, with an extraordinary range of restaurants and small bars for the hipster crowds. But night and neon can be deceptive – in the harsh daylight its imperfections are obvious. The street is pockmarked with a dozen backpacker hostels with names like the Original Backpackers, Backpackers Hotel, Zing, Kanga House and Chilli Blue. The drab Travellers Rest, at 156, is the former home of the artist and teacher Lucien Henry.

There is a constant stream of backpackers down the street. The residents might whinge about them but backpackers are crucial to the economy of the Cross. Practically every bar and café has them on staff, many of them – as I can testify from personal experience – with little interest or pride in their jobs; they're more focused on saving for the traditional trip to far north Queensland or recovering from another night of binge drinking.

Hidden among the hostels, cafés and terraces near the southern end are two discreet dwellings that typify the Cross and its ability to assimilate radical social services that would be anathema to the rest of Australia. At number 180 is a new clinic, an adjunct of the Kirketon Road Centre, which has provided counselling and methadone programs for a quarter of a century. After outgrowing the K2 centre on Darlinghurst Road, Clinic 180 was opened in 2012. It provides testing and treatment for sexually transmitted infections, HIV and hepatitis, as well as counselling, first aid, injecting equipment, condoms, and help for local sex workers. Although a handful of residents opposed the centre, it was a relatively uncontroversial decision compared to the hysteria about the injecting rooms on Darlinghurst Road. As a sign that the Cross can 'normalise' what disgusts other parts of Australia, the centre was opened by Governor Marie Bashir. Next door to Clinic 180 is Lou's Place, a terrace catering for battered, drug-addled, mentally disturbed, hungry women and their children.

Amidst this miscellaneous collection of buildings and dowdy houses was once a café called Roy's Famous. It has had several reincarnations since, including, for a short period, as a Japanese restaurant. Back in the late 1990s Mandy and I would sit at an outdoor table and enjoy the entertaining passing parade of the hip, eccentrics, zombie junkies, backpackers, businessmen and beggars. The trouble with Roy's was that the owner was in financial difficulties. The food began to get so bad that we brought our own and the white wine list was reduced to only one cheap and undrinkable brand. The waiter stole from the increasingly unkempt owner, who fired him not long before he walked out of the café himself one day and never came back.

Directly across the road is a large anonymous-looking terrace. Inside is a brothel in which an acquaintance of ours worked as a tradesman, creating exotic Egyptian and African themed rooms. One time we watched as a hooker in her early twenties was dragged kicking and screaming from the brothel, her hair unruly, her eyes electric with drugs. Even after she was thrown into the back of the paddy wagon, you could still hear her foul-mouthed tirade as she was driven away. On another occasion a young man, about nineteen, emerged from the front door and when he walked down the footpath he began to skip with happiness until finally he jumped up, yelling out 'Yes!' and punching the sky with unbridled joy. The bordello is now called the Golden Apple and is described as 'Sydney's busiest establishment'. The theme rooms have been replaced by stylish modern rooms with moody lighting and luxurious spas. Next to the brothel is the Piccadilly Hotel, an exquisite example of art deco both inside and out. It's most famous for its upstairs Soho Bar with its labyrinthine series of bars and pool rooms, and its downstairs bar, the Piccadilly Room, its old-fashioned ambience reinforced with leather club chairs. My ex-partner wanted to be married on the roof, which duly happened with a bemused marriage celebrant and guests watching me attempt the bridal dance to Jayne Mansfield's caterwauling on a ghetto blaster, and being entertained by the Sisters of Perpetual Indulgence, a group of gay men dressed as nuns playing piano accordions. Perhaps the parodic elements were a sign that the marriage would last only eighteen months.

About fifty metres further on, past several restaurants – one of which used to be the celebrated Arthur's in the 1980s, with its three storeys of diners and much sniffing and giggling in the toilets – is the Butler Stairs. Here is a second memorial plaque devoted to a famous past resident of the street. The brass is corroding but the words are still visible:

> *Mick Fowler, Seaman, Musician & Green Ban Activist ...*
> *They were hard old days, they were*
> *battling days, they were cruel*
> *times – but then*
> *in spite of it all, Victoria Street will see*
> *low income housing for workers again.*

The steep stairs are a vivid example of the height differences between the ridge and Woolloomooloo. There's still a sense that the working class live below, while the gentry live up in genteel Potts Point. This distinction was even greater in the late nineteenth and early twentieth centuries. If anything showed the popular view of Potts Point it was two films made in the twenties. The comedy romance *Sunshine Sally*, released in 1922, was set in working class Woolloomooloo and the palatial houses and gardens of Potts Point. Sally works in a sweatshop called 'The White Laundry'. After she is rescued from drowning in Coogee by Basil, a lifesaver, she becomes involved with his mother's rich Potts Point lifestyle which is played for comedy as Sally tries to mimic the social etiquette of Potts Point. Five years later a children's film, *Kid Stakes*, was made based on the Fatty Finn comic strip. It's the story of a group of roughneck Woolloomooloo children who want to enter their goat Hector in a race. The once delightful Woolloomooloo is depicted as a treeless slum of a port town, with ships and warehouses the permanent backdrop. The dilapidated terraces and hovels are surrounded by concrete and asphalt. Hector escapes up into Potts Point and wanders into the grounds of a mansion. The contrast could not be greater. The enormous gardens are like a verdant Eden which the starving goat begins to destroy; he eats his way through copious amounts of flowers, devouring 150 chrysanthemums, 200 roses, fifty (very rare) orchids, and thousands of pansies and violets. At the same time the spoilt son of the Potts Point mansion ventures down into the bowels of the 'Loo. Bespectacled and dressed like a Little Lord Fauntleroy, he is taunted as a 'sissyboy' from Potts Point and set upon by the local boys, but he proves his mettle. He leads the 'Loo boys and girls up the Butler Stairs, a hair-raising adventure because a corpulent policeman guards the top of the stairs to stop such riff-raff from entering. But the cop falls asleep on the job and the children sneak past him into the forbidden and intimidating Potts Point; the symbolism of the huge class divisions could not be greater.

Crossing to the other side of the street – making sure to avoid the increasing numbers of joggers and dog walkers – the flâneur can dawdle up the narrow and short Orwell Street. It's hard to imagine now but once it was one of the most charming avenues in the Cross. When the Minerva Theatre opened in 1939, on the former site of Orwell House, and the plush Roosevelt nightclub, one door away, in the same year, the street was filled with people dressed in their finery, basking in the searchlights, the glamour and the excitement of being in the slightly wicked Kings Cross. The Minerva became a cinema and then a theatre again for *Hair.* The Cross was the perfect location for a musical that exalted 1960s hedonism, dope smoking and hippie values. After a run of two years the space reopened as a shopping centre. Its most recent incarnation has been as a production office for the Kennedy-Miller film company, producers of *Mad Max* and *Happy Feet.* Its façade is peeling and it looks determinedly drab, though you can still see its softly rounded feminine shapes, which give you a flavour of just how stunningly beautiful the building must have appeared when it opened.

Back in Victoria Street on the eastern side, it's a short walk to Hughes Street. At the corner is number 2, where Commander H.C. Brewster, author of *Pearls of Papua*, co-wrote with Virginia Luther the delightful *King's Cross Calling*, which provides a valuable record of the Cross during the Second World War. Hughes Street is an inconspicuous street, which is why in the 1960s it was the perfect place for the Cobweb Coffee Lounge. It had a gay bar out the back, which was carefully hidden. A patron had to go through a trapdoor to gain admission into what was thought to be the first gay disco in Sydney. Inside it was black and full of smoke, with fake cobwebs hanging from the ceiling. Hippies and drag queens mixed together, smoking joints and drinking cocktails.

Hughes Lane, which runs off the street, is even more unassuming and discreet. A month or so before the injecting centre opened on the main drag, Mandy and I went there to look at a house for sale and, because there was no way we could get inside, we decided to look at the rear of the building where there was a tiny lane. Four junkies were sitting on the ground, one of the men bleeding from his left arm. While one woman waited for her fix, the second man was preparing to plunge a needle into his arm when he noticed Mandy and me standing close by. He glanced up at us and said in a genteel voice, 'Sorry, youse shouldn't have to see this,' and pressed the plunger. Blood rushed into the syringe and his eyes rolled back in pleasure. He had just enough energy to hand the needle on to the impatient woman at his side before sprawling on the ground.

Back in Victoria Street there could not be a greater contrast to what Mandy and I experienced than the long row of elegant terraces restored to their former beauty on the western side, just past the Butler Stairs. Some are set back from the street and are obscured by leafy gardens with a thick profusion of shrubs, flowers and ferns that have a tropical prodigality. In summer the late afternoon sun finds it hard to pierce the leafy shield of the plane trees and the crepuscular light has an eerie green glow that's strangely comforting, as if time has regressed and the sound of cars has been replaced by that of horses and carriages.

The plane trees help define the area. First planted in 1935 they were a glorious addition to the streets. Where the ubiquitous evergreen gum trees gave no hint of the changing seasons, locals see the plane trees as a seasonal clock. The barren boughs of winter bud in spring (releasing blizzards of pollen that cause hay fever, runny noses and severe coughing as the pollen insidiously works its way down throats and inside noses) and then burst into the magnificent green foliage of summer. Viewed from the top of apartment buildings, Victoria Street seems like a lush green river. A few months later dead leaves pile up in gutters and footpaths, creating a crackling accompaniment to the flâneur's footsteps.

Hidden behind one of the gardens is Hordern House. It sells antiquarian books and also publishes studies on exploration and colonial history. The rooms of the terrace have a graceful simplicity and there's a hushed, sombre quality to it that can be intimidating for the first-time visitor. One day, when I was broke, I tried to sell them the first book written on Australian mushrooms, the 1892 *Handbook of Australian Fungi* by M.C. Cooke, a man who had never been to Australia. My first edition copy had several marks in it which meant it had little monetary value and I was politely sent on my way, still broke but retrospectively thankful to have kept it.

These gorgeous buildings face the eastern side of the street with its tawdry backpacker hostels, take-away cafés, cheap restaurants and a miscellany of tacky facades and weary buildings. It's only when you reach the Victoria Court Hotel that the eastern side of the street starts to look like the fashionable boulevard it once was. The hotel trades on that reputation with four-poster canopy beds, chandeliers and a forced Victorian charm.

But the western side of the street can be deceptive. Just past the terrace where my wife Mandy lived in the basement flat as a nine-year-old, there is a basic entranceway in a lane between two houses. Only when you step back across the street and look up do you see that behind the Victorian terraces are two high-rise apartment blocks with grubby cream bricks, dreary red corrugated roofs and all the architectural élan of a kid using a Lego set for the first time. Their brutal plainness and cheapness is apparent to all and an indictment of 1970s political and bureaucratic corruption, police immorality and government sponsored violence and stupidity. This is how the whole of Victoria Street could have looked if it hadn't been for the Green Bans.

It's about here that the eastern side starts to have terraces as beautiful as those facing them from across the street. These finish at St Vincent's College, established by the Sisters of Charity and one of the oldest Catholic girls' boarding schools in Australia (its 150th anniversary was held in 2008). The boarding wing of the school backs onto Tusculum Street, which may seem a secluded and decorous stubby cul-de-sac, but for a time it became a site that typified the tensions that have erupted over the years in the Cross between the blatant commercialisation of sex attempting to co-exist with more traditional values. The school fought a long legal battle to prevent Misty's, a brothel at number 3, gaining approval to operate ten prostitutes until 4 am on weekdays and 6 am on weekends.

One of the school's criticisms was that the brothel's front door was next to the school's entrance. Residents in the quiet street often complained about Misty's clients urinating on walls, smoking marijuana, littering and parking illegally. Some of the noise was caused by 'girlfriends of brothel clients screaming from cars the entire time their partners are inside'. A judge ordered Suzelle Antic, the manager of the 'massage and masturbation parlour,' to shut down within four months. Antic hired private investigators who, instead of finding evidence that contradicted the school's complaints, admitted to the court that they had seen groups of young men 'smashing bottles on the road, hitting a road and traffic sign with a stick, urinating on the trees ... on nearby apartment

block walls and even on the tyres of the private investigators' car'.
St Vincent's won its case and the brothel closed.

It's not as if this was a protest by cloistered nuns. Lay teachers
have gradually taken over and by the 1990s none of the Sisters of
Charity remained at the school. Of the 750 girls enrolled in Years 7–12,
140 are boarders. In the morning it's a familiar sight to see the day
girls streaming out of the underground train station, like hunchbacks
bent forward under the weight of heavy backpacks, marching down
the street to the college in groups of two and three, giggling, chatting
and sharing an iPod. On weekends it's common to see flushed,
anxious boarders rushing back to the school in time for the start of
the curfew. For many of the boarders, especially those who come
from distant suburbs or the country, the location of the school can be
alarming. Melinda Gainsford-Taylor, an Olympic athlete, remembered
leaving her home near Dubbo in 1985:

'Looking back it was hard because I was a country girl going to
the city. It was a culture shock being near Kings Cross.' She and her
friends would sneak up on the roof at night, which was forbidden, and
gaze longingly at the Harbour Bridge and Opera House that seemed
almost within touching distance.

As you walk down the western side of Victoria Street, the terraces
finish at number 55, which borders the McElhone Stairs, 120 steps
that lead down into Brougham Street. Behind this beautiful last
terrace are more of those hideous, grim 1970s apartment buildings.
At the top of McElhone Stairs is a 30-metre high vent releasing the
toxic air from the Navy's underground carpark. It is a long grey tube,
braced by horizontal steel grids that hold the metal pipe upright.

A month after she tried to commit suicide on Christmas Day by
threatening to leap off the William Street overpass, the Aboriginal
woman, her brain a noxious stew of ice, clambered to the top of
the pipe and perched up there screaming out that she was going to
jump. The police and ambulance workers tried to talk her down but

she jumped, or fell, no witness is certain. Instead of clearing the reinforcing horizontal steel grid, she fell directly on to it and, as her broken body remained caught in the spokes, coins slowly fell from her handbag at the feet of her stunned would-be rescuers onto the path below. (Six months later I was drinking outside at the Old Fitzroy Hotel in Woolloomooloo when she hobbled up on two steel crutches, her body twisted out of shape. She was tipsy, happy and begging for some money to play the pokies.)

It anything proves that the Cross is a port town it is the roof of the naval car park. Now called Embarkation Park, the site was occupied by ramshackle wooden warehouses used by the Fitzroy Stevedoring Company from 1899 until the 1970s. Standing in the park with its delightful formal displays of Australian shrubs and flowers, one can see down to Woolloomooloo Bay where warships are docked, the hum of their engines reverberating across the Bay and up into Potts Point, a constant reminder of their presence.

'THE GOLDEN AGE'

THREE YEARS BEFORE THE OUTBREAK of the First World War, the New South Wales government declared war on the terrace house. The Labor politician John Rowland Dacey remarked that 'The day is past when free Australians were content to be herded together in terraces of mere dog boxes [where] they are compelled to live together like flies.' Since the 1890s the inner city had become known as 'Slumdog Sydney'. With the rapid rise in population there was limited housing and many working class people found themselves at the mercy of unscrupulous landlords who charged high rents for seedy flats. In order to be able to pay the rent many tenants sub-let the rooms, creating a crowded, unsanitary, ugly inner city whose running sores of slums would stretch from the Rocks to Darlinghurst and Surry Hills. Some thirty-five per cent of inner city homes were considered unfit for human habitation. The dilapidated and congested terraces were also seen as breeding grounds for vice; adding further to the immorality were the countless hotels in the same streets.

Dacey was able to realise his plans to create a working class suburb which would be 'slumless, laneless and publess' when Labor was finally elected to government in 1910. In 1912 the *Housing Act* was passed and the first such project was initiated. Dacey died of nephritis in the same year and was never able to see his vision realised. Australia's first public housing scheme, to be called Daceyville, was constructed between 1912 and 1920 six kilometres south of the city. The single-family suburban homes and their gardens would combine the most attractive elements of city and country life. It was a deliberate act of social engineering and also about improving the morality and respectability of its inhabitants.

In 1912 something else happened that was just as significant as Daceyville. The highest apartment building in Australia was completed in Kings Cross. Kingsclere, at 1 Greenknowe Avenue, was the first of what would be a vast number of large apartment blocks in the area. Built on the estate created by the demolition of the 1840s mansion Greenknowe, it was the first multi-storey apartment block built in Sydney. It was owned for much of its life by the Albert family of music publishers and promoters who, for nearly seventy years, rented the flats out to visiting singers and music hall performers. The red brick construction was fitted with the latest American technology such as 'telephonettes', intercoms, automatic lifts and an open-air cinema on the roof. The seventeen apartments were spacious, with four bedrooms, kitchen, pantry, two bathrooms, lavatories, linen cupboards, cook's and housemaid's cupboards, two balconies and fire escape stairs from each flat. Despite the self-conscious technological modernity of its interior, the building itself had a Victorian gravitas to it. Unlike Daceyville, only the wealthy could afford to live in Kingsclere.

Both the working-class suburb and the high-rise apartment block were foreshadowing two very different Sydney lifestyles. By the end of the Great War 60,000 Australian servicemen had been killed, another 156,000 men wounded, gassed or taken prisoner. The hundreds of thousands of returning soldiers needed to be housed and Daceyville was transformed from a working-class rental scheme into a suburb for returned servicemen. The huge death toll meant that there were thousands of women who would remain single. Daceyville was meant for families. For many single women the cheapest rentals were the inner-city terraces and flats, and if you were employed in the CBD then it was only a fifteen-minute walk to work from Kings Cross.

With the car giving people much more mobility, the suburbs began to expand, especially into the North Shore. The terrace houses of Victoria Street, once the epitome of prestige and wealth, were abandoned for the bungalows and gardens of the suburbs. Darlinghurst Road in the 1920s was very different from now. According to Robin Dalton's evocative and amusing memoir of the period, *Aunts Up the Cross*, it was 'a dusty hodgepodge of low-built buildings'. She lived in number 107, near where the entrance to the railway station now is. It had cast iron balconies, a swing gate and a porch. Outside grew a plane tree, the only tree in the street.

Behind the main road was a squiggle of poorly lit lanes and streets, a ragbag of cottages and houses. Some of these, like Earl Place, were grim, pinched thoroughfares with white-ant-infested crumbling back fences, outside dunnies and backyards filled with scrawny fruit trees. Maramanah, on the present Fitzroy Gardens site, represented the glorious past. Built it the nineteenth century, it had a distinct Georgian influence, featuring an impressive ballroom and an elegant entrance hall with a floor made of marble. When Dalton's Jewish great-grandfather Jacob Hollander bought it, he added turrets, towers and balconies until it resembled the spooky mansion of the Addams Family. He and his family were obsessed by music and if they weren't holding musical soirees then the twelve children would be practising their instruments. Any musician of note passing through Sydney would be invited to play; even Nellie Melba had sung there.

Perhaps the most celebrated occasion was at the turn of the nineteenth century when a wedding was held at Maramanah between Mr Harry Morris Cohen and Mr Hollander's third daughter, Juliet. The ceremony was held in the ballroom, which was decorated with flags and floral arrangements. The traditional Jewish service was celebrated by the Reverend Rabbi Davis, with the bridal party standing under a crimson canopy suspended from silver poles. Juliet wore a beautiful trained gown of white duchesse satin, trimmed with rose point lace, a small coronet of orange blossoms and a tulle veil. She carried a shower bouquet of white flowers and wore a pearl and diamond pendant, the gift of her bridegroom. At the end of the ceremony the reception was held in a large marquee erected on the lawn, where a sumptuous dinner was served and then, before the dancing, guests were treated to the talented Hollander family playing a selection of orchestral pieces. The married couple were to return from their honeymoon to reside just down the road in the glamorous Alberto Terrace (where the library now is).

For outsiders, life at Maramanah may have seemed glamorous, but Dalton's mother detested living there, not so much because of the house itself but because she found herself endlessly quarrelling with her four younger aunts (Lilla, Mina, Netta and Anys) who were 'jealous and unmarried'. She took the opportunity of marrying the young Kings Cross doctor Jim Eakin to leave Maramanah. Even though for thirty-five years she lived only two blocks down the road from her aunts, she never spoke to them again. The official reason was that she, as a Jew, had married outside her religion – Eakin was a northern Irish Protestant – but the truth was that she loathed her aunts.

During the early 1920s the area was still a slow-moving hamlet and on Darlinghurst Road itself there were no restaurants, food stores or hotels. They were in William Street, or more correctly the northern side of it, as the southern side had been flattened and it would be 1923 before new buildings were constructed. However, by the middle of the 1920s the landscape of the Cross began to change. The City of Sydney experienced the construction of more blocks of flats than any other area in the state. Nearly a quarter of all flats built were in Kings Cross and a number of these were high-rise (eight storeys) and reached the height limit established in 1912 that dictated that all buildings be capped at 150 feet (45.72 metres), which would define Sydney's urban landscape until 1957. Like Melbourne, which had created a height limit of 132 metres, the object was to avoid the boastful skyscraper mentality of Manhattan.

Blocks of flats began to appear down at the northern end of Potts Point. Number 13 Wylde Street featured the increasingly popular Spanish Mission style with its twisted columns, arched entry and tiled parapet. In nearby St Neot Avenue (named after one of the early houses), rows of flats were built. One of the most regal blocks of flats was Byron Hall in Macleay Street, completed in 1929. Designed in a Beaux Arts style by Clive Hamilton, it pioneered the concrete frame. It had a facade of 'liver' bricks, projecting balconies and facetted bays of windows. It was privately owned with renters on long-term leases. The forty-two apartments were serviced, with meals delivered to the tenants and laundry collected.

The rapid conversion of the area was so dramatic that a 1927 sales brochure for Elizabeth Bay House observed that:

> *In the history of Sydney's real estate no centre has been more*
> *rapid in transformation and in rise of values than Kings Cross,*
> *Darlinghurst extending to Elizabeth Bay. The interchange*
> *of properties has recorded figures that have bewildered many*
> *experienced speculators in real estate.*

The building boom meant the great houses of the nineteenth

century were in danger of demolition. Thomas Mitchell's Craigend was demolished in 1922 to make way for flats. The mansion Tusculum, which had frontages on Manning, Tusculum and Hughes Streets, was sold in 1927 and its lavish garden reduced to a fragment of its former glory, while the rest of it, except for the house itself, was bought by property developers. In the same year Elizabeth Bay House was put up for sale. From 1875, when the first sub-division of its land was created, there had been a gradual but inexorable carve-up of the estate. Out of this came new routes like Onslow and Billyard Avenues. The last remaining portion of the estate was sold in 1927 and Elizabeth Bay House was bought by the art collector and prominent lawyer Arthur Allen for £14,000. An extension of Onslow Avenue encircled the house and isolated it from what was left of the once magnificent gardens. The problem for Allen was that he did not know how to make money out of a mansion which was in a state of disrepair. In 1930 it ended up a storage facility for paintings belonging to the estate of George Lambert, a flashy and very successful society painter who died in that year.

For most people the gradual disappearance of the mansions was not an occasion for nostalgia but an opportunity. A 1926 newspaper article was thrilled at the demolition of one of the great homes: 'Three hundred flats in eight blocks will be built on its extensive grounds. Thus more than a thousand people will live where only ten live now.'

Some may have called the apartments 'dog-boxes' but for the tenants they were adventures in modern apartment living. The first trader to be listed as 'interior decorator' in Sydney was Margaret Jaye, who opened a store in Darlinghurst Road in 1925. It was a gift shop stocked with antique furniture, ornaments and French and Italian fabrics. Most of its customers were women following the latest trends in decor, sourcing them from magazines like *Home* and Hollywood movies.

Mainstream Australians saw the flats as a denial of family life and they were also rumoured to be dens of depravity. The unsupervised mixing of single women and men in apartment blocks created moral panics which were exploited by the tabloids, like *Truth*'s campaign against the immorality of 'flat life'. Sexual promiscuity was not the only temptation in flats – there were the drinking parties that got out of control. In one notorious incident in 1929 a group of men and women began a drinking party in a block of flats on a Wednesday night and continued until Sunday. It would have gone unnoticed except that a beautiful girl, Della Hutton, went missing. After being questioned by police, the drunken crew recalled that some time on Friday night Della had gone to have 'a lie down' in a distant bedroom. It was determined that she died between Friday and a Sunday from an overdose of the sedative veronal. Incidents like these only confirmed what dangers lay in flat life for young women.

But for the women themselves life in the Cross had a freedom that was not available in the suburbs or country towns. Dulcie Deamer, who regarded herself as an archetypical flapper, extolled the Kings Cross lifestyle in a 1926 article:

> *The flapper ... goes her blithe Twentieth century way. The world is her oyster. As long as she keeps within the police regulations she can do as she likes ... She is sleekly or fluffily shingled, well groomed, well fed and fairly complacent unless Reginald 'phones to say that he has the 'flu and can't take her to the studio party where there will be wine cocktails and a jazz saxophonist.*

If the flappers had an ideology then it was against maturity, maternity, marriage and domesticity. Their bobbed hair and knee-length crepe de chine tube dresses emphasised a slim girlish look that had nothing maternal or mature about it. The young women courted the male gaze and shocked conservatives with their sexual frankness. They were influenced particularly by Hollywood movies, for which women made up seventy per cent of the audiences. The flapper was unchaperoned and an exhibitionist, obsessed with popular art. She symbolised novelty, youth, constant change, technological innovations and natural exuberance, embracing the idea that she was consciously performing a role. Perhaps Elizabeth Wilson's theory is right when she says of the impact of the flapper that 'only by becoming part of the spectacle can you truly exist in the city'. And if anything represented an urban space where self-display and a sense of performance could be possible, then it was the Cross.

Deamer herself was to play an important role in the creation and reputation of bohemian Kings Cross. Born in 1890 in New Zealand, her father was a doctor and her mother extremely supportive of her daughter, allowing her to study acting from the age of thirteen. When she was eighteen Deamer fell in love with a fellow actor, Albert Goldie, who was twice her age. They married and toured Asia and the United States. She had six children in quick succession, two of the sons dying early. To supplement her income she wrote articles for newspapers and trashy novels like *The Suttee of Safa* ('A hot and strong love story about Akbar the Great'). By 1922 the marriage was over and Deamer suffered a nervous breakdown.

During her convalescence she decided to totally change her life. She deposited her four children with her mother and turned up in Kings Cross, determined to enjoy life unencumbered by marriage or children (she showed a chilly indifference to her children all her life). One of the attractions of the Cross was its cheap rents.

Deamer had been shaped by her time in the United States ('I'd learned to jazz in the States') and the *joie de vivre* of the jazz age epitomised by the flapper, dancing, movies and popular music. For her, and many young women in the Cross, the 1920s was what she called the Golden Decade. She saw these sparkling years as a release from the horror of the war: 'the out-of-school feeling, and our share of the lovely, irrational, general conviction that every-thing was going to be good-oh'. Her trashy novels were set in the past, whether it be the time of Jesus or witchcraft in the medieval era. Their steamy plots generally revolved around a teenage girl becoming a woman. The money she earned from the potboilers and ephemeral journalism funded her bohemian lifestyle, which revolved around parties and cafés. She knew her fiction wasn't high art; the more important thing was to live according to the bohemian credo: live one's life as a work of art.

She became the face of bohemia at the age of thirty-two. The first annual Artists' Ball had been held in 1922, copying the Eng-lish Artists' Balls where bohemians and artists came dressed as pirates, princesses, skeletons, policemen, Chinamen and clowns. Homosexuals wore drag knowing it was against the law but they could get away with it in the Dionysian atmosphere. One polit-ician worried over 'the presence of a notorious type of effeminate male who dressed in female attire'. To the tabloids the balls were a drunken orgy where semi-naked men and women danced las-civiously and groped and fondled each other. The following year Deamer created a sensation by arriving at the Town Hall dressed like the chaste goddess Diana in a leopard skin and a dog-tooth necklace. The skimpy outfit was slipped over a body stocking but still the effect was, as she had hoped, shocking. After revealing her outfit she danced frenetically and then concluded her perfor-mance with the splits. From that moment on she became known as the Queen of Bohemia and revelled in her fame.

Plain and vain, Deamer loved attention and was a relentless flirt whose wild sex life existed more in the minds of others than in reality. She treated parties with more reverence than her plays and novels and spent much time writing skits for them. She became a seminal example of the Bohemian life (which traces its origins back to Henri Murger's *Scenes de la Vie Boheme* of 1851, later becoming famous as the Puccini opera).

The Jazz Age bohemians rejected the bush culture promoted as quintessentially Australian by Henry Lawson and *The Bulletin* school. They celebrated urban living and, although they lived in poverty, each aimed to become the artist of the heroic ideal and, as such, developed an attitude where it became more important to act the part of the poet rather than excel at writing poetry. Driven by romantic narcissism and a sense of moral superiority over the philistines and wowsers, they set out to outrage the middle class and flamboyantly rejected the family, the church and the materialism of the bourgeoisie.

The low rents and its location close to the heart of the city meant that Kings Cross became a sought-after place to live for bohemians. As Deamer said of the Cross during the 1920s, its 'half-broke, sanguine, visionary world of artists, sculptors, poet-scribblers, holed-up in basements, third-storey attics, any living crevice that was cheap'. She was often on the poverty line and lived such a life, renting dives in grubby Woolcott Street (its name changed to Kings Cross Road in 1926, in the hope that would remove the stain of its foul reputation) and ending up in a bug-infested third-storey room in Victoria Street. The flats were conductive to the lifestyle of the bohemians and its obsession with parties. As Peter Fitzpatrick writes of this era in *The Sea Coast of Bohemia,* 'A party was the focal ritual ... anyone could participate who had friends or the wherewithal to obtain grog. A liberal attitude to life was all that was required.'

Deamer once boasted that she had been to 2000 parties. With the popularity of the gramophone growing (and complaints from neighbouring flat dwellers rising), parties were loud, with boisterous drunks and much dancing. For the modern Australian girl jazz meant dancing. As Kathleen Mangan recalled of the 1920s:

> *... you danced; in the afternoons, in the evenings, at night in*
> *dimly lit cabarets you danced until the small hours, and your feet*
> *ached and you could scarcely hold your head up.*

In order to benefit from this craze, the Palais Royal was built to hold 5500 people, with 3000 of them able to fit on the dance floor. Jim Bendroit, a Canadian who lived in Kellett Street, was one of the most successful and innovative entrepreneurs. He booked Billy Romaine, one of Australia's first jazz groups, and then he imported the first American jazz bands, including Ruth Varin's Maryland Maids. (Later Bendroit opened the chic Princes nightclub and the celebrated Trocadero.)

For women, jazz – meaning dance – became 'the pre-eminent musical expression of women's emancipation'. There was something uncomfortably sexual about jazz dancing, in its flaunting of a woman's body and her torrid physical movements. Deamer didn't deny it, saying of women that '... we *do* jazz in order to experience a mild – very mild – sex adventure and to allow our repressed polyandrous instinct to get a breath of fresh air'.

Flat life not only meant parties, but a loosening of sexual morality and the freedom that the anonymity of the Cross gave people. Joan Lindsay Burke, once married to Norman Lindsay's son Ray, recalled in the 1997 documentary *Bohemian Rhapsody* that sexual promiscuity was a crucial part of their transgression against bourgeois morality: 'The sex life was really rampant ... everybody had a very, very, very active sex life. They really did, including me.'

What made this Sydney bohemian world different from that of Melbourne of the 1890s was that women were included.

Bohemian life had previously been male-orientated for the simple reason that the social life was in pubs and women were excluded from them except for the ladies' lounge. The 1920s freed women to find their own careers in the arts, whether as a writer, illustrator, designer or painter and crucially the bohemian social life was centred on the cafés and restaurants, which meant the participation of women. Cafés became a meeting place for both sexes, and pick-up joints.

This is not to say there was equality between men and women despite the supposed sexual frankness. Women such as Deamer realised that to gain attention she had to act in a provocative manner in order to be noticed by men. Not that she was a proto-feminist; she once cracked, 'A woman, like a dog, needs a master.' Her need for attention was endless. Joan Lindsay disliked the exhibitionism of someone like Deamer, thinking her a 'crashing bore': 'We would groan every time Dulcie came out to do her party piece splits in her leopard skin, and we'd think, "Oh, Christ, not again."'

Joan Lindsay summed up bohemian life as 'cocking a snook' at the establishment, but like all bohemians there was a contradiction at the core of their beliefs. They may have despised the middle class but were dependent on it to finance their vision. As the Australian designer George Taylor pointed out, bohemians were a hypocritical lot, 'The poetic ones are so unpractical as to forget that it is the *Soulless Philistine* who keeps poetry and art alive by his purse.'

One of the formative influences on the King Cross bohemians was Norman Lindsay, an artistic reactionary who loathed the new European art movements of post-impressionism, surrealism and fauvism and mocked modernist writers like James Joyce. The guiding light was Nietzsche and the concept of the artist as hero. The aim was the creation of an artistic aristocracy where artists and writers would become the new gods of modern life. Lindsay's son Jack helped found and edit a magazine, *Vision,* to espouse his father's philosophy. Published in 1924 the magazine lasted only four issues. It was artistically conservative and backward looking:

'We wanted,' wrote Jack, 'not any sort of futurism, but a new grand art linked with Praxiteles and Rubens, Rembrandt and Turner, Aristophanes and Shakespeare, Catullus and Keats, Rabelais and Blake.'

Even the young poet Ken Slessor (Jack Lindsay thought he was the only decent writer in *Vision*) found it difficult to extract himself from Lindsay's fairy goo of centaurs, fauns, leering satyrs and buxom nymphs.

Yet Slessor, like the Lindsays, viewed art with a greater seriousness than Deamer did and, in so doing, revealed that there were two strands of bohemians; Deamer represented one and the poet and academic Christopher Brennan the other.

Brennan was born in 1870 to a publican father. He had a precocious academic ability and was a brilliant classical scholar at the University of Sydney. He was appointed assistant lecturer in French and German in the department of modern languages and literature and also wrote poetry influenced by the French symbolists, especially Mallarmé. He married a German woman who had four children to him, but his heavy drinking and spendthrift ways created considerable tensions in the family. His marriage broke up in 1922 and he began living with Violet Singer, seventeen years his junior. In March 1925 she was killed by a tram. Two months later he had to resign from his university post because of adultery.

From then on it was a descent into alcoholism and bohemian excesses. He left his Newport home on the coast and drifted into the Cross. His poetical output slowed dramatically and he became a feature of the area, wandering from hotel to hotel cadging drinks from his acolytes who would listen in rapt silence to

Brennan's monologues (he was never a conversationalist) as he showed off his prodigious learning, especially in the classics. During the middle 1920s he became a habitué of the Mansions Hotel where he would improvise ribald verses in Latin and ruminate aloud about completing a definitive edition of Aeschylus, which he never did finish. His poetry, in fact, wasn't very good. Laced with esoteric symbolism and clotted rhythms, it showed off his supreme erudition but had nothing to say – any meaning was lost in misty verbiage. For bohemians, part of Brennan's appeal was that despite his great promise as a poet and scholar, he achieved little, but that didn't matter because he himself had become a piece of art. Dressed in a voluminous black raincoat, with watery eyes, long black greasy hair, a mouth that emphasised his lack of a chin, a body reeking of BO and stinking of stale beer, he redeemed his appearance with exquisite manners and an attractive voice. Still, there were locals who would cross to the other side of the street to avoid him when they saw him pub crawling up William Street into Kings Cross. Women may have been wary of his squalid appearance but he had plenty of star-struck male fans.

His most intense relationship was with his daughter, Anne, a gorgeous blonde with vivid blue eyes and a body riddled with TB. They fought constantly and yet seemed to many to have a curious incestuous connection that sometimes became an erotic display when both were drunk. Anne was considered to be her father's intellectual equal but revelled in besmirching his reputation by whoring on the corner of William and College Streets near the museum, letting her clients know that she was the daughter of a famous professor and poet. Her nickname around the traps was 'German Annie'. Brothers like Jack and Ray Lindsay were enthralled by the woman they called 'the bitch' and viewed her intimidating allure with a corrosive mixture of lust and bitterness. When she wasn't living in her Victoria Street digs she stayed at the Café la Boheme (or Betsy's as it was always called) where she loved to show off by dancing on the tables between the wine bottles and glasses. The only way Ray Lindsay could describe her beauty was through the eyes of a painter:

> [who] would have to possess the bravura of an Augustus John, the sentimental sensitivity of Greuze, and the bitch-insight of a Toulouse-Lautrec. Despite her selfishness ... she retained an extraordinary and uncanny ability to arouse love.

His real thoughts were more vulgar, however; he called Anne one of 'Those-Women-One-Could-Have-But-Never-Did-Fuck'.

Her colossal wreck of a father spent much time at Betsy's, always drunk. Ray Lindsay remembers hanging out the window of the café and vomiting on the head of Brennan attempting the same from the next storey down. After a moment of recovering from shock, Brennan cried out, 'Some filthy bastard has emptied the contents of his stomach onto my cranium.'

Deamer had an exasperated affection for the eccentric poet Geoffrey Cumine. Grubby, shabby, and often drunk, he had the words *To Let* permanently tattooed on his forehead. One night she had to lug a smashed Cumine down to his William Street lodging but, as she marvelled, 'Thanks to the mind-your-own-business Kings Cross creed, nobody took any notice.'

Cumine adored Brennan and in 1928 he convinced Deamer to invite the poet to Christmas lunch in her Victoria Street flat. Deamer did not mix in Brennan's circle and neither did her attractive friend Cecily, who was thrilled to be meeting the famous man for the first time. Cumine escorted the unfit Brennan up the three flights of stairs and the four of them managed to fit around a small table in the tiny living room. Brennan was hungry but Deamer could not afford turkey so they had reheated baked rabbit, a few greasy sausages and a tin of peas. The two men had brought alcohol. Once the wine was finished the men tackled the rum and Brennan grew progressively more drunk and sleazy, making coarse passes at Cecily and trying to fondle her. The women were horrified and somehow Deamer managed to push the walrus-sized Brennan and his mate onto the third storey landing and locked the door.

The incident left her shattered, but to someone like Brennan this was not an unusual occurrence. This inglorious lunch showed just how different were Deamer's and Brennan's bohemian behaviour and attitudes – he treated art seriously, she treated it as a means to an end; the result was she performed her life, even if that meant a determined frivolity. They also came from opposite ends of culture, he representing the highbrow, she the popular culture of the jazz age. Deamer lived in a bright bubble of exuberance and performance where Brennan's bohemian lifestyle embraced the squalid and the constant reminder of his failure as a poet and scholar.

Self-disgust and a feeling of existential emptiness led Brennan back to the Catholicism of his youth. In 1930 he found some sort of financial stability, and even happiness, as a teacher of modern languages at St Vincent's College at the end of Victoria Street. His daughter married and moved to Bondi, only for a shark to take her husband in 1929. Later that year Anne succumbed to TB. Her father died in 1932, largely forgotten. Brennan and Deamer were crucial players in creating the bohemian reputation of Kings Cross. So successful were they that by the end of the roaring 1920s it was increasingly compared to France's famous Montmartre.

Neon

IT WAS THE RAZOR GANGS who brought light to Kings Cross. By the end of the 1920s the Cross may have been described as Sydney's Montmartre, but its reputation was also that of a wicked dark place festering with crime. John Milton wrote, 'When night darkens the streets, then wander forth the sons of Belial, flown with insolence and wine.' This baleful observation was something that the Sydney City Commissioners agreed with and in 1929 they determined that Kings Cross and William Street would be so brightly illuminated 'that it will be impossible for a visitor from "the Loo" or Surry Hills to strop a razor in the street without attracting undue attention'.

The plan worked so well that crime quickly retreated into the penumbral back lanes and side streets. It meant that the main streets were safe, even for women. By 1932 light was so synonymous with the Cross that the *Sydney Morning Herald* published a poem called 'Lights of King's Cross' by a Muriel Feldwick, an occasional writer and admired soprano who sang often on the radio (her repertoire including the now seldom heard 'Two Little Curly Headed Coons'). For Feldwick the neons and bright lights were like a glittering galaxy that had the alchemical power to make 'day out of night'.

When the Frenchman Georges Claude introduced neon signs

to the United States in 1923, they became immediately popular and chic. Earning the soubriquet of 'liquid fire', the signs had such a hypnagogic intensity and enchanting brilliance that some people would stare at them for hours, mentally giddy, mesmerised by the reds, blues and greens that gave the illusion that the buzzing light inside the tube was a pulsating, living entity.

It wasn't long before the first neon lights came to the Cross and by the early 1930s they were one of its most celebrated attractions. There were locals who objected to them. In 1938 several residents in a Bayswater Road wanted an injunction taken out against York Motors and its neon sign of red and green that blinked out the commercial haiku, *The peak of perfection – Chrysler, Plymouth*. As far as the tenants of 40a Bayswater Road were concerned, the neon sign was so bright that 'Photographs of their flats can be taken by it and newspapers can be read in the flats.' As one plaintiff put it, 'We cannot go to sleep with this bright light shining upon us – or play cards or enjoy a book.' The tenant also said that although the sign went off at 11.30 at night, he needed to go to sleep before that. Justice Boyce, hearing the case, made a crack about the reputation of residents in the area: 'From what I have heard I would imagine that any earlier hour than that for going to bed would not be general at Kings Cross.' But the plaintiffs won the case, when the Judge – who inspected the sign one night – granted the tenants a restraining order on York Motors preventing them from illuminating their neon sign between 8.15 pm and sunrise.

For most people, however, the neon signs were magical and inviting and, as a practical Kenneth Slessor was to remark, if he wanted to sleep at night it was an easy matter to cover his bedroom window with a canopy of shirts or a dressing gown to shut out 'the viridian green moonlight streaming from the largest and most illuminated bottle of beer in the world'.

As more neon signs lit up the top of William Street, they became a psychedelic siren call to beauty, excitement and entertainment. The Cross became an incandescent beacon and William Street the yellow brick road to this luminous Oz on top of the ridge. There is a newspaper photograph from early 1939 entitled 'Nightly Brilliance of King's Cross'. The shot was taken across the waters of Rushcutters Bay, on the eastern side of the ridge, and the dark waters are radiant with reflected light from the Cross where light streams out of flats, from streetlamps and outdoor neon advertising so that it seems a luminous oasis amidst the Stygian gloom of the city and suburbs.

By the time he came to publish his volume of light verse, *Darlinghurst Nights*, in 1933, Slessor had been enthralled for years by the neons and how they altered the very concept of the heavens. In his imagination the stars became neon 'alphabets of lights' and, from the heights of a flat, the whole of the nocturnal Kings Cross took on the appearance of a permanent solar eruption or, as he puts it, a 'fiery hedge'. Even the hazy brilliance of distant constellations didn't match up to the neon's nebulae, and who wouldn't be seduced by William Street's, 'red globes of light, the liquor-green/the pulsating arrows and running fire'?

Just as parents take their children to see the department stores' Christmas decorations, so people visited the Cross during the Depression just to gaze in awe at the neon lights and the brightly lit shops that stayed open until midnight.

All that changed with the fear of Japanese invasion. The government claimed that Sydney would be the second largest city in the British Empire to be blacked out. The first test blackouts in late 1941 had mixed results at best, with Kings Cross as usual acting as if it were a law unto itself. In spite of intense work by 10,000 wardens during the blackout, the worst area proved to be Kings Cross, where 'innumerable' lights were reported. There was such disregard for co-operating in the exercise that a government spokesman said that Kings Cross had caused observers considerable alarm with one spotter plane reporting that its neon signs could be seen at 5000 feet. It was not only the nonchalance of the Cross that irritated the government but the attitudes of the people themselves. Instead of remaining indoors, thousands of residents paraded through the streets laughing and joking in what was called 'a carnival spirit'. They were guided by the glow of thousands of cigarettes that from the sky resembled an immense swarm of fireflies or, as one astonished pilot reported, 'Kings Cross looked like a large birthday cake with all its candles alight.' The authorities ordered the residents to install black curtains on their windows and forbade them to go out onto the streets when the air raid sirens sounded, but as soon as the all clear sirens went off, they were back on the streets again. As one woman remembered, 'It was all very foolish but I think we thought nothing would or could ever happen to the Cross – she was safe and beautiful and she loved us.'

For locals the end of the war meant the lights returning to the Cross. As Virginia Luther evocatively put it in 1945:

> *That breathtaking beauty which flashes so briefly in all large cities lingers longest here on wet evenings when, without the bitter need for blackouts, the Neon signs redden the glistening drops as they slant to the black pavements, covered in little puddles reflecting the lights of car, bus and tram.*

The flashing red and green neons came on again but it was a gradual process to return to the glory days of light. By 1954 the City Council was trying to restore the pre-war nightlife of Kings Cross and promised that 'the night lights of Kings Cross are rapidly being turned on again.'

And they were. By the 1960s there were more lights and neon signs than ever before. In 1962's *Kings Cross Caper*, Gordon Flanagan describes their appeal:

William Street was alive with colour as neon-magic transformed the dusty and sometimes depressive slope into a tiny replica of America's famous Great White Way, and at its peak, squatting insolently at the summit like a colourful and arrogant queen, was King's Cross.

There were neon signs that became instantly recognisable like Dulux Paints, Phillips Electrics, Penfold's Wine and Pamm Paints. They and other neon signs, plus scintillating lights, were so dazzling that film stock right through to the 1980s couldn't handle the intensity, so that in documentaries or newsreels of the time the top of William Street became as incandescent as a sunspot and seemed to burn a hole into the retina of the celluloid.

But as the sixties wore on the lights became not so much a site for enchantment but 'moving signs of advice and temptation'. The signs advertising striptease joints and nightclubs became more figurative, explicit and sexually alluring. Not everyone could see their seductive beauty. To the teenage Kate Fitzpatrick the neons made everyone look diseased, and for the novelist Kenneth 'Seaforth' Mackenzie, the pulsating lights created 'a gleaming nightmare of faces' as though the people were drowning in greenish-red water. The signs became an enticing call to sin that would 'wreck the well-ordered, narrow suburban lives of people'. Once the lights represented the beauty of urban life, but now they began to be seen as a feral neon jungle where the unwary would get lost in 'Australia's most notorious network of vice', as the author of 1966's *Vice Trap, Kings Cross,* put it.

The most famous neon display is the Coca-Cola sign which

dominates the intersection of Darlinghurst Road, Victoria and William Streets. The red and white neon billboard was erected in 1974. It is made up of eighty-eight vertical bars of red tubing concealed behind reflectors; 800 fluorescent lamps projecting a total of 13 different patterns, controlled by a computer behind a sign totalling 41 metres in length and 13 metres in height. *(Enjoy Coca-Cola.)* It's considered the premier billboard sign in Australia due to its central position and is often referred to as 'the Gateway to the Cross'. It looks dull and uninspiring in the daytime, but as Richard Flanagan wrote in *The Unknown Terrorist,* 'of a night it transformed into a latter-day Lighthouse of Alexandria, a small sea of rolling red and white neon waves announcing … the entrance to the Cross'.

The Baz Luhrmann movie *Strictly Ballroom* (1992) featured the sign in a long sequence and, although on one level it could be seen as an advertisement for Coke, Luhrmann realised that the sign had transcended its original purpose and had become a pulsating symbol of the promise of illicit excitement and bohemian excess.

Under the Coca-Cola sign is the Santa Barbara, an Asian-American themed barbecue restaurant that was converted from the trendy black marble Piano Room nightclub, partly owned by John Ibrahim, whose meteoric rise to become King of Kings Cross features in the crime series *Underbelly*. The other part-owner was James Miller, Ibrahim's protégé. Handsome and a party animal, Miller died at the age of thirty-eight after a cocktail of cocaine and sleeping tablets (having the same dealer as Miller I can confirm he was also an enthusiastic dope smoker). His death caused the King of the Cross to lament after the funeral, 'James Miller I cried for you today my friend, not in the dark and behind closed doors but in a packed church in broad daylight where we gathered to say goodbye to you.'

It's when you sit at one of the restaurant's windows at night that you realise the Coca-Cola sign of red and white neons perfectly mirrors the car lights of the William Street traffic; the red lights heading into the city and the white lights of vehicles coming to the Cross.

During the major refurbishment of the Cross in the early years of the millennium, the Sydney City Council wanted to abolish neon signs altogether. It offered $1000 to businesses to replace the existing bright lights under the street awnings with sedate small metal signs. It also determined that any future signage that used fluorescent colours, flashing lights or 'words or phrases which are lewd or offensive' would be banned. This puritan directive was greeted with a local campaign to save the signs, including those regarded as 'lewd' – *Playgirls International, Love Machine, Stripperama, Porky's* and *Showgirls.*

It was an attempt to tame the unruliness and neon sexiness of the Cross. The Council was joined by a handful of wowsers who thought the signs were sleazy, but there were so many residents in favour of them that the Council overturned its decision, belatedly realising that neon lights and the history of Kings Cross were inextricably linked. Its first action was timid, but positive. It placed a heritage order on an innocuous small green-and-red sign – *BOOKS* – outside the Roslyn Street adult bookshop that had been erected in 1974. The Coca-Cola sign has become such an intrinsic feature of the Kings Cross landscape that it has been placed under a National Trust order.

Realising the historic relationship between lights and Kings Cross, the Council gave the go-ahead for neon lights to be installed in the refurbished Llankelly Place. Eleven lights were suspended down the length and centre of the lane. They are two metres in diameter and range from red, orange and yellow to green. The colours of these eleven lights are said to represent the transition from the 24-hour culture of Darlinghurst Road to the green space of Springfield Gardens at the northern end of Llankelly Place. They are turned off at 1 am. Not everyone likes them. Some residents complain that the art works keep them awake. As in the 1938 court case, proof that there will always be people who should never live in Kings Cross.

THE UNDERBELLY OF
AUSTRALIA'S MONTMARTRE

ON ST VALENTINE'S DAY 1916, 5000 Australian soldiers at a training camp in Casula went on strike, protesting against the bleak conditions and an increase in drill hours. Not content with a vocal protest, they hurried on to Liverpool, where hundreds of other troops joined them, the protest forgotten as they drank two hotels dry. After a drunken mêleé at the railway station, which caused the death of one man and the wounding of six others, the soldiers hijacked a train and headed to the city, where the thousands of intoxicated soldiers, like a plague of voracious khaki coloured locusts, descended on Sydney, damaging shops, restaurants, hotels and, out of drunken self-righteousness, the German Club. They assaulted any man or woman who got in their way. The debauchery continued for three days. The reaction of the appalled Army chiefs was swift and five days later over a thousand soldiers were discharged from the AIF for drunkenness, misconduct and being absent without leave. Another 116 were ordered to be court martialled.

The riots occurred during an intense public debate about restricting the consumption of alcohol. There was a strong temperance campaign to limit the hours that hotels could trade. At the time they opened at six in the morning and closed at 11 pm. The temperance movement was driven primarily by women, but was also backed by newspapers like the *Sydney Morning Herald* and the churches – except for the Catholic Church, which made sense given most of the publicans were Roman Catholic. The *Sydney Morning Herald*'s reaction to the drunken mayhem was typical of the public's horror, saying it shamed Australia and confirmed that 'no amount of clever dodging or denial can mask the demands of people for early closing'.

A referendum was held on 10 June 1916 on the issue of hotel closing hours. The rioting soldiers created a wave of public sympathy for the cause of the temperance movement and it gained an overwhelming majority of votes for six o'clock closing. It may have been a moral victory but it was to also have disastrous consequences for Kings Cross. Since the rum-soaked days of early settlement Australians have been great drinkers. Six o'clock closing wasn't going to change this. The era of sly grog had arrived.

Drinking is as elemental a part of Australian society as gambling. For example, in 1926 there were 8896 Sydney men and women charged with public drunkenness. It is no wonder that thirsty Sydneysiders were quite prepared to pay inflated prices for their illegal alcohol, despite some of it being of dubious quality, especially the so-called 'pinkie' – new wine fortified with cheap spirits that could result in hospitalisation. As Prohibition proved in the United States, the popularity of alcohol didn't diminish but flourished underground with the help of the criminal element.

Besides prostitution and drugs, sly grog became endemic in Surry Hills and East Sydney. These poor areas were crammed with slums, decaying terraces, rat-infested lanes and houses and flats swarming with cockroaches. There were sly grog outlets scattered throughout this mucky honeycomb of East Sydney streets. The selling of illegal alcohol became so common in the Cross that some sly groggers didn't hide what they were doing. In 1926 a barman, Richard Moss, openly sold four bottles of beer to two men who were standing on the footpath of Victoria Street. Marie Williams, in her early forties, sold illegal alcohol from her home in Kings Cross Road. She had been arrested and fined in 1927 but continued to trade out of her flat. Three years later she was caught selling beer to an undercover policeman who then searched her premises and found half a dozen bottles of beer and a bottle of whisky. She was fined the huge sum of £100. But one of the consummate sly groggers of the era was Kate Leigh.

Born in rural Dubbo in 1881, she was one of thirteen children and a problem child from the beginning. A proverbial bad seed, she was violent and a compulsive thief who eventually made her way to East Sydney as a teenager. She gravitated to prostitution, where her good looks made her highly sought-after, but she retired from street walking when she realised there was more money in operating a brothel. Even though she didn't drink, or take drugs, she also moved into selling illegal alcohol and, at her peak, she had between twenty and thirty sly groggeries, from stinking dives to up-market rooms (there were three alone in Devonshire Street, Surry Hills, including 'Mum's', the largest, at number 212). She bought the alcohol at wholesale prices from breweries and corrupt hotel staff. The men and women could drink on her premises or take the alcohol home. Her mark-ups of up to 100 per cent made the illegal trade a highly profitable one. She also home delivered and her men would push handcarts full of beer up William Street to the Cross, supplying brothels and thirsty drinkers in seedy Kings Cross Road and the badly lit lanes and alleys around Kellett Street.

Leigh's arch enemy was another woman. Tilly Devine arrived from England in 1920 after marrying a thuggish Australian soldier, 'Big Jim' Devine. She had been a prostitute back in London. Considered beautiful by some, with cute blue eyes and alabaster skin, she was foul mouthed and had a vile temper. She continued her career as prostitute in Sydney with her husband acting as her pimp. According to Larry Writer in his book about the period, *Razor*, Tilly not only worked in sleazy East Sydney but also Macleay and Kellett Streets and Bayswater Road. She charged ten shillings to a pound for sex at a time when domestic servants earned between one and two pounds a week. A favourite ploy was to use a large Cadillac to solicit and service her clients and, of course, the four-wheeled bed could be driven away if they saw the police.

Tilly and her husband began to realise that there was more money in being a brothel keeper and in 1925 they opened their first bordello. By the late 1920s she had eighteen brothels dotted around the streets and lanes of East Sydney, Surry Hills and Kings Cross Road. Tilly's successful shift from whoring herself to being a madam was in part the result of the vagrancy laws of 1905 and the *Police Offences (Amendment) Act* of 1908, which criminalised street prostitution and made it illegal for men to operate brothels or profit from the earnings of prostitutes. As usual the government's good intentions became an opportunity: this time women became the faces of crime. Women like Tilly evaded the law because the acts did not forbid women to run brothels. Tilly brought the girls in from the street, making it safer to ply their trade. Her girls gave half their money to her, while 'Big Jim', pimp, brutal stand-over man and drug dealer, sold cocaine to the sex workers, knowing full well that addicted whores were easier to control.

Cocaine had been introduced to the slums of Surry Hills, Woolloomooloo and parts of Kings Cross by servicemen returning from the First World War. It could be bought from shady chemists or illegally obtained from dentists. Kate Leigh was a prominent dealer, nicknamed 'the Snow Queen', her cocaine business earning her the newspaper epithets of the 'Most Evil Woman in Sydney' and 'A monster in human disguise'. There were two gangsters who also dealt in large quantities of cocaine. One was Charles Passmore, the dealer of choice between 1924 and 1928. One exasperated policeman commented in court that, 'You can see [Passmore] any evening about 11 o'clock standing at the corner of Woolcott (Kings Cross Road) and Craigend Streets ... handing out the deadly contents of an innocent-looking package – cocaine – to scores of addicts.' Another dealer was an English spiv, Harry 'Jewey' Newman, who targeted dentists, buying their supplies of cocaine from them. If they tried to stop selling it to Newman he would blackmail them into continuing the supply by threatening to take them to the police. His mark-up was remarkable, even for a dealer. He bought cocaine for one pound and sold it for fifty. He diluted it with boracic acid, which had the effect of drying out the mucus membranes of the nose and causing the soft cartilage to collapse. Many an addict ended up with hideous facial disfigurement. This didn't stop the whores from using it. In fact, it was thought that seventy-five per cent of prostitutes were cocaine addicts. As Newman once said, 'These fucking women have to have snow.'

In 1924 the government passed an anti-drug law that allowed police to arrest drug dealers caught in the act of selling, but strangely you couldn't be arrested for possessing the drug. In 1927 possession of cocaine was made illegal. Authorities began monitoring the cocaine supplies of dentists, so Newman began to import from overseas, but the spiv was an unpredictable blend of vanity and low intellect. He grew careless and when police raided a shop of his they discovered packets of cocaine hidden in a drainpipe. He was sentenced to nine months in jail and vanished from sight after serving it. The 1927 law caught up with Passmore a year later when police raided his flat and uncovered a stash of cocaine. Smart, cunning Leigh continued dealing, her gang buying the drug from Asian seamen who docked in Woolloomooloo Bay.

The effects of cocaine on women was graphically realised in a vicious brawl on a cold winter's night in 1928. A policeman, Constable Sweeny, was on duty in Kings Cross when a taxi pulled up and a woman screamed out for help. She was virtually incoherent but mentioned cocaine and a fight with razor blades. The policeman found a razor in the cab and Sweeny, with the help of another policeman, rushed to a flat in Victoria Street where they came upon a naked woman dancing around a heater in what they said was 'a wild hysterical fashion'. The woman who had alerted police said that the naked woman had attempted to murder her with a razor but she had wrested the weapon from her in a fierce struggle which resulted the other woman's hand been sliced open. She said her own hand was cut when she prevented her throat from being slashed. The constables, unable to figure out who was telling the truth, arrested both women and after dressing the naked woman in an overcoat and slippers, took them to Darlinghurst police station. On the way the two women went berserk in the car and thrashed around, fighting and abusing each other. It took some effort for the two men to pull the women apart. At the police station the screaming women made charges and counter charges against each other and shouted out the names of cocaine users and dealers. After restraining the two the police placed them in separate cells where it was reported they 'created further uproar'.

Larry Writer says that police estimated that by the late 1920s there were about 5000 drug addicts in Kings Cross, Darlinghurst and Woolloomooloo dependent on marijuana, cocaine, heroin, opium and speed. John Rainford in *Consuming Pleasures: Australia and the International Drug Business*, is much more conservative about the figures. He believes that in 1926, for instance, there were probably only about fifteen women who were regular coke users or addicts. That year there was only one prosecution for cocaine but by 1929 prosecutions had risen to thirty-four. Two years later it had dropped to five and by 1933 there was just one prosecution.

Two acts passed by the New South Wales government in 1927 were to result in gang warfare so violent that *Truth* declared Sydney 'the Chicago of the South'. Early in 1927 the *Pistol Licensing Act* outlawed the carrying of concealed firearms and handguns. Writer says that the first recorded use of a razor was soon after the Act was passed when a sailor visiting a sly grog joint in Womerah Avenue used a cut-throat razor to defend himself from an attacker. The brutal evidence on the victim's face convinced local gangsters that the razor was the perfect weapon; it looked frightening, it was silent and it could be used for both for intimidation and disfigurement. But it seems razors had also been used on victims before the Act was passed. In 2012 a police mug shot was found of vicious Frank 'the Little Gunman' Green taken in 1923 in Long Bay Jail. It shows the then 21-year-old gangster with a horrifying L-shaped scar stretching from his right cheek to his lips, a wound that earned him the appropriate nickname of 'Scarface'.

In August 1927 the *Dangerous Drugs Amendment Act* was passed, making it illegal for anyone to manufacture or distribute a drug without a licence, and possession was made unlawful. The lethal animosity between Tilly Devine and Kate Leigh was reflected in open warfare over the drug trade, sly grog and prostitution. Leigh's mob slashed the faces of Tilly's prostitutes and in retaliation Devine's gang would do the same to Leigh's drug dealers. There were constant tit-for-tat battles where Tilly's bordellos were trashed by Leigh's gang and in return Tilly's goons would smash up Leigh's sly-grog joints. The years between 1927 and 1931 have been called 'the worst mob wars in Australian history. Nothing before or since has approached them for ferocity.'

Devine's pet thug Frank Green was a reliable hit man, mugger and chilly psychopath with a great dose of small man's syndrome. In 1931, with the help of his accomplice 'Big Jim', Tilly's husband, Green murdered Barney Dalton at the Strand Hotel on William Street. Green's inability to control his temper was legendary. It was said he had killed three or four men and had been shot himself several times. His great rival was Guido Calletti, boss of the Darlinghurst Push gang. Calletti had spent his childhood in reformatories and knew no other life than that of the criminal. He instilled fear in others and his own sidekicks. A vicious stand-over man, thief and killer, Calletti targeted SP bookies, forcing them into buying protection from him. This illiterate brute, flamboyant dresser and dancer was, like Green, highly attractive to women.

Frank Bongiorno in *The Sex Lives of Australians: A History* also makes the observation that in those years, 'Nowhere else in Australia did the world of organised crime and prostitution become so entwined as in Sydney.' Gangsters like Green and Calletti fought over the favours of the beautiful prostitute Nellie Cameron, as did others over the striking blonde Ginger Rogers look-alike, Dulcie Markham. At their peak Cameron and Markham could earn £2 a client, double the usual rate.

Cameron and Markham became minor celebrities and the tabloids closely followed their unruly lives. Dulcie Markham was nicknamed 'the Angel of Death' because eight of her lovers were shot or stabbed to death. She was shot herself three times and her body was a coarse road map of knife and razor scars. As her contemporary, the policewoman Lillian Armfield observed:

She wasn't happy unless she associated with violent men, and it is beyond any doubt that she encouraged them to violence ... Jealousy over her was responsible for more than one murder.

Paranoid and ill, Nellie Cameron gassed herself to death in 1953 at the age of forty-one. Despite having being forgotten by the press, 700 people attended her funeral. Markham, crippled by a client who threw her over a balcony, died at the age of sixty-three in an all-too-common fashion when she went to sleep leaving her cigarette burning. The mattress caught fire and she suffocated in the acrid smoke.

There were other gangsters who took advantage of the razor and one of the first was Norman Bruhn, whose gang terrorised the back lanes of the Cross. An alcoholic and coke user himself, Bruhn liked to prey on prostitutes, sly groggers and drug dealers, threatening to kill or disfigure them with razors. Bruhn and his thugs were determined to annex Tilly Devine's empire but he underestimated her. In 1927 she ordered Frank Green to kill Bruhn, which Green did with typical gusto.

The razor attacks grew more frenzied and in one month alone in the year the acts were passed, St Vincent's Hospital treated twenty-two victims. Like the huge majority of the 500 slashing victims between 1927 and 1932, none of the men would say how they got their wounds. Sydney's *Truth* observed:

> *Razor gangs are terrorising the underworld of Darlinghurst, that region of bohemia, crime and mystery. The razors its members carry in their hands are feared far more than the revolver of the ordinary crook.*

Four months later in dingy Kellett Street, just up from Eaton Avenue, another serious outbreak of the war between Leigh and Devine's gangs occurred. Leigh was in Long Bay Jail again and the Devine mob took the opportunity to destroy her enemy's gang. On 8 August, Tilly's armed crew marched into Leigh's territory in Kellett Street, a grim place known for its brothels, sly grog houses and violence. There the Devine mob taunted and yelled abuse at Leigh's gang through the afternoon and into the night, both sides – probably up to forty gangsters all told – sitting in the gutters or leaning against houses seeking courage from beer and cocaine. The tension intensified, both sides waiting for the other to make the first move, yelling obscenities and throwing empty beer bottles.

One resident who'd had enough was J.C. Bendroit, the celebrated manager and jazz entrepreneur of the huge dance hall the Palais Royal in Moore Park. Bendroit leant out his window and told them to stop. Both gangs turned on him, throwing bottles through his window and threatening to kill him. Bendroit may have been a flyweight who looked like Fred Astaire but he had been a lumberjack and professional boxer and wasn't easily intimidated. One reporter said of him, 'he was renowned for his ability to evict cantankerous drunks during an era when the razor was a weapon of choice'. Even at the age of seventy, he looked like 'a man that had lived, but one you didn't mess with'. Deciding he had had enough, Bendroit grabbed his revolver and fired a warning shot.

It was the catalyst for an all-out fight in the street. The men used revolvers, razors, bottles, stones, boots and fists to inflict maximum damage on each other. Even though the two mobs had been in Kellett Street for hours, the police only got to hear of the violence when five people were rushed to St Vincent's, including Leigh's protégé, handsome 22-year-old Bruce Higgs, his clothes soaked with blood and his face and hands criss-crossed with eight razor wounds. He lived, as did the others, but was permanently scarred. Some of the mob, still exhilarated by the battle, marched on the Red Mill Café around midnight and when the manager wouldn't allow them in they attacked him and smashed the front window.

This was the tipping point for law officers and the government. New laws followed quickly. Later in 1927 the *Vagrancy Act* was changed to sentence criminals to gaol terms for consorting with 'reputed thieves or prostitutes, or vagrant persons who have no visible or legal means of support'. In other words, criminals were prevented from associating with each other. This draconian law was almost immediately successful, as was the 1930 *Crimes Amendment Bill*, which sentenced anyone who unlawfully possessed a razor to a six-month jail term. This law worked. In its first year fifty-four men and sixty-two women were arrested; of these sixty-eight went to prison. The next year 121 were gaoled.

What is fascinating about these figures is that more women than men were arrested. It's a mistake to think that the razors were only used by criminals and drug dealers. Women resorted to the razor as eagerly as men but for them there were other issues at stake, mostly personal. In 1929 Stanley Quinn, who lived in Springfield Avenue, was walking along the disreputable Kings Cross Road one Monday night when a woman jumped out of the darkness and savagely slashed him across the face. Almost blinded and bleeding profusely, he was taken to St Vincent's where his nose was stitched back together. Quinn told the police he knew his attacker's name but he didn't know where she was.

Women slashed other women in the street and others took revenge on their two-timing boyfriends or husbands. Jealousy also festered in men and only a razor could lance it. John Mc-Fadden, forty-four, was in Kellett Street in the early hours one morning, talking to a girl, when a young man walked up to him, accused him of stealing his girlfriend and then manically slashed McFadden's face before disappearing into the darkness, leaving a screaming girl and a victim whose face was a patchwork of cuts and blood.

Although the razor violence stopped and cocaine usage slowed drastically (to almost cease in the coming Depression because of the law and the high cost of the drug), Tilly and Kate continued their illegal activities, concentrating on sex and booze while at the same time Calletti was growing greedy, coveting the proceeds of protection money the Brougham gang were earning off bookies in Kings Cross and Woolloomooloo. His gang fought bitter battles with the Brougham Street mob. Calletti's ego and self-importance produced in him a sense of messianic invulnerability. On 6 August 1938 he and his amour, Dulcie Markham, attended a funeral. Afterwards he decided to gatecrash a birthday party for one of the Brougham Street gang's girlfriends in the street of the same name, and therefore on their territory. In the beginning he was diplomatic and convinced the mob that he had come in peace, but he got drunk and became abusive, shouting that 'I'll fucking-well fix all you fucking bastards.' Things became heated, a brawl erupted, the lights suddenly and mysteriously went out, shots were fired and when the lights came back on, a horrified Dulcie saw that Calletti was riddled with bullets. He died a couple of hours later in St Vincent's, refusing to name his killer. Five thousand mourners attended his funeral, while his mistress wept theatrically by his splendid coffin, her face radiant with grief.

The killer and thug Frank Green fell into the lethargy of alcoholism and died drunk and nearly penniless after being stabbed with a carving knife by his de facto in their kitchen. He was fifty-four years old. The autopsy revealed numerous knife scars on his flesh and eight bullets inside his body.

Devine and Leigh continued their enmity and their nefarious careers. In 1936 the incorruptible Sydney Police Commissioner, William Mackay, convened a meeting in his office with the feuding women and offered them a deal. The police would go easy on sly grog sales and prostitution but in return both women had to agree to stop the gang warfare. Mackay had come to the conclusion that the best way to control the crime was to confine it in one area and therefore have it under control. This was a pivotal point in the policing of Kings Cross. From now on morality was relative. Policing the Cross would be done with the knowledge that the area was the one place in Australia where certain criminal activities would be tolerated in order to stop their spread into the rest of the community. As events would prove, the elastic morality of the Cross would corrupt many a policeman.

Both women realised that Mackay's compromise would make life easier for them without the continued police harassment and, for the older woman, 56-year-old Leigh, it was probably a relief. The two women were exhausted and agreed that the wars were over.

After the Second World War Leigh's empire began to decline as the liberalisation of liquor laws took effect. In 1955 when hotel trading hours were extended until 10 pm the sly grog era was over and she was bankrupt. The tax department financially ruined Tilly. Like most criminals she liked to think of herself as a victim. She moaned and whinged in the press about the tax department hounding her and wondered aloud how she was going to get the money to pay the fine. She had few assets, except for a house she had bought in Brougham Street, but it wasn't enough.

Leigh died of a stroke in 1964 aged eighty-two. One policeman who knew her summed up her up as 'a bad insane woman'. Devine survived her arch enemy by six years, dying aged seventy in 1970. At the end she too was broke. Like a scorpion that dies of its own poison, cancer ate away her insides, reducing her once voluptuous body to something resembling a piece of dried-up gristle.

Although Devine and Leigh were folk heroes to some, the fact is that their vile behaviour and squalid lives were far from glamorous. Devine was arrested 204 times for soliciting, drug trafficking, robbery, assault (she razor slashed a man) and manslaughter. Leigh had 107 convictions, thirteen gaol terms for perjury, illegal liquor sale and manslaughter. This is not say that they were heartless. Both understood that the area they lived in was a breeding ground of poverty, bad education and early death. Devine gave gifts to poor children and organisations like the Salvation Army. Leigh became famous for her Christmas parties at her Lansdowne Street home where her henchmen, dressed as Santa, gave out gifts and money. Both women were vigorous campaigners for the Labor Party which they saw as the party that tried to help the dispossessed. It was said that they viewed crime as a product of social circumstances and were 'socialists at heart' (though the quality of their hearts is far from certain).

The two criminals became part of Sydney's history. The character of Delia Stock in Ruth Park's *The Harp in the South* and *Poor Man's Orange*, both novels set in the slums of Surry Hills and Darlinghurst, was cunningly assembled from both Leigh and Devine. In theatre there have been plays devoted to Devine, such Peter Kenna's 1958 play *The Slaughter of St Teresa's Day*, a story about Oola Maguire, a queen of the underworld, holding her annual St Teresa's Day party to celebrate her miraculous recovery from a bullet wound eight years before. There was Ken Horler's *Tilly's Turn*, which premiered at the Kings Cross Stables theatre in 1998. Recently a one-woman show, *Mum's In*, has been playing at various Kings Cross venues.

In 2011 the TV series *Underbelly: Razor* told the story of Tilly Devine and Kate Leigh. It was heavily romanticised, the storylines heavy on fiction and gossamer thin on the facts. The ugliness and brutality of slum life was brushed over and the two lead actresses remained disturbingly beautiful over the years, unlike the original women, whose looks disintegrated alarmingly; Leigh became flabby, with a face like wet dough with two dry raisins for eyes, and Devine's desiccated body seemed more mummy than human.

In reality both women had little emotional empathy. The German philosopher Martin Buber originated the terms *Ich–Du*

(I–thou), where the person has the empathy to relate to others who also have thoughts and feelings, whereas those who are *Ich–Es* (I–it) see others as objects to be used for their own self-absorbed ends. The latter seldom feel guilt or remorse, and therefore don't care about the feelings and thoughts of others. The description fits these two women perfectly, and most of the gangsters they associated with.

Robin Dalton remarks in her memoir that towards the end of the 1920s Kings Cross in daytime was safe for girls and boys, who were allowed to wander the streets from Woolloomooloo down to Elizabeth Bay. That may have been so, but the sinister influence of Devine, Leigh, Calletti and Green, like a toxic sludge, permanently seeped into its nocturnal side streets and alleys.

Last orders

A WOMAN STANDING ON A bed is drawing a sketch of a voluptuous nude on the ceiling with a felt pen. A person I have never seen before is trying to wrench a lamp from the wall. The man from room service steps over people who have spilled out of the room into the corridor. On his platter is a red felt pen. Someone grabs it and starts to draw on the wall. It's 10 o'clock and I fear things can only get worse.

It all started innocently enough. Mandy and I booked a room at the Sebel Townhouse to celebrate and mourn its closing. We had planned part of our anthology of writing about Kings Cross, *In the Gutter ... Looking at the Stars*, downstairs in the bar and thought it would be appropriate to say goodbye to the hotel that was remembered fondly by so many people. Curiously, we didn't include anything about the hotel in the anthology because the best stories were unpublishable. In a way, even though the Sebel was in Elizabeth Bay, it had the spirit of the Cross with its tolerance of diversity, eccentrics and the morally dubious behaviour of some guests.

It was so well known that I had heard of it before I came to live in Sydney. Built by Harry Sebel, a property tycoon, after the local council put paid to his attempt to build flats, it opened in December 1963. Fourteen storeys high, it became famous for its style, conviviality and reputation as one of the classiest hotels in Australia. No request seemed too eccentric or demanding and its staff became legendary for their diplomacy and ability to improvise. Over the years, the hotel's guests ranged from Frank Sinatra to the Bay City Rollers, from David Bowie to the pelican that starred in the film *Storm Boy*. One of its most loyal guests was Elton John, who was a regular from 1974 to 1994. The largest bar tab ever was the night that Elton announced his engagement to a woman called Renata. The marriage didn't last long, given that groom was gay.

In the 1980s and early 1990s it seemed that every rock and roll group stayed there. You always knew when a band had arrived because the teenage girls would perch on the rocks across the street. I remember a couple of dozen of them wearing their private-school uniforms gazing up at the room where their favourite band was staying and shouting out: 'Come down here and fuck us, come down here and fuck us.' All the virtues of a private-school education had been overwhelmed by raging hormonal lust.

The rooms were comfortable, almost quaint, but it was the bar that everyone remembered, or could barely recall next morning. Absurdly small, it was covered in signed photographs of actors, musicians and celebrities. It was in this bar that Bob Dylan met his nemesis in Gypsy Fire, who soon afterwards was on the front pages of tabloids calling herself Dylan's 'sex slave' (a claim that later earned her a defamation verdict). One of the loneliest men I ever saw was in the restaurant. It was the artist Brett Whiteley, just before he died of a drug overdose, looking more a cadaver than a living human being, his face the texture of rough sandpaper, sitting in a corner dreamily picking at his dinner.

When I was going through a personally troublesome time I used to go to the bar late at night for a martini or two. I took my chihuahua, Ren. She would sit in the pocket of my leather jacket.

While I sipped my drink at the bar Ren would poke her head out of the pocket and eat peanuts from a champagne glass thoughtfully provided by the barman. I always knew who the alcoholics were because they would pretend not to notice what looked like a large rat eating peanuts at the bar, just in case people thought they had the DTs.

It was becoming obvious that the Sebel was struggling to attract its former classy clientele. Examining the signed photographs, I noticed that most of them belonged in a time warp that stopped in the early 1990s. Even the names attached to several young faces didn't ring a bell, and the photographs merely proved the axiom that whom the gods wish to destroy they make into a soapie star.

As Australian hotels became minimalist and generic, the Sebel began to seem tatty and old-fashioned. Rock stars stayed elsewhere and the guests were older and more conservative. The hotel was sold to the Mirvac Group in the late 1980s but the personal touch of Sebel and his wife, nicknamed 'Queenie', was sorely missed. It came as no surprise that it was to be demolished to make way for luxury apartments.

It was fitting that on its last night the hotel would host a party for the music industry after the ARIA awards. After all, over the years probably every major musician had stayed and partied at the Sebel. If anything, I wanted to celebrate a hotel whose staff didn't bat an eye when I would turn up with my chihuahua, and also to honour a Kings Cross institution.

My idea was that Mandy and I would invite our friends for a few drinks. I expected a tame night. After all, the friends were publishers, film directors, writers, tradies, dope dealers and ex-prostitutes – certainly not rock 'n' rollers. Most of the guests had Sebel stories; many of these revolved around sex. There was the familiar anecdote about the gay rock musician having his bum hair shaved by a boy while a 'media personality' was in the bathroom being serviced by a piece of rough trade he had picked up at Rushcutters Bay Park. There were stories of illicit affairs and one friend told us about her time as a prostitute, when the only time she ever robbed a trick was at the Sebel because 'he was such a bastard'.

The staff arrived with more felt pens. By midnight every part of the ceiling and walls was covered in drawings or graffiti, much of it more suitable to a urinal. The music was at top volume. The handwriting on the walls was becoming shaky and the misspellings frequent. Someone went downstairs to the post-ARIA party and was profoundly shocked, saying it was mild compared with ours. Someone drew a large cheque on the wall, signing my name to an amount of $250,000 addressed to the hotel. Then a fellow I barely knew, wanting to emulate rock 'n' rollers, was vainly trying to push the window open wide enough to throw out the television while a woman passed out in the corridor.

All this seemed like a dream when I finally awoke late morning. As I stumbled my way to the bathroom I stopped in my tracks. The walls and ceilings were covered in graffiti and indelible ink drawings of earthy naked women and male and female buttocks. The room looked like a rubbish tip, food was splattered the floor and couches and light fittings had been ripped out. I noticed the mini-bar had not been touched; this was a miracle up there with the Resurrection and the Virgin Birth.

After packing our bags we went downstairs. The staff were already stripping the rooms. Peeking in at those where the ARIA crowd had stayed, I noticed that they were neat and tidy. This was a new generation of rock 'n' rollers. They behaved more like the Brady Bunch than Led Zeppelin. Although I did hear a rumour that Fatboy Slim had trashed the boardroom. It took a Pommie to honour Harry Sebel, who was also from England.

As I signed out at reception I was congratulating myself on not having to pay for the minibar when I looked at the bill and saw I was being charged an extra $300.

'What's this for?' I asked.

'Property damage,' the girl said sweetly.

I was going to argue but thought better of it. Mandy and I stumbled, hungover and blinking, into the sunlight carrying two suitcases full of nicked Sebel memorabilia.

The Sebel was one of twelve hotels to be closed after 2000. Most were turned into apartments but the Sebel was razed and became a white minimalist block devoid of personality or a sense of the past.

'THERE WAS A DISGRACEFUL STATE OF THINGS GOING ON THERE'

FOR DULCIE DEAMER THE COMING of the Depression in 1929 changed everything: 'The bright lights had started to dim down … earnings dwindled, jobs were lost, and pretty soon one heard that this one and that one were *on the dole*.' During the depths of the Depression there would be thirty-two per cent unemployment nationally but the rate rose to seventy per cent in the slums of East Sydney and Surry Hills. Yet it was during the 1930s that Kings Cross became a name synonymous across Australia with all things modern, foreign, cultural, bohemian and immoral.

Criminal activities became more entrenched, especially gambling and sly grog. During the thirties it became almost impossible to thwart SP bookmaking and the sale of illegal booze. Police raided Kings Cross night clubs, restaurants and flats. Among the hundreds of raids, one on Christmas Eve 1932 is typical. Police burst into the Monte Carlo Club at 86 Darlinghurst Road. A waiter was charged with having sold beer without a licence and eight men and seven women were arrested for drinking on the premises. The raids were incessant, with thousands of customers and hospitality staff arrested over what seems now to be a petty amount of alcohol (the proprietor of the Claremont Café was fined £30 for having sold a bottle of wine to an undercover policeman while not holding a licence).

By 1936 the police were fighting a losing battle. Ronald Hudson, a labourer, had rented a flat in Acacia Flats in Kings Cross Road for the sole purpose of selling alcohol. Sergeant Jennings, the policeman who arrested Hudson, was exasperated at how futile policing sly grog sales had become, saying in court, 'There was a disgraceful state of things going on there [in the Cross], and the police found it hard to put down.' He was right. In early December Lionel Lindforth was charged with being a person in control of an unlicensed premises, the Tabarin Cabaret. Before he had taken over the venue the premises was a well-known sly-grog shop and had been raided several times. Lindforth's lawyer argued that the police had 'incited' the staff to sell liquor to several plainclothes officers, who had been accompanied by women. But, like the frustrated police, the magistrate argued that the only way to stop the infernal trade was for 'the police … to meet cunning with cunning'.

Illegal liquor was not only sold in nightclubs and out of flats. One of the most well-known sly grog joints was a delicatessen halfway down Victoria Street. If the owner trusted a customer, he'd lift up the wooden flap on the front counter and escort him out the back into his living room where he sold alcohol and his patrons could play his piano if they wanted to. When he closed the shop at night, his customers could exit or enter via a rear entrance in the lane.

The locals may have regarded the Cross as culturally and socially distinct from the rest of society, but it still had the same fascination with gambling and cards that was pervasive across the whole nation. Two-up, baccarat and poker were banned but they were played everywhere. Manila Poker, a variation of American poker, was rife in the Cross. Bridge was an obsession for many and housie (bingo) was played near Barney Allen's fruit shop on the corner of Penny's Lane for years.

The Cross gained a reputation for its illegal card games and roulette clubs. The undermanned police conducted raids, like one that occurred in March 1932 when they burst into a room in Kings Cross just after midnight and arrested forty-one people. In the chaos and confusion one man managed to escape. This was no dive but an elegant room, with smart furnishings, a bar and a waiter. Among those arrested for playing faro (a game where players bet on the cards of the dealer's or banker's pack) were prominent business and professional men.

Raids continued throughout the decade. In the early hours of 24 September 1937 police stormed two flats in Kings Cross and arrested thirty-five people who were playing pontoon (a variation of 21 or blackjack). One flat was in Roslyn Street, where the police found £16 on a table. A woman was charged with being the occupier and a man with being the croupier. The gamblers, four women and five men, were charged with being found in a common gaming house. But unless penalties were higher the raids were pointless as those arrested were generally bailed out within the hour and paid a minuscule fine.

In a newspaper article headlined 'Gambling's Big Grip', it was reported that card games were in evidence everywhere, ranging from chemin de fer (at Macleay House), bridge and pontoon to faro. Two-up and 'mosh' (faro) were popular in the slums of Surry Hills, but in the Cross there were sophisticated clubs where 'society folk wager with almost reckless abandon'. These were clubs whose clientele was wealthy, important and glamorous. At the other end of the spectrum there were gambling clubs that were basically dives.

Perhaps even more popular was gambling on the horses. As Dalton remarks in *Aunts Up the Cross*, 'I was brought up in an atmosphere where gambling in all its forms, but especially horse racing, was an important and integral part of our lives.' Dr Eakin and his wife were addicted to it – he was constantly working out a system and her 'fiscal week was ruled by Saturday's betting results'.

What this meant in practice was that Dalton's parents, like a majority of Australians, regularly broke the law. In 1906 the *Gaming and Betting Act* had been passed, which made off-course track betting illegal. The law allowed people to bet at the race-track but for many, especially as the Depression took hold, going to the races was too expensive and time-consuming, so off-course betting using SP (starting price) bookmakers boomed. Journalist and poet Kenneth Slessor would spend hours in his newspaper office on Saturday morning drawing up a list of bets to lodge with his bookie. He bet in tiny sums, sometimes backing two or three horses in the same race. Bookmakers worked out of hotels, shops and their own homes. The popularity of SP bookies is reflected in the fact that between 1930 and 1936 over 20,000 arrests were made.

The trade in cocaine continued but not to the levels prior to its being banned. Besides sales made in back lanes, flats or hotel rooms, there was a coffee shop in Darlinghurst Road which sold it. One contemporary resident remembered that the clients were in their forties and fifties and were 'looked upon as rather depraved individuals'. Cocaine dealing may not have been rife as in the 1920s but there were addicts who still craved it. Acting on a telephone tip-off, two detectives, Brown and Strachan, plus other police, hurried to the Mayfair Hotel early in the evening of 7 September 1937 and confronted a Geoffrey Robinson in the lounge, telling him that they had information he had cocaine in his possession. Robinson knew the jig was up and said there was no need to search him.

'I'll give it to you,' he said, handing detective Brown a phial and four small packets. 'Look, give us a go,' he pleaded. 'It's coke all right. It's not mine. I'm minding it for a sheila.'

Brown questioned him as to where he got the drug and even though Robinson said he had been 'dumped cold with it' he wouldn't squeal. It turned out that he had been selling cocaine to Kings Cross prostitutes out of hotels for three to four months.

Violence percolated through the streets. The gang wars may have petered out but acts of aggression were becoming part of King Cross's unsavoury reputation. Razors were still used but as weapons to solve personal grudges. In March 1931 an angry and jealous 20-year-old storeman, William Bennett, went to a flat in Victoria Street and confronted his 16-year-old girlfriend, Patricia Kelly. They argued and he whipped out a cut-throat razor which he used to slice open her throat and, if that weren't enough, he slashed at an ear, nearly severing it. Neighbours heard the girl's screams and rushed into the apartment to find her lying on the floor in a pool of blood, her hands gashed by the razor when she made a desperate attempt to ward off her attacker. Bennett remained in the flat and when the police arrived he calmly told them, 'I did it ... she double-crossed me.' With that he handed an officer the bloody razor.

Almost without anyone noticing, another gangster began to lay claim to being King of the Cross: Phil 'the Jew' Jeffs, a Latvian via London, where he had lived a homeless life as a boy. In 1912, aged sixteen, he sailed to Australia as a kitchen hand and jumped ship in Sydney. With plump lips, prominent nose and jug ears, Jeffs's weird face looked as though it were permanently in a stocking mask. He had ambitions to become a crime boss but he spent the early 1920s operating a fruit barrow, slowly graduating to mugging and working as a cockatoo. His prospects seemed dim; still, he was persistent, and he started to run sly grog shops, deal cocaine and work prostitutes out of Kings Cross flats. He cultivated the image of a well-read autodidact but he could be a nasty brute of a man. One evening in early 1928, he and four of his mates dragged a married woman from Bayswater Road into an apartment at 2 King's Lynn, where the men took turns in raping her. They painted their victim as a prostitute and had alibis strong enough to get them off the charges.

Not content with rape, Jeffs also cut his cocaine. It was this that caused the 'Battle of Blood Alley' on 7 May 1929. Tired of Jeffs adulterating the cocaine with boracic acid, the Woolloomooloo gang came up into the Cross and challenged Jeffs's mob to a fight in Eaton Avenue, a bleak lane just off Bayswater Road known as 'Blood Alley' because of the muggings that took place there. The two armed gangs assembled at around 10 pm and started brawling. For half an hour the men shot, kicked, clubbed and slashed at each other, only stopping when the police arrived. Jeffs escaped, but was shot twice later that night while in bed at his Kensington home. Miraculously he didn't die, but knowing his life wouldn't be worth much if he stayed in the Cross, he slunk off to Woy Woy, where he made a slow recovery from his wounds and pondered the direction of his criminal career.

He returned to Sydney in 1932 after his enforced sabbatical determined to become wealthy by other means. He reinvented himself. He dressed soberly and read widely. He opened nightclubs; perhaps the most notorious was 50-50 on the corner of William and Forbes Streets. Here one could drink sly grog, snort cocaine, dance, gamble, and have sex upstairs with the many prostitutes. He understood that although it was important to buy off the cops – as had the Devines and Leigh – his survival depended upon the good will of politicians. He started a precedent, which would later be refined by Abe 'Mr Sin' Saffron, of bribing politicians and government officials. That he succeeded well was reflected in one newspaper report which described the ambience of 50-50 as 'painted women of the street mingling with well-known scions of Society, prominent actors and actresses and the leading lights of our legal and medical professions'.

Jeffs later retired, spending the rest of his life in Ettalong where, as Larry Writer says, 'he entertained often, had many lovers and, he liked to boast, read and re-read his library of philosophical works'. He died in 1945, aged forty-nine. It's said his death was the result of the bullets remaining in his body from his attempted murder turning septic and poisoning him. He was buried under the alias of Phillip Davies.

Of all the gangsters of the 1920s and 1930s, only Jeffs had the nous to leave the crime business a wealthy man.

The Cross became a fertile ground for con-men and tricksters. Although the locals prided themselves on their worldliness, they could be as gullible as anyone else. Near the end of 1934 three men exhibited what they called the only dancing duck in the world. They'd pick a popular corner for their pitch, place an upturned tin on the pavement and on top of it a duck. One of the men whistled a tune, another addressed the crowd about the wonders of their bird, and the third carried around a hat while the duck jogged up and down on the tin in time with the music. Over several consecutive nights the men collected a small fortune from 'amazed onlookers'. The dancing duck act came to the attention of the police, who raided the show. The three tricksters escaped through the throng of spectators who must have been astonished when the police removed the tin to discover the cause of the duck's 'dancing' was a lighted candle beneath it.

As for prostitution, many girls worked out of terrace houses in Kings Cross Road, Royston Street, Kellett Street and, more discreetly, in Victoria Street. As Brewster coyly writes in *Kings Cross Calling*: 'Without doubt various forms of vice exist, but one must dive well below the surface to find it.' Hookers also worked in the side and main streets where they devoted their attention to kerb crawlers. Lydia Gill, in her affectionate memoir *My Town:*

Sydney in the 1930s, recalled that when she and her girlfriend walked home at night they wouldn't go near the gutter, because 'the girls' did a lot of business in and with passing cars. One night as she was walking down Macleay Street with her girlfriend:

> *... a big black expensive car pulled into the kerb, a girl pushed the passenger door open, climbed out, then slammed it with all her strength. Turning to us, she said, 'What did he expect for two and six?' after which she turned and walked away.*

One of the most frequent come-on lines used by the prostitutes was the crisp offer: 'Looking for company for the night, love? C'mon, thirty-bob, strip to the earrings.'

Fire

JOCELYN MARTIN-BROWN WAS A familiar figure in the area. She was a restaurant photographer and for forty years traipsed up and down the streets of the Cross asking people if they wanted to be photographed. Apparently an attractive strawberry blonde when she was young, I saw her only towards the end of her career when she seemed so forlorn that when she approached you in a restaurant you had merely to start shaking your head for her to sigh in resignation and quickly turn her attention to someone else. By this stage was she in her late sixties and her high heels were scruffy, her stacked hair a windblown mess, and she generally sported one or two black eyes (courtesy, it was rumoured, of her alcoholic partner). In 2007 she was in her eighties, and the digital camera had finally made her job redundant, when a fire broke out in her apartment and she died of smoke inhalation.

It's a rare way to succumb now, but in the twentieth century fires were a common way to expire in the Cross. Many a person died after smoking in bed. What made these incidents potentially catastrophic was that the fires were frequently in apartment buildings and affected other tenants. The causes of the fires could be unpredictable. In 1938 Frederick Collins went to attend to the furnace for the hot-water service in a block of flats he owned. A few minutes later he rushed out into the rear lane, his clothes blazing. People smothered the flames but he was badly burnt and died soon afterwards. It was thought that Collins had methylated spirits with him when it caught fire.

Another man, Frederick Pritchard, was in his flat cleaning his clothes with benzine when it caused an explosion. He was found groaning on the floor, severely burnt. In 1946 a fire broke out in the Roosevelt nightclub at 4 am. It was caused by a red-hot electric iron that had burnt through an ironing board. The building was saved by the resident cat, Rosie, who woke up the caretaker with her crying. Another cause of fires was electrical faults. A short circuit in the switch room of the eight-story building containing forty flats on the corner of Tusculum and Hughes Streets started a fire that fused the electric lights and the wiring of the lift. Residents had to flee down the stairs or rush onto the roof. The kitchen of the California Café burst into flames early one morning, which resulted in the typical sight of residents running outside in their pyjamas and adjoining flats being evacuated.

But who can predict fate? In 1944 lightning struck the Hampton Court flats during a heavy electrical storm and started a fire in the lift.

The causes of some fires were inexplicable. In 1930 two women were rearranging furniture in Carisbrook, Springfield Avenue, when 'a column of smoke burst in on them'. The intense heat and fumes sent them staggering backwards and they fell to the floor. As flames enveloped the room, a large chandelier fell from the ceiling and struck one of the women on the head, almost knocking her unconscious. The other woman managed to call 'Fire' and drag her friend downstairs, leaving behind a severely damaged room and smouldering possessions.

There were also frequent examples of people coming home to find their flats on fire, the cause of which was never discovered. The constant fear for Kings Cross residents was that the fires could easily spread through a whole building. In 1954 fire destroyed two big storage rooms on the roof of Gowrie Gate, considered at the time to be one of the tallest and most luxurious apartment buildings in the area. The flames were seen from the city. Occupants of the sixth floor flats were driven out by water and heat. If anything typified a resident of Kings Cross it was their reluctance to leave their flats. One blasé woman said, 'I can't be bothered, I'm too busy.'

By the 1940s Maramanah was a fading and isolated relic of the glorious era of the great mansions. One night it burst into flames, and as Robin Dalton writes in *Aunts Up the Cross*, she was awakened by her mother jigging with excitement as the fire engines caterwauled down Darlinghurst Road. Her mother told her that Maramanah, the house that contained the aunts she had always loathed, was on fire and urged her daughter to come with her and watch it burn:

> *Down the street we pelted; [my mother] always loved a good fire anyway, and as she rarely went to bed, the fact that it was two in the morning was no deterrent to her enjoyment. Indeed it was an exceptionally bright blaze: the towers and turrets and iron-laced balconies showed up beautifully; and my mother was only disappointed that there was no sign of the aunts being lowered by ropes.*

After the fire the aunts never went back. They settled in an apartment nearby and the Navy used Maramanah as a canteen during the war before the City Council bought it with the idea of demolishing it and extending the gardens to an adjoining park.

In March 1946 ten squatters took possession of the vacant mansion. Most of them were returned servicemen who were homeless. As a spokesman put it:

'We have done everything to find a home, but it is hopeless ... it is disgraceful that the council should tear down a beautiful old building like this when thousands are homeless in Sydney alone. We can sleep here. We cannot sleep in the parks.'

This action captured the imagination of Sydneysiders who were all too aware of the desperate housing shortage after the war. Though there were others who thought it was a Communist plot and pointed to the fact that the Communist Party held meetings and weekly dances at Maramanah. Even so, the authorities realised that the squatters had the public on their side and did nothing to evict them.

In 1953 a fire took hold in one of the squatters' rooms and spread. A resident of Cahors, across the road from the burning mansion, thought the flames were so intense that he hurried a few doors down to 52 Macleay Street where his mother lived and brought her back to his apartment as he feared the flames would spread to her units. It was the end for the stately home and it was razed to the ground to make way for the Fitzroy Gardens.

Just after the Second World War Nora Willis, a landlady in her early forties, went into the room of her tenant Barbara Zenda and set fire to Zenda's clothes, saying dreamily as she stared at it, 'What a lovely fire.' When she was arrested Willis refused to wear anything other than her pyjamas and a great coat. An officer asked her how many people were in the house and the demented woman replied, 'Fourteen thousand.'

During the Cold War the Communist Party had a branch in a four-storey block on William Street and in the early hours of 1949 a fire broke out which was extinguished with great difficulty. At first police believed the fire had been accidentally caused by a passer-by throwing a cigarette butt into paper and other rubbish in the doorway, but later conceded the bleeding obvious – that the fire may have been deliberately started – although they had no suspects.

Two of the most persistent arsonists of the Cross were the gangsters Jim Anderson and Abe Saffron, partners in crime. Anderson liked to become personally involved in the arson. In the early hours of 26 November 1973 he staggered into the casualty department of St Vincent's Hospital, burns covering half his body and his clothes smouldering and blackened. When the police interviewed him he told them that he was driving past the Staccato Club (partly owned by Saffron) at 101 Darlinghurst Road when he saw two men acting suspiciously. He decided to investigate and, finding the club's door was open, walked inside but tripped over. He was smoking a cigarette and when he stood up the whole room exploded in flames. Although he was burning, he managed to escape the club and drive himself to the hospital.

The story was a lie, of course. His shoes reeked of petrol and there were other questions, such as why would he leave his gun behind in his car when a potential confrontation with the two men could have led to violence? And petrol fumes would not have ignited from a cigarette; a naked flame would be required. Anderson spent five months in hospital. His body a lattice of scars from the fire, he returned to work for Saffron. 'Mr Sin', as Saffron was known, had almost a pyromaniac's fascination for fires. Between 1979 and 1981 six of his premises were destroyed by fire – all of them insured – including the Wonder Centre, a brothel, the Peak Room and the Venus Room. One of the reasons the buildings burnt so quickly was that despite the venues having been ordered to upgrade their fire safety precautions they seldom had. Saffron and Anderson paid off the fire inspectors just as easily as they paid off corrupt police and politicians. It's estimated that over the years nineteen properties owned by Saffron were damaged or destroyed through arson. Even though Saffron was a major insurance risk it did seem odd that a lone insurance clerk had been involved in most of the pay-outs.

Kings Cross attracts the sane and the mad – sometimes it is hard to tell the difference – but many disturbed people find refuge and solace in the Cross where their delusions and strange behaviour are, if not accepted, at least tolerated until they dangerously impinge on other lives. The unfortunate aspect is that some, a tiny group, act out their harmful fantasies. Raymond Lyttle (or as some newspaper reports say, Little) was a 23-year-old gay cook. Born in Newcastle, at the age of four his parents sent him to a boys' home, where he remained until he was fifteen. By 1975 he had a history of arson convictions including setting fire to a shop.

If people recognised him it was because, ironically, he had played a prominent role in a campaign to fireproof Kings Cross's old buildings. At around 5.30 am Christmas Day 1975 he went into the basement of the Savoy Hotel (45–47 Darlinghurst Road), and used his cigarette lighter to set alight several bundles of newspapers. The fire quickly spread, and with no means of escape from the second and third floors of the 1925 building, fifteen of the sixty guests died in the blaze. Those who perished were either asphyxiated, burnt or killed jumping for their lives. Many others were injured. Bumper Farrell, who was at that time in charge of Darlinghurst Police Station, was called out of bed to investigate. He was greeted by the sickening sight of burnt and charred bodies. He recognised one of the victims, the stripper Kerry Green who worked under the *nom-de-strip* of 'Baby Doll' at the Paradise Club. Eventually suspicions fell on Lyttle, who was staying at the hotel.

He had started the fire out of anger at his male lover not visiting him. As he said to the police, 'I seen the newspapers stacked inside the door and I just lit the fire with a cigarette lighter ... I was just trying to relieve some tension in me.' For the ageing cop Bumper Farrell it was impossible to forget the horror of the crime scene and he was frequently heard lambasting 'fucking poofters'.

Lyttle was sentenced to life imprisonment with a minimum of twenty-eight years.

Another dangerous arsonist was Gregory Allan Brown, who was arrested in August 1990 while staring at a blaze he had started in Woolloomooloo's Matthew Talbot Hostel. The police were soon to realise that Brown was the firebug who set fire to a settee in the foyer of the Downunder backpacker hostel at 43 Darling-hurst Road at 4 am on 17 September 1989, killing six people and injuring another eighteen. He confessed to his crimes, including his involvement in starting the 1983 Ash Wednesday bushfires, which killed forty-six people in Victoria and destroyed more than 2000 homes. Before setting fire to the backpacker hostel he had lit more than 200 blazes during a year-long arson spree in Melbourne and Sydney between July 1989 and July 1990.

The clearly insane Brown was aggressive, a social misfit at school and spent six months in a psychiatric hospital at the age of eighteen after trying to strangle his father. He had started to light fires as a teenager. A forensic psychiatrist, Dr Rod Milton, interviewed the proud arsonist and was horrified by Brown, warning police that the firebug was beyond reform and he couldn't recall ever seeing 'anyone as dangerous to others as the arsonist'. Brown was found guilty of the manslaughter deaths of three British backpackers and one each from Sweden, Austria and Denmark and jailed for a maximum of eighteen years. A fellow prisoner told the court that far from being concerned about the six deaths, Brown told him, 'That's why I lit it. I love hearing people scream and watching them die.'

In a way Abe Saffron was to blame, too: after all, he owned the Downunder. An investigation later revealed that the local council had issued three fire notices on the building since 1980, ordering it to comply with fire safety regulations. Nothing was done and the building had no fire escape, an inaudible fire alarm, no sprinkler system and the only stairway in the hostel that had fire doors to contain a blaze had those fire doors permanently wedged or latched open. No doubt Saffron had paid off the fire inspectors again.

REACHING FOR THE SKY

THE GENERAL ECONOMY MAY HAVE been bleak, with unemployment reaching nearly thirty per cent by 1932, but Kings Cross experienced a building boom in the Depression that was to radically transform it into Australia's vanguard of cutting-edge architecture. It became a focal point for all things modern: innovative food, ethnic mix, technology, music, design, contemporary buildings and a community quite distinct from the rest of the country. It also became the most densely populated spot in Australia.

This physical transformation had evolved gradually during the 1920s. Robin Dalton mentions none of this in her *Aunts Up the Cross*. She insists that the Cross was quiet, insular, almost like a country town, but there was a range of impressive apartment blocks being built. One of the handful of architects who radically transformed the area during the 1920s and 1930s was Claude Hamilton, who designed the Savoy just after the First World War, Regent's Court in 1925, and Byron Hall in Macleay Street four years later. Like the Regent's Court 1929 facade, Byron Hall has liver-coloured bricks, but is more dramatic, with projecting balconies and facetted bays of windows as well as an appliqué of classically derived detailing both in the entranceway and at the top of the building.

Within five years from 1920, Walter Leslie Nielsen created in Springfield Avenue what some believe is one of the most beautiful streetscapes in Australia. He began with the understated but fine Carisbrook, then Kentwood Court, and finally Carinthia. Their simple porticos with columns and long entrance halls soothed by soft lighting and panelled with polished wood have a refined, genteel ambience. The graceful white buildings, like stately wedding cakes, have distinct similarities to London's Knightsbridge.

Nielsen's masterpiece, Franconia, on Macleay Street, opened in 1930. This elegant block of nine storeys with forty-two apartments, has Gothic wrought-iron gates, softly glowing gold lettering and art deco lamps lining the richly polished wood-panelled corridors. It had a restaurant, a concierge and a live-in caretaker who had to wake several times during the night to shovel coal into the basement boiler to make sure all the units had hot water. And if staff or residents ever got bored, there was a mini golf course behind the building. It says something about Nielsen's pride in the place that he decided to live there with his wife.

Throughout the 1930s the major architects strove to break the decorative tradition and to reinforce streamlined design, to rid the façades of as much ornamentation as possible and to install the latest technology from electric elevators to telephones. These graceful designs made a building like Kingsclere, constructed twenty years before on the corner of Greenknowe Avenue and Macleay Street, look heavy and almost Victorian in its ponderous certainty.

Another significant architect was Emil Sodersten (he changed his name from Sodersteen). Born in 1899 in Balmain to a Swedish mariner, he studied at Sydney Technical College and attended lectures at Sydney University. An exceptional artist and, although short (5 feet 3 inches) and bulky, he was also a brilliant sportsman with a liking for skiing (then a very adventurous sport) and polo. He was the leading architect working in the art deco style and his fastidious, imaginative planning and lavish brickwork earned him 'the contemporary appellation of a modern Horbury Hunt'. Sodersten's affection for intricate and decorative brickwork developed a strong tradition in the Cross of ameliorating the austere look of American modernist architecture. He designed Kingsley Hall (an odd but charming wedge shape to fit in a tiny pocket of Barncleuth Place) and Werrington and Wychbury Towers, side by side in Manning Street.

His masterpiece is Birtley Towers, an enchanting nine-storey art deco block with six flats per floor in a U-shaped plan that maximised the use of light. When it was completed in 1934 it was one of the largest blocks in Australia, with fifty-four flats, six per floor. It brought a sky-scraper style to Australian apartment design with its textured brick and dramatic sunbursts and finials at the top, an impressive porch entrance and a shiny maple veneer foyer. Unlike his gifted architect friend Charles Dellit (who was to later design the Minerva theatre and shopping complex), Sodersten had studied how the American skyscrapers played with gradations of colour – the brick facade is graded from dark tones at the base to light red at the skyline to emphasise the illusion of height. Dellit didn't know this so his early attempts had brickwork darkening towards the summit.

These extraordinary, elegant buildings were looked on with awe. One reporter marvelled at 'those soaring sky scrapers of King's Cross which people see from incoming ships and imagine are the city itself'. A year later in 1936 another journalist wrote that Kings Cross had become a hive of flats: '... great modern buildings rearing eight to ten storeys high. Their lights against the dark heavens present a striking picture'.

What enthralled people was the very concept of height and the rare sensation of being up so high. For some years Kenneth Slessor lived in a flat on the seventh floor at the top of William Street, high up above the noise and dirt of the city ('... eating, sleeping, loving, arguing, sausage frying and head scratching in a small room of stucco, wallpaper and brick, on top of a layer of steel in a structure of cement'). It was here he could look down on his beloved neon-lit Cross and its 'spider web of living'. The women in his light verse are so high up it's as if they are in heaven and party girls are said to '[live] in the sky'. Residing in a high-rise flat became almost a transcendental experience. The vogue for the exhilaration of being so high was exploited by the Mansions Hotel in Bayswater Road, which boasted that it was 'the highest and most convenient position in Sydney'.

For flat dwellers there was also a voyeuristic appeal in being able to peer into other people's apartments, which were almost within touching distance. The action of Ray Mathew's play, *The Life of the Party*, takes part in a Kings Cross flat ('in the Bohemian section of Sydney'). For its protagonist Alex, the famous radio actor, the attractions of living in such a building are obvious. From his balcony he can see into the opposite windows:

It's like being God ... You get to know lives ... the couple over there ... no children. They both work but different hours. She runs a sailor as well as him. He doesn't know, or at least we don't think so. She never lets them meet ... There's a writer in that white block. His light stays on; all night he works or reads ... The place under his has a dry cleaner. He's got a truck and a daughter who can talk and call him daddy, so he doesn't seem to mind his wife. That flat is shared by two girls – air hostesses. They wear uniforms ... They come home at all times, at all months, escorted by prosperous-looking beasts in Bentleys.

With the erection of these apartments came a huge influx of residents. By the late 1930s the Cross was said to be home to about

60,000 people in an area of barely one square mile. Ernestine Hill, novelist and journalist, in an article headlined 'An Anthill of Human Life', was amazed at the transformation:

> *Twenty years ago it was tenements fast falling into slums. Then Sydney began to sell the sky, and today it is a cosmopolis – flats, flats and flats – flats over butcher shops, flats over florists, flats in their own right, sumptuously set apart and these in the great majority.*

She was thrilled how a doctor's charming residence in Macleay Street which boasted eight servants was demolished to make way for a towering block of eighty-seven flats which would house 380 people. It was no wonder Kings Cross real estate agents worked through Sundays.

The hazards of living in flats were cheerfully endured. One reporter was passing through the Cross when he saw a man in a towel and bathrobe climb an unsteady ladder to his third-floor flat. He had left his key inside when he had gone down to the communal bathroom. Trying to keep the ladder steady for actor Cecil Perry was his mate, fellow actor Peter Finch. And this was another extra benefit of living in the Cross: you got to mix with people you wouldn't ordinarily meet. Lydia Gill's fellow residents were a wonderfully sundry bunch:

> *There was Selena who made junk jewellery from glass beads and copper fuse wire, Nancy who believed in the curative powers of carrot juice and who worshipped her cat, the lass who took university extension courses and one who travelled with a circus and was cut in half at every performance.*

There were also the unavoidable noises seeping out from the flats where the personal lives of others became public in the concrete and steel hive. Ronald McCuaig, an exceptional though underrated poet and friend of Slessor, wrote several poems about apartment living. In 'The Letter', a man writes to his beloved and at the same time is unable to keep out the sounds of a couple making love in the flat above, a shouting match in another flat between a man and woman (the husband calling his wife a whore), an argument going on into the early hours of the morning, a conversation downstairs between two men about one of them not loving a girl; in one flat a young woman has sex with a married man, while in another a husband has spent the rent money, and in an adjoining flat another husband, drunk, punches and then rapes his wife.

One inescapable aspect of living in high-rise buildings is the prospect of loneliness. In Slessor's *Darlinghurst Nights* (subtitled: 'Being 47 strange sights/ Observed from eleventh storeys') the lively world of the party girls and kept women residing in their flats also has a darker side – that of the solitary, loveless life. In the poem 'Lonely' a young woman stares out of her high-rise apartment looking down at the glowing shops and lovers on the street:

All the windows shine with things for Other People Only,
All the world is kissing, and I'm lonely, lonely, lonely!

In Mathew's *The Life of the Party,* a disturbed European woman poisons herself and a lonely musician blows out his brains. There were suicides by jumping, gassing or poisoning, sometimes the body not found for days, only confirming the social isolation of the sufferer.

Besides the new high-rise apartment buildings there were guest houses. One of the most expensive was the Cairo at 52 Macleay Street, which advertised itself as an exclusive hotel for ladies and gentlemen, with prices starting from ten shillings a day to £20 a week. It was a glorious mansion (later the site of the Chevron Hotel) that had been a private home. It had a circular drive leading from the main gates through luxuriant gardens scented with camphor laurel and magnolias. Behind the Cairo were tennis courts.

There were many guest houses scattered throughout the area, but not so exalted as the Cairo or Mrs Freda Buswell's swish Number 9 Springfield Avenue. At 44 Macleay there were one hundred rooms with hot water, a telephone in every room and bedsitting rooms with bathroom and highly sought-after harbour views. The prices ranged from £3 10 shillings to £6 6 shillings per week. At the Imperial, 'Sydney's most modern guest house', there were 160 bedrooms each with hot and cold water, an electric elevator, a roof garden and harbour views, with prices ranging from £2 15 shillings per week to ten shillings and sixpence per day. In Bayswater Road there were furnished self-contained flats for rent which were a particular favourite of country visitors who had to keep to a tight budget.

Dozens of terrace houses had been converted into flats and 'flatettes'. In *Kings Cross Calling*, the authors write of them with a shudder:

> *Many of the slums of today were the mansions of yesterday with strange and jerry-built additions ... Victoria Street is filled with attics ... in summer the tin roofs and narrow windows make them unbearable, the enamel wash basin leaks, the wardrobe is a row of hooks behind a dingy curtain.*

Dorothy Drain, a young journalist renting a flat in 1936, recalled that you could rent a bedsitter for twenty-five shillings a week but 'if you wanted a ray of sunlight and some air you might have to pay thirty shillings'. As a lowly D-grade reporter on *The Sun* she earned £6 a week and before long she was spending a third of that on her tiny flat. Cam Bone, who ran a corner shop in Victoria Street, recalls in her memoir *Knock Around the Cross* how the once grand terraces were divided internally with cheap boards so that sometimes as many as twenty people shared a single house. For artists, 'rents were low and one could starve much slower in the Cross than anywhere else in Sydney'. Rooming houses, dubbed residentals, could be had for as little as ten shillings a week. These rooms or flats included a shilling-in-the-slot meter, a gas ring or small stove, but no hot baths, unless you paid extra.

With the rise in the number of cheap flats came the iconic figure of 'the Landlady', a Medusa-like figure whose only friends were other landladies, or what one local called 'the acid camaraderie of Kings Cross landladies'. There was her constant mantra: *No radios after 11 pm. No noisy parties*. If she said to the prospective renter, 'You'll like it here. It's a quiet place,' it was a subtle way of saying there were to be no noisy parties. Landladies wanting late rents lay in wait for lodgers on the stairs and turned off the gas at eleven. It was said that one landlady, known as Irish Mary, was imbued with a sixth sense which led her unerringly to the culprit who had plugged an iron into a light socket and blown the fuse.

They not only made sure that single women had no male visitors past a certain time but were grimly efficient in collecting rent and displaying handwritten notices in corridors and bathrooms:

> *Kindly do not read the newspaper when using the toilet. There are others waiting. Don't bother to break open the gas meter in search of pennies. It is cleared every day. If you must sing or whistle when taking a bath please do so quietly, to avoid annoying other tenants.*

Other signs were taped on the toilet wall: *This seat is for convenience not for meditation*. In George Johnston's *Clean Straw for Nothing*, there was a framed printed sign screwed above the ring-marked bathtub which stated, in plain English, *Guests are politely requested please not to shit in the bath*.

Lydia Gill remembers as a sixteen year-old living in a larger-than-normal bedsitter in Rockwell Crescent with a tiny kitchenette, a dining suite and a daybed for furniture. Her bathroom was down half a flight of stairs ('Only in the Cross did one find half a flight of stairs'). Her first landlady was an English woman with a peculiar American accent. She and her husband 'ruled everybody's coming and goings in the building with a rod of iron'. Gill had been in her first-floor flat for only a short time when the landlady asked her to move into a smaller flat on the first floor because she could get eighteen shillings and sixpence per week for Gill's flat, which was classified as a double flat, and Gill was only paying fifteen shillings per week. It was the Depression and the landlady was keen for the extra money.

The Kings Cross landlady became a key ingredient of radio drama and theatre. In Bob Herbert's evocation of Kings Cross during the Second World War, *No Names, No Pack Drill*, it is the landlady's nosy interest in Kathy, one of her woman boarders, that sets in train a series of dramatic events. Kathy, an Australian girl (loosely based on my mother and her time in the Cross), is harbouring Rebel, an American deserter. The action is set on the second floor of an apartment building in Kings Cross. Mrs Palmer, the landlady, is described as 'a tall Englishwoman of about fifty who affects a certain cheerful refinement'. This nosy termagant was based on a despot Herbert had had to endure in Tara, Greenknowe Avenue. Mrs Palmer has 'a large-tooth smile which assumes at times the proportions of a tour de force'. She is not only a gossip but she informs on the local black marketeer, telling the police where the character Tiger sells 'sly grog' and where he hides his car (in Manning or Crick Streets). Near the end, just when you think the illicit lovers might get away, with Rebel about to abscond on a ship, the landlady is discovered listening at the door. Kathy has been pretending to the police that Rebel is her brother, but Mrs Palmer tells the police it isn't him. The stage direction says there is a 'heavy silence', which on the several times I've seen the play, is always the spot where you hear an audible gasp from the audience, as the landlady from hell ruins the young lovers' lives.

Beggars

LATELY I'VE BEEN HAGGLING OVER money with Vince. I tell him that I'm quite prepared to give him one payment per week, instead of spreading my money over four or five nights. He shakes his head when I offer him the deal.

'I don't know, Louis,' he says. 'I'd like to think about it.'

Vince is a beggar. He has staked his spot a few metres from my apartment, strategically placed between the liquor shop and the junction of streets and roads that gives Kings Cross its name. He is not the only beggar in the area. There are many. If one is to give a rough summary of the types of beggars that proliferate in the cramped area that includes the higher regions of Darlinghurst Road down to the halfway mark of Macleay Street – the main drag of the Cross – then the most common are the temporary beggars who, grimacing with severe hangovers, crop up of a Sunday and on Monday mornings wanting money for extra drinks or just enough money to flee back home from their disastrous weekend in Kings Cross. I answer their importuning with 'No, thank you, I don't want any,' which gives me a few seconds to move on as their addled brains try to process what I've said, before realising and crying out after me, 'No, it's me that wants the money, stupid!'

Then there are the men and women who hover around the railway station pleading for money to buy a train ticket. Their familiar cry is for 'spare change', or a small but uncommon amount like forty cents, in the hope that the impatient commuter will offer a fifty-cent coin or a dollar just to get rid of them. Before the recent makeover of Kings Cross, they would succeed more often than now, because the professionals and yuppies who have since shifted into the area have no time for these dishevelled losers. Strangely, these city workers often give money to a quiet scruffy man waiting outside the entrance to the station. What they don't know is that this is Ed, a go-between for junkies who have been told that a bearded man with a silky terrier outside the station will take them to a drug dealer or tell them where drugs are being sold. Women especially take pity on the unkempt tiny dog always sitting patiently at his feet and give Ed money without him asking for it.

Then there are the severe alcoholics who need just enough change to dash off to the hardware shop to buy their metho. They slump in alcoves or on the doorsteps of apartment blocks and shops, their faces like giant bruises, holding out trembling hands, giving a hideously bad performance as someone who needs enough money to get a train home to the most distant suburb they can think of. One haunts the doorstep of a friend of mine and begs for spare change with an accent that would not be out of place for an actor playing an aristocrat in English repertory. Most do not stay long; they either die or end up in a drying-out facility.

Let's not forget the crazies; the last twenty or so years has seen a growing influx of madmen. Thrown out of asylums because of government cutbacks and society's indifference, they wander the streets muttering to themselves, cursing God, or suddenly looming in front of you with wild grins and demanding money. Ice addicts make the worst beggars because by the time they get up enough courage to beg they are simmering with hostility, having been up for two or three days without sleep, and any knock-back is an affront to their self-esteem. They yell and hurl abuse at the frightened man or woman whom a few seconds ago they were addressing with a brittle charm that barely concealed their impulse to attack.

A couple of years ago I saw a well-groomed man in a business suit carrying a briefcase hurrying towards me. He must have been taking a shortcut to the Kings Cross railway station because he seemed out of place in malodorous Barncleuth Lane. He grabbed hold of my arm.

'You'd better be careful,' he warned. 'There's a guy just over there and he's shooting up.'

The ashen-faced young man hurried off. I walked on and stopped. Sitting on the kerb, surrounded by the squalor of plastic bags full of garbage he had collected from rubbish bins, was a tiny fellow locals nicknamed 'the Rat Man'. His hair was wild and dirty, his face blotched with veins and pustules, his clothes filthy. He was injecting into his leg the dregs from a syringe he had found.

'How you going, John?' I greeted him. He looked up at me and smiled.

'It's a really good morning 'cos I found some good stuff in the rubbish, Louis,' he remarked cheerfully, and went back to eking out the residue of the drug.

If anything indicates the great social and economic divide that now exists in Kings Cross, it was that encounter. John was harmless. He haunted the back lanes and side streets in a constant and thorough search through the garbage, looking for used syringes that may have the dregs of drugs or any sort of pill that may give him a high or just alter his metabolism. Paramedics from St Vincent's Hospital knew him well, as they had to save his life on a regular basis. It's one of the marvels of life that he hadn't died many times over and residents speculated that his blood must be a Petri dish of disease. He stank and had the gauntness of an anorexic, but also the manners of a Victorian gentleman. Once when he asked my wife for a cigarette she handed him one and he slightly recoiled when his grubby fingers touched hers as if she were the tainted one. He wanted her to light it, but not when he had the cigarette in his lips because she would be too close, so he held it out with suspicious fingers in the hope he wouldn't catch a disease from her.

John's begging mantra never changed. He asked for spare change in a casual manner that suggested he didn't care one way or the other whether he was successful. One of the problems was that he seemed too cheerful, too full of an optimistic bonhomie weirdly at odds with his sickly body. No doubt his odour was off-putting, and his face had more than a hint of a death mask, but he never took offence at rejection – it's as if he expected it. When my wife gave him money, he thanked her in a courtly fashion, almost bowing from his customary position sitting on the footpath sur-rounded by the garbage he was sorting through.

'You are most kind, Mandy.'

We knew his life had been saved again when he would return from St Vincent's hospital with his straggly beard shaved off and his mucky shrub of hair gone. One Saturday afternoon we saw a waiter ejecting him from the side door of a restaurant into Kellett Way after he had gone in there to buy some food with money he had earned from his begging.

'I only wanted to buy a schnitzel,' he complained to us, still indignant.

One sunny morning as I was coming back from the post office I saw him sitting in the Fitzroy Gardens on a bench under a pair of palm trees. He was naked except for a hospital blanket deco-rated with the words *Property of St Vincent's Hospital*.

'As you can see, Louis, I need some change.' I handed him a

few dollars, and as he stared at the glittering coins he vomited on them. He looked up at me, smiling apologetically. 'Sorry about that, Louis. Must be something I ate.'

Despite his appearance, John collected a lot of money. I saw people throw coins at him from a distance as if they were afraid of catching a virus. Once he had made enough he indulged his one passion besides drugs – gambling. The only time he was seen indoors was when he was in the pokies section of the Darlo Bar or the Vegas Hotel. He always played alone because, quite simply, he stank so much he'd send even gambling addicts fleeing from the pokies room. He sat on his stool like a wizened imp with one rigid finger monotonously tapping a button until he ran out of money, then he'd quietly slip out of the hotel, leaving the bar staff to wipe down his seat with disinfectant.

He became so well known that he's mentioned in Clinton Ca-ward's novel *Love Machine*. When the narrator passes Dean's Café in Kellett Street he sees 'the Rat Man, impossibly skinny, lank hair falling to his dirty, unshaven cheeks, squatting in his nest of pa-pers and old clothes'.

But John tempted fate once too often and died of an over-dose in 2008. His story was in the newspapers for several days because it had been revealed that he had cost taxpayers $500,000 in welfare payments, hospital visits, and rehab. The public was supposed to be outraged by this. Mandy and I went to St Canice's down in Roslyn Street for his funeral service. It was a Thursday morning but there was an impressive turnout of about a hundred people from all walks of life: nurses, doctors, lawyers, the home-less, Kings Cross 'identities' and Coco my chihuahua, whom he loved. When one person announced that they would put 'sym-bolic' objects on the altar I inwardly groaned; what a twee ges-ture to make, I thought. A woman put a plastic bag filled with the sort of miscellaneous stuff he collected on the altar. It looked exactly like John's bags and the whole congregation laughed. It was a totally appropriate reminder of him. There were prayers, songs ('Let it Be', of course) and some of his friends and nurses spoke about him, many not shrinking from how much of a pest he could be – and even that behaviour seemed comical in retrospect. As I looked around I realised just how much John had been part of Kings Cross and how much this beggar meant to our community. It was an example of how long-term residents do not judge or reject those who are less well-off, as would happen elsewhere.

If John looked like a permanent passenger on the ferry crossing the River Styx, Rose resembles a troll. She has been begging for almost a decade now. Like most professional beggars, she has her own territory. I first saw her working the Darlinghurst Road restaurant precinct at night. Her clothes have never changed. She wears a battered windcheater, baggy trousers and scruffy runners. Stocky, with a brown face like weather-beaten leather, she shuffles back and forth, covertly eyeing off her marks. She's Aboriginal, a fact that is vitally important in making her the most successful beggar in the Cross. Her targets are couples, especially young professionals who are in the early stages of dating. She approaches the man, never the woman, and asks for money in a simpering, servile voice, grinning shyly. Few of the men fail to give her money. After all, they want to look charitable in the eyes of their girlfriends, especially towards an Aboriginal woman.

One evening, as I was sitting outside a restaurant watching as she unctuously approached couples, she spied me and tried her technique on me.

'I like the way you play on white guilt,' I remarked. 'It's very good.'

The angelic expression immediately transformed itself. 'Get fucked,' she snarled and then turned on her heel to stalk an unwary couple.

From then on, we had a combative relationship. Whenever she saw me she would sidle up to me and whisper, 'Get fucked.' Having learnt her name, I would answer back, 'Now, now, Rose, remember to play to white guilt.' But I did admire her, especially as I was to learn even more about her. Rose is a junkie and earns enough not only to feed her habit but occasionally to dispense extra to other Aborigines, which she bestows with the hauteur of Marie Antoinette handing out cake to peasants.

One night I was walking Coco in the small St John's churchyard. Coco was off the leash and ran into the shadows. I heard a female voice impatiently telling her to go away. I went to get Coco and saw that it was Rose, huddled up in the darkness between the sandstone steps and a crevice in the wall. She was injecting into a vein. I grabbed Coco, who was trying to smother her with affection, and a weary Rose glanced at me, saying in a sweet voice, 'I'm sorry about that.'

This exchange didn't mean there was any softening of our relationship. On the contrary, a few weeks later she was still addressing me as 'Get Fucked'. Finally I stopped her at the corner of Darlinghurst Road and Macleay Street and, with mock anger, told her that she should be ashamed of herself. Coco had been severely traumatised by seeing her shooting up. Her eyes narrowed. Was I having a lend of her? Unsure, she shuffled away, but from then on she avoided me. I didn't see much of her for some months because she changed her beat. Now that cashed-up yuppies have flooded into the area, the financial demographics have changed. The money is now down in Macleay Street. I hear from friends that Rose is making a killing with her guilt shtick. Those young white professionals are easy prey.

Meanwhile at the Kings Cross dog show, held in the Fitzroy Gardens, Coco won a trophy by dancing, doing high-fives and begging. About a fortnight later, I was walking Coco down the main drag when Rose approached me in her usual stooped shuffle.

'I saw her win first prize,' she cooed. 'She's beautiful, isn't she?' She was grinning, and for the first time I detected a maternal warmth to her.

'Thank you,' I said, moved by her obvious delight. Coco adopted a begging position that makes her resemble a meerkat.

'She's quite good,' said Rose, with a professional discernment. Then she looked at me through the wild tangle of hair obscuring much of her face and grinned wickedly. 'Not so traumatised now, is she?' With that she was off, heading down to the posh end of Macleay Street. We have a truce now. If she says she's desperate, I know she needs it for her habit so I give her something.

With Vince, I have a different arrangement, constantly negotiated for some six years now. I first saw him sitting on the doorstep of an apartment block a few doors up where he has become a permanent fixture. 'Got a couple of bob?' was his constant cry. One night I gave him twenty cents. He held it in his gnarled hand, gazing at it with contempt.

'I said a couple of bob,' he complained.

'Well, that's twenty cents. That's a couple of bob,' I said, not a little miffed.

'Look,' he replied, 'a couple of bob now means two dollars.'

'Well, why don't you ask for a couple of dollars then?'

Vince rolled his eyes, incredulous at my stupidity. 'People give a couple of bob, they won't give a couple of dollars.'

That's how our relationship began. He worked his pitch at night and whenever he saw me he'd ask for a couple of bob and gradually, without me being aware of what was happening, this became a daily event.

His face is the colour of dirty beetroot. His standard outfits are a scruffy tweed jacket and baggy trousers in summer and he adds an extra jacket in winter. When he stands, which is not often, he is short. From a distance, as he sits hunched up on the doorstep, he resembles a gargoyle. His clothes and hair hide his great distinguishing characteristic – tattoos cover his body. When he has a haircut you can see, because you're generally staring down at him, that even his scalp is covered in tattoos.

Vince is prey to wild mood swings. Sometimes he is so morose he cannot even say the words 'two bob'; at other times he is so jittery with excitement that he can barely sit still. The first time I saw him in a euphoric mood was in the video shop across the road. As I worked my way from new releases to cult films, I noticed Vince lying supine on the concrete floor. He had arranged himself in a crucifix position. Surrounding him were empty DVD cases. His eyes opened when he heard footsteps.

'Hi, Louis,' he greeted me casually. I took in the covers of the DVDs. At the end of both hands he had placed religious movies like *The Passion*, at his feet he had arranged comedies like *Porky's* and *Police Academy*, and around his head was a halo of three horror movies.

'I like your choice in movies, Vince,' I said.

'Shit,' he groaned and jumped up. 'Shit, shit, shit,' he kept on muttering to himself as he hurried from the store.

When he was on a manic high he would give me tongue twisters to pronounce like 'AWoopBamABooBamLoopBangDoBang'. If I repeated them exactly he would grow angry, yell 'Shit!' and storm away, forgetting to ask me for money. Sometimes the mania would possess Vince utterly, and he would chase after me if I were on the other side of the street. I would know he was crossing Darlinghurst Road because I would hear screeching brakes and blasting horns. He'd arrive breathless and grinning, not wanting money but just to say hello. It became obvious when he was on medication because his mania vanished. If he took his medication too soon after assuming his regular spot for the night, then he was withdrawn and almost incapable of communicating. One evening I asked him if he were schizophrenic. He nodded calmly.

'Everything was all right until I was about eighteen,' he said, 'then my life went haywire, but I'm OK now.'

Vince and I established a rough sort of etiquette. I would run into him frequently during the day away from his pitch, but he never asked for money. We would chat a little and then he would scurry off, as if he were late for some appointment. Sometimes when he saw me leaving the liquor shop he'd smile and ask me how much I spent on the wine. I never told him, but he'd shake his head ruefully as if I had and remark, 'That's quite a lot of dosh, Lou.' He used the shortened form of my first name when he was taking the piss out of me.

Everyone in the area knows him by name, and when they return from a holiday or business trip he knows exactly how long they've been away. Once when I came back from a research trip, I handed him some money. He stared at the coins for a time and said, 'I want some notes.' I wasn't going to put up with this kind of blackmail.

'Look, Vince, that's pretty much what I give you every night.' He stood up on the step of his pitch so he was nearly my height.

'You see, Louis, I've counted up the days you've been away and I've worked out you owe me notes, not coins.' I was irritated and told him that if I gave him notes then he would continue to demand them.

'Maybe,' he replied carefully, 'it all depends what mood I'm in.'

Late one afternoon I saw him in his regular place, drinking a can of beer – which was unusual. He patted the space next to him and asked me to join him. I told him I didn't drink beer.

'That's OK, Louis, just sit here.' So I sat with him and talked.

It was fascinating to see the world from his perspective. It was amazing how many businessmen looked down at him (maybe us) with expressions of absolute contempt. Others passed by, pretending indifference. A few locals greeted him by name, which pleased him no end. During our conversation I wondered if he had ever been beaten up.

'Once or twice by hoons, but you gotta accept that.' I asked him why he didn't stay at the hostel where he slept and get the dole.

'That's a living death. A real living death,' he replied. After an hour, I stood up. 'This is my world, Louis,' he remarked cheerfully.

KINGS CROSS IS DIFFERENT

IN THE DIZZY RUSH TO be modern and to accommodate a huge population by constructing new apartment blocks, towards the end of the 1930s some people belatedly realised that the heritage of the past was being destroyed. The grand homes and mansions of the nineteenth century were disappearing. In a 1937 newspaper report photographs showed the magnificent Kinneil mansion reduced to a bleak and decrepit shell; sombre, spooky Orwell House in the street of the same name, soon to be demolished to make way for the Minerva Theatre; and Roslyn Hall in ruins.

Roslyn Hall had been bought by Alfred Parry Long, the Registrar-General, at the beginning of the twentieth century from a Major Chauvel, who was well known for his fashionable garden parties, dinner parties and musical evenings. It had a unique stone-flagged entrance hall, the biggest drawing-room in Sydney, and an enchanting ceiling painted pale blue with gold stars to resemble the evening sky. After her husband died the widow Parry Long lived there for twenty-five years, doting on her daughter, whom she wanted to make the richest woman in Australia.

Mrs Long was obsessed by property and owned the nineteenth-century mansions Grantham, Orwell House and even Cheverells for a time. She bought several houses in Roslyn Street, the imposing terrace at 10 Challis Avenue, land and properties in the city and in Newtown, Petersham and Picton. This massive property and land portfolio was intended to be inherited by Eliza, but she died in 1930. The devastated mother continued to inhabit the crumbling Roslyn Hall with a small retinue of servants, her loneliness compounded by living alone in such a huge house. She retreated to the comfort of the past by driving round Kings Cross in a pony-drawn Victoria. A special wooden shelter was built in the grounds of Grantham (which she ran as a boarding house) to give her pony fresh grazing land. She continued her buying sprees, even acquiring shops, stock and all. She was reputed to be in possession of one hundred pairs of spoonbill corsets after she snapped up a drapery store. She died alone and intestate in 1935, her properties eventually divided amongst several claimants.

Many of the mansions that were the area's remaining links with the nineteenth century were demolished around this time. Only a handful survived, not in their original state, but as a giant boarding houses (the once grand Elizabeth Bay House was subdivided into fifteen tiny bedsitters for artists) or, as in the case of Tusculum, becoming a hospital that specialised in drying out alcoholics and then ending up a squalid boarding house.

Near the end of the 1930s *Building* magazine commented that the Kings Cross flat dwellers seemed to:

> *... subscribe to some extent to the modern conception of living in which the home is but a place to hang the hat and that living should be done in the restaurant and theatre.*

Indeed there had been an astonishing transformation since the former American serviceman, the dapper Dick McGowan, opened the California Coffee Shop at 41 Darlinghurst Road a few years before in 1931. It featured American-style percolated coffee, steaks and club sandwiches and could cater for up to 300 people. Its walls were light green, the floor was green and so was the upholstery. It had an impressive fireplace and its staircase, with chromium-plated handrails, led up to the first floor where jazz bands and pianists performed.

The accelerating population of the Cross needed places to eat. Many of the apartment kitchens were small or non-existent. The area quickly gained a reputation for its cafés and restaurants, with one reporter asking rhetorically, 'Is it not a legend that no-one in the Cross can cook?' By the mid 1930s it was said there were more cafés per square yard in the Cross than there were hotels in a mining town. There was a thrilling range of restaurants and cuisine to choose from. As one admiring witness wrote:

> You can eat in nine languages up at the Cross – English, American, French, German, Swiss, Russian, Chinese, Mexican and Hebrew. American 'quick-fire service' wins in the popularity stakes.

Restaurants not only catered to a variety of tastes but also budgets. The Hasty Tasty at 86 Darlinghurst Road opened in 1940. It was Sydney's first 24-hour fast food café. It was very popular and cheap, with basic food like hamburgers and sandwiches, though cynical locals nicknamed it 'chew and spew'. Its clientele were weary-eyed taxi drivers, sailors and shift workers. In Penny's Lane, the Vienna Café, near the tram depot in Bayswater Road, had a three-course dinner for only a shilling and threepence. At Mintons restaurant, on the first floor of Minton House, dinner cost one shilling and sixpence. At the other end of the scale was the Kinneil, in a row of large expensive terraces on Elizabeth Bay Road, regarded as the best restaurant of its time. The newly opened Mayfair Hotel (1937) offered afternoon teas and an *à la carte* menu. At the Top Hat, afternoon tea was served daily and, while you savoured the scrumptious cakes and sandwiches, dainty asparagus rolls and scones 'as light as air', you could listen to the Top Hat Band, conducted by Buddy Smart. Greeneagles offered exclusive suppers from 9 pm to midnight and light meals were available at the Knickerbocker for theatregoers after a show. If you wanted a themed restaurant then it was hard to go past the Elizabethan Inn with its mock Tudor front, overhanging eaves, kitschy carved chairs and tables and rich panelling.

There was a vast range of coffee shops, some of them gleaming with nickel and enamel, 'definitely futuristic even to the precarious seats', while others were small intimate places with low lighting 'Where,' wrote one entranced tourist:

> ... *people smoke, and gaze into each other's eyes, and talk in low voices so that you wonder if they're lovers or students or gangsters or just plain people like yourself, enjoying a cup of Arabian coffee.*

The Arabian coffee shop was owned by Ursula Schwalbach, an elegant willowy blonde with Eton-cropped hair. A White Russian, she was never far from her Alsatian dog, Mitzi. A cup of coffee cost fourpence. The popular place to sit was upstairs, where there was a balcony hung with coloured lights like gorgeous balloons and you could indulge in the Kings Cross pastime of watching the entertaining passing parade below. The joke in the Cross was that the Californian was for loud extroverts and the Arabian for the introvert: 'The Arabian loves to brood alone in the dim lights, or sit tête-à-tête at the intimate little round tables hiding in corners and behind curtains.'

For those who wanted to take food home, plenty of fruit shops and delicatessens were available. Lydia Gill remembered that:

*Little food shops were everywhere ... Just before Macleay Street
there was a ham and beef shop and mixed business. One could
leave a dish or plate in the morning on the way to work and
collect it on the way home; on the plate would be an inviting
salad of tomato, lettuce, spring onion, radish, a piece of cheese
and a slice or two of hard-boiled egg, all for sixpence. In cooler
weather one left an enamel dish, preferably with a lid, and
collected a generous serve of something hot.*

Another woman who came to the Cross in 1938 found she could
get a good loin chop, beans and peas and half a pound of onions
for threepence, when the basic wage was £3. A threepence in the
gas slot would cook a meal.

It was the range of food that staggered tourists. One visitor
from Perth was amazed, telling his readers back home about the
wonders of Kings Cross:

*Imagine fruit-shops piled with every fruit you can think
of – bananas, paw-paws and custard-apples, mangoes from
Queensland side by side with apples and oranges and strawberries
and – yes, grapefruit imported from California.*

There were Swedish and Swiss bakeries, untold Continental lux-
uries in the delicatessens (pretzels, black bread, caviar, herrings,
imported cheeses, anchovies, coleslaw and an infinite variety of
sausages) and food most Australians had never tried. Victoria
Street had many shops owed by a diverse bunch of nationalities
including one run by a Greek family that sold smallgoods hard
to get anywhere else. There were fruit stalls (with their vibrantly
coloured awnings) scattered around the streets, including one in
Springfield Avenue. Jimmy the Chinaman sold fresh vegetables
from a cart (his horse was hit by a trolley bus outside Manar in

Macleay Street and the police had to shoot it). There were hamburger stalls and a hot dog seller with his interminable cry of 'Hot dawg! Hot dawg!'

Unlike the rest of Australia, fruit shops could stay open until 11 pm on Friday and Saturday nights, but some continued to trade until after midnight. Henry Virgona, owner of two fruit shops and part-owner of two others in the Cross, boasted that none of his shops would close at the time the government regulations demanded.

'The law may be an excellent one for parts of Sydney but Kings Cross is *different*. Flats here are too small to store up food. People buy it when they want it. At night we don't get busy until half-past nine.'

One of the central attractions for visitors and stickybeaks was the nightlife. The neon lights were spectacular enough but it was the electric light and its impact on window and gleaming metal counter displays, plus brilliant new artificial colours, that delighted the eye. People came from the suburbs not only to enjoy the restaurants but to window shop even knowing they couldn't afford to buy the top hats, suits and frocks from Gerrecks at 76 Darlinghurst Road or furniture and knick knacks from Ye Old Antique Shoppe or the millinery, frocks, furnishings, perfumes and furs on display in the shop windows where goods were theatrically presented under bright lights to create a gleaming site of enticement and enchantment.

If anything symbolised the feminisation of the Cross then it was flowers. There were flower shops and stalls everywhere. Sellers went from street to street calling out 'Fresh flowers! Fresh flowers!' with butcher baskets full of golden marigolds, wallflowers, petunias, violets 'all held high on the breast and in contrast to the swarthy face above them'. The popular Chantal Flower Shop was on the corner of Kellett Street and Bayswater Road and also sold chocolates. Shop windows glowed with groves of flowers, nosegays for pinning on women's shoulders, trails of frangipani, pinky-cream, and great armfuls of roses and carnations. At certain times of the year flower shops became effusive bowers of chrysanthemums, mimosa, poinsettia, baskets of roses and orchids. One of the reasons for this obsession with flowers was quite simple. As the character Cressida in *Clean Straw for Nothing* realises, flowers made her pokey, grim room happier and it sparked up her spirits to look outside and see the gorgeous flower stalls down below. Flowers gave her a sense of optimism that things would be all right, despite her lack of money and the oppressive drabness of her flat.

By 1937 the *Kings Cross Times*, which sold about 10,000 copies weekly, thought the shopping precinct was different from those springing up in the rest of the country:

> *There are no large general stores ... like the substantial*
> *emporiums you may see at suburban shopping centres. What*
> *we have in this district is a large number of small service shops*
> *catering for provisions and refreshment in great variety, florists,*
> *small lending libraries, a multitude of trading conveniences*
> *particularly suited to a large population of flat dwellers living in*
> *rented apartments.*

The popularity of the Cross, both as a place to live and an entertainment and shopping district, meant thousands of people poured into it of an evening and weekend. Newsreels of the time show a never-ending stream of people, cars, taxis and trams heading into the Cross or using Bayswater Road to pass through to the eastern suburbs. Complaints about traffic congestion became more urgent. The *Kings Cross Times* constantly pointed out that because the Cross was also the main gateway to the eastern suburbs it had become a principal traffic thoroughfare, with the result 'that it is possibly the most dangerous traffic centre in the City of Sydney'. One letter-writer found that when he returned from the city at night he had sometimes had to wait thirty minutes before crossing the road after alighting from a tram. Some thought the traffic problem was even worse than in New York. A candidate in the 1938 election, Commander R.G. Bowen, gained first-hand knowledge of the problem during his campaign when he found himself having to cross Kings Cross streets several times a day, saying, 'Narrow escapes from sudden death have given me uncomfortable proof of the traffic dangers.'

It's not until you see newsreels of the period that you realise what a perilous situation was developing. It needed two policemen to try and control the flow. When people stepped off the trams in the middle of the Bayswater Road they had to wait for a break in the traffic and then scurry across to safety. Accidents involving workers, commuters and hapless pedestrians were frequent. Trams cost tuppence from the city and ran through the Cross half-hourly to 2 am. Collecting fares was a dangerous occupation. The conductor had to balance on the external footboard, rain, hail or shine – which meant he was in constant danger of falling ill, slipping off the footboard or being hit by passing cars. There were many accidents and deaths for both conductors and their passengers. One woman got off in a tram in Bayswater Road and was run over by a car in sight of her home in nearby Kellett Street. In late August 1932 a nine-year-old girl, Peggy Houlihan, was run over by a tram and was pinned under it for a quarter of an hour as tram workers struggled with a jack to raise the tram-car. The girl's injuries were horrific, with her left leg almost severed. Eventually the wheels were raised ten inches and the terrified girl was given a shot of morphine before she was slowly and with great difficulty pulled out. Her leg was later amputated. The bottleneck that Governor Darling had created a hundred years before was causing such intractable problems that it was thought at the beginning of the Second World War that it would be impossible to successfully evacuate Kings Cross because of the traffic chaos.

Even the traffic jams didn't stop people coming to the Cross. There was so much to see and do and eat. The cinema at the corner of Darlinghurst Road and Victoria Street, built in 1916, the present site of the Mercure Hotel, was one of the first picture theatres to convert to sound in 1929. It was popular with both children and adults. There were nightclubs and hotels where one could listen to music and dance. Even though the arrival of the talkies had meant the end of live musical accompaniments in the cinemas, musicians found plenty of work playing in bands or orchestras in the Cross or city. There were hundreds of musicians who lived in the area. In recalling the era residents described the atmosphere as 'Bohemian and musical'. It was common to see people carrying music cases and their instruments. There were other entertainments, including novelty acts such as Argus, 'the world's greatest mind reader and world famous telepathist'.

Argus always had an assistant in his act. When blindfolded, he could describe any article the audience might show him, could tell them the dates of their birth and describe what was in their pockets. When someone wrote down a question on a piece of paper he could say what the question was without looking at it. His act even hoodwinked Joseph Lyons, the Prime Minister, and, years later in *Memories: Kings Cross 1936–1946* one man who saw the 'Boy Wonder' was still astonished by his ability: 'How he knew all the answers I just can't imagine.'

For women living in suburbia the Cross had become a tempting atoll of mystery and sexual enticement. In Dymphna Cusack's novel *Jungfrau,* a woman:

*... listened to the faint roar of the trams in Kings Cross. Like
a jungle, the city with its dark, stolid buildings all cramped
together. Hiding what? You could imagine strange, secret vices,
turbulent dreams, mad passions. She laughed ruefully ... Probably
they hid only frivolling and boredom; at worst a querulous
irritation with life.*

Middle-class women flocked to the flats. *Art and Architecture* believed that the 'women of today have other outlets for such energy as they possess – and hence the demand for flats'. Moralists associated flats with childlessness, as more and more women embraced high-rise life. One conflicted woman journalist wrote in the *Sydney Morning Herald*:

*It is curious how many of us agree that living in a flat is the so-
called wrong way of life. But we do continue to live in them, and
they spring up on every side like mushrooms after rain. So their
advantages in modern life must outweigh their supposed evils
after all.*

It meant that the unmarried middle-class women had more money to spend on themselves than their sisters in the suburbs. The Cross became a fashion hub. In the area between Springfield Avenue and Victoria Street there were three frock shops, half a dozen dressmakers and several dry cleaners. Women were also the forerunners of the art of interior decoration, which assumed great cultural importance in the decade. One of the pioneers of interior design was Miss Molly Grey, whose flat was featured in a 1934 issue of *The Home* magazine. The photographs showed that the intense Grey, with her close-cropped hair, was a decorator with a discerning, uncluttered eye. Women in fashionable flats were a crucial element of the city's social life; the changing trends in interior decoration were slavishly followed in *The Home* and the women's section of the *Sydney Morning Herald*.

There's no doubt that moral panics about women living in flats had some semblance of truth. Living in apartments allowed women much greater sexual freedom. Betty Roland, journalist and dramatist, had many one-night stands and affairs during this time. She believed it was inevitable that she would choose the Cross as the place in which 'to exercise my right as a fully liberated woman'. When the urge was upon her, she gratified it in as cold and dispassionate a manner as a man going to a brothel to satisfy himself. She had some uncomfortable and scary moments.

> *How I managed to emerge unscathed I do not know, but I did, and I can't help feeling that I became a better person because of the things I learned about my fellow creatures in the process. Be that as it may, it explains why Kings Cross does not surprise or repel me; it is an integral part of myself.*

Bohemian lifestyles almost demanded that the men and women live sexually permissive lives. The Cross was one of the few places where couples could live in sin or shack up when married not to each other, but to others. Certainly for actors like Errol Flynn and Peter Finch, Kings Cross was the perfect place to meet women. Flynn knew the Cross intimately in the late 1920s. As one friend said of his charisma and attraction to women, 'Walking through the Cross with Errol was almost embarrassing.' Flynn, who starved, did odd jobs, and even modelled for a tailor, moved between his grandmother's cottage at Bondi and a mate's 'love shack' in the Cross. Peter Finch lived in numerous dives and flats around the area for six or seven years. He used to frequent three well-known underworld night spots – the 50-50, the 400 Club and a squalid dive called The Palms down in Rushcutters Bay, which had steel front doors as a precaution against criminal gangs and police raids. When broke, he and his fellow libertine, Cecil Perry, visited a high-class brothel in Bayswater Road to read poetry to the madam, a tall, gorgeous redhead with a body, according to Finch, 'like a sexy serpent'. Her favourite poem was Walt Whitman's *Leaves of Grass*, which she listened to in a state of ecstasy as the two men took turns to read to her. She paid the men handsomely for their recitations.

Which is not to say that Finch and Perry never used the services of a brothel. Finch's biographer, Trader Faulkner, said of him, 'as an indoor sportsman he could have won the Olympics for Australia'. About five o'clock one morning he and Cecil were walking down Victoria Street very drunk when a group of attractive whores on a verandah invited the pair up. They forgot to pull down the canvas awning and Finch ended up on a balcony caught in the act by workers on their way down to the Woolloomooloo docks who applauded and cheered him on.

His choice of women came in all shapes that Kings Cross had to offer. The Lothario had girlfriends in Macleay and Victoria Streets, Rockwell Crescent, Challis Avenue – in fact, a map of Kings Cross dotted with his conquests would look like fly-speckled paper. His sexual promiscuity extended to men. He justified this by saying he came to homosexuality out of 'penury, propinquity, a high libido and a sense of life's absurdity at times can breed queer bed-fellows'. He slept and stayed with Donald Friend, the artist, and of an evening the pair of them would trot off to a nearby flat where a gay man held open house for 'whores, pimps and squares'. At midnight the host would put on a one-man drag show. Friend lived with his male lovers in attics, his aunt's apartment, flats in the Cross and finally a bedsitter at Elizabeth Bay House having 'a marvellous bloody time ... a sort of

Sydney bohemia'. And that was another thing about Kings Cross that made it special – it had a wary openness to homosexuality when the rest of the nation thought it disgusting and depraved.

For young people it was an intoxicating time. Even without money there was friendship, social mixing on a level one couldn't get anywhere else, opportunity to explore one's sexuality, endless coffees, conversations deep into the night about art and the future, much alcohol and freedom from the family and responsibilities.

Errol Flynn and Peter Finch acted together in a 1955 film shot in England called *The Dark Avenger*, a ludicrous concoction where Flynn plays the Black Prince who must crush the restless nobles in English-held Aquitaine and defeat the duplicitous count, played by Finch. During filming they often reminisced about their time spent in 'the dirty half mile that lay between Kings Cross and Darlinghurst.' They thought it was the best time of their lives, a sentiment that echoes down the decades as each generation looks back at their carefree youth spent in the Cross. One night, two years after filming *The Dark Avenger*, a drunken, drugged Flynn moored his boat in Rushcutters Bay. He sat on the deck and looked up at the twinkling lights on the hill and with a bottle of rum toasted 'the fun of those early days when I didn't have a penny and slept like a tramp'.

If Kings Cross had become a rite of passage it was, as the poet Judith Wright said, also notorious 'as a hot bed of political radicalism'. One reporter rented a flat where all the other residents had formed a communist cell. Throughout the decade there were ferocious skirmishes between right-wing and left-wing mobs, especially in the early 1930s when the right-wing group the New Guard fought running battles with communists in Darlinghurst and Kings Cross. In one flare-up in Springfield Avenue, police went to restore order only for one of the communists to throw pepper into their eyes. Days later one policeman still hadn't regained his sight and was in acute pain. The worst clashes were at open-air meetings. During one mêlée a crowd hostile to the communists heckled them until eventually fights broke out. One communist smashed a policeman with a rubber hose loaded with lead. The leader refused to halt the meeting and called on his comrades to sing 'The Red Flag'; the crowd responded by singing 'Rule Britannia'. The police decided it was time to move the crowd on but the communists, thinking the plainclothes police were members of the New Guard, attacked them. A fierce brawl erupted between the policemen, members of the crowd and communists. Many were injured and six men were arrested.

Springfield Avenue was also bedlam during elections when politicians and those seeking votes would use it as a soapbox, much to the delight of locals who liked to heckle them.

The political clashes added to the Cross's reputation as 'a den of iniquity'. When Kenneth Slessor's mother heard he was going to rent a flat in Kings Cross she was horrified, believing he would end up living with a prostitute. Judith Wright's parents were equally shocked, thinking the Cross was 'infested with prostitution and drink'. In order to quell her family's fear, Wright told her parents she lived in Elizabeth Bay. In *Memories: Kings Cross*, one woman relates how she was disowned by her aunts and brother-in-law because 'all the single women living in the Cross turned into prostitutes'. The rift continued all her life. When another woman first came to Sydney and applied for a job at a leading department store she was asked three questions: Did she belong to a union? What religion was she? Where did she live? 'My first two answers were satisfactory, but I was not given the position until I moved from Kings Cross.' Newcomers quickly learned that the reputations of Kellett Street and Kings Cross Road were even worse and, if they lived there, they had to keep the fact secret from their employers. There were even calls

that these public perceptions of Kings Cross would be altered if
it changed its name.

What impressed and sometimes overwhelmed visitors was the
extraordinary blend of people. One bedazzled visitor wrote:

> *In its ever restless streets in the daytime you can pick out among
> the crowds a Count and a counterfeiter, a blonde who has been a
> leading lady in two underworld murders, nuns sedately pacing,
> a sloven out shopping in kimono and slippers, and a fur-coated
> plutocrat with two black eyes. A doctor hurries out to the call
> of life and death, and coming home in the small hours, stops
> for coffee at a hamburger café, and makes friends with a Negro
> boxer, an Australian tram conductor, and a lady with a Budapest
> past.*

To a journalist the Cross was a fantastical place:

> *All life therein is self-contained. When a man presents a visiting
> card that features King's Cross, he may be a governor's aide, a
> gunman, a gigolo or a garbage contractor.*

For locals the Cross had a village atmosphere. Because they lived
in such close proximity to each other, and in such a small area, it
was easy to get to know your fellow Cross-ite. Perhaps it was because many residents did not have children that the Cross became
known for its innumerable cats and especially dogs. In a late 1920s
newsreel on Kings Cross what becomes apparent is the huge number of dogs being carried or walked on a leash by as many women
as men. In 1939 one journalist reported – with some exaggeration
– that Kings Cross's population was 100,000 and that there were
as many canines: 'every human being dandles some monstrosity of
dog, be-ribboned, be-curled, at every street corner'. Or as another

man remarked, 'pampered little dogs on leads in fancy dress' were everywhere. It was an exaggeration of the numbers of both humans and canines but there was an exceptional number of dogs.

The most celebrated was Bob, a fox terrier, whose 'countenance is as familiar to newspaper readers in New South Wales as that of the Prime Minister of the Commonwealth'. It was said that even visitors from overseas knew about him.

As a young dog Bob lived with his master at the corner of Darlinghurst and Bayswater Roads. When Bob's owner died, the 'disconsolate but determined' dog lived on the corner for twelve years, refusing to leave it. His faithfulness touched the locals as did his sparky nature, happy personality and intelligence. His annual registration was paid for by a resident who also bathed him once a week. He was given a handsome collar with *King's Cross Bob* inscribed on it. He was immensely popular and made sure that no other dog attempted to invade his space, even for a moment. He enjoyed a scrap as he did the offerings of cake and chocolates that would oblige him to undergo weight loss treatments at a veterinary hospital.

His large personality suited the Cross. He liked to lie in the sun or, like some canine flâneur, saunter through the streets, accepting food, praise and pats from the locals. It's hard to overestimate his popularity; he was said to have thousands of friends. If he were ill it was treated almost as a public calamity. He was a familiar figure with a collection box strapped to his back, used to raise funds for charity. Because of his popularity and charity work he was given a party in December 1936 for his eighth birthday by the Royal Society for the Prevention of Cruelty to Animals. Each dog on its arrival was presented with a 'jazz cap' and Bob, being the guest of honour, was given a large sombrero with the words *I'm a Sheik* sewn on it. To the strains of 'See the Conquering Hero Comes', played by two Army buglers, Bob made his entrance escorted by twelve children. There was a special birthday cake with eight candles which was cut into several helpings and distributed to the dogs. Bob was also given a medal conferring honorary membership of the Tail Waggers' Association.

Few dogs had been more feted than Bob. An admirer even took him for a trip by car around Australia. His devotees were many. One gave him breakfast every morning and he took supper at the sophisticated hour of 10.45 pm as the guest of a local restaurant, after which he'd return to a comfortable couch in a garage near his stand on the corner. One of his many fans was F. Thompson, who had lived in Sydney for twenty-four years and for about eight years helped feed, bathe and shelter him. The terrier came to identify him easily in the crowded streets and even to recognise the sound of his car horn in dense, noisy traffic.

Then in 1939, much to the consternation of Kings Cross residents, Bob vanished. A few months later he was reported to be living with Thompson in the small town of Cygnet, Tasmania. The locals wanted Bob returned but Thompson vowed that he had no intention of doing so. As far as he was concerned Bob was in poor health and was too old to live on the streets of the Cross. Apparently contented, although in bad health, Bob died in Cygnet. There is a sense that the Cross took to Bob for reasons peculiar to Kings Cross. The dog had a gregarious personality, was ferociously independent and had an individual character as unconventional as some of the bohemians and artists.

What became a defining feature of the Cross was the how it changed from day into night. During the day locals went about their business, working, shopping and creating, but at night it became an alluring stage set, or as one man remarked, 'At night she blossoms forth like Cinderella going to the ball in her spangled gown.' Part of that transformation reached its apogee in 1939 when the Minerva Theatre opened in Orwell Street.

Built by the theatre entrepreneur and property investor David Martin, the Minerva, designed to seat 1000 people, was part of a complex which included shops and a nightclub. Martin was bald with a fondness for loud, bright ties. He neither drank or smoked and had two strong dislikes – comedians who worked 'blue' and fat chorus girls, for whom he keep diet charts in his desk. The opening was one of the gala events of the decade and it added to the glamour and sophistication of the Cross. It also did something else. For people who were unsure about the raffish Cross, going to the chic Minerva had an exciting prickle of a dare about it and there were the potential thrills of mixing with the demimonde and bohemians after the show.

The productions were regarded as some of the best in Australia and its spectacular lighting even impressed the visiting actress Vivien Leigh. Many well-known actors performed there. Ron Randell, who went on to star in Ken Hall's *Smithy*; Peter Finch, who won a posthumous Oscar for *Network*; Sumner Locke Elliott before he became a writer; the comedian Gordon Chater (who supported himself for two years by washing dishes down the road at the Hasty Tasty); and the actor Trader (Ron) Faulkner, who became Finch's eventual biographer. Finch saw the avant-garde Bodenwieser Ballet at the Minerva in 1939 and fell for Tamara, one of its dancers, whom he later married.

The theatre added to the stylish atmosphere of the Cross. Men in tuxedos, women in evening dress headed 'up to the Cross' to nightclubs or restaurants after seeing a show in the city. As the modish Mayfair Hotel put it in its advertisements, Kings Cross was the dress circle of Sydney. The promenade of a Friday and Saturday night became a distinctive characteristic, with people crowding the footpaths window shopping and gawking at the bohemians and eccentric characters. Even if you didn't have the money it was a night's outing to go to the Cross:

*The coffee shops were lovely, the boutiques had lovely lingerie,
the fruit shops were beautiful to look at and one was sure to meet
friends ... the liveliness and the colour, and the fun of seeing so
many types.*

Girls and women could go about knowing they were not in danger. Residents were bemused by the Cross's criminal reputation because they regarded it as a much safer place than the dark, lonely streets of the suburbs.

The Cross became the epitome of sophistication. Perhaps the best illustration of this is a photograph taken in the winter of 1941 of two women, one of whom was Valma Ashcroft, a beautiful 20-year-old model who had been on more *Australian Women's Weekly* covers than anyone else in her day. The two women were tall and perfectly dressed in fur stoles and perky hats posing outside the Perfumeri shop on the corner of Orwell and Macleay Streets. Ashcroft wears a tartan themed short-sleeved dress and black gloves and carries a shoulder bag; her friend wears a long black dress with a fur stole and a large brooch glorifying her throat. Their beaming smiles and elegant clothes summed up the urbanity and refinement of the area.

Since the twenties there had been an increasing sense that Kings Cross made the rest of Australia seem staid and parochial. But it was more than that; locals saw the area as an island, a refuge that was isolated from the puritan values and cultural desolation of the suburbs. Their attitude was the same as fruit shop owner Henry Virgona's: 'Kings Cross is *different*.' He put into words what residents thought. They felt separate from the rest of the country and, like Virgona, they were proud that Kings Cross was different. And it was. It was also the most vital, dazzling and sophisticated place to live in Australia.

KELLETT STREET

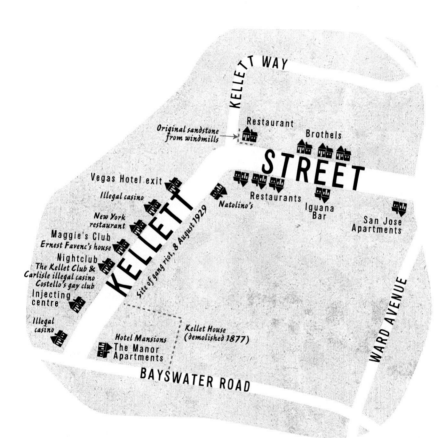

Original sandstone from windmills →

Restaurant

Brothels

Vegas Hotel exit

Illegal casino

New York restaurant

Maggie's Club

Ernest Favenc's house

Nightclub

The Kellet Club &
Carlisle illegal casino

Costello's gay club

Injecting centre

Illegal casino

Hotel Mansions
The Manor
Apartments

Restaurants

Natolino's

Iguana
Bar

San Jose
Apartments

Site of gang riot, 8 August 1929

Kellet House
(demolished 1877)

KELLETT WAY

KELLETT

STREET

WARD AVENUE

BAYSWATER ROAD

AT THE TURN OF THE millennium I shifted into an apartment at the top of a three-storey terrace in Kellett Street. It had a tiny kitchen, a living room and a bedroom. Outside the window was a robinia tree whose delicate lime-green leaves shielded the flat from the summer sun. On the ground floor the owner of the building ran a caviar and smoked salmon importation business. Next door was the Iguana Bar, its thumping techno music of a night and noisy bottle collection of a morning frequently keeping me awake. On the other side of my apartment was the San Jose, built in the Spanish mission style, which was a popular place for theatre people to stay in the 1950s and 1960s. My uncle, Bob Herbert, rented there when he was working for the theatrical producers J.C. Williamson's. He once told me, with a knowing wink, that it was the sort of place where *What happens on tour, stays on tour.*

One afternoon when I returned to my apartment I opened the door and found someone was on the other side trying to push it closed. I knew instantly it was a thief and, beside myself with anger at my personal space being violated, I slammed myself as hard as I could against the door until it gave way. I grabbed at a thin guy in a grey tracksuit as he was making his escape, but he pushed me off and rushed into the bedroom, slamming the door behind him. The key was on my side so I locked the door and called the Kings Cross police. They said they wouldn't be long. While I waited I heard the sound of smashing glass. It could only be my window, which overlooked the courtyard in the rear. Assuming he must have jumped, I grabbed a bread knife from the kitchen to protect myself and unlocked the door. The window was shattered and he was gone. I looked down expecting to see his dead body spreadeagled on the bricks. Instead I heard the thief clambering over my roof and jumping onto the roof of the Iguana Bar. There was blood on the broken glass and he had dropped his mobile on the floor in his panic to get away.

The cops didn't arrive so I took the mobile and my story down to the police station. The officer I dealt with showed no sympathy and no interest. I handed him the mobile phone, saying he might want to check the numbers on it.

'Oh, it's probably stolen,' he sighed. I asked him if he wanted to see the crime scene. 'Oh, no,' said the bored cop, 'we know who it is. He just got out of Long Bay yesterday and has already burgled a couple of places. He always comes in through the roof.'

Kellett Street is a living demonstration of the two major preoccupations of the Cross – sex and food. There are usually about half a dozen restaurants or more and about the same number of brothels in the dog-legged street. The restaurants stick to one side while the brothels face them on the other, both serving the two great human appetites.

On a hot summer's night if you walked past Manhattan Terrace there was a tell-tale red light out front and blowsy whores sat at the open windows behind bars, peering through the grating asking men passing by if they wanted to come in. When you said no they would laugh as if you were too afraid. It's closed now and for sale, as the real estate hoarding says: *D.A. approval for a bordello.* A few years ago when Mandy and I were taking a group of American university students for a tour of the Cross they stared in amazement at a similar sign advertising a brothel. The immoral pragmatism of Kings Cross was too blatant and vulgar for them.

If they were shocked by the unabashed flaunting of our sex industry, then it was probably good that they didn't know that number 52, a dark crimson terrace with shutters permanently closed on its front windows, was a male brothel, Alexander Male Escorts. The business was run by two men. One of them was Brian Roberts, who was jailed for four years in 1996 after he forged the will of his murdered client Ludwig Gertsch and stole $500,000. The ostentatious Gertsch was gay and a millionaire. He was killed in 1990, six months after inheriting $2 million dollars on the death of his lover. The last person to see Gertsch alive was Roberts, who said he had picked him up from the Ashfield apartment of Gertsch's boyfriend, Vince Esposito, and dropped him at Oxford Street. After Gertsch disappeared, and before his body was found in the Blue Mountains, Roberts transferred $89,000 to himself from Gertsch's account for 'legal fees'. The coroner said that he did not believe the evidence of either Roberts or Esposito and ruled that Gertsch had died at the latter's apartment at the hands of persons or persons unknown. Alexander Male Escorts is gone now and the address is home to a heterosexual brothel called Star 52.

Cleopatra's is an up-market bordello with a discreet neon sign saying *Open* hanging from the awning. It also has an electric sign advertising a VIP spa room. (I drink with a tradie down at the Old Fitzroy Hotel in Woolloomooloo who used to install spas, and he once had to repair one in a Kings Cross brothel. 'You wouldn't want to know what was in the pipes,' he recalled with a shiver.) Inside are life-sized statues of black Egyptian pharaohs. Its internet advertisements feature lithe Asian girls in lingerie sipping champagne, stripping seductively by candlelight and enjoying the spa. It's all soft lighting and the interiors verge on the kitsch. The prices range from $150 for thirty minutes, $220 for forty-five and one hour will set you back $280. Their motto is: it's a business doing pleasure.

The most indiscreet brothel is Maggie's Club for Gentlemen, its name scrawled across two large shop front windows. Instead of the old-fashioned red lamp, it has a red neon sign announcing it's open. A few years ago I was walking past it when I saw a high-ranking American naval officer in his forties talking to Maggie herself on the footpath. He had a warm Southern drawl. She was dressed in black and wore her greying hair in a tight bun. It was as if they were discussing the price of eggs.

'Well, Maggie, that's a rather steep price for your girls.'

'Those are the prices,' she said firmly in a broad Australian accent adding, 'My girls don't come cheap.' He sensed she couldn't be budged on the price.

'I appreciate that, Maggie,' he said without rancour, and tipping the brim of his cap like a true Southern gentleman, he nodded and walked off.

If there is a pertinent example of the Cross having a tolerant attitude towards people whom other communities would reject then it is Maggie Krauser, the eponymous owner. Regarded as one of the community's most affable and successful businesswomen, she was elected President of the Kings Cross Chamber of Commerce in the late 1990s. She considers herself 'Just an old fashioned girl from Newcastle' and has no shame at being the owner of a bordello. As she once said, 'Except for when I go out to dinner or sit down to listen to a couple of Barbara Streisand records, my life is one hundred per cent business and probably always will be.'

Her business partner is a tall, stooped white-haired man in his late sixties. One afternoon I was in the local supermarket when I saw him talking to the manager of a brothel in Victoria Street. The younger man was tubby with a dramatic shiny black quiff. They were bemoaning the running costs of their businesses and how rapacious landlords continue to raise the rent. Any passer-by would have thought they were two ordinary businessmen. The younger bloke announced that his takings were up fifty per cent on Good Friday Eve.

'What about Good Friday?' the older guy asked.

'Slow. Slow. No point in really opening,' replied the younger and the older agreed with a sad understanding nod.

A common feature of these brothels is that they are mainly staffed by Asians, principally Thai. In 2007 immigration officials conducted a series of raids on brothels across Sydney in a crackdown on illegal immigrants, searching for sex workers breaching their visas or women being held in sexual servitude. Maggie's was raided at 2 am. Unlike other brothels in the suburbs, immigration officials found no illegal activity, but they did find that the attractive young women were not quite what they seemed – according to official documentation they were men. Many a client who had paid for a girl at Maggie's must have shuddered on reading the story the next day.

There was one prostitute at Maggie's who was one of the few non-Asians working there. She was blonde, attractive and in her mid-twenties. She must have decided, for reasons I don't know, that she'd work for herself on Darlinghurst Road. She did the day shift and at about four o'clock her husband would park his car in Kellett Street and wait with their nine-year-old daughter for his wife to finish with her last customer. He was always grim-faced, as if still mentally processing the fact that his wife was a hooker and he was living off her earnings. Sometimes the wait was a long one and the daughter would get out of the car and practise her tap dancing on the footpath. She was always provocatively dressed, like a miniature hooker in tiny skirts and tight tops. She had long blonde hair and her mother's beauty. When her mother turned up, she'd get into the passenger seat and the daughter would silently climb onto the back seat and without a word or gesture of affection the trio would drive away.

One afternoon I saw the mother behind the telephone booth near the cake shop in Bayswater Road. She was dressed in a black mini skirt and black bra and was passionately kissing a handsome man, not her husband. I began to see them together more often, frequently hand-in-hand like young lovers. Her face, once a defensive mask of watchfulness, was glowing with love. Her husband and daughter no longer picked her up. As frequently happens in the Cross with people you see all the time, you take their presence for granted until one day you realise you haven't seen them for some time. I became aware that she had vanished from her pitch. I haven't seen her since. What stayed with me was how love softened her. Who knows when and if her pragmatic cynicism about men returned.

The other great necessity of humans, besides sex, is food. The turnover in restaurants is phenomenal. As a restaurant reviewer wrote in 2006, Kellett Street has always been something of a Bermuda Triangle: restaurants go in there and are never heard of again.

Many of the restaurants in the street are hidden behind fig trees and shrubbery. The Iguana Bar features an enormous liquidambar tree squeezed between verandah and restaurant, as if nature is merging into the very building itself, desperate to become one with it. The restaurant has been a stayer, less for its food than for its nightclub ambience. In the early hours of the morning the patrons' eyes take on a sparkling quality, the hubbub grows louder, the women's voices shriller as the cocktails take effect and the trips to the toilets more frequent, the purpose of which is obvious when they return to the main room with a tell-tale rubbing of the nose, brightly alert eyes and high-pitched stream-of-consciousness monologues.

On the other side of the street, on the corner of Kellett Way, is a Czech restaurant. Its painted sandstone walls and those next door seem old and indeed they are; the friable sandstone blocks used to build both cottages are the remnants of Barker's windmill and are the only remaining evidence that Sydney's nineteen windmills ever existed at all. A development company bought the two buildings in 1975 and had planned to demolish them as part of a big redevelopment plan but a union ban prevented them.

Perhaps the two most well-known restaurants were Natalino's and the New York. During the 1960s and 1970s Natalino's was one of Sydney's premier restaurants. It was started by Natalino Proietti and his wife Norma, who had come from Rome in the 1950s. The clientele was a heterogeneous mixture of movers and shakers, celebrities and suburban couples wanting to experience sophisticated Kings Cross nightlife and gawk at 'colourful Sydney identities'. Natalino liked to tell the story about the wealthy mistress of a Sydney crime figure who entered the restaurant alone one Saturday night, drunk and wearing a floor-length mink coat. She asked for a table in the centre of the

restaurant where she quickly downed two martinis with her entree.
The maitre d' asked if she cared to remove her coat. Certainly,
she said, standing up and removing it. She was stark naked and,
oblivious to the stares from the diners, nonchalantly handed over
the coat to the stunned maitre d' before sitting down to resume her
meal. In 1992 at the age of seventy-two Natalino sold his restaurant
but it quickly went downhill and has since gone through several
incarnations from Thai to a pizza restaurant.

Directly across from it was the New York restaurant, a Kings
Cross institution since the late 1940s. Refusing to keep pace with
culinary trends, the menu was a relic of 1950s dining: fried fillets of
whiting, chips, lettuce, tinned beetroot, lamb chops, veal schnitzel,
T-bone steaks, rice pudding with prunes, cheesecake with an eerie,
fluorescent glow, plus orange cordial.

It moved six times over the years around the Cross until it ended
up in Kellett Street. The cook and part-owner was 'John' Kakaris,
who got his first job in Australia as a kitchen hand in 1955. Like the
previous owners, Yanni Kakaris was a Greek migrant. By the time the
New York closed in 2010 Kakaris reckoned he had made about two
million meals.

The restaurant was a telling contrast to Natalino's, which had
expensive decor, snug tables and chairs and dim lighting. The New
York was the opposite of pretentious. It had hardy plastic chairs,
Laminex tables and fading 1970s reproductions of tableaux of fruit
and grains on the walls. While Natalino's customers began arriving
around 8 in the evening, the New York, which opened six nights at
4 pm, closed at 8. The ceiling lights were fluoro tubes that harshly
emphasised the peculiar or eccentric contours of faces so that
sometimes when you walked past its windows it was like looking into
a gallery of caricatures or something out of Dickens.

These were haggard, worn, aged, mainly Anglo faces that
hinted at hard lives, bad luck and, occasionally, defeat. No-one

came from suburbia to eat at the New York; in fact the facade was
so unprepossessing that the restaurant went unnoticed by visitors,
which is how the locals liked it. Its regulars, many of whom were in
their sixties and seventies, were the poor of Kings Cross, those who
had scrabbled enough money for a feed, pensioners and students
in need of a cheap meal. Known to the locals as the Diner, it offered
basic comfort food at ridiculously cheap prices. It was also a homely
place where the waiter greeted regulars by name. Outside scruffy
dogs waited for their owners and one time even a Shetland pony was
tethered outside, waiting patiently in the drizzle.

It was the last of its kind. The well-known Sydney restaurateur Gay
Bilson ate there and compared it to trendy Oxford Street, 'where all
the shops, cafés and restaurants were designed for the same people.
The New York is for everybody else.' It was still popular but the
landlord had upped the rent again and Kakaris couldn't make the new
overheads so, after six decades in the Cross, and the last of its kind,
the Diner closed. It's now empty.

Next to where Natalino's used to be is the Kellett Lodge ('No
lease. No Bond. Short term and long term stays') whose permanent
lodgers often ate at the New York. Just up from the Lodge is the five-
storey, 888-square-metre Mansions Hotel. Like most of the hotels in
the Cross it has closed down and will reopen as managed apartments.
It has undergone several refits recently, none to any avail (even the
pokies and Tuesday night bingo run by drag queens didn't help). In
2010 the asking price was $25 million but it sold for just under $17
million the following year. The new owners think they're on to a good
thing. After all, across the road the Hampton Court Hotel's reinvention
as apartments has been a total success, all 125 apartments selling off
the plan in just six hours and proving just how chic and hip the Cross
is becoming again.

During the 1980s and 90s the Mansions Hotel was no longer the
beautiful building it once was, but a tough pub with such a rough

clientele that the Maori bouncers wore T-shirts emblazoned with the cocky announcement, *We don't call the cops!* It was in that era that a friend of mine, the chef there, dropped a tab of acid and, waving a carving knife, threatened a customer who had bad-mouthed his food (thankfully other customers pulled him away before he could use the knife). I always wanted to go upstairs to look at the enormous ballroom and large dining room but the floors were unsafe, the wood rotten and the dust so thick you had to scrape it off. Those empty, dusty, decaying rooms now only held ghosts of the long-dead, their stories having died with them.

My last memory of drinking in the Mansions was when I was there to watch a short documentary about the Cross and some of its famous identities. It was a small crowd and Abe Saffron was there with his mistress, who wore enough earrings and rings to furnish a jewellery shop window. The 80-year-old Saffron had recently been in a gossip column extolling the virtues of Viagra. A local photographer, Roz Sharp, wanted to replicate the famous photograph of Saffron framed by the legs of a showgirl. The photograph was taken when he was young and running the Roosevelt nightclub. Roz wanted Mandy to act the part of the showgirl but she refused. I thought it just as well. Saffron, who was to die soon, looked like a used condom.

Of a daytime Kellett Street looks dull and empty, except for a few locals and husbands in track suits hurrying into Maggie's for a quickie after pretending to their wives they were going out jogging. Hard to avoid are the junkies who lurch out from the rear of the injecting centre, carrying plastic cups of instant coffee, with their large pupils or dazed expressions and nasal accents so mucus-thick that it's impossible to know what they're saying. They make their wobbly way around the corner into Bayswater Road to the cake shop, where they stare at the cream cakes, mesmerised by the range of choices, finding it almost impossible to choose, their brains bubbling with drugs, their taste buds demanding anything sweet.

There are always maddies wandering around. I was heading towards Kellett Way late one morning when I heard a man shouting out, 'You're fucking dead! You're fucking dead, you nigger monkey. Fucking nigger monkey. Suck more VB, you fucking cocksucker.' He continued to scream out as he walked up Kellett Street, the trees dripping on him after torrential rain overnight. He was thin with a straggly beard, possibly only in his middle thirties and alone, but he was consumed by an inner fury at someone who had wronged him. He was still yelling out, 'I hate your fucking guts, you fucking nigger monkey,' when he turned into Bayswater Road. Who he was venting his anger on, it was impossible to know. A man passing by looked up at one of the grinning office girls leaning out of her window listening to the tirade:

'They're out today, mate.'

'Yeah,' she said ruefully.

Around the corner on the right-hand side of the street are two nightclubs, one next to the injecting centre, number 14, and the second further up, the Sapphire Club, with its harsh facade of narrow panes of dark glass bordered by shiny chrome strips. Number 14's most recent reincarnation, after being a billiard room; an illegal casino; Costello's, the infamous male brothel; and Melt, a trendy nightclub, is an even more prestigious nightclub called Number 20, reputedly financed by one of Kings Cross's 'colourful identities', John Ibrahim. It's strange to think that a hundred years before, Ernest Favenc, the explorer, alcoholic and author of the magisterial *History of Australian Exploration,* spent the last years of his life at the address before his death in 1908. Kellett Street was a long way, physically and spiritually, from the outback where he had earned the title of 'the Last of the Explorers', and it must have seemed all very different in 1851 when he lived as a child in Cahors, a mansion his father, Peter, built in Macleay Street. When Ernest was six the family were broke and his humiliated father took his wife and brood far away from the Cross because the family 'could not bear to remain there after having lost all their property and beautiful home'.

The best time to see Kellett Street is of a warm summer's night. The robinia and liquidambar trees are engaged in a symbiotic embrace of iron spiked fences and nature as if they are a merging of the animate and inanimate. The trees on either side of the street bend towards each other creating a natural bower-like archway with a scent that is musky and rich. The tiny bright lights wound around the tree trunks and boughs seem like fireflies. The air is deliciously pungent with the odours of food from restaurant kitchens. The brothel and restaurant windows are open to let in the softer warm night air. Lovers, arm-in-arm, come searching for a restaurant, or single men, or sometimes a small group of them, wander from brothel to brothel haggling over the price of sex or the quality of the girls. The gigantic fig tree that grows in the small front yard of the restaurant at number 7 dominates the end of the street before it takes a dogleg right. Its thick smooth naked boughs and dramatic buttress roots glow from the strategically placed lighting, reflecting eerie yellow and blue colours that give the street the feel of an enchanted wood in a fairytale. It's at times like these, with the smell of food, the red neon signs and lamps advertising the bordellos, the wrought iron balconies of the terraces, the sensual scents of sub-tropical nature, that you could almost believe you were in the French Quarter in New Orleans.

Little Europe

DURING THE 1930S THE WORD that began to be used more frequently to describe Kings Cross was 'cosmopolitan'. People of diverse races and ethnic groups, especially Italians, Greeks and Jews, had settled into the area. But the real transformation came in the middle of the decade when Austrians and Germans, escaping from the Nazis, started arriving. They were attracted to the Cross for several reasons: it was a short distance from the docks, they were used to apartment living, the rents were cheap and, like many migrants, they sought their own kind, finding solace in the same language and culture. Many of the new arrivals were sponsored by the Jewish Welfare Organisation, which had an office in the Cross.

Despite the fact that Jews were being persecuted in Europe, Australians were generally not welcoming. In 1938 Thomas White, Minister for Trade and Customs, was appalled by the prospect of large-scale Jewish immigration, saying, 'As we have no real racial problem, we are not desirous of importing one.' Around the same time the Immigration Department analysed the quality of Jews, and came to the conclusion that Berlin Jews were good, the Viennese had bad characters, Budapest Jews were even worse, Polish Jews were thieves and Romanian Jews were gangsters.

They stood out in their appearance for a start: 'They wore long overcoats, heavy material and padded shoulders. Their hats were different and they always carried a briefcase with them and the men had money purses.' The women, on the other hand, were thought to be shorter than Australians and plumper, with some residents finding the Jewish women had 'a kind of excessive femininity about them'. The refugees were arrogant and they treated locals as inferior beings; the Russian Jews were said to be particularly haughty and 'glib'.

Racial generalisations were common:

The Jew has the perfect poker face, as inscrutable, as immovable as the Sphinx. His womenfolk fall broadly into two groups. These are the pampered petulant wives and daughters upon whose plump shoulders hang heavy furs, whose black or hennaed hair, glistening with health, sweeps upward from their olive skinned foreheads and fine dark eyes. And there are the Intelligentsia, the broad hipped, large nosed Jewesses one always seems to meet in flats at the Cross at three o'clock in the morning after a party.

Residents bemoaned the fact that their 'Little Paris' had turned into 'Little Vienna'. One café proprietor wanted to put up a notice *English Is Spoke 'Ere* because, she explained, the Australians didn't know where to go to eat. The refugees seemed to be taking over the Cross and *auf wiedersehen* was heard as often as goodbye in English. Even their cooking could be offensive to Australians, as Lydia Gill remembered: 'Strange and sometimes overpowering cooking odours wafted out of the many kitchens.'

There seemed to be so many refugees that by 1939 newspapers began to report that Kings Cross was threatening to become a Jewish colony. The joke that went the rounds at the time was, 'Tell Hitler he can have Danzig, if he'll give us back Kings Cross.'

Even those who believed that Australia should take in the refugees – or reffos as they were colloquially known – thought that the Cross was 'full to bursting point' and had become 'a Mecca for Jews'. Australians could be cruel and a frequent response to a refugee's thick accent was the savage, 'Why don't you reffo bastards learn t' talk English!' There were serious complaints that Jewish families were not trying to learn English and refused to send their children to public schools. Examples were reported of a block of ten flats where only one flat was occupied by an Australian family, and that some of the cafés were not welcoming to the locals but used exclusively by refugees.

The Australian Jewish Welfare Society denied that Jews wanted to form a colony and believed that part of the locals' reaction was because they had a tendency to class all people of foreign appearance as Jewish refugees. The spokesman also added that he didn't know of one example of Jews refusing to learn English or not sending their children to local schools. The aim of the refugee was to be naturalised as quickly as possible.

What was forgotten was that Jews had been a part of the Cross since William Street and Woolloomooloo Hill were settled. They had been prominent in making William Street a vibrant shopping district during the Victorian era and some of the glorious mansions that were first built in the area were owned by Jews. They attended the synagogue in the city, which was within the prescribed distance to walk on the Sabbath, and observed many of the Jewish festivals and rites, but they had also assimilated quickly.

These attacks were an added burden to the refugees, whose qualifications were not recognised and who found themselves having to forsake their professions, some ending up selling bathmats for a living or taking a menial job as a caretaker of flats.

Walter Magnus is a case in point. He wasn't allowed to practice dentistry in Australia so he opened up a restaurant called the

Claremont on Darlinghurst Road, next to where Mary Gilmore resided in her first-floor flat.

His had been a long journey to Kings Cross. He had been born in 1903 in Westphalia, Germany, one of three children. His father was a cigar manufacturer who died when Magnus was six. He didn't get on with his stepfather, so he was sent to rabbinical school where he became fluent in Hebrew (he had a natural gift for languages). He was fit and healthy when young and enjoyed boxing, was an enthusiastic cyclist, and excelled at tennis and soccer. He became a dentist but fled Germany when Hitler came to power. It was the start of his peregrinations, travelling through various European countries, then on to England and when even that seemed too close to Nazi Germany, Magnus and his wife, Hedwig, joined his sister in migrating to Australia in 1937.

It wasn't such a jump for him to segue from dentistry to being a restaurateur, as he was a splendid cook. His cheap and hearty menu focused on schnitzels, Hungarian goulash served in earthenware bowls, and spatchcock with garlic. The Claremont became an immediate success due, in its early stages, to the artists, actors and bohemians who were attracted to the food, the large helpings and its cheapness.

William Dobell adored Magnus and painted his portrait, *Chez Walter*, which shows a very different fellow from the fit young sportsman. Magnus revelled in his role as bon vivant and cheerful host, whose thick German-accented English was often parodied. A learned man, he was a lover of classical music and food and wine and smoking. The result was that he became grossly fat or, as one customer noted, 'heroically corpulent'. A bundle of sweaty energy, he greeted each customer fluently in Spanish, French, German or English. He had a raucous laugh and a fierce but short-lived temper. His clothes were in impeccable taste and he affected a monocle, furthering his eccentric appearance. If he had any philosophy of life it was epicurean: '... I like everything the very best there is. Once I have a beautiful Rolls Royce but when I can no longer afford such a car I run none at all. I drink only the best wines, for bad wines are like harsh women.' He became a naturalised Australian just after the end of the war, dying in 1954 of a weak heart and rich diet.

There were other Jews like the members of the Weintraub Syncopators, who arrived to play music and escape from Hitler. They were one of the most successful jazz bands in Germany during the late 1920s and early 1930s. You can see them accompanying Marlene Dietrich in Josef von Sternberg's masterpiece *The Blue Angel* and they were the band that sat for the expressionist Max Oppenheimer in his painting *Jazz Band*. Germans were attracted to their highly theatrical act and their specialised genre of 'nut jazz'. This was a loony mixture of miming, musical clowning, and freakish musical accomplishments like playing two woodwind instruments at once. By 1938 the band claimed they had played in 459 places, in 230 cities, in twenty-one countries and travelled 105,000 miles.

When they came to Sydney in 1937 they were seen as a threat because they took the jobs of local musicians. Frank Kitson, secretary of the Professional Musicians Union, was determined not only to stop them from playing but to have them deported, claiming they were non-British, Jewish, and therefore enemy aliens. Kitson was furious when clubs offered them work, complaining to one reporter 'that Sydney café society, titled people and wealthy playabouts have developed a distinct fondness for foreign musicians'. Kitson rejected any attempts by the band to join the union, claiming his members were fervently opposed to the importation of foreign musicians, even those 'exiled from Germany as a result of the Hitler regime'.

As time went by Kitson made it plainer that he didn't like

them because they were Jews. The union secretary did his work well and in June 1940 three members of the band were interned, two of them being released a year later. The band folded as the musicians went their own ways. Two became naturalised Australians and Leo Weiss, who was finally admitted into the union in 1945, changed his name to Leo White and became a successful band leader and recording artist. Another played cello in the Sydney Symphony Orchestra. All of them at one time or another lived in the Cross, discovering that it was indeed a refuge for the refugees and an antidote to the pervasive and pernicious anti-Semitism that existed in Australia.

Despite the ambivalent reactions of some locals, the refugees flourished in Kings Cross, helping to create a cosmopolitan ambience that had no equivalent elsewhere in White Australia. Australians and their government may have had an ambivalent attitude to the Jews but they needed them and Kings Cross for propaganda in the Second World War.

In comparing Australia to the Nazis, government publications and newsreels emphasised how a tolerant and democratic Kings Cross had taken in refugees who were 'directly and indirectly opposed to the doctrines of Hitler'. As one resident said of Kings Cross, the refugees made their home in the only part of Australia that could truly be called 'grown up'.

Still, there were people who continued to dislike the reffos. In Colin Sherwood's memoir of the Cross in the 1960s he tells the story of how his mother would never take a taxi if she thought it was driven by a 'reffo'.

There were others who remained stubbornly anti-Semitic. In 1949 Isaac Kahn, owner of the Oriental Hotel in Victoria Street, went to court to have a tenant evicted from a lock-up shop on the ground floor of the hotel. Kahn, Jewish and a noted philanthropist (he had given £125,000 to various charities), told the court he had been 'disgusted and outraged' by anti-Semitic notices the tenant had exhibited in her shop window. Miss Claire Louise Peters, a middle-aged spinster, had displayed placards that read in part:

> *Menzies and his gang going around the country with the*
> *Capitalist mouse-trap, putting in the cheese of cunning and deceit*
> *to trick the workers. Non-Christian Jews and Capitalists who*
> *join with them are the cause of all evils. Non-Christian Jews who*
> *never work are living in luxury on noble workers. If that is not*
> *injustice – what is? These evil, non-Christian Jews are flocking*
> *into the country, and live on the best the country can produce.*

Kahn had complained about the notices many times but Peters had refused to remove them. In her defence she said hundreds of people had commended her for placing the placards in the window. She denied that she had been insulting or had annoyed other tenants except for the Jewish Mrs G. Rothschild who occupied the shop next to hers and annoyed her so much that she would bang on the wall in retaliation. In her defence she said that her notices only dealt with current affairs and added that, 'I have no personal animosity against non-Christian Jews, but only to the things they do in a body. They don't trade under their own names, which is another of their tricks.'

Peters lost her case and the magistrate, deciding that the placards and her behaviour were 'provocative and inflammatory', ordered her to give up possession of the shop.

The reputation of Kings Cross as a refuge for reffos and a Babel of foreign languages was so widespread that even in the early 1960s radio comedians on national shows could always be sure of a laugh with the standard line:

'Hey, what do you think happened to me at Kings Cross last night? Somebody said goodnight to me – in English!'

The Devil is a woman

IT IS EARLY MORNING ON 9 March 1956 and a Qantas aeroplane has just landed in Sydney having flown all the way from London via Darwin. Descending the steps of the Constellation is a silver-haired 62-year-old man, Sir Eugene Goossens. The title Sir is brand new. Just a few weeks before in London he was invested with his knighthood for services to Australian music. He is a world famous conductor and composer. He is wealthy and married to a beautiful young woman. He strolls across the tarmac, goes through the arrivals door and picks up his six large suitcases. He has done this trip many times before and has always been waved through the Nothing to Declare aisle without being stopped. But this morning is different.

Half an hour away, in Kings Cross, a woman called Rosaleen Norton is blissfully unaware of what is about to happen. Secretly waiting for the conductor is a special team of detectives and customs agents. They will ask to inspect his luggage. He will pale and nod a yes. In a few hours his career and reputation will be ruined. And the incident will confirm for Australians that Kings Cross is a cauldron of sexually depraved, morally bankrupt women corrupted by the sordid nature of the place itself – it's a space that you enter at your moral peril.

It is said that the Goossens family were to music what the Sitwells were to literature and the Barrymores to the theatre. Eugene was born on 26 May 1893. His brother Leon became a brilliant and successful oboe player and his sister Sidonie (Annie) a celebrated classical harpist. Eugene was naturally gifted at music but also had a 'mania about gargoyles'. This preoccupation with these grotesque creatures and the occult continued into the 1920s. His interests were further stimulated by his close friends Cyril Scott, author of *An Outline of Modern Occultism*, and the composer Philip Heseltine, who was so obsessed by black magic he changed his name to Peter Warlock.

On the other side of the world in New Zealand, Rosaleen Norton had been born during a violent thunder-storm. She came into the world with a sinewy strip of flesh extending from her armpit to her waist, a deformity she would later cite as confirmation she had been born a witch. Born in 1917, Norton was the third of three sisters in a Church of England family. Her father was a mariner and was frequently away at sea. In 1925 the family migrated to Australia where they lived on Sydney's North Shore. When she was seven she noticed two small blue marks very close together appeared on her left knee and remained there. As an adult she was to learn that two (or sometimes three) blue or red dots together on the skin are traditional witch marks.

By the time he was in his middle twenties Goossens was so famous as a conductor and composer that Noel Coward wrote a song in praise of him ('My heart just loosens when I'm listening to Mr Goossens'). He mixed with important and famous people, like Stravinsky and Picasso. In the 1920s he went to live and conduct in the United States. The prestigious English magazine *Musical News and Herald* remarked of him:

> *Eugene Goossens is the most outstanding figure in the younger musical generation. He's been lionised by the press, almost*

*canonised by the musical public; and subsidised by himself. He
has earned the interest of the press and praise of the public by his
musical genius and his fearless enterprise in the cause of musical
progress.*

He was very attractive to women and hired a valet called Billings,
who had to protect him from female admirers who would push
their way into the dressing room and try to cut pieces from his tie
as if he were a film star. He composed an opera, *Judith*, which was
performed in 1929 but it was not a success; his next opera was *Don
Juan de Manara*. His Don Juan is an amoral lover and a murderer
who drives women to murder and suicide. It premiered in 1937
and had decidedly mixed reviews, with one reviewer aptly sum-
ming up his talent as 'a rather sterile brilliance'.

At the age of fourteen Norton was expelled from school for
her eccentric and 'depraved' behaviour. Relieved to be out of
school, she went to East Sydney technical college where she studied art for two years. She also wrote macabre tales and several
of them were accepted by *Smith's Weekly*, the famously irrever-
ent newspaper, when she was fifteen. Impressed, the newspaper
employed her as a cadet journalist and illustrator when she was
sixteen years old.

Unable to produce the right sort of illustrations for the paper,
she was fired after eight months. But she had had a taste of freedom and now that her mother was dead, she left home. For the
next few years she worked as a kitchen maid, a PMG telegram
messenger and as a model for Norman Lindsay. Over the years
she would try to deny the huge influence he had on her but you
can see strong similarities to his art and subject matter – pagan
parties, naked women, Pan and satyrs. Lindsay didn't much like
her, saying of her: '[She's] a grubby little girl with great skill who
will not discipline herself.'

At the age of seventeen she married Beresford Conroy the day before Christmas 1940. He went off to fight in New Guinea and when he returned she wanted a divorce, which finally became official in 1951. The end of the marriage took the pressure off to be a mother:

> *Nothing would ever induce me to have a baby. The very idea of it was always repugnant, chiefly because I feel it would detract from my own completeness.*

By the beginning of the Second World War Norton had read widely on such subjects as witchcraft, Carl Jung, Freud, the occult and pantheism. She became a close friend of Dulcie Deamer. Rowie, as she was known to her friends, was a self-proclaimed black witch; Deamer labelled herself the white witch of the Cross. Norton drew the cover for Deamer's *The Silver Branch*, a book of poems. Given that Norton was a supreme narcissist it was no surprise that instead of putting Dulcie's portrait on the cover, she put her self-portrait on it. This was not unusual. Near the end of the war the author of *Kings Cross Calling*, H.C. Brewster, commissioned Norton to design the cover. The central face was of a leering Norton with a slight devilish countenance. This aspect of her personality she developed as skilfully as an actor becoming a character. She had naturally spiky ears but filed her teeth to make them pointed. Her hair was dyed jet black, her extreme arched eyebrows were painted a theatrical black and her lips were a flaming red; she liked to wear trousers and, like a prop out of a 1930s farce, she smoked from an ornately carved cigarette holder. Where the reality of her life and the performance of it left off is difficult to say, except the two probably merged so seamlessly that even Rosaleen couldn't tell the difference.

She came into contact with the thirteen-years-younger Gavin

Greenlees, a slight, bespectacled bookish man with a fragile mind; a poet who wrote jejune surrealist verses. He was homosexual but that didn't stop Norton becoming his lover. She enjoyed sex with gay men, saying of their virtues that they were soft and rounded and let her do what she liked with them. In the libertine atmosphere of the Cross she discovered that she liked oral sex and sadomasochism. She enjoyed being tied up and beaten and when having sexual intercourse would urge her master to be forceful and hurt her more. In lesbian sex she was always the dominant one, fantasising about having a penis so she could have sex with a woman like a man.

Goossens's marital history couldn't have been more different. Instead of living in bohemian poverty like Rosaleen, he inhabited a privileged upper middle class world. He went through two marriages and married his third wife, Marjorie Foulkrod, in 1946. She was a divorcee, wealthy, glamorous, a piano graduate of the Juilliard Music School and nearly twenty years younger than her husband.

A year later Goossens came to Australia to conduct the Sydney Symphony Orchestra and become Director of the Conservatorium. He was in love, happy, and Australia rejuvenated him. His task was to build up the Sydney Symphony Orchestra and raise the standards of Australian musical tastes. His three-year contract as permanent conductor of the SSO and Director of the Conservatorium earned him £7000 a year at a time when the Prime Minister was being paid only £5000. He discovered the soprano Joan Sutherland and gave her the main role in a local production of *Judith*. A stern taskmaster, it only took him two years to develop the SSO into the sixth best orchestra in the world. At the Conservatorium he sacked staff and failed whole classes of senior students. Richard Bonynge, later to become a conductor and husband to his famous opera singing wife, Dame Joan Sutherland, remembered his time as a final year student at the Conservatorium when Goossens would 'sail into diploma classes with this great fur coat around his shoulders. I won't say pompous, but very autocratic. A proud man. We were in awe of him – even frightened some of the time.'

In 1949 Norton scored her first major exhibition at the Rowden-White Gallery at Melbourne University. The exhibition attracted much press coverage, most of which dwelt on the extraordinary subject matter of the works, her unconventional lifestyle and occult interests. It was her first taste of media sensationalism and she liked it. What she didn't realise was that the public outrage was real, and two days after the exhibition opened the Vice Squad raided the gallery and seized four of the pictures, alleging that *Witches' Sabbath*, *Lucifer*, *Triumph* and *Individuation* were decadent, obscene and likely to arouse unhealthy sexual appetites in those who saw them.

She went to court on obscenity charges, the first such case against a woman in Victoria. The act under which Norton was prosecuted was based on a case first heard during Queen Victoria's reign in 1836. The magistrate found in her favour, dismissing the charges against her and awarding her costs against the police department.

Norton and Gavin were now living together as a couple, she the dominant partner. Greenlees, a mild-mannered and highly strung man, was prone to epileptic fits and unexplained attacks of panic and rage. They lived at 179 Brougham Street in a grungy three-storey terrace in a state of permanent disrepair. The basement where she held her coven meetings was decorated with occult symbols and a rudimentary altar was used for the witchcraft rituals. Outside in the corridor was a sign that read: *Welcome to the house of ghosts, goblins, werewolves, vampires, witches, wizards and poltergeists.*

In mid-August 1952 a collection of her illustrations accompanied by impenetrable poems by Greenlees was published as *The Art of Rosaleen Norton*. Controversy continued to shadow her. The book's publisher, Walter Glover, was charged with obscenity and Norton found herself back in court defending her art in terms of Jungian archetypes. Such arguments notwithstanding, the magistrate fined Glover £5 and ordered that two pictures (including one of *Fohat*, a cheeky demon with a snake for a penis), be obliterated from unsold copies of the book because they were obscene and 'an offence to chastity and delicacy'.

Norton's behaviour and her art were perfect for tabloids, which salivated over the sexual images at the same time as denouncing them. Reports of the book were accompanied by headlines such as 'Witches, Demons on Rampage in Weird Sydney Sex Book' (the *Sunday Sun*). Several newspapers ran stories deliberately goading irate readers into denouncing the book. Some called for it to be banned, although one woman reader decreed that, 'Burning isn't good enough; all copies should be burnt and the plates destroyed.'

These two very different people, Norton and Goossens, living in completely separate social circles, seemed unlikely ever to meet one another until one day in early 1953 Goossens came upon the book *The Art of Rosaleen Norton* in the Notanda Gallery in Rowe Street, just off Martin Place. It rekindled his occult interests from when he was a young man. He wrote to Rosaleen saying how much he enjoyed her art.

And it's at this point in the story that the very topography of the Cross plays a fateful role. Thrilled that someone so celebrated liked her work, Norton invited him to tea in her studio. The orchestra's rehearsal studio was above the Woolworths building on Darlinghurst Road, so Rosaleen's terrace was literally just a couple of minutes away. Goossens's biographer Carol Rosen describes perfectly the peculiar sight of 'the distinguished maestro, immaculate in Savile Row suit and Homburg hat, disappearing into the dubious recesses of the rundown three-storey house tenanted by vagrants and beatniks'. Goossens was enthralled and he began to visit Rosaleen often.

As their friendship grew closer, Norton often went to his concerts at the Town Hall. Goossens had found her a useful source of material for the Satanic scenes in the world premiere of his cantata, *The Apocalypse*. Their relationship became intimate and took on a compelling sexual urgency. While away he wrote her many letters, addressing her as 'Roie' or 'Roiewitch':

> *Contemplating your hermaphroditic organs in the picture made me nearly desert my evening's work and fly to you by first aerial coven. But, as promised and when a suddenly flapping window blind announced your arrival, I realised by a delicious orifical tingling that you were about to make your presence felt ... I need your physical presence very much, for many reasons. We have many rituals and indulgences to take. And I want to take more photos.*

Goossens was aware he was now living a double life and he frequently cautioned 'Roie' not to tell others about their friendship and to destroy the letters. But of course she didn't, and kept them in a bundle hidden behind her sofa.

Marjorie and her husband maintained the image of the devoted couple but by this stage they had grown apart and slept in separate bedrooms. She was the sort of woman who needed constant male admiration to reaffirm her desirability and had many affairs. For Goossens, the worship of Pan provided sexual excitement that was both exotic and illicit, yet there was more to it than that; he was convinced that the rituals of Sex Magic he and Rowie practised together were an invaluable source of inspiration and aid to his creative powers which he felt, like his sexual energy, were fading. Rowie's world now began to seep into the house in suburban Castlecrag: he painted the walls of his bedroom ox blood red, highlighted by red and gold pelmets.

The following year started out as if it were to be just as successful for the Englishman as previous years. On 17 May 1955 the State Cabinet announced that the Opera House would be built at Bennelong Point. The Premier, Mr Cahill, spoke glowingly of the originator of the idea:

> *The main hero of the Opera House site choice is Mr Eugene Goossens. His artist's eye picked out the site within a year of coming here in 1947. For six years Mr Goossens worked to rally public opinion and force official action.*

For the Witch of Kings Cross 1955 also looked like being a good year. The coffee shop the Kashmir showed her work and the Apollyon had a permanent display of her paintings. She would linger long over cups of coffee, secretly pleased to see visitors to the Cross who had come especially to see the Witch of Kings Cross surreptitiously gawping at her.

But on 14 September the police picked up a homeless adolescent girl, Anna Hoffman, who blamed her sorry plight on Norton. Hoffman had first met Rosaleen a few months earlier, telling the police:

> *Roie was already famous – perhaps one should say notorious – as an eccentric artist and bohemian practitioner of witchcraft. I also yearned to be a witch and made an absolute neophyte of myself hanging around her basement flat. I was hoping she would divulge to me her occult secrets ... I once smelt a secret perfume wafting from the smoke filled room behind her. I knew she smoked hashish*

*to open doors to her subconscious for painting and to prepare for
magical rites while in a self-induced trance.*

The mentally unstable Hoffman retracted her allegations but
the scandal added to Norton's notoriety, though as Rowie tried to
point out, she had never taken part in a Black Mass and, in fact,
her god was horned Pan, not Lucifer. Hoffman was sentenced
to two months jail for vagrancy. The incident sparked a series of
stories on Satanism in Kings Cross. One particularly spectacular
headline from the *Australasian Post* verged on the hysterical: 'A
Warning to Australia: DEVIL WORSHIP HERE!' It was accompanied
by a photograph of Rowie in pagan dress kneeling before a painting of the god Pan.

The same month that police arrested Hoffman, two men,
Frank Honer and Ray Ager, tried to sell to newspapers a roll of
undeveloped film stolen from Rowie's flat, asking £200 for it. The
tabloid *The Sun* had the film processed but decided that the photographs were 'too hot' for publication. They were staged acts of
sadist sexual poses, featuring Norton and Greenlees wearing cere-
monial garb while they performed what the newspaper described
as an 'unnatural sexual act'. *The Sun* gave the photographs to the
New South Wales Police Vice Squad.

On 3 October 1955, using the excuse of the obscene photographs, the Vice Squad, lead by Detective Bert Trevenar, raided
Rowie's flat and charged her and Gavin with making an obscene
publication and 'the abominable crime of buggery'. The detectives
allowed Joe Morris, a crime reporter from *The Sun*, to accompany
them on the raid. Searching the flat, Morris reached behind the
sofa and found a bundle of letters to Norton signed 'Eugene' or
'Gene', together with photographs.

The same afternoon, the newspapers had their headlines: ART-
IST IS QUESTIONED and ARTIST FACES CHARGE OVER OBSCENE FILM. A

panic-stricken Goossens hurriedly burnt his private collection of pornography and black magic paraphernalia. But the tenacious Trevenar would not be easily put off. He was sickened by the letters, which clearly indicated 'that Goossens was involved with the practice of Panthiasm [*sic*] and the resultant sex perversion with Norton and Greenlees'. Energised by his own disgust at the Witch and the Englishman, he was determined to arrest the conductor.

The year that had begun with such promise entered turbulent times. Gavin collapsed under the strain and was admitted to Callan Park asylum in October. This was not so much a matter of his going mad – the stress was more a trigger for what was already inside him, impatiently waiting for the moment to bloom like a gaudy poisonous flower. He hallucinated voices and was diagnosed as a schizophrenic and, according to Dr Sands, the acting medical superintendent, Greenlees was 'obsessed with sex'.

Around the same time as Greenlees was committed, Goossens left Australia for a five-month tour of Europe and to receive his knighthood for 'services to Australian music' from the Queen. By the time Bert Trevenar was ready to issue a warrant, Goossens had left the country. Trevenar discovered that the New South Wales Police didn't have the resources to track down his movements in England and Europe so the frustrated detective made a deal with *The Sun*. If Joe Morris could convince some Fleet Street journalists to tail Goossens, then the tabloid would be given a sensational 'exclusive' when the newly knighted conductor returned. The English connections were as good as their word and they reported back to Sydney that the famous conductor was seen in seedy newsagencies and dirty book shops in Soho and Leicester Square.

It's important to pause and recall just what Australia was like in the middle 1950s. Television had just been introduced. Men's magazines included the innocuous *Man* and *Man Junior*. The Censorship Board banned many novels including *Peyton Place*.

The majority of wives didn't work. A man's income was almost sufficient to support his family, pay a mortgage on a modest suburban bungalow and have an occasional night out at the pictures by public transport. Hotels were not open on Sunday and neither were the cinemas. Sunday night meant listening to the radio for most people. Around a quarter of all families still had no refrigerators. More than half of all homes did not have hot water on tap. Most clothes washing was still being done by hand in a copper. Six o'clock closing had just finished but as for dining out, there were few places to go if you didn't live in Kings Cross. The owner of the Moulin Rouge Café in Kellett Street was fined £5 for having a reproduction of Toulouse-Lautrec's *The Salon* because it depicted a near-nude woman adjusting her stocking.

At 8 am on 9 March 1956, confident and smartly dressed as always, Goossens walked off his plane at Sydney. What surprised him was that for the first time in his many trips through customs he was stopped. He was asked if he had anything to declare and he shook his head. The customs inspector motioned to Goossens's briefcase and asked what was in it. The composer replied that it contained only musical scores but the inspector opened it anyway. By now Goossens knew that there was something ominous in this line of questioning and the light blue collar of his shirt began to change to a dark blue as he began to perspire heavily.

It was the beginning of a seven-hour nightmare. The prosecuting counsel would describe the contents of his luggage thus:

> *The articles in the briefcase were contained in folders of heavy paper, sealed with adhesive tape and bearing on the outside the names of composers, presumably with the object that they should be taken as containing sheets of musical scores. A series of envelopes was attached to the inside of each folder and the photographs were contained in these.*

Also hidden among Goossens's luggage was a substantial collection of pornography, masks, a film viewer and some incense sticks. There were 837 photographs, a set of prints, bizarre personal letters and postcards written by him, eight books and a spool of film. At first a rattled Goossens blamed his London valet, 'I told Billings my valet not to put them in here ... it's his mania. He packed them about a week ago.' But as more suitcases were unpacked he began to wilt until the evidence was overwhelming and he resigned himself to his fate, saying more to himself than the many customs officers, 'All for a stupid private collection.' A few moments later he thought he could wiggle out of his predicament by saying he had bought the material in Paris. When that sad ploy didn't work he pleaded with them not to let the news out and finally, the last resort of the desperate, he hinted at paying a bribe.

It was not only the filthy photographs that interested the officials – there were also books with titles like *Sharing Their Pleasures, Continental, Flossie, Nancy's Love Life* and – amusingly – *Catcher in the Rye.* By now Goossens had given up and with a sigh said he welcomed the seizing of the material, adding that it was not for anybody's use or purpose except but his own.

The terrier-like detective could hardly contain his impatience as he waited for the thorough Customs officials to finish. When they did he escorted Goossens to the Vice Squad's Bathurst Street office where they were greeted by reporters and photographers from all four Sydney newspapers. Goossens knew then that there was no way of avoiding a scandal.

An exultant Trevenar enjoyed interrogating a man he considered a despicable pervert. He questioned him about the magic ceremonies, especially their sexual component. Goossens explained that the rite was conducted in the nude with everyone sitting on the floor in a circle. Norton intoned incantations calling up Pan and then the Englishman would perform 'sexual stimulation of her'. Trevenar, an Australian man of his time, was appalled that any one would indulge in the unnatural and disgusting act of cunnilingus. He showed Goossens the photographs *The Sun* had obtained. The Englishman admitted that some were of the Sex Rite which he had participated in with Norton and Greenlees, some 'four or five times'. At the end of Trevenar's interrogation a crushed Goossens dictated a two-page statement. Before he left the conductor turned to his triumphant nemesis and said quietly, 'You have been most understanding and sympathetic and I am sorry to have caused you so much trouble.'

The press camped outside his house day and night. On 22 March when his case came to court he was too ill to appear and his barrister pleaded guilty on his behalf. This plea ensured there would be no display of the material that customs officials had confiscated. He was fined the maximum of £100 for 'having had obscene books and pictures in his possession'. Four days later Goossens resigned from his positions at both the SSO and the Conservatorium. He was sixty-three and would remain, in the words of his biographer, 'a non-person for the next twenty years'.

On Saturday 26 May Goossens, under the assumed name of Mr E. Gray, flew out of Sydney bound for Rome. He briefly met up with his wife in Nice. They never lived together again. As far as Fred Blanks, the *Sydney Morning Herald* music critic was concerned:

> *Under his direction of the Sydney Symphony Orchestra and Conservatorium from 1947 to 1956 we experienced a unique musical awakening. For Sydney it was the decade of the century. But Sydney repaid him miserably.*

Rosaleen rarely mentioned the controversy – given her egocentricity there was no doubt she enjoyed it and, like Marlene Dietrich's character in *The Blue Angel*, cared little for the man whose reputation and life she shattered forever. It was another scandal that added to her infamy as the Witch of Kings Cross. As she told the *Australasian Post* the following year:

> *I have been described as eccentric, decadent, exhibitionist, crank, genius, witch, freak and so on, both in public utterances and private conversations. Yes, I am all of these things and glad of it. My first act of ceremonial magic was in honour of the horned god, whose pipes are a symbol of magic and mystery and whose horns and hooves stand for natural energies and fleet-footed freedom. And this rite was also my oath of allegiance and my confirmation as a witch. If Pan is the Devil, then I am indeed a Devil worshipper.*

Seven years later, in early 1964, Greenlees was given a temporary release from Callan Park. He returned to Brougham Street but soon went berserk, threatened to kill Rowie and threw her furniture into the street. She called the police. An officer found Gavin leaning over a sink running a knife across his throat.

'Did you harm anyone?' the policeman asked.

'Not yet,' said a calm Gavin, 'but it is time for me to kill her.' He then pointed to the basement, 'She is in there.' The policeman went downstairs and found the Witch of Kings Cross kneeling before an altar, muttering to herself.

Goossens's career never recovered. The conductor Richard Bonynge and his wife Joan Sutherland went to see him several times in his London flat. Bonynge said: 'It was tragic to see him. Tragic. It seemed he'd become half his size. He was absolutely destroyed physically. Definitely. He was pilloried by a very insular society.'

As for Rosaleen, she continued to paint occasionally, but her art never graduated from its immature preoccupation with goblins, ghouls and Pan. To earn money she sold charms and hexes and developed a habit for drugs like Methedrine and Dexedrine (soon to become popular in the late 1960s). She was still feared by people. The exotic dancer Roberta Sykes was scared of Rowie, especially after the witch fell in love with her and would stand outside her window of a night calling her name. Ayesha, who was a performer in Les Girls at the time, told me that Rowie had such a wicked reputation that Ayesha would have to hail taxis for her because if the drivers saw Norton they wouldn't pick her up. As a thank you, Rowie drew a Celtic symbol on Ayesha's dressing room mirror in Les Girls to ward off the evil thoughts of others.

As she aged, the Witch of Kings Cross retreated into her dingy flat, a haggard, exhausted figure, where she looked after her beloved cats (as suits a witch) and listened to classical music. The younger generation either hadn't heard of her or were not so much frightened of her suspected powers as amused by how she seemed to have become a caricature of herself. She died of cancer in late 1979 in the Sacred Heart Hospice, Darlinghurst, tended by nuns but an atheist to the end.

DARLINGHURST ROAD

BAYSWATER ROAD

PENNY'S LANE

WARD AVENUE

Entry
Zenith
Apartments

GODERICH LANE

Diamont
Hotel

Original terraces
and apartments

Café
Hernandez

*
Elan
forecourt
sculptures   Elan

KINGS CROSS ROAD

118 properties demolished 1975

Altair

Woolcott Street ['The Dirty Half Mile']
Upper William South

Cross City Tunnel

IT WAS A PLEASANTLY HOT summer's day in 1950 and Mrs Jessie Querns and her seven-year-old daughter, Dolores, were in the laundry at the rear of Moonbi Flats in Kings Cross Road. While the mother did the laundry Dolores pottered about in the backyard. A few moments later Querns heard her daughter's terrified screams. She rushed out into the yard and was astonished to see a huge wedge-tailed eagle, its eight-foot wings stretched out, its beak open and its claws at the ready, advancing on the little girl. The mother screamed at the raptor while Dolores ran back and locked herself in one of the laundries. The eagle advanced on Querns.

'You should have seen its eyes – blazing they were and fierce.' She held her arms up to defend herself and the eagle rose up, circled and swooped on an arm, missing it the first time, but in a second attempt it sank its claws into her flesh, leaving a serious and bloody gash.

Querns beat off the eagle and locked herself in the other laundry where, in a frenzy, it clawed at the door and flapped its wings in attempt to get inside, like something out of Hitchcock's *The Birds*. Querns screamed for nearly half an hour hoping to be rescued because others in the flats were afraid they would be attacked if they came to her aid.

Eventually the eagle flew away and landed in the doorway of a residential just down the road. About sixty people tried to trap it but it defended itself, its wings stretched out, pecking savagely with its sharp hooked beak at those who came near or slashing at them with its two-inch talons. By the time the law turned up the eagle was 'fighting mad'. The policemen chased it up the stairs and captured it by throwing a blanket over it.

It turned out that the eagle's owner, William Norkett, managed the residential to which the bird had returned. He had owned it for a decade, ever since it was ten months old. Apparently the eagle had escaped from its netted exercise yard after being frightened when a fire started suddenly nearby. Norkett claimed it was a harmless pet which he let out of its cage every morning and was so tame that he could fondle it and that it liked to kiss him on the chin. To prove to the police how harmless the eagle was Norkett kissed it. Even so, as the police noticed, he had warnings on the entrance to his home, *Enter at Own Risk* and *Danger – Keep Out*.

Norkett was not arrested or fined because eagles were not protected and there was no regulation prohibiting them from being kept in captivity. This didn't mollify Querns, who, after she had recovered from her wound and shock in hospital, said that it was 'a scandal that anyone should be permitted to keep an eagle as a pet – especially in Kings Cross'.

Kings Cross Road is no longer called the Dirty-Half Mile or Douche Alley. All traces of its former notoriety as a haunt of prostitutes, sly grog dealers and gangsters, the road littered with rubbish and used condoms, has gone. Most of the residential blocks, including Moonbi Flats, have also vanished. As one critic bitterly remembered: 'The whole of Kings Cross Road area was demolished in one of the most brutal incidents of environmental butchery to be seen in the City of Sydney.'

In 1969 the government finally decided to solve the traffic problems created 140 years before and build a four-lane highway for through traffic, leaving William Street near Dowling and joining Bayswater Road, east of Neild Avenue. It would pass under Victoria Street and emerge some 240 metres to the east and from there lead directly to the eastern suburbs. The cut and cover tunnel required resumption of about one hectare of residential area between Craigend Street and Kings Cross Road. A total of 118 properties were to be razed, plus the Kings Cross Post Office, with its exquisite Italianate sandstone façade and Georgian windows. The unfortunate aspect to this was that it was the southern side, those of houses of uneven numbers, which would bear the brunt of this destruction.

After the residents had recovered from their shock they held many meetings, angry that they hadn't been consulted; as Colin Sherwood says in his memoir of those times, 'What gave the government the right to destroy an extremely close-knit society?' His mother was caretaker of the Harvard Flats at 13 Kings Cross Road. Marien Dreyer, the left-wing, one-legged writer, lived in Flat 28 in the Harvard and arranged meetings with politicians and a protest march down Macquarie Street. But it was a losing battle. The residents were issued with eviction notices and given eighteen months to quit. Sherwood and his mother were some of the last to leave. By early 1971 they were the only ones left in the building and they too were forced to leave. The Harvard, Kingsway, and ninety per cent of the buildings in Kings Cross Road and its immediate vicinity were all demolished. One of the buildings to be flattened was the sumptuous and sophisticated Belvedere Hotel, a white Victorian-style mansion with wisteria-twined balconies, marble statues and an ornate fountain. Once a stately home in the 1930s, it became a private hotel with a five-star dining room serving French cuisine, its name synonymous with grand European service. Its unique New Orleans Belle Époque atmosphere attracted celebrated guests such as Margot Fonteyn, Yehudi Menuhin and the Opera House architect Joern Utzon. Now there is only a vacant patch of land where it once stood and the only reminder of this gorgeous hotel is a small plaque commemorating it, plus Gaby Naher's evocative memories of the hotel and her adopted father, who owned it.

Sherwood never recovered from the eviction and the destruction of his home, calling it a massive removal of the heart and soul of Kings Cross.

The tunnel opened on 15 December 1975, costing $21 million. Two-thirds of that money had been spent buying up land and properties.

The road is empty of character now and, after it dips down and crosses Ward Avenue, it dribbles past a shabby backpackers hostel before being passively absorbed by Bayswater Road. The southern side basically consists of two apartment blocks, the Altair and the Elan. During the construction of the 40-storey Elan, a dozen or more homeless Aborigines and junkies had to be evicted from under the top of William Street where they lived a Morlock-like existence. Completed in 1997, it's a prosaic-looking building, most of its balconies never used because of the punishing winds that buffet it.

The Elan may have an anonymous feeling to it but it is the sculpture that is planted on the open plaza of the building that is its most controversial feature. Created by the well-known sculptor Ken Unsworth for $35,000, 'Stones Against the Sky' features seven steel columns mounted with artificial stones. From the moment it was unveiled on the site locals considered it 'bloody awful' and dubbed it 'Poo on Stilts' and have consistently tried to get rid of it. In 2003 a group of art teachers and students calling themselves 'the Revolutionary Council for the Removal of Bad Art in Public Places' threatened to destroy the much-maligned sculpture if it wasn't removed in three months. The Elan management took the threat seriously and issued a warning that the police would be called if any harm came to it, as the critics would be destroying private property. Tired of the ridicule, all the resigned artist would say was that he 'didn't have a problem if they decided to remove it'. The deadline of three months passed and nothing happened to the sculpture except that the Elan believed that its ugliness would be minimised if the ochre red stones were painted charcoal. The sculpture is less obtrusive but the sticks now seem to hold up seven black tumours on toothpicks.

Next to the Elan is the Altair, which is also built above the Cross City Tunnel. It's a sleek, minimalist building, its strong horizontal lines helping hide the fact that it is a sixteen-storey block. Costing

$80 million it was designed by the Sydney architecture firm Engelen Moore, who emphasised its environmentally friendly design. It went on to win the prestigious Best Multiple-Housing Award in the World Architecture awards run by *World Architecture* magazine.

Both apartment blocks face the Diamant, opened in 2007. It's described as 'a contemporary boutique hotel' and features moody lighting, and sober coloured rooms with black bedheads, armchairs and cupboards. It has a twenty-four-hour gymnasium which I use. The clientele is mostly men and at the time I attend in the early afternoon those working out are waiters, bouncers, doormen, Muscle Marys and the bulked-up steroid users. Below the gym is the corner ground-floor restaurant, which has gone through several owners and cuisines. The space has never worked, not helped by the grimness of Penny's Lane itself which, because it is sandwiched between tall buildings, is gloomy even in the daytime. Goderich Lane, which runs off it, and was once part of the charming grounds of the Goderich mansion, is now a rat-infested bleak conduit to the sunlit Ward Avenue.

It's only when you drift over the incline and cross Ward Avenue that you strike a vestige of the old Cross. Café Hernandez has been operating in the same spot since 1982. Open twenty-four hours a day, its regular customers include firemen, police, taxi drivers and locals. Over the years the owner, Federico Sabrafan, has been variously described as being an Argentinean-born Spaniard or being born in La Mancha, Spain. He arrived in Sydney in 1970 knowing little English and having to borrow money to start a coffee shop. As he was to say, 'It was cup of tea time in Australia and I want to change it to a coffee culture.'

Sabrafan started out as a wholesaler and in only a few years Juanita Nielsen wrote about him in the local newspaper *NOW*. He sells fifteen blends and varieties from Cronulla blend to Ethiopian and Brazilian. It's not a large space; it has ten small tables inside and four outdoor tables. A piano sits in front of the enormous roasting machine which runs all hours of the day and night creating a permanently inviting, sensuous coffee aroma. Sacks of beans surround the machine like sandbags shoring up a levee. It's a café where people can sit alone, think and read or enjoy it with their friends. Sabrafan's English can sometimes verge on the eccentric but it matches his florid bushy moustache. Locals like to tell the story of how he ordered Gerard Depardieu to take his feet off the table not knowing who the French actor was. In 2003 his son, Joaquin left his engineering job and joined his father.

Opposite Café Hernandez there are no buildings remaining, only a long concrete wall hiding the entrance to the tunnel and the Ronald Shores Memorial Park, a sliver of land seldom visited or used. What strikes one is just how forlorn it seems, with its tiny park and one bench. The concrete wall that runs down the southern side hides the tunnel entrance and obliterates any sign that the street once buzzed with life, with prostitutes, gamblers, crooks, ordinary families and artists. Six hundred people were uprooted and a vibrant community shattered.

The road itself, since the demolition of the terraces, has become a wind tunnel. Still, as Sabrafan has said: 'A lot has changed outside but nothing has changed [inside] here for the past twenty-five years'. And the reason he venerates coffee?

'You drink coffee, you can think; you drink alcohol, you no can think.'

SEPTIC TANKS

TO ONE MAN IT SOUNDED like the beating of a carpet. To others it seemed it was merely another bout of blasting for the Garden Island graving dock. But for the artist Donald Friend, it was 'a brilliant display of Eastern pyrotechnics'. On the night of 31 May 1942 he was living in Elizabeth Bay House, in the room above the portico, where he had a panoramic vista of Sydney Harbour and so had a spectacular view of a Japanese mini submarine attack on Allied shipping.

The three mini subs had slipped into Sydney Harbour at around 11 pm. One became entangled in the boom net near the entrance to the harbour and was destroyed by its crew. The second submarine simply vanished and the third fired two torpedoes at the US cruiser *Chicago*, which was illuminated by the floodlights of Garden Island. Both missed their target, one running aground on Garden Island and failing to explode, the other passing under a Dutch submarine and the converted harbour ferry, the depot ship HMAS *Kuttabul*, striking the sea wall just behind them. The blast damaged the Dutch sub and sank the *Kuttabul*, killing twenty-one men and wounding ten others. Throughout the night the sound of depth charges going off in the harbour was deafening.

The sneak attack was a total surprise and not far down the road in Kings Cross wild rumours began to circulate that the

Japanese would soon be invading. The next day the streets of the Cross were filled with removalists' trucks. One man remembered standing outside the Macleay Regis and counting twenty-eight flats that had suddenly been abandoned. Franconia had only fifteen residents left in the building. Frightened people headed for the safety of the Blue Mountains.

The dread and panic was very different from the excitement two years before when huge crowds welcomed in 1940. The largest crowds were in Kings Cross, where up to 40,000 revellers took 'complete charge of Kings Cross' and sang and danced and brought traffic to a standstill. Local shopkeepers boarded up their windows with wooden slats to protect the glass. Wrote one reporter, 'Essentially [Kings Cross is] an area in which self consciousness is unknown and the residents gave themselves up to unrestrained hilarity.' The police, resigned to anything that might happen, advised drivers to avoid the area. People wore fancy dress and masks, and others dressed as parodies of Allied and enemy leaders. Women embarrassed policemen by kissing them, men drummed on the sides of buses. There were trumpets, tin whistles and fireworks and some young soldiers clambered up on awnings to watch the spectacle. Even though war had been declared, the European front seemed so far away from the delirious Kings Cross party welcoming in the New Year that it was impossible to imagine Australia would be attacked, let alone invaded.

The Cross had made preparations for war. There were wardens who took it in turns manning their posts all night. They had been instructed in dealing with incendiary bombs, the art of fire fighting and rudimentary first aid. There was a warden's post in the basement of the Piccadilly Hotel in Victoria Street and one in the back room of a flat in Manar, where the publisher Sydney Ure Smith was a warden. During the war years all shop windows were boarded up against bomb blasts and many of the windows of flats and houses were criss-crossed with sticky tape to minimise glass shatter.

Locals helped in other, more curious ways. In early 1942, three water diviners, clutching a bent piece of fencing wire, a hacksaw blade and twisted steel bar, worked their way through the streets of the Cross trying to locate underground streams. The diviners had volunteered to help the Darlinghurst section of the People's Defence Auxiliary which was mapping emergency water supplies. They had been chosen from three hundred volunteers who had offered their services. The three consisted of a local woman from Springfield Avenue, 58-year-old Mrs Madeline Sloan, and two men, one aged thirty-five, the other seventy-four. As they moved slowly through the streets, followed by dozens of curious spectators, Mrs Sloan used a bent piece of number 8 wire, one of the men carried a hacksaw blade fitted with a copper cup and the other had a twisted steel bar with a leather sheath to establish the type of water they found. Mrs Sloan said her power was like a magnetic ray. 'I have located water blindfolded in a car, driving around my husband's properties in Corowa'. One of the men described the power as 'a mighty atom, like light'. Working independently they each located a major stream which ran under the fire station, agreeing with each other that it was about 13 feet wide and 33 feet down. The Auxiliary announced it was very grateful to the diviners but as it turned out there would be no need for the emergency water supplies.

Rationing was introduced in 1940, petrol and liquor became hard to obtain and this was followed by the rationing of clothing, tea, sugar, butter and meat. Yet it was as if the Cross didn't notice; there was a thriving black market in the rationed goods and a sense of euphoria, even decadence. As far as Donald Friend was concerned, it had 'a genuine Berlin air. *Everybody* is wicked.'

After the attack on Pearl Harbor the war came closer to Australia when the Japanese captured Singapore and bombed Darwin. The Americans retreated from South-East Asia to Australia as did the Dutch from Indonesia. Soon it seemed as if the whole world had come to Sydney: Americans, British, French, Dutch sailors, soldiers and airmen. Kings Cross was the favourite destination for American troops for their five to ten day furloughs. At the peak of the war it seemed to locals that there were six Americans to every Australian soldier.

Two large apartment blocks were taken over in Macleay Street. Maramanah was commandeered for a barracks. Tusculum had been a private hospital but was transformed into an officers' club for the American Red Cross. The posh Kinneil guest house in Elizabeth Bay Road was leased for the duration of the war to the Australian and Allied forces. Run by the Australian Comforts Fund, the Kinneil Officers' Club accommodated about 130 officers each night. Cheverells, a three-storey building (where the Gazebo now stands), was another officers' club. Volunteer women served as the household personnel and held Sunday afternoon teas, bridge tournaments and musical performances. During its three-year use by the Thirteenth Air Force, 68,000 men lodged there and 194,000 meals were served. American nurses were allotted buildings for their clubs in Manning and Macleay Streets. And as for food, the stylish Balcony restaurant on the first floor of the Woolworth's building became the Australian Combined Services canteen.

Because the Americans had commandeered so many buildings and also rented out rooms in other blocks, Australians found it hard to find flats or boarding houses from the second half of 1942, especially after those residents who had fled fearing invasion returned to their apartments as the threat receded. What was available were luxury flats at cheap rents because the top floors of buildings were considered the most vulnerable. Landladies rented out their flats to Americans because they would pay more. Some charged such extortionate rents that they were prosecuted. But the American servicemen, who earned much more than Australian soldiers, were willing to pay any price for all kinds of goods and services.

The Kings Cross streets were filled with hundreds of swaggering Yanks. What amazed locals was that it was 'the first time any of us Australians had ever seen a male carrying a bunch of flowers'. The flowers were to impress women, of course, and it was women the Americans wanted. The Cross served as a major location for brothels. US officials also rented houses and flats where they set up prostitutes for their servicemen. Landladies made money by renting out rooms by the hour for the Americans and their 'girlfriends'. One of the most popular spots for prostitutes to work was the corner of Roslyn Street and Darlinghurst Road, dubbed Battleship corner. The whores had a special come on for airmen, who were nicknamed blue orchids: 'Would you like a little jig-a-jig, Blue Orchid?' Taxi drivers were a conduit for sex. When a soldier asked a cab driver if he could take him to a prostitute, the Australian would make the rules clear (no kinky sex, etc.) before dropping him off at an address where he was paid a commission by the girl.

Black American servicemen had their own club, the Booker T. Washington, down in Surry Hills away from the white troops. The Negroes were popular with Australian girls because they paid twice as much as the white soldiers. US military police cooperated with brothel owners to make sure certain rules were followed. One Sydney prostitute recalled that she 'moved straight from the Depression into a time of money ... The Yanks were here and they were good with money, buy anything you wanted.'

The veteran policewoman Lillian Armfield, one of the first plain-clothes female detectives in New South Wales, was horrified that she had to allow the brothels to flourish despite finding girls as young as twelve working as prostitutes for the black troops. Even homosexuals were available for gay Yanks. The going rate for giving a head job to an American serviceman was two shillings and sixpence. The gay writer Sumner Locke Elliott was impressed by their hair cuts and their 'marvellous teeth'. Of course there were scams and American servicemen were rolled for their money or found themselves being gingered – a sting where a woman would take a man back to a room and while they were having sex an accomplice hiding under the bed would stealthily steal the man's wallet from his trousers. Just as climax neared there'd be an angry knocking at the door. The prostitute would pretend panic and say it was her husband or the police and tell the serviceman to leave by the back door. The client skedaddled, not realising until too late that his wallet had been stolen.

But there were plenty of women who came to the Cross just to have sex with the Americans. Prostitutes sneeringly called them 'charity molls'. For many of these women, the Americans were more attractive than Australian men. American servicemen wore svelte uniforms that made the Australian baggy outfit seem daggy; they had more money, they were more romantic and Hollywood movies had given Americans a mystique that Australian men didn't have. The Yanks were sophisticated, brought their dates flowers, took them out to dinner, held out a chair for a woman as she sat down, opened a door for her to enter first and said please and thank you. It seemed that the average American was more knowledgeable, more interested in the world and had more wit and confidence. They also loved swing music and the latest dance crazes; their ability to jive and jitterbug thrilled Australian women.

With so much money pouring into Kings Cross, things such as Lucky Strikes and Camel cigarettes by the carton that had been unavailable became commonplace, as did chocolates, nylon stockings, and hard liquor. Taxis and tables in restaurants were scarce unless the woman had an American escort. It was no wonder Australian men were jealous. Most of the fights between them and the 'Septic Tanks' were over women. But for many women it was wonderful.

My mother was one of those women and she came up from Melbourne to Kings Cross when she was about seventeen. She was always proud of the fact that she had two marines go AWOL for her. Sometimes late at night in our housing commission home I would overhear my Aunt Nell, who had been with my mother at the time, reminiscing about their adventures together in the Cross. It was easy to tell by their girlish excitement, knowing laughter and sighs of regret at their present drab circumstances that this had been the time of their lives and nothing in peacetime had ever come close to matching it.

If Australian men were envious of the Americans, so were some Australian women jealous of other women who had success with the Yanks. Betty Roland, by this stage in her early forties, was constantly frustrated that the place may have been crawling with Americans but they were only interested in young, attractive women who were naive and not very bright.

'I marvelled to see them sitting in the most expensive restaurants, orchids cascading down their bosoms, not knowing which fork or spoon to pick up first, totally overwhelmed by the visitation of these god-like creatures from another world.' Roland stewed over the unfairness of it all: 'We wanted the attention, nylon stockings, good manners, good looks and tailored uniforms of Uncle Sam's brave boys who had swept into Sydney like an army of conquerors and claimed the spoils of war.'

Teenage girls flocked to the Cross to meet American men whom they had only seen in the Hollywood movies that so bedazzled them. The girls were from middle-class suburbs, broken homes or had run away from Girls' Reformatories, many making themselves available as 'pick-ups'. Some were as young as twelve and thirteen and they came to the Cross mesmerised by the very notion of being with an American. They met servicemen in the cinema, on the streets at certain corners (Roslyn Street and Roslyn Gardens were popular spots), cafés or in hotel foyers. One of the most notorious venues was the Oriental in Victoria Street, which was considered just a notch above a bordello: 'its tawdry lobby was a hive of tarty girls trying to pick up Army and Navy officers who couldn't get in anywhere else'.

The servicemen on R&R were in the Cross for a week or so. In that brief time the girls were the centre of attention, given flowers, taken out, wooed, loved; the intensity of it would approach the heightened level of a Hollywood melodrama or love story. Then there was the bittersweet moment of goodbye, not knowing whether it would be permanent or not. The girls may have had romance in their hearts but the Americans had lust in their loins. For the teenage girls who came to the Cross it was the sex that shocked. Most of the girls were unprepared for it, having had no sex education, and blamed their parents or schools for not teaching them about 'life and sex'.

The behaviour of the girls could range from the naive to the calculating. Joan, a teenager, was born in Homebush, left school at fourteen and fled her home soon after Pearl Harbor. The Manpower Department forced her to work stints at canning factories and as a maid, but most of her time was spent outwitting Manpower and having fun in the Cross, where she rented a flat with her best friend. In two years she had spent £500 on rent, clothes, living expenses and cosmetics (her favourite lipstick was Victory Red). This was truly a considerable amount of money given to her by Americans. When asked how many she had met, all she could say was it 'might be dozens – or hundreds, I don't know'. As she remarked defiantly, 'There's the war and all this money. Why shouldn't girls have a good time?'

There were girls who were victims of their own romantic fantasies and caught venereal diseases or fell pregnant. The proportion of children born out of wedlock rose from well under five per cent in 1940 to a peak of seven per cent in 1944, and the number of girls between twelve and sixteen who were made wards of the state increased from twelve per cent at the beginning of the war to thirty per cent in 1943. There were also those women who robbed or conned the Americans and were demonised as 'gold-digging harpies' and 'Lounge Lizzies'.

Male writers like Kenneth Slessor and George Johnston may have concentrated on the war in the Pacific and Europe, but the phenomenon of American servicemen fraternising with Australian women attracted novelists such as Kylie Tennant and Dymphna Cusack, who tried to make sense of it all. Tennant was a rigorous researcher, even getting herself arrested once so she could experience jail. Her novel *The Joyful Condemned* is about fifteen year-old 'Big' Rene McGarty, a delinquent girl in wartime Sydney. It's an epic canvas of young girls escaping from reform homes, basement flats in the Cross, upper class parties and gangsters. The characters range from welfare workers, prostitutes and criminals to shady landladies. A central scene is that of the young unmarried mother, Marie, washing the diapers of her illegitimate baby and telling the kindly old Archdeacon Aumbry the technique of an American serviceman propositioning a girl. It is disarmingly simple. The American compliments her dress or comes on to her with the line 'Hello, Sunshine'. Then he takes her to a nightclub and maybe a restaurant. Marie believes that it's only fair that the girl contribute by having sex with the man who paid for the evening. The Archdeacon asks her if she ever felt what she was doing was morally wrong. She doesn't feel guilty at all and he despairs that all Marie is doing is producing another generation of children without fathers or moral guidance.

Come in Spinner was written by Dymphna Cusack and Florence James. Like Tennant, Cusack based her novels on a solid foundation of research. In 1941 she managed a block of flats, Karoon, at 10 Orwell Street where she was known as 'the Sky Pilot of Orwell Street'. This nickname came from her attempts to clean up the flats in which the family money was invested. During a period of neglect it had become a haven for prostitutes and bludgers and her arrival was not welcomed. One night she threw out a group of soldiers who had come with one of the tarts to continue a drinking party. As she said later, 'I must say that my experience in six months at the Cross enabled me to write *Come in Spinner* with more accuracy.' The novel offers a vivid picture of the impact of American forces on the city and traces the fortunes of a group of young women who work at a beauty salon. One woman's younger sister succumbs to toiling in a brothel and there is a scene where the mistress of an American soldier dies as the result of an abortion, dramatising the fear of Americans morally contaminating Australians. But the novel doesn't whitewash Australian men, who complained bitterly about the success of the Americans with their women. The character Guinea expresses the common thought that Australian men who whinged about the success of the Yanks with their women were hypocrites: 'You'd think they were a lot of monks themselves.'

H.C. Brewster, writing at the end of the war, remarked that, 'Although it may seem to the casual observer that the American has stolen the Cross's thunder, his passing, like the passing of time, will leave no mark.' But the American influence had taken deep root in the Cross, whether it be their movies, fashion, dancing, music or food. The appeal of the idea of being with an

American was a statement of how these teenage girls and young women viewed the world. England was old-fashioned, unlike the United States, which symbolised everything that was modern, sexy and glamorous.

'You find this ugly,
I find it lovely'

WHAT'S CURIOUS ABOUT THE BOHEMIANS of the 1920s and 1930s is how they would live nowhere else in Australia other than Kings Cross but never wrote about it. Jack Lindsay's pretentious and convoluted verse had nymphs, mermaids and the Doge of Venice for subjects. Dulcie Deamer's novels were set in past Biblical and medieval times. It was only years later that both Lindsay and Deamer wrote memoirs about living in Kings Cross during that era.

Kenneth Slessor's early poetry was similar. Through these poems Pans, satyrs, nymphs and gods gambolled. Slessor was reacting against the pervasive bush ballads of Banjo Paterson and grim realism of Lawson but his subject matter had all the substance of fairy floss. And yet he was to become one of Australia's marvellous poets and the unofficial poet laureate of the Cross.

He was born in 1901 in Orange of German–Jewish–Scottish background. The family name Schloesser was Anglicised at the start of the First World War. He married in 1922 when he was twenty-one and his wife, Noela, sixteen. It was a tempestuous relationship with infidelities on both sides. At first he was a journalist for the Sydney *Sun* but left it for one of the most seminal, original and unconventional newspapers in Australia, *Smith's Weekly*, staying there for fifteen years and ending up its editor. Widely read, he spoke French, was excellent at chess and had a life-long passion for music. He was fastidious about his appearance and dressed like a dandy with bow ties, sharp suits and waistcoats, cultivating the air of an aristocratic dilettante, and backed it up with scrupulously good manners.

Slessor began writing poetry as a child and in his early twenties he fell under the influence of the artist and writer Norman Lindsay. He collaborated with Lindsay and his son, Jack, on the production of *Vision*, a short-lived arts magazine that centred on Lindsay's crackpot aesthetic that amalgamated Nietzsche, anti-modernism and the Victorian idealisation of art that transcended drab reality. If anything indicated its contents it was the Norman Lindsay drawing on the cover of a dancing faun chasing an elusive butterfly.

It seemed as if Slessor would continue to write mediocre poetry with inane subjects, but *Smith's Weekly* would change all that. He was an intensely private person and disliked personal intimacies, but in the strongly informal and masculine world of the satirical newspaper he began to loosen up. Most of the staff were heavy drinkers and in the male ambience of the pub he could be warm and funny, with a liking for vulgarity.

Smith's Weekly had the finest collection of black and white artists ever seen in an Australian newspaper, among them Joe Lynch and Virgil Reilly. Lynch, a tall, gaunt, red-headed Irishman sometimes illustrated Slessor's humorous articles. Lynch's nihilism ('[he] said the only remedy to the world's disease was to blow it up and start afresh') and his stamina for alcohol appealed to Slessor, but it was the poet's partnership with Reilly that helped Slessor realise that the subjects for his light verses were right in front of him in the Cross. The cartoonist was celebrated for his 'Reilly's girls', beautiful, elegant flappers, in various stages of undress, but never naked. The gorgeous pin-up girls were at odds with their creator, who was a small hunchback, unlucky in love, who often referred to himself a leprechaun.

These light verses were nearly all focused on urban girls, whether they be on the game, a gunman's moll, a cocaine addict, a lift attendant, telephone operator or shop assistant. They were the types Slessor saw every day of the week, whether in the city or the Cross. The verses had a journalist's eye for detail, as in his description of residents of flats where,

> The stars are lit by neon,
> Where the fried potato fumes,
> And the ghost of Mr Villon
> Still inhabits single rooms,
> And the girls lean out from heaven
> Over lightwells, thumping mops.
> While the gent in 57
> Cooks his pound of mutton chops.

Slessor had abandoned his stiff baroque symbolist poems with mythological creatures and become a poet who took the city as a subject, 'then so little celebrated in Australian verse', as his biographer Geoffrey Dutton put it. The verses were eclectic: Choker's Lane full of thieves, prostitutes on the prowl, murderers, beauty parlours ('She has Venus in a bottle, and beauty in a jar/ She can turn a little typist into a motion-picture star'), or the Kelvinator refrigerator replacing the ice man.

These poems were published as *Darlinghurst Nights* in 1933 and, even though Slessor was dismissive of them, the subject matter and a more simple diction influenced his major poems, which were obsessed with the passing of time, as an unstoppable and remorseless tide with an indifference towards humans that verges on the cruel. His light verse focused on girls, not women, and for all their romantic dreams the subject of love is rarely mentioned. He had an aversion to revealing himself and that meant writing about love or, as he put it, 'Lyrical poetry is extremely bad manners ... it's an exhibition of private experience.' His attitude towards sex was a mixture of revulsion and attraction, as is evident in one poem where he describes businessmen using whores as 'a cheap convenient sewer'.

Although he enjoyed the company of writers and artists who considered themselves bohemians, he never did embrace the lifestyle. As he once commented ruefully, 'I was a very amused and detached observer ... I didn't belong to it mainly because I'd committed the unpardonable offence and got myself a steady job at £4 ten shillings a week, which put me beyond the pale.' He loathed the bohemian ideal of the romantic, Byronic image of how a poet should behave and perform. He rarely discussed his work and only talked about poetry to a few intimates. Women were kept at a distance. Elizabeth Riddell, a poet and journalist who was one of the few women who worked at *Smith's Weekly*, summed up most women's feelings about Slessor: 'Ken was a cold fish and the man least like a poet you could possibly imagine.'

He may not have loved women but his great love was Kings Cross. He lived in many apartments in the area over three decades and wrote prose pieces in praise of Kings Cross that were to define its allure for many readers and how the decision to go there or to live at the Cross is, as he put it, 'expressing a state of mind'. When he did try to define its actual location his personal belief was that it encompassed Darlinghurst, Elizabeth Bay, Potts Point and the fringes of Woolloomooloo and Rushcutters Bay. His writings on the Cross infuse it with an erotic sensuousness and he is defiant in his belief – almost unique in Australian poetry of the time – that urban life can be as beautiful as any country landscape. In William Street he found the neon lights as delightful as any constellation and even the prostitutes and greasy takeaways had an uncommon beauty:

> *The red globes of light, the liquor-green,*
> *The pulsing arrows and running fire*
> *Spilt on the stones, go deeper than a stream;*
> *You find this ugly, I find it lovely.*

The refrain 'You find this ugly, I find it lovely' acts as a manifesto. It's a silent accusation against those many Australian poets for being deliberately blind to the charms and dangerous attractions of the city. Kings Cross was crucial to Slessor. The diverse range of people, restaurants, entertainments and foods energised him and made him open to experiences that his reserved self would not have had anywhere else. As a journalist he was enthralled by apartment living, which forced the individual to connect with others or face the horrible slow death of loneliness.

One of the great Australian poems is 'Five Bells', his lament for his friend Joe Lynch. In 1927 Lynch and a few of his boisterous mates caught a ferry to attend a party on the North Shore. It was on the way there that someone noticed that Joe, wearing an overcoat, its pockets filled with beer bottles, had vanished. The ferry turned around and there was a wide search for him but he was never found and was presumed drowned. Slessor, who liked Lynch's 'mad Irish humour and mad Irish rages', was grief-stricken and ten years later wrote about his dead friend. 'Five Bells' is a melancholy meditation at night, while Slessor looks out at Sydney Harbour and hears the cold hard fact of time – the five bells or half-past ten bell, rung from a ship at its moorings below his apartment. His Lynch had '… gaunt chin and pricked eye' and told

... raging tales
Of Irish kings and English perfidy,
And dirtier perfidy of publicans
Groaning to God from Darlinghurst.

This moving poem about the relentless movement of time is not only an elegy for Lynch but also a requiem for Slessor's youth when the world held so much dreamy promise and possibilities. It was a time when Kings Cross invigorated him and, because he was in his twenties, '[it was] the right age for appreciating indigestible food, dubious drinks, prehensile women, exhausting conversation, hair-raising gymnastics and about two hours' sleep a night.'

Even when he had departed the Cross to Chatswood on Sydney's North Shore, after having lived in the area for forty years, he still was drawn to it and penned a luscious love note to it in 1965's *Life at the Cross*:

> *King's Cross, with its 100,000 human beings, cats, dogs and budgerigars packed into a square mile of hilltop in the heat of Sydney, is one of the most thickly populated focal points of white men's habitation on the face of the earth. Layer upon layer of humanity lives, loves, suffers, exults, despairs or dies at every moment in the great antheap of its brick and concrete. The streets are perpetually crowded day and night, 1 am or 1 pm, not only with residents but with equally vast swarms of 'foreigners', visitors, tourists, adventurers, merrymakers, gourmandisers, businessmen, tradesmen, conmen, longhairs, shorthairs, beatniks. Honeymooners, housewives, de facto wives, policemen, firemen, ambulancemen, sailors, millionaires, crackpots and deadbeats.*

Many people who have left the Cross for the suburbs return years later only to find that the area has changed and it doesn't seem as exciting or as potent as they remembered; their criticisms of the changes are really mourning for their youth. Slessor felt the same. Like many long-term residents he thought of it as his personal fiefdom. His affection for it lasted all his life: 'Whether it was any better or worse than today's King's Cross I wouldn't know. But I loved every inch of it.'

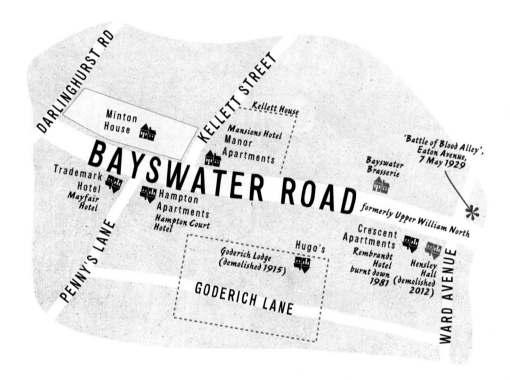

FOR GEORGE SPROD, WRITING ABOUT Bayswater Road in the late
1980s, the two main hotels, the Mansions and Hampton Court, both
built in the 1930s, had become seedy parodies of their former splendid
selves. The major attraction for George was a large terrace house a
few doors down from the Mansions. It was a brothel called the Nevada
and boasted 'Australia's Largest Bed'. The prostitutes would stand on
the balcony wearing only lingerie or mini-skirts and wink at the men
below or brazenly shout out to them to come and test out the bed. At
the time the only restaurant of any significance was the Bayswater
Brasserie, which had opened in 1982. Influenced by Parisian
brasseries it had tessellated floors, simple wooden chairs and tables
and a bar out the back. It became the home of the long lunch, where
tipsy diners stayed on for dinner. It was a much-loved haunt of film
producers, directors, writers, publishers, actors, businessmen and
shady characters organising deals. One of the most attractive features
was not the food, but the broad-minded friendly staff led by Sunny,
a cheerful Thai who stayed for twenty years after arriving in Sydney
without a work visa. For its regulars it was simply known as 'the
Office'.

Before the 1960s the road was considered a stylish part of the
Cross but after the Second World War, it became a by-word for
sleaze and excess; a party-hangout at night with sex, drink and
illegal gambling and casinos up until the late 1980s at 17, 20 and 26
Bayswater Road. Since 2000 the road has undergone a remarkable
conversion. Even the Brasserie underwent a refit in 2002; the ugly
deli bar was replaced it with an oyster bar, and the back room given a
sleek make-over. They broke the 20-year-old tradition of leaving the
tables bare by having white linen and paper.

It was only natural that this was where Mandy and I would have
our wedding reception. I had spent a considerable amount of money
there during the late 1980s and early 1990s and, when we were
courting, Mandy and I were frequently the last to leave of a night,

having consumed much liquor and scant food. We were married at St John's Anglican church in Darlinghurst Road by the Reverend Greg Thompson who, much to the displeasure of the church hierarchy, dispensed charity to the homeless and disturbed. (His slip of the tongue, 'lead us into temptation', at the wedding ceremony was probably his unconscious religious ideology.) Afterwards the congregation of about eighty walked to the Bayswater Brasserie, led by a jazz band, and had a memorable reception, which included live music from 1930s swing to a Nine Inch Nails song, the chorus of which – 'I want to fuck you like an animal' – everyone, including the staff, sang along to. My last memory of the reception was waiting in the taxi as Mandy's girlfriends heaved her on their shoulders and carried her outside, minus her high heels, so that she was thrown in the car, dirty feet first.

In 2003 there was a proposal for a mega-brothel in the former 40-room Barclay Hotel. It had cost $7.5 million to buy and the new owners said they would have a 29-room five-star brothel with $2.5 million spent on the refit and would include a licensed bar and restaurant, with the brothel staffed by fifty sex workers at any one time. The Council objected and the plan didn't eventuate – probably just as well, as over the next few years the majority of the brothels on the road went broke. There are now only two or three left. For a couple of years Dancers, the pole dancing club on the corner of Bayswater Road and Ward Avenue, played host to the New South Wales heats of Miss Pole Dance Australia. But it closed soon afterwards and re-opened as the Lincoln after extensive renovations costing $10 million. It had an art deco theme with black and gold décor, several bar areas, a downstairs dance spot, and upstairs a dimly lit lounge/supper club with white and caramel art deco armchairs and dining tables with crisp damask. The refit didn't work and it closed.

This didn't stop many other restaurants from opening up on the strip, including Hugo's Lounge, the modern Mexican Barrio Chino, and contemporary rotisserie Concrete Blonde. The only time I went to Hugo's was to propose to Mandy. It was a softly lit space with deep comfy seats, handsome staff, glowing table lamps and exotic furnishings that made it hard to tell if it were a restaurant or lounge. Most of the diners were under thirty and many of the girls seemed to be models, judging by their walk (the long legs moving forward with the top half of the body following behind). The staff called you 'guys' whatever your gender. When I went to the toilet to calm myself, because I was so nervous, there were two men and one girl in a toilet cubicle sniffing cocaine. Before I could propose I drank enough to quell my jitters. When I eventually asked Mandy to marry me she smiled and said, 'What took you so long?'

The restaurateurs in Bayswater Road were determined it become an over-35s dining mecca. Peter Polovin, of Concrete Blonde, commented that the restaurant owners were helping to change the reputation of the precinct: 'We're all coming together to try and make this place a real eat street.' Barrio Chino was once the pricey Darley Street Thai, run by the highly influential chef David Thompson, who revolutionised Thai cooking in Australia. The new owners turned it into a place described by one restaurant reviewer as 'a rough and ready, dark and loud drinking den'. Concrete Blonde had a 'rustic-industrial fit-out' with a metal studded bar, shiny exposed ducting, a glass wall of wine bottles and cow-hide walls. The food was described as having Mexican, Mediterranean and Asian influences. As I discovered, the chicken and meat cooked on a state-of-the art rotisserie was pleasant but not exceptional, the servings small and the lighting so dim that it was hard to know exactly what you were eating. For all its owner's optimism, the restaurant went bust.

This is not say that Bayswater Road as a foodie destination thrilled all critics. The *Sunday Telegraph* reviewer Elizabeth Meryment wrote:

Walking up Bayswater Road at 10 pm on a Friday is an eye-
opener. Girls channelling Kim Kardashian on a bad night spilled
from the nearby bars and clubs, their bum-high skirts unable
to disguise mountains of fluttering cellulite on their fake tanned
legs. Pissed blokes stood around ogling the girls, with the luckier
ones getting a handful of that delightful cellulite. Bouncers
observed this soft porn performance with indifference.

Dismayed by the location, she wondered why 'chefs and restaurateurs make the real estate decisions they do'. Meryment craved a quiet and 'respectable' dining street, something she felt Kings Cross could never provide.

She had dined at the Ortolan on Bayswater, which had opened on the former Bayswater Brasserie site, after the Brasserie had suddenly and mysteriously closed its doors. The Ortolan was a curious beast. The casual front verandah area become a fine dining room with a $130 ten-course degustation menu and out the back, on the deck, was a less expensive French bistro. Eating there was a dispiriting experience. The front room on the night we ate there was empty, except for a couple at one table, and the staff, seemingly under sufferance, also had to serve us in the bistro. I grabbed a chance to have lamb's brains for $16. They were fried and dry with a bland sauce and nothing else. The portions were smaller than those served in the front. Despite it trying to have a casual bistro ambience the waiters were, like the maitre d', stiffly formal and humourless, as if the food was a sacred experience rather than a part of an enjoyable night out. It was no surprise when the Ortolan curled up and died of its own solemnity.

The Mansions closed, to be replaced by apartments called the Manor, and as if to cleanse it of all associations with Kings Cross, the tagline for the Manor is: *Get a (potts) point of view!* Across from the derelict Mansions is the Minton building, which had been saved from becoming a hostel for three hundred backpackers. It's now suites of up-market offices on the second and third storeys and on the ground floor are shops and cafés.

Down the road there is the august and imposing row of the Bayswater terrace buildings, most of them bars and clubs, including the World Bar (a backpackers' favourite for its cheap drinks and casual atmosphere), Le Panic and Candy's Apartment, which features live bands and DJs, the latter describing itself as 'a club that dares and wins by pushing the limits and barriers on music genres. Nu-Wave, underground and cutting edge, distinctly electro with solid influences that include House (and its sub-genres), Rock and Hip Hop and when the time is right even a solid set of party tunes.' The eclectic music mix is a long way from the single-minded jazz clubs of the 1960s and grungy rock and roll venues like the Manzil Room.

These bars and clubs are opposite a sterile U-shaped group of buildings at 31–35, including serviced apartments, Hugo's and coffee bars. Once it was the site of the Rembrandt Hotel. The multi-storey complex burnt down in 1981, causing nineteen deaths. The fire was apparently an accident and not the result of deliberate arson. Next to it was and still is Hensley Hall, a rotting hulk of a building, boarded up and empty. It was a 36-room private hotel/boarding house built in 1912 and originally known as Mercedes. Advertisements for it began to appear in the 1930s, emphasising its history (*Established a quarter of a century*), its cheapness (*Very moderate breakfast and terms for permanent or casual guests*) and extras (*Unfailing hot water, laundry facilities free*). Some time during the Second World War the name was changed to Hensley Hall. Its main inducement was the low rent – a sign the place was in irreversible decline. The author of *Razor* (about the Razor gang era), Larry Writer, lived there in 1957 at the age of seven when his parents separated, forcing Writer and his mother to room with her sister in her flat. His major memory is of 'people sitting around in their singlets and braces watching the horse racing on television'.

By the 1980s Hensley Hall was falling into disrepair. Over the decade dozens of tenants were evicted by the owner, except for five former soldiers. Eventually only two remained: Ernie Joyce, who was a Rat of Tobruk, and his mate Austin Roonan. After Austin died Ernie was too frightened to live in the increasingly decrepit building on his own, so he moved out. Instead of the building becoming a home to squatters as locals thought would happen, a man called Barry Minhinnick shifted in as a self-proclaimed caretaker–resident in 1992. With his hint of Asian features and long flowing greying hair he was a common sight either playing guitar outside Hensley Hall, riding his bike through the Cross or developing his extraordinary 'art' garden on a narrow strip at the side of the building on Ward Avenue. The garden was created out of sculptures and chairs, and the plant beds were made from old spring-beds, ovens, fencing and found objects salvaged from construction sites and dumpsters. It was a luxuriant and eccentric garden and even featured on the television show *Gardening Australia* in a 2011 segment called 'A Kings Cross Treasure', as indeed it was.

In the same year he was on television Minhinnick was threatened with eviction. A friend of mine, the photographer John Webber, and Violet Tingle, author of the informative blog *My Darling Darlinghurst*, toured the hall. John had first seen it in the middle 1990s, when as a rock photographer he paid Minhinnick $100 to use the ornate stairwell as a background for the rock band the Screaming Jets. In those days the stairs were in good condition but by the time John saw them again they were treacherous. Everything about the building was unsafe, with rotting floorboards, frail ceilings, buckets for the rain, crumbling stairs, falling plaster and aggressive rats.

Minhinnick fought his eviction in the courts but by the following year, after twenty years of being the caretaker and only person living in the building, he was kicked out. The name Hensley Hall was removed from the façade but you can still see the ghostly outline of the letters, as if the building itself is fighting the threat of anonymity. It's locked up now and cyclone fencing covers the windows to keep out vagrants and squatters. The garden has been trashed and little remains of its former beauty. There are rumours that the building will be converted into fifty-four apartments, although apparently the City of Sydney has insisted that the façade, an important historic feature of Bayswater Road, should be kept.

Whether this happens or not Hensley Hall joins a long line of buildings with historical associations whose demolition will sever a connection with the past and will exist only in the memories of an increasingly diminishing older generation of locals.

THE NEON LIGHTS ARE
BEING TURNED ON AGAIN

THE ONLY MAJOR NIGHTCLUB OPEN to celebrate the end of the war was the Roosevelt in Orwell Street. It had started out as the Barcroft cabaret in 1943 but quickly gained a reputation for sly-grog and prostitution. Its unsavoury character even came to the attention of Prime Minister Curtin. It was declared a disorderly house and closed, to reopen as the Roosevelt, a swanky, glamorous nightclub with a dance floor, excellent food and cigarette girls in short, sexy skirts. It was *the* place to be seen, and men wore suits or tuxedos and women gorgeous evening gowns. The Roosevelt had swing bands, late night floor shows, chorus girls, and superb singers like Nellie Small and Barbara James, who lived in the Cross and was one of the first singers to use the microphone to shape and style her intimate and erotic vocals.

On 15 August 1945 there were so many people wanting to get tickets to the nightclub that over a thousand lined up in Orwell Street from 10 am to 8 pm, but many missed out. Those that got in found it was so packed that dancing was impossible. Hundreds of people who were unable to get in danced outside in Orwell Street to the music of the band inside. The man who made all this happen was Abraham 'Abe' Saffron, a man who had made his money selling sly grog. He was born of Russian–Jewish origins in Sydney in 1919, the fourth of five children. His father ran a drapery store, a vocation that didn't appeal to young Abe, whose criminal tendencies started early when, at the age of eight, he sold black market cigarettes. At nineteen he was fined £5 for allowing premises to be used for gambling. Two years later he was sentenced to six months hard labour for receiving stolen goods. The magistrate gave him a suspended sentence, hinting that it would be a good idea if Saffron joined the Army to fight for his country.

He enlisted in the Citizen Military Forces but never served overseas. It took him two years to reach the rank of corporal and even then he was considered so useless that the Army discharged him. He quickly saw that there were fortunes to be made in sly grog, especially in a nightclub, when patrons would pay a premium for a drink. He was only twenty-three when he took over the running of the Roosevelt. A few months later he bought the Gladstone Hotel in William Street, just a five-minute walk from his nightclub, but, because an individual was entitled to only one hotel licence, he convinced his family to pretend it was their licence. Beer was in short supply in the war and hotels were given a quota of bottles, but by buying up hotels Saffron cornered the market, selling the illegal booze out of the nightclub and also to sly groggeries.

Only 5 feet 6 inches tall, he had a swarthy complexion and grey reptilian eyes. His sense of the truth was slippery, he had a formidable priapic drive and a greed that would result in beatings, even murder. He had a shrewd and masterful grasp of the weaknesses of others based on his belief that every woman and man had a failing or moral flaw that he could exploit, whether it be sex or money, the only two things that he cared about himself. In order for his budding empire to survive and flourish he bribed the police and important officials and he picked up a valuable lesson from Phil 'the Jew' Jeffs's experiences in running the 50-50 club: to also pay off the politicians who in turn controlled the police. He became so successful doing this that he ended up corrupting the New South Wales police force, the judiciary and even premiers themselves.

But that was to come. Kings Cross tried to reclaim its pre-war glory now that rationing was over. The delicatessens were acclaimed for their range of products: German liverwurst, Italian mortadella, tinned Italian mushrooms, herring fillets soaked in wine and Swedish and Russian caviar. The locals were proud of the variety and vast selection of food; as one merchant said, with a touch of superiority, 'We cater to sophisticated eating. We try to please the palate of fastidious Europeans and advanced Australians.' This was not just the opinion of a smarmy local, others thought it too. The Brisbane *Courier-Mail* recommended that some Queensland storekeepers would benefit if they visited the Cross and 'learned the A.B.C. of food delicacies'.

On the surface things may have returned to normal, but this was a different era from the 1920s and 30s. Building stagnated; in fact, only one new block of flats appeared in the 1950s. Neon lighting banned during the war was not as brilliant as before. Few new restaurants opened, though in 1954 residents were excited by the addition of two new ones, both serving up continental food, one with the bonus of a gypsy band. The City of Sydney talked up this development, promising that the new venues 'would help restore the pre-war nightlife of Kings Cross. The neon lights of Kings Cross are rapidly being turned on again.' When 3000 American sailors from Admiral Halsey's 'Goodwill Fleet' arrived in 1954 they had all heard of the famous Cross, but those who had experienced it during the war remarked that it was much quieter now.

But it still beguiled and enticed those who wanted to flee the torpid world of suburbia. One woman left her husband to become an escapologist. Mrs Jean Moore, twenty-three, married William Moore, thirty-eight, in 1940. He was a carpenter and she a waitress.

After the marriage they lived in Castlecrag, but Jean felt suffocated in the suburbs and told her husband she wanted to live in Kings Cross. She stuck it out for a year and then suddenly left him after she developed what she called 'itchy feet'. She found her vocation in the Cross when she was drawn to acrobatics and escapology.

As an acrobat and escapologist she performed at carnivals and in clubs. One of her acts was to swing twenty feet in the air over a fire and wriggle free of a straightjacket. One time while she was performing, the fire burned through a rope supporting the scaffolding from which she was swinging. The scaffolding collapsed and she fell into the fire, breaking an arm and injuring her back. Her husband rushed to her hospital bedside on hearing of the accident and begged her to come back to him. She said she might return, but 'only for a week or so' as she would undoubtedly get itchy feet again. He waited for her but she never returned. Instead he received a letter telling him she was pregnant to another man and would marry him once he returned from active service. 'Please, please,' she wrote in a second letter, 'leave the way clear for somebody else. I know you don't want me.' The stigma of adultery didn't bother her at all and she didn't contest the divorce.

For a woman like Faith Bandler, the daughter of a South Sea Islander who had been blackbirded from Vanuatu in 1883 to cut sugar cane as a virtual slave, Kings Cross represented one of the few parts of Australia where she was accepted without reservations. Her father had escaped the cane fields of Far North Queensland, married a Scottish–Indian woman and started a farm in Murwillumbah where Bandler grew up. She worked as a dressmaker's apprentice after she left school. During the Second World War she served in the Australian Women's Army working on fruit farms. After the war she shifted to the Cross to study music and attend WEA classes to further her education. She was exhilarated by the people, the nightclubs and cafés. She had *her* own coffee lounge, the Arabian, where 'you could sit there all night, over one cup of coffee, and they wouldn't dare disturb you. It had very much a touch of the Old Vienna where you didn't go to drink the coffee. You went to met your mates and read the newspapers … I'd go up there with this trek of men trotting up the stairs behind me and we'd sit out on the verandah … and look down onto Darlinghurst Road.' The intense and invigorating discussions in coffee lounges and flats helped her to articulate and refine her politics, especially in regard to indigenous issues.

An attractive woman, she was always surrounded by male admirers. She had a long affair with a Finnish sailor and in 1952 married Hans Bandler, an engineer and Jewish refugee from Vienna. Before long they shifted to the northern suburbs. She would lead the campaign to remove discriminatory provisions from the Australian constitution, which resulted in the 1967 referendum granting voting rights to Aborigines. When she reflected on her life she was always nostalgic for her times in the Cross. It was not only that she was young and carefree, but there was an egalitarian element to the area that was not found anywhere else in Australia.

For the locals the pleasures were many. George Johnston, returned from overseas as a war correspondent, and still married to his first wife, lived in sin with Charmian Clift, an unmarried woman, a state of affairs that would have had them socially ostracised anywhere else. Like Bandler, the main characters in his novel *Clean Straw for Nothing* feel that they have discovered places that belong only to them. They choose a flower stall as '*our* flower stall' and designate their favourite coffee lounge as belonging solely to them, '…we can hear *our* songs on the jukebox, "Laura" and … "Night and Day".' The Cross had a beauty and charm, especially for lovers: 'And in the evenings we can walk through the light-dazzle and cacophony under the bronzing leaves, and nobody takes any notice of us or cares who we are.' But John-ston also reckoned that there was another, more malevolent side to the Cross, which was coarse, tough and 'poised on the edge of violence'.

He was right. Although the Cross was no longer riddled with black marketeers and racketeers, there was always violence in the air. Belligerence and vendettas were common in the criminal underworld. One such hoodlum was Stanley Birch. He couldn't stay out of trouble. In 1942 he was shot in the stomach in a shoot-out at a two-up school. Three years later he was getting drunk with a dozen men and women in a flat when an argument broke out. Guns were drawn, four shots were fired and a bullet pierced Birch's liver. The police only learned that there had been a shoot-out when the unlucky ruffian arrived by taxi at hospital near death.

These gangsters and malevolent oafs operated in their own criminal world and residents were seldom affected by their ac-tions. It was as if the criminals operated in a parallel universe that didn't impinge on locals – but when it did, the results could be horrifying.

In 1952 Ernest 'Dickie' Devine was a 48-year-old hoodlum nicknamed 'the Great Lover' who had a reputation as a Casanova with eclectic tastes in women. He didn't care if they were young or old, as long as they had sex with him. A brute, he had been jailed many times for offences such as assault, robbery, carrying a loaded gun and housebreaking. For three years he lived with a divorcee, Joyce Vining, who was thirteen years younger than him. She had two children to her former husband and a daughter to Devine before they separated.

A few months after the separation, at about six in the even-ing, Devine went to Vining's flat, which she shared with her three children, her mother and stepfather. They were preparing dinner when Devine turned up, demanding that Vining come back to him. When she said no, he took out his revolver and fired three bullets into her head at close range. She collapsed onto the floor and lay still. Devine took one long last look at her and then put a bullet through his own forehead. A crowd of about two thousand gawking, excited locals had gathered outside the apartment block by the time the police and ambulance arrived. Both Vining and Devine were rushed to hospital. She died as soon as she was admitted. Devine's condition was so critical that doctors couldn't operate. He breathed his last the following day.

Illegal gaming prospered, especially baccarat schools. It had become blatantly obvious that the police were deliberately turning a blind eye to their existence. Despite newspapers exposing the gaming schools and publishing their addresses, they operated with impunity. One reporter watched outside a Kings Cross school while a uniformed policeman strolled by and spent several minutes in idle chit chat with the den's doorman/cockatoo before sauntering off on his beat.

Sydney's major baccarat school in Kellett Street was run by 'Joe the Pig' and 'the Greek', who had no trouble with the police whom they bribed. They had bought the Kings Cross den when the founder Siddy Kelly – who introduced baccarat into Sydney in 1944 – died in 1948. Takings after Kelly's death were so lucrative that the two owners were able to pay a relative of Kelly's a £50 a week pension. Their clients were racecourse gamblers, crooks and the general public. The house took four shillings out of every pound wagered. On a big night when £10,000 was bet, the house took £2000.

A problem for the honest cops was that the dens were heavily barricaded and by the time they had smashed their way in, the gamblers were pretending to play ludo, draughts and dominoes and openly laughing at the raiders. In order to surprise the gamblers, police resorted to unusual tactics. For one early morning raid in Roslyn Gardens the police drugged an Alsatian guard dog which was kept in the backyard of the gaming house and forced their way in through the rear of the three-storey building. Forty-five people were arrested, including Jack Davey, one of the most famous radio comperes of the day and a gambling addict. Nine of those charged with being found in a common gaming house were women. More than a thousand pounds was taken from the premises. Most of the players were fined three to five pounds and their names printed in the newspapers. Nearly all the women were described as domestics; the men were clerks, dentists, salesmen and shopkeepers, but most described themselves as labourers. A 76-year-old man was fined £25 for having acted as a doorkeeper of a common gaming house.

Drugs were still available as before the war, but marijuana was gradually becoming the drug of choice to a small but growing circle. The police reported that teenagers were smoking it. A kitchenhand, Eric Cook, was caught with marijuana in his possession. It turned out he was a dealer and sold it to restaurant staff. Found guilty, he was sentenced to twelve months hard labour. The detective who arrested him described marijuana as the worst drug that could be let loose on the community. It was a drug of exhilaration that removed all inhibitions and anyone under its influence gave in to immediate gratification 'in all its forms', which is why people considered it a 'sex drug'. It was thought that if it were given to children it would cause them to become violent. A 36-year-old Maltese wharf labourer was arrested when police saw him staggering about the streets of Kings Cross. After searching his flat they found a partly smoked marijuana cigarette, plus cocaine and more marijuana secreted in the toe of a shoe stashed under his bed. Cocaine hadn't entirely disappeared. Chemist Henry Eyre, forty-three, lived in Kings Cross Road and had been an addict for two years. He pleaded guilty to having stolen a total of 324 grains of cocaine from pharmacies where he worked as a relief chemist, and three charges of having administered the drug to himself. His addiction was obvious but, as he said to the sympathetic magistrate, 'It is correct that the drugs were taken, but it caused no suffering to any other than myself.' He was sentenced to a year in the hope he could be cured of his addiction.

Prostitutes worked the hotel foyers of the main hotels like the Mayfair, Mansions and Oriental, some of them housewives who commuted to the Cross during the day to earn extra money. One man who enjoyed their favours was the Third Secretary of the Soviet Embassy in Canberra. Vladimir Petrov would frequent the Cross when he was in Sydney. It was the Cold War and 'it seemed like the Kings Cross and eastern suburbs area was a hotbed of spies working for one side or the other'.

ASIO's Sydney headquarters was in the Agincourt building down in Wylde Street in Potts Point and they had two rooms in the elegant art deco Cahors, with its unique blue-tiled frontage and blond brick facade. Brigadier Charles Spry, chief of the spy agency, believed Petrov was willing to defect. In 1954 he took him out to many dinners and plied him with whisky. Petrov liked a drink and would often eat at the Adria café in Kings Cross Road with Feodor Nosov, a TASS journalist who lived in the Cross and was the Soviet 'handler' of Australian communist and traitor Wally Clayton. Petrov got drunk there often and when he was inebriated he was obnoxious. His other major vice was women, and Michael Bialoguski, a doctor, musician and ASIO agent, would arrange for Kings Cross prostitutes to service Petrov, sometimes in one of the Cahors apartments, the squat, chubby Russian not realising that the rooms were bugged and there was a listening station in the adjoining flat.

Eventually he was persuaded to defect in April 1954. He and

his wife were granted asylum under assumed names in return for evidence of Soviet espionage. He was quite a catch, not only for his knowledge of Soviet penetration of Australia, but also because he knew the secret codes of the Soviet Embassy which enabled ASIO to read their communications. But there was one more connection to Kings Cross. Three months later, a local café proprietor, 'quietly spoken' Joe Gottwald, who everyone agreed was the perfect double for the Russian defector, told newspapers that he feared he would be killed by 'a Communist fanatic' trying to assassinate Petrov and mistakenly kill him.

For the public, bohemianism meant artists and, as art publisher Lou Klepac once said, a whole book could be devoted to the astonishing number of them who inhabited Kings Cross and Potts Point from the 1930s to 1960s. Two of the most significant ones were Donald Friend and William Dobell. Both were gay and they spent time together when they lived a hand-to-mouth existence in London. The shy Dobell liked the gregarious Friend, but he in turn found Dobell infantile, not very intelligent and with appalling taste, although, when he relaxed with his friends, Dobell's wit could be touched with 'knife-sharp bitchiness'. Dobell returned to Australia in early 1939 and rented a flat on the corner of Roslyn Gardens and Darlinghurst Road. Friend had lived not far from Dobell's studio in a flat in Elizabeth Bay House.

Dobell thought that Australia couldn't provide the social and cultural milieu necessary for great art and reworked a lot of the material he had done in England. Though when war came, he became intrigued by the American servicemen, specially the sailors who roamed the streets of the Cross looking for women. He also painted Australian girls who came to the Cross looking for a good time and sex. His *Woman in a Hamburger* is of a heavily painted woman, her hat, long gloves and flimsy dress a striking combination of black and white, broken only by her heart-shaped red lips. She sits at a bar, cigarette in her hand, a glass of liquor and a straw before her. She has the bored and worldly air of someone who has been through this before. Behind her stands a leering American sailor. A companion painting to this is a moral commentary as strong as Hogarth's *The Rake's Progress*: *The Souvenir* shows a young single mother playing with her demonic-looking illegitimate child, a dubious souvenir of the long-departed American serviceman.

By 1957 he was famous and painted a portrait of the then 92-year-old writer Dame Mary Gilmore, who had lived at 99 Darlinghurst Road since the mid 1930s. She was the most famous woman in Australia and his painting was controversial. Gilmore looked like a piece of ancient parchment paper, beyond gender, not so much a human being but an idea of one.

Dobell had been the centre of controversy before when, in 1944, he won the Archibald for his portrait of fellow artist Joshua Smith, painted in his Kings Cross studio (the lights of Sydney Harbour can be seen in the background, and it's easy to make out Springfield Avenue as it dissolves into nocturnal murk). He made his friend look like a bug-eyed piece of ectoplasm in a brown suit. It was said that Smith was so horrified by the portrait that he wouldn't speak to Dobell, but the truth was probably that Smith had entered a portrait of Mary Gilmore and Dobell was certain that Smith was miffed he didn't win:

'He was sure his would win and mine he regarded as a joke. He got a shock when I won.'

Two unsuccessful artists, Mary Edwards and Joseph Wolinski, brought an action to overturn the award, saying it was not a portrait but 'a caricature'. Dobell admitted there was 'a slight exaggeration' in the portrait but for all intents and purposes it was a good likeness of his character and body language. The appeal failed, but Dobell was devastated by the court case. People sent him abusive letters; others spat on him in the street. The result was a nervous breakdown and a severe case of agoraphobia. His only escape was to retreat permanently to Wangi Wangi, near Lake Macquarie.

Like Dobell, Friend devoted few works to Kings Cross. On VE Day, Friend went in search of people celebrating victory but there were none, but the next day he found an amazing scene of people linking hands and dancing in the streets. His sketch of the scene has a vivid immediacy and exuberance that captured the excitement and joy. Sali Herman, another contemporary of the two, used the Cross and Woolloomooloo as subject matter, especially slums and the low life. His painting of McElhone Stairs is one of his best. The many stairs rise up from the Woolloomooloo basin, the steps dotted with sailors, children and women struggling up to the heights of Potts Point like pilgrims heading towards a sacred mountain top. Yet it's strange that these artists seldom painted the Cross, although they lived in it. One of the best depictions of an interior is Herbert Badham's picture of the Hasty Tasty, *Snack Bar*, painted in 1944. The busy restaurant is crowded with happy, gregarious people, a man eating with relish, American sailors flirting with local girls, a GI leaving arm in arm with his girlfriend, and smiling women. This is a place for gossiping, community chat, quick food, rapid turnover and quick pick-ups.

For long-term residents, Kings Cross's appeal in the somnolent Australia of the 1950s was not only its bohemians, cosmopolitanism, artists and eccentrics but also the exotic nightlife, the illegal activities of criminals, gamblers and sly grog merchants. Even though it was densely populated, it was still like a village where many knew one another. Even the plane trees contributed to the mood of the place. For the journalist and later editor of the *Women's Weekly* Dorothy Drain, the locals were 'almost entirely dependent for our signs of the seasons on the plane trees which line some of our pavements'. It was why the trees were held in affection by the residents. In summer, with neon lights shining through them, she thought they looked so pretty 'that the young poets in the coffee shops are almost moved to abandon their stark, modern rhythms and go back to nature poetry'.

WOMEN ON THE EDGE

SHE HAD ONLY SEEN HOW to load a rifle once in her life. Her hands shook as she placed the bullet into the chamber. It was 1954 and Shirley Beiger, twenty-two, beautiful, blonde, and one of Australia's top models, had had enough of her duplicitous lover, Arthur Griffith.

Beiger lived in a Kellett Street flat. Although Griffith lived with his father in Rosebery, he sometimes stayed with Beiger or Don Lee, who rented a flat in the same building. Lee, a waiter who worked at Chequers nightclub, had known Griffith for two years and Beiger for one. Earlier in the day Griffith, a 23-year-old bookmaker's assistant, had promised Beiger that he loved her and would marry her when he came back from an overseas trip. But she still had her doubts. He had been going out nights 'with the boys' and she suspected he was seeing other women. After telling Beiger he'd marry her, Griffith dressed up in his best clothes and said he was going to the dentist. Beiger's jealousy got the better of her and she rang the dentist, who told her that Griffith had no appointment that day.

She suspected he may have gone to Chequers, his favourite restaurant and nightclub, so she hurried into the city and spotted his truck parked outside. Just after half-past eight she arrived in Coogee where her mother was visiting her brother and asked her mother to accompany her into town. The mother and daughter sat in the black Ford Consul outside the nightclub on the corner of King and Pitt Streets, where they saw a grinning Griffith, arm-in-arm with a girl, head into Chequers around 11 pm. They followed him inside and Beiger told him their relationship was finished. She was sick of being the girl who washed his clothes, cooked his food, ran errands for him and even cleaned his shoes, 'so that he could be nice for other girls'.

Consumed with jealousy, anger and despair, she asked her mother to drive her to Kellett Street where she would gather Griffith's belongings and take them to Chequers. The first thing Beiger did was go to Lee's room, where she took down the .22 rifle she knew was on top of the wardrobe, found a cartridge and loaded the weapon, then hid it under her coat. She grabbed Griffith's bag of golf sticks and threw them onto the back seat. The mother and daughter drove back to the nightclub. When they arrived Beiger told her mother to go inside and tell Griffiths to come and get his things. Beiger waited in the car, holding the rifle. He came out and stuck his head inside the car. There was an argument. The barrel of the rifle was only a few inches from Griffith's forehead when it went off. The bullet shattered his skull, the force of it sending him backwards onto the pavement; he was dead before he hit the ground.

Beiger became hysterical when she saw the bloody face of her dead lover. She ran inside the nightclub, rushing down the stairs and shouting out to Lee, 'Donny, Donny, I've hurt Arthur!' Then, in a blind panic she went back up into the street and began to flee from the crime scene before a policeman stopped her.

In late November 1954, three months after the shooting, Beiger stood trial for murder. The media and the public were gripped by the case. The courtroom was packed with 200 people, some of them models. Griffith was seen as a cad whom many thought deserved to die. Women supported Beiger by waving to her or blowing kisses. Her clothes were impeccable. On the first day she wore a tight-fitting black high-necked dress and a short grey top coat and carried a small posy of roses. She wept throughout her one hour's evidence with a policewoman occasionally handing her a tablet. The judge even allowed the distraught Beiger to leave the stand so she could regain her composure. Her defence was that she had merely wanted to frighten Griffith and had forgotten the gun was on her lap. She knew she was gripping something tightly but because she was so fraught had no idea what it was. Griffith stuck his head through the window and they had a brief argument. As usual, when he won, he gave Beiger a push, which caused her to accidentally pull the trigger.

The prosecutor argued that the angle at which the bullet struck the dead man did not tally with her story. After a two-day trial the all-male jury took just two and a quarter hours to acquit her. Beiger wept on hearing the judgment and her mother cried, murmuring, 'I thank God, I thank God.' Outside the court room the women who had been unable to get in cheered on hearing the news.

The public's fascination with Beiger went beyond how a beautiful woman came to shoot her bounder of a boyfriend. There was the dubious life Beiger lived. It was clear that the closest she came to being photographed nude was when she modelled lingerie, but what appalled moralists was that she lived in a de facto relationship which, said the judge, made 'a sad although somewhat sordid picture'. It seemed to people that part of Beiger's problem was she hadn't married Griffith, and in such situations women invariably got hurt. As one newspaper commented, 'In such an atmosphere reactions of jealousy, distrust, and fear of insecurity tend to become abnormal.'

There was also the Kings Cross taint. What sort of woman

would live there in sin? The area seemed to bring out violence in women that wouldn't be tolerated anywhere else. There were even brawls between females. Just after the war, four women, two of them wearing scanty clothes exposing their mid-riffs, fought in Victoria Street. While 2000 people egged them on, the screaming women punched and pulled each other's hair. While the spectators were enjoying the donnybrook, pickpockets set to work, stealing £11 from two soldiers. Police had to force their way through the crowd to reach the women, who were later charged with offensive behaviour.

They could be as violent as males. Dorothy Craig was charged with intent to murder two men. The 26-year-old was married to a seaman with a criminal past, John Christie. They had a tempestuous relationship and he was often cruel towards her. They had been drinking with Christie's mate, Alfred Laffey, a labourer, also with a criminal record, on New Year's Day 1945. Things were becoming heated and there were increasingly bitter comments between the two men and Craig. At about 2 pm seven-year-old Vince Martyr and his father arrived at the Kellett Street flat in a taxi. When they entered, the trio were arguing. Craig's face showed the effects of a beating. Vince's father surreptitiously gave a revolver to Craig and fled the apartment, leaving his young son behind, who was at a loss because he didn't know these men or the woman. Craig hid the gun in her frock until she could put up with the men's abuse no longer. Then she pulled out the revolver and shot Christie in the shoulder and Laffey in the right arm. The wounded men staggered outside with the young boy following. They hailed a taxi and, as Vince said in evidence in court, 'I went … with the two strange men to hospital.'

By the time Craig came to trial, Christie was in jail on a charge of having stabbed a man to death in an underworld mêlée in a Kings Cross flat. He was sentenced to ten years. In court Craig admitted she had fired the two shots but said it had been in self-defence. She was acquitted.

It was not only women shooting men but women shooting at each other. One early afternoon in 1951 residents of St Julian's flats heard shots in a second-floor flat and called the police. A Constable Cooper rushed there on his motorbike and ran up the stairs where he saw a woman, 43-year-old Patsy Day, on the landing, aiming a smoking revolver and firing bullets at a glass door. There were also shots coming from inside the flat. The glass door had been shattered by the bullets. Cooper arrived as Day was going to shoot again. He crept towards her but on hearing the policeman she swung around as if to shoot him. Cooper grabbed her right arm, which held the gun, and snatched a hammer from her left hand. At the same time there was an explosion from inside the flat and a bullet blew plaster off the wall, just missing him. Determined to do his duty, he marched Day into the flat where he saw a woman, Barbara Thompson, with a repeating rifle, while a man, Kevin Connolly, stood nearby, his arm bloodied from the flying glass. Still furious with him, Day shouted, 'It was about time somebody did him in!' and added that Connolly had been violent towards her and had been sponging off her for years and she was sick of it.

Day had become pathologically jealous of the 30-year-old Thompson and the trio had been involved in a feud for some time. The younger woman said that 'Patsy Day had gone mad' and started firing into the flat trying to kill Connolly. Thompson had returned fire in order to frighten her. These weren't middle-class women like Shirley Beiger – all three had been in trouble with the law. Both women were bailed and were to report daily at the police station, but given their enmity, they were to do this at separate times.

Since the 1920s Kings Cross was seen as a moral danger for

women, especially single women, either tempted into sinning or victims of a man's betrayal like Shirley Beiger. The Cross attracted women with 'itchy feet' and enabled them to express themselves in ways that were puzzling and even abhorrent to many Australians. Police had been horrified by how young women would come into the Cross and fling themselves at American servicemen not only willing but desperate to fornicate with them. It seemed that the area contaminated women so deeply they lost their moral bearings, their sense of decency and respectability.

If anyone epitomised the dangers of the Cross for women then it was Abe Saffron. Sly grog made him rich and he could now indulge his insatiable sex drive. He was inordinately proud of his penis and as a party trick would whip it out and compare it favourably to those of his cronies. He was married to a long-suffering wife who tried to commit suicide several times because of his compulsive adultery. He could be charming in the practised manner of the criminal who enjoys his own performance as much as the person who is charmed. If he couldn't get want he wanted then he was vicious and unprincipled. The writer Roberta Sykes, who performed a snake act in the clubs on Darlinghurst Road, once rejected his advances. He made sure she didn't work again and there was the unspoken threat of being beaten up, a threat she took seriously, given that he like to watch his thugs bash any of his mistresses seen with another man.

He had a penchant for orgies and sadomasochism. He held sex parties, many of them in the Appin private hotel in Springfield Avenue, which he owned. On 24 June 1956, when he was thirty-six, he and two other men and two women held an orgy at Palm Beach, where he enjoyed whipping the girls and he in turn was beaten. He also took photographs of the sexual high jinks to sell. The party moved to a Kings Cross flat where he again whipped the women and photographed them. A few months later one of the women had a falling out with Saffron and told the police what had happened. The men were charged with scandalous conduct and the other woman was charged with 'scandalous conduct which openly outraged public decency by taking part in lewd, obscene and disgusting exhibitions'. The police also found pornography in Saffron's flat. The prosecutor called him 'completely sexually depraved with no moral sense whatsoever'. Nine more men and another woman were also arrested. Saffron had the added charge of committing 'an unnatural offence' (sodomy) with a woman. All told, eleven men and 'three pretty girls', one of them 'coloured', were up on morals charges. Through bribery and the intimidation of witnesses, all the charges were mysteriously dropped, except for possession of obscene publications, for which Saffron was fined £10. He appealed and won.

According to Tony Reeves's biography of Saffron, *Mr Sin*, not long afterwards Saffron, who now believed that pornography was going to be big business, bought 35,000 pornographic books and magazines. He made an estimated one and a half million dollars profit from their sales. In 1994 the National Crime Authority was to report that Saffron had been and was still 'heavily involved in vice, obtaining financial benefit from vice engaged in by others. He controls prostitutes. He produces and imports pornography and distributes around Australia.'

Far from being cowed by the revelation of his sex parties at the trial, he saw them as a lucrative source of money and, most importantly, as a way of blackmailing people. He held orgies and arranged for men to indulge in whatever sex acts they desired. The parties were attended by gay men, S&M aficionados, and others with sexual kinks that would have outraged mainstream Australia. And in order to fulfil the dissolute tastes of some of the clientele, he brought in young children to service them. His guests included businessmen, politicians, judges and lawyers. They thought the orgies were secret but Saffron had the sessions photographed through a two-way mirror. It was a masterstroke that only a man with the amorality of an Iago could come up with. If any of his guests were ever to side against him, especially lawyers, politicians and judges, he had the visual evidence to blackmail them. One notable example, as Reeve documents in *Mr Sin*, was alleged to have been the activist Federal Court Justice Lionel Murphy. He had a weakness for young Filipina girls which Saffron serviced. Murphy became one of Saffron's blackmail victims and the evidence was kept for safe keeping when the need arose to pull the judge back in line or ask for a favour.

The success of his pornography business, the sly grog and the sex parties convinced Saffron that he could continue to push the moral boundaries of conservative Australia and the only place where that could happen was Kings Cross which, because he paid off officials, policemen and top politicians, was becoming a law unto itself. He also recognised more quickly than anyone else that the conservative morality of the times was fraying and he would become wealthy by exploiting women for pornography and prostitution.

The fear that police had in the 1940s that striptease clubs would open in Kings Cross was realised by Saffron who at the end of the 1950s planned to open the first legal strip club. Called Staccato, it was only a few doors down from the old Roosevelt site at 6–8 Orwell Street. It was a hit. Saffron opened a number of striptease joints or had a financial investment in them. Women became a commodity, whether they worked for him as prostitutes or else stripped naked in clubs full of men. By commercialising sex he altered the public's perception of the Cross. Its reputation grew as a depraved place of sexual excess and debauchery, where girls and women who ventured out were at risk of becoming entangled in its insidious vices. If the moral guardians were outraged by what was happening in the Cross in the 1950s, then they were going to be appalled by what was to come in the next decades.

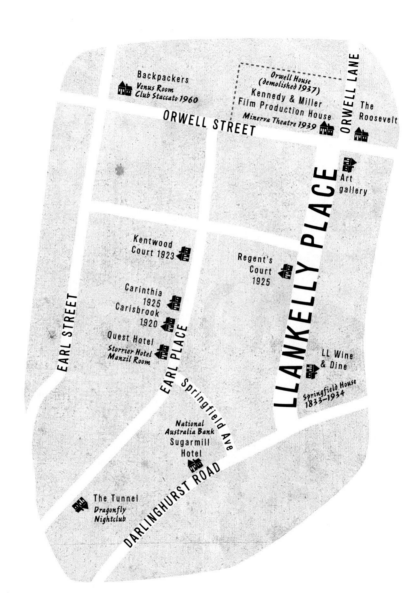

Backpackers
Venus Room
Club Staccato 1960

Orwell House
(demolished 1937)
Kennedy & Miller
Film Production House
Minerva Theatre 1939

ORWELL LANE

The
Roosevelt

ORWELL STREET

Art
gallery

LLANKELLY PLACE

Kentwood
Court 1923

Regent's
Court
1925

Carinthia
1925
Carisbrook
1920

Quest Hotel
Storrier Hotel
Manzil Room

EARL STREET

EARL PLACE

LL Wine
& Dine

Springfield House
1833-1934

Springfield Ave

National
Australia Bank
Sugarmill
Hotel

DARLINGHURST ROAD

The Tunnel
Dragonfly
Nightclub

ON BOXING DAY 2000, a woman, woken up by screams, peered
out of her apartment window in Llankelly Place and saw two young
Korean men kneeling submissively on the ground while they were
slapped and kicked in the face by two other Koreans. She grabbed
a video camera and filmed the enforcers punching, slapping and
kicking the kneeling men outside the dilapidated Village Centre. A
third thug bashed a young Korean woman, who screamed and wept.
He eventually knocked her down before stealing her wallet. When
the police finally arrived the victims were bruised and bleeding but
none of them made a complaint, so the police were unable to make
an arrest. The enforcers told them it was a Korean matter; the young
woman had married outside her clan and class and they wished to
settle the dispute amongst themselves. The hoodlums were allowed
to walk away without being arrested. The woman who filmed the
incident told reporters:

'This happens all the time. The streets are theirs.'

By that she meant the Korean criminals. During the 1990s they
regarded bleak Llankelly and Earl Places as their private domain.
One night in 1997 in Earl Street, outside the Ewha Karaoke Club, two
Korean gangsters were made to kneel and bow their heads while they
were ceremoniously beaten with clubs and kicked. After being beaten
the victims were dragged off the street into the Ewha Club where they
were forced to kneel while the group hit them with wooden clubs,
one of the yobs shouting, 'You have the hide to come here. You die!'
Both victims, one twenty-seven and the other thirty-one, died of their
wounds in St Vincent's Hospital. The police arrested the manager of
the club on two counts of murder. Another three Korean thugs were
eventually tracked down and arrested.

The Springfield Village Centre, constructed in the late 1960s, had
once housed popular food, clothing and tourist shops, but by the time
the Korean gangsters had claimed the strip as their own, the Centre
was in a sorry condition. Most of the shops were closed, the waxworks

had long gone (together with its gruesome portrayal of a shark attack victim with a bloody left stump and savaged right leg), and pigeons nested on the second floor; their droppings splattered everywhere and stank. There was a small, dispiriting supermarket, a tawdry TAB, a Korean restaurant and a pinball parlour where heroin addicts shot up, dealers sold drugs and junkies slept.

The strip may have looked dismal and depressing of a day but of a night it hummed with menace. A producer friend took a short cut one early evening down Earl Place only to be mugged by a mob of Aboriginal boys. Drugs were openly sold in Springfield Avenue and tourists and even locals tried to avoid the area at night. It was labelled 'the epicentre of sleaze'.

By 2012 Llankelly Place was almost unrecognisable. The Hayson Group bought the old Village Centre, demolished it and erected a block that houses an excellent greengrocery and fish shop, plus another sixteen speciality shops and five levels of office space that overlook both Springfield Avenue and Llankelly Place, which now has coffee shops, bakeries, restaurants, a voguish hairdresser, plus the Funkhouse backpackers.

If anything typified the gentrification it is the LL Wine and Dine restaurant. Started by three brothers, Matt, Chris and Tim Barge, it opened up in February 2010 serving contemporary Asian food and also operating as a small bar. The interior is black and red and exposed wood, with an outdoor area that's popular when the weather is good. When the brothers took over the building they found two illegal gambling dens in the rear, which were sealed with a hydraulic steel door. It was a spot where bookies, crooks and corrupt cops used to meet in the early 1960s and 1970s. In the 1980s it became the Ecstasy Adult bookshop and sex club. Down in the basement were swings and ropes for the sexually adventurous gays. The Barge brothers had to use thirty-five garbage bags to get rid of the X-rated porn videos hidden in the ceiling. As homage to the sordid past, the interior in the back of the restaurant has colleges of sexual images from the former adult bookshop. The handsome brothers, progeny of an attractive Chinese mother and Australian father, were successful almost from the beginning. Their modern Asian-fusion food was extremely popular and the boys had an easy charm that was most attractive to women.

This is not to say that tourists have embraced the cleaner streets and lanes around Springfield Avenue. In 2008 the Storrier Hotel opened on the corner of Earl Place and Springfield Avenue. A five-storey red brick building built along art deco lines, it had seventy rooms and was the first in a projected series of establishments to be named after Australian artists. Tim Storrier attended art school in Darlinghurst in the late 1960s but, as he said, he avoided spending too much time down the road in Kings Cross:

'It certainly wasn't my bloody stomping ground. In those days, it was basically whores and bad booze.'

Evening Blaze, a large painting from his well-known but glib 'burning rope series', hung in the lobby, while his photographs and prints decorated the corridors and rooms. As for the hotel being in Kings Cross, the ever-modest Storrier replied, 'I wouldn't care if they put it in the Sahara. I like it that it's named after me.'

On the ground floor there was a restaurant with transparent Philippe Starck-designed Louis Ghost chairs, and the rooms had views across the Sydney skyline. The beds had faux-fur covers and the bathrooms were tiny (one critic commented, 'I've seen bigger bathrooms on sailing boats'). Still, despite the owners trying to sell the hotel as 'inner city funky', the Storrier was difficult for taxis to find and tourists shied away from its position next to the dimly lit Earl Place that led down to a nightclub variously named the Dragonfly or Tunnel.

Over the years the spot has gained a squalid reputation for bashings, including one where a 24-year-old man was nearly killed breaking up a fight. Shots have been fired outside the club by drug-addled patrons and in 2009 the president of the vicious Notorious bikie gang, Alan Sarkis, and three other high-ranking members of the club were jailed over a fight at the nightclub. It's no wonder the weapons check at the door is decidedly uninviting for tourists. For many visitors the area is not so much funky as grungy. The Storrier closed down within a year, as did the restaurant. It's now serviced apartments with a hideous lime-green coating on the brick facade.

The Storrier never developed the 'street cred' of Regent's Court. The boutique hotel faced Springfield Avenue and continued back to Llankelly Place. It is a liver-brick block built in 1926 and renovated as a hotel in 1990. The Regent's staff, led by the vivacious Paula MacMahon, were exceptional in their down-to-earth friendliness. Frequently Paula would invite her guests for a wine or champagne (on several occasions I enjoyed a drink with her when I was catching up with friends staying there). Its corridors were vibrant with enormous vases of orchids and agapanthuses. The lift was an old cage one. And the large rooms had high ceilings, mushroom coloured walls, wooden Venetians and kitchenettes. There was a rooftop garden with pots of gardenias and roses, wooden tables, BBQ and kitchen. The views of Sydney and the Opera House were spectacular and a brilliant background to the literary events and readings that were held up there.

Guests ranged from film directors and producers to actors, singers, lawyers and visiting luminaries from overseas, no doubt attracted by the praise in such magazines as *Hip Hotels, Vanity Fair* and *Wallpaper**. The London *Financial Times* summed it up: 'For the arty set, the sort of person who in London would probably stay at Blake's.' Like many other hotels in the area it was bought during the new millennium and reopened in 2010 as apartments, or what are called 'residential chambers'.

Despite the gentrification of Llankelly Place, it is still a quintessential Kings Cross space where the lowliest denizen exists side-by-side with the affluent locals and tourists. The lane is a conduit that continues across Orwell Street down Orwell Lane, where its one footpath is frequently strewn with dirty mattresses and garbage bags full of clothes, and on to the Wayside Chapel in Hughes Street.

One of the favourite pastimes of residents and visitors is the great Kings Cross spectator sport of people watching. Weekend afternoons are the best time to take in the human traffic that flows down to the Wayside and back again out into Darlinghurst Road. The homeless, the insane, the junkies, the lonely, the poor, the abused and the losers make up a constant stream that passes back and forth. Sitting behind the timid red picket fence outside LL Wine and Dine is a good place to watch the ceaseless ebb and flow of those heading to the Wayside Chapel or back into the streets to find drugs or alcohol. It's easy to spot the Wayside clients: gaunt and hollow-eyed, with weather-beaten features, their bodies an epidermal canvas for tattoos, grubby runners, dirty clothes, straggly beards, and voices so nasal they sound as if they're perpetually moaning. In the mornings, vacant-eyed with weariness or suffering from the entropy of hangovers, they shuffle slowly to the Wayside for something to eat, but as the day wears on, anxiety sets in and groups of three or four head into the Cross itself to search for a source of drugs, any drug will do, whether it's prescription (Oxy, Xanax), heroin or ice. By late afternoon the angst spills into angry outbursts over money and/or the failure to find a dealer. These arguments are loud and foul. They are so caught up in their own concerns they don't notice any of the diners and tourists a few metres away.

Once a source of drugs is known, then, as if by herd instinct, there's a stream of people from Wayside hurrying down Llankelly place in what I call the junkie canter, a cross between a fast walk and a jog. Their eyes are feverish with expectation and now they are united with a sole purpose there is no swearing or talking except to confirm where they're going.

Sometimes the drugs are available outside the Wayside, and the addicts, having just shot up or swallowed pills, slowly shuffle and lurch and stagger up the lane, glassy-eyed, wonky and, if affected by bad ice, as happened one weekend, even crawling along the ground, babbling incoherently and resembling not so much living human beings as zombies engaged in a farandole dance of the damned. They make their clumsy, uncoordinated way to the main street, in the hope that there will be more drugs, or if not, cheap alcohol, which they will return with, swigging directly from the paper wrapped bottle, so stoned or drunk that the women, unable to balance on their cheap high heels, tumble over unaware that their tiny mini skirts fail to hide their lack of undies. Only occasionally does a drunk or someone on ice who hasn't slept for two days show anger at the way the diners view them as an amusing public spectacle. But that is rare because although they inhabit the same physical space, their world runs parallel to and only infrequently crosses over into that of the locals and tourists. It's hard to know sometimes whether it's a sign of the mutual tolerance that the Cross is known for or an unconscious and determined effort to treat the Other as invisible until it remains impossible to ignore them.

THE GLITTERING MILE

IF ANY ONE WORK BURNISHED the myth of Kings Cross it was the 1964 television documentary *The Glittering Mile*. This hour-long portrait about the most densely populated 'white area in the world' was highly controversial for its scenes shot at a strip club and the drag acts of Les Girls. Yet there was nothing deliberately sensational about it, and the producers tried to depict the area as objectively as possible. The title is based on the spurious belief that a mile is the distance covered walking Darlinghurst Road from William Street into Macleay Street and back again.

The documentary develops the idea of the striking contrast between day and night in the Cross. Daytime belongs to the locals and their prosaic daily activities of shopping, cleaning and relaxing in sun-dappled outdoor restaurants. Fitzroy Gardens is filled with residents escaped from their dingy lodgings and flats, listening to live opera. We hear the description of the Cross as a friendly village with its Parisian atmosphere. The drabness of the apartment buildings and streets of a day is exaggerated in order to distinguish it from the neon-lit brilliance of the night. Local identities are interviewed. Dulcie Deamer, seventy-four at the time, with the benign, saggy face of a grannie, represented the bohemian past. As far as she is concerned the youth of the 1960s are not bohemian, but then, as usual, her opinion is that Kings Cross has gone downhill since her heyday. Rosaleen Norton sits in the Apollyon café, where the walls feature her paintings and drawings. Her garish make-up, with sharply defined eyebrows and exaggerated lipsticked lips, is that of a performer who courts attention. But the viewer is drawn towards her mouth and its filed down, rotten teeth that resemble miniature tombstones and a tongue that seems desperate to slip out of its dental cage and makes her difficult to understand. She confirms she's always been a witch and when asked if she ever wanted a 'normal life' of husband and children she lets out a horrified, 'I'd go mad.'

What remains familiar is the constant whingeing of residents about noise and the behaviour of others, just proving nothing ever changes. The documentary does a fine job showing the distinctive transformation from day into night when the Cross becomes a temple of entertainment, invaded by packs of holidaying footballers making for the striptease joints, suburbanites dining out or the 'rubber neckers' driving up and down the glittering mile for the voyeuristic pleasure of ogling prostitutes and strippers on their way to work. What's extraordinary is how the place is still teeming with people at four and five in the morning, many of them, as the narrator says, 'in a search for something, whatever it is, [that] goes on all through the night.' In 1962 *The Bulletin* reported that the traffic jams of a Saturday night were so bad, that by 8 pm 'there is complete bedlam'. During the early 1960s Kings Cross had around 800,000 visitors a year, but to the chagrin of locals like Kenneth Slessor, it seemed his beloved Cross was being invaded by 'foreigners from the suburbs'.

The portrait that slowly builds is of a place at odds with the rest of Australia and yet a magnet for people wanting to experience what the co-owner of the Hasty Tasty calls the 'off-beat pleasures of gambling and prostitution'. In his interview he talks of the Cross as a playground where people find a release for their desires and needs that can be found nowhere else. The documentary's conclusion that Kings Cross is not so much an actual place but a state of mind would become a cliché, but even so, true.

The most thrilling section of *The Glittering Mile* is its portrait of the nightlife; the infinite variety of food (there were 250 restaurants in the area), the exceptional number of women on the game, the exotic nightclubs, striptease joints and the Les Girls drag shows. The excitement and electric buzz of Kings Cross is palpable and some visitors are quite simply wide-eyed in amazement.

At the time the Cross emulated the chic nightclubs seen in American movies and were regarded as the height of sophistication. There was the classy Chevron Hilton down in Macleay Street, built only a few years before with its elegant Silver Spade Room where Sarah Vaughan, Nat King Cole and Shirley Bassey performed. At the Club Folies Bergère a topless Ruriko Oka ('specially contracted') wearing a large wide-brimmed hat, had an act where a boa slowly and sensuously wound itself around her thighs. There must have been great interest in exotic performances aping atavistic dance moves, because another nightclub's headlining act was 'Anna, the world's greatest primitif dancer'. At the Flamingo, 101 Darlinghurst Road, the billboard out the front had an image of Rosita, wearing a two-piece bathing suit, with a peacock-feathered hat and a florid spray of peacock feathers attached to her bikini bottom as she stares passionately at a New Guinea carving. Tabou, on the corner of Macleay Street and Darlinghurst Road, was one of the most stylish, with a Latin American band and Egyptian food overseen by the owner, Gaston. Or you could go to the Fox Hole Nite Club which had three shows nightly with Frank Newall, a juggler, the dancer and singer Ingrid Hart (big earrings, notable breasts, white fur stole) and the 'Foxettes' dancing to the George Sanders Band.

It was the sexual content of the documentary that caused most of the controversy, especially the scenes of strippers performing at the Pink Pussycat. Abe Saffron had opened the first strip club in Australia, Staccato, in 1959 in Orwell Street. By the time *The Glittering Mile* aired, there were many strip clubs, like the Pink Pussycat, the Pink Panther, the Paradise Room, the Crazy Horse, and the Pigalle Club in Bayswater Road. Some of the strippers became well-known names. Miss Subtle Sex was a 'Negress' who swung her breasts in time with the music, and there were lesser lights like the Eurasian Sex Kitten and Sexy Sabra. Although the wowsers complained, the strip clubs were highly lucrative. There was a concerted effort by the owners to portray stripping as a tasteful art and something to aspire to. The Pink Panther promoted an attractive deaf mute who used sign language as one of its featured artists. Visiting strippers from America and Europe were photographed and interviewed when they arrived at Sydney airport, all of them promoting their performances as artistic and not tacky or salacious. Their modest but fashionable clothes, bee-hive hairdos, heavy make-up and cigarette holders added a touch of refinement. The police also helped to maintain decorum. If the women didn't cover their nipples, or if they showed an inch too much thigh, they'd be arrested. Police used tape measures to make sure that the sides of the bottom of women's two-piece costumes were no narrower than four inches.

Some strippers did their own choreography, but the Pink Panther had Judd Lane, who was trained in classical ballet and jazz dance. He worked out movement patterns and gestures to suit the skills of the strippers. As society grew more permissive by the late 1960s and 1970s the girls ended their performances in just a G-string and stick-on tassels. For the young actress Kate Fitzpatrick the most spectacular occupants of the Cross in the late sixties were the strippers who worked between the Pink Pussycat and the Pink Panther. The clubs were on opposite sides of the road and the dancers worked both joints. She liked to watch them criss-crossing the road:

> ... *sure footed in ridiculously high heels, young, tall, fit and stacked ... They looked like double-breasted Amazons ... They proudly sported gigantic, decorated beehives that would have made Marie Antoinette jealous. These often almost metre-high masterpieces were created weekly and kept in place with shellac.*

The public face of stripping became Sandra Nelson. Born in Russia, she ran away from a migrant camp in Wollongong and started stripping at the age of sixteen, lying that she was two years older. Tall, gorgeous, blonde, with peculiar blue-green eyes and breast measurements that had started out at forty inches in the beginning of her career and increased to a hyperbolic forty-three inches at the end, Nelson worked mostly at the Paradise Club. A keen self-promoter, she became immediately notorious in July 1964 when she conducted a tour of Sydney wearing a black topless dress in a publicity stunt for her strip club. She finished her tour with a trip on the Manly ferry, still proudly showing off her bare breasts.

She became one of Australia's premier pin-up girls, appearing in nearly every issue of *Dare, Topless, Australian Models* and *Gentleman's Choice*. She posed naked for the first issue of *Censor* on the steps of the Supreme Court Building. The Chief Justice, Sir Leslie Herron, was dutifully outraged, considering the photograph 'at the very least ... a shocking breach of bad taste. I was greatly offended that the Supreme Court was used for the material.' She appeared regularly on the front page of the *Kings Cross Whisper*, an extremely successful satirical paper with corny gags, pin ups and ridiculous headlines: 'Indonesia captures Darwin', 'Queensland ban on custard pies'. Max Cullen, actor and artist on the paper, said of her, '*The Whisper* without Sandra Nelson (our first topless dancer) would be like Playboy without a Bunny!'

The Cross's blonde bombshell became the Antipodean equivalent of Jayne Mansfield or Marilyn Monroe. Her effect on men was legendary. According to Frank Black, who later ran the Pink Panther, she was 'a mad lay. If you looked sideways at her breasts she'd look for a fight.' One man who grew obsessed with her was Lim Yew Hock, the Malaysian High Commissioner. Every time he was in Sydney he'd hightail it to the Paradise Club to watch her strip. She gave him the affectionate nickname of 'Hocky'. One day the love-stricken, lust-driven diplomat flew from Canberra to Sydney under the alias of 'Hawk' and disappeared – and so did Nelson. There was nation-wide coverage of their disappearance, but when she turned up a couple of days later she protested that she had no idea where he was. There was a massive but unsuccessful police search. Lim's wife and daughter went on national television to plead for his safe return. Even the Malaysian Prime Minister was concerned and sent his chief of protocol to Sydney to help. Then Lim mysteriously turned up after being missing for ten days. Nelson was quick to point out that her relationship could not be compared to the Profumo sex scandal in England where espionage was believed to have played a role: 'I'm not Mata Hari. I can assure you we never discussed defence secrets.'

Two years later in 1968 she married Les Ramsay, manager of the Paradise Club. Her fame was such that a nightclub was named after her, the Sandra Nelson AO Club (aka the Pink Panther). When Ramsay died in 1971 she gave up stripping, married the owner of a health-food shop and left the Cross for good, going to live in the United States, where, according to James Cockington in *Banned,* she reverted to her original Russian name.

What was slyly introduced into the strip shows were men pretending to be women. These drag queens were promoted as real women. They were more sexually aggressive and invited audience contact, whereas women were content to merely display themselves. It was to be an American who exploited this growing drag scene.

Lee Gordon, brash, optimistic, small, and with the supreme confidence of a snake oil salesman, arrived in Australia in 1953 at the age of 30. He was born in Detroit and became a bookings manager for the renowned Tropicana nightclub in Havana. After that he started up a chain of electrical stores, selling them off for half a million dollars which he lost in three years of backing unsuccessful Broadway shows. He began a marketing business in Sydney and then established himself as a concert promoter working out of his office in 151 Bayswater Road.

His first major concert tour in 1954 of jazz legends Ella Fitzgerald, Buddy Rich and Artie Shaw was a flop. He soon realised that it was the youth market he should be catering to and he brought out Johnny Ray, whose second tour was so successful that he was mobbed by 10,000 fans at the airport. Gordon imported many other rock and rollers including Bill Hayley, Little Richard, Buddy Holly and Jerry Lee Lewis, but his favourite performer was probably Frank Sinatra, whom he toured in 1955 and 1957 and who was best man when Gordon married his Australian wife, Arlene.

At times he was stunningly successful and wealthy but the money quickly evaporated when he imported the American Roller Derby (it was ahead of its time and would become hugely popular at the end of the 1960s) and the Lenny Bruce tour, when the comedian was banned from performing because of his obscene language. Gordon converted the Kings Cross cinema into one of our first discotheques (the Birdcage), introduced the Twist to Australia and, with Abe Saffron, opened up several striptease joints. The relationship was one of opposites: Saffron was quiet, guarded and careful with his money; Gordon was gregarious and a spendthrift.

Gordon's mental condition was always fragile and he spent much of 1958 in a Hawaiian asylum after experiencing a severe nervous breakdown. He returned to Australia with new plans for the future but he had to sell off his record label and then his company verged on bankruptcy. His alcohol and drug problems became worse. In 1963 he was charged with attempting to obtain pethidine without a prescription. After fleeing Australia and trying to find work in the United States, he flew to England, and was found dead in the same year of a coronary occlusion in a cheap hotel room.

His talent was recognising popular cultural and musical trends. He may have been before his time with some of them but he tapped into the sort of spectacle no other city in Australia would dare – drag shows. Of course, drag was not new in Sydney. After the First World War there were men who liked to dress as women who paraded around College Street, risking arrest because it was illegal to dress as a woman under the *Offensive Behaviour Act*. To avoid the law gays gave private performances in flats. There was a curious caveat to wearing drag; if a real woman was present at a drag party then the men weren't doing anything illegal. But even this law did not stop the police from raiding the parties.

In Jon Rose's vivacious and moving *At the Cross*, an autobiographical novel of the early 1940s, he writes about a party held in a hall in Macleay Street run by Milly, a woman who adores gays and drag queens. Milly herself is drunk and dressed in a top hat pretending to be George Sand. Two hundred exotically and lavishly dressed men attend and are entertained by singers and an orchestra. To Rose it is:

> *... all gorgeous bedlam: half the theatre and radio world seemed to be there, as well as quite a few people who, one would have*

*thought from listening to their usual comments on life and
people, would sooner have been found dead in the nearest gutter
than be seen at such a degenerate 'do'.*

There is a Queen of Sheba, at least eight Carmen Mirandas, a few
Dolores del Rios, a Lana Turner and one Dame Nellie Melba.
Everything is heady and wonderfully decadent until the police
raid it, turning the party into pandemonium. The vicious cop in
charge walks over people or knocks them flying, calling the men
'poftas' [*sic*]. Men jump out of the window in fright and flee back
into the heart of the Cross.

*Lights started up in many flat windows. People no-one even
knew came up saying, 'It's a stinking disgrace, why don't they
leave the boys alone, and get after the black market gangsters and
molls?'*

The reaction of the locals was typical. Kings Cross had become
a place of refuge for homosexuals. It offered men and women of
the same sexual persuasion a place to gather and find some sort of
social acceptance they wouldn't find anywhere else. George Johnston, a journalist for *The Sun*, wrote about them in 1949 and how
they gravitated to the Cross:

*Most of Sydney's homosexuals form an almost self-contained
social section of the city, and to this community (in which most
members are known to each other) there is a regular stream of
recruits. Many so called 'pansy parties' are held fairly regularly
– sometimes with as many as 100 to 150 guests – but are usually
much more intimate. At the much larger gatherings, it is
sometimes the curious practice to invite a few women. They are
invariably prostitutes and are never touched by the male guests.*

The hub for gays during the 1950s and early 60s was the Rex. When it opened in the mid-1950s it was a swish hotel but with the arrival of the Chevron in 1960 it rapidly went downmarket, and its 'Bottoms Up Bar' out the back was frequented by queens and rent boys. The hotel was raided often. According to *Truth*, hundreds of 'effeminates and known perverts' drank there every Saturday. Perhaps the most celebrated incident occurred in 1956 when police caused a near-riot after they arrested two queens who 'resplendent in the latest fashions, had minced from group to group, trilling in high pitched voices ... but downing their beers with all the aplomb of thirsty wharfies'.

Lee Gordon noticed just how significant the camp scene was in Kings Cross and he and his wife Arlene inaugurated drag shows at the German-themed restaurant the Rheinschloss (where Porky's is now). The touts out front were dressed in lederhosen, long socks and hats with feathers in them. Arlene choreographed the routines and her husband paid for the costumes. One of the drag artists Gordon employed in 1962 was a pretty young man, Richard Byron, who took the stage name Carlotta. When she arrived in the Cross she felt like Dorothy in the Land of Oz: 'There were flashing neon lights like a mini Las Vegas, bohemian people. Colour, glamour and noise.' Although she still dressed as a man of a day, she quickly realised that this was the only place where she could become the woman she wanted to be. Lee and Arlene took a shine to her, so when they started up another drag venue, Carlotta was the centrepiece of the show.

Dubbed the Jewel Box, it was a dingy room at the back of Nick's Inn at 41 Darlinghurst Road. Audiences had to walk through the milk bar, past its slot machines and up the back stairs to enter. Owned by a 'homespun' Greek family, it had grey columns with coloured chips of glass cemented into them. There was a long narrow stage with a dance floor in front of it and the backdrop curtains for the stage were made out of hessian with sequins randomly stuck on them. The room held only eighty people who paid seven shillings and sixpence to get in, bringing their own flagon of wine. A year later it was looking decidedly shabby because Gordon lost interest in the running of the club when he became obsessed with a guest performer, the beautiful blonde Coccinelle, a French transvestite. Often drunken fights broke out between the patrons. Performers thought the Jewel Box sleazy, but as Carlotta said, 'We [drag queens] didn't mind because we were getting paid $35 a week and a chance to strut our stuff as girls.'

For adventurous Australians it was their first glimpse of drag. It proved to be one of Gordon's successes and he and Sammy Lee, a Canadian Jew known for his cigars, gaudy clothes and vile temper, opened up Les Girls on the corner of Darlinghurst Road and Roslyn Street just before Christmas 1963. Downstairs were dress shops, a restaurant, hair salons and that indispensable feature of the Cross, a pawnshop. The cabaret and VIP rooms were upstairs. The walls were bright red flock wallpaper. The colour scheme extended to the red velvet drapes with gold trimming and red tablecloths with candles. An enormous chandelier hung from the ceiling, giant mirrors reflected the audience, making the room seem larger than it was, and there were photographs of the 'girls' in gilded frames on the walls. This was the Cross's version of a Las Vegas 'glitz and tits' show – individual acts, bawdy comedians, strikingly attractive impersonators, and everyone on stage for the spectacular finale.

Part of the art was to create the illusion of being a woman, but the performers also had to make certain there was no evidence of their manhood, as everyone in the business knew that the crotch was the focal point of a drag show and a site of bemused speculation in the minds of both men and women in the audience. One of the exotic additions to the show was Ayesha, who looked Asian or, some thought, Native American. Her impersonation of Shirley Bassey (apparently her version of 'Fascinating Rhythm' was a knockout) was so spectacular that some thought she was channelling Bassey's spirit. The shows were changed every six weeks with two performances nightly, one at 9.15 and the second two hours later, with an additional show at 1am on Fridays and Saturdays.

The venue originally attracted an audience of men, some arty types and a few slumming socialites, but Carlotta believes that it wasn't until *The Glittering Mile,* which featured a long section on Les Girls containing a rousing Carmen Miranda production number and an interview with Carlotta, that women understood that it wasn't sleazy but an intriguing mixture of 'high gloss and illusions'. The documentary made Les Girls a success and curious women dragged their husbands and boyfriends to it. One of their biggest shows was 1966's *Yankee Doodle Dandy*, to celebrate the visit of President Johnson to Australia. The Cross was teeming with American servicemen who filled the venue.

Lee was tough. He wouldn't let the performers fraternise with the patrons unless they were fully made up and wearing full-length gowns, and used threats and menace to keep them in line. The girls were often at the mercy of violent men. Police took especial pleasure in hurting them and stealing their money. The legendary tough policeman Bumper Farrell was a particularly nasty piece of work and Lee could be particularly brutal. Dressing as a woman was still illegal, unless you were on stage, so the boys tolerated being smacked around by gangsters, bad cops and even worse, bosses, just for the pleasure of pretending to be a woman and earning a living from it, even though the pay was lousy. As Carlotta relates in her memoirs *Carlotta, I'm not that type of girl*:

Kings Cross was a place that controlled you ... we were terrified of putting a foot wrong [and] you wouldn't dare complain about the bad working conditions. Once they broke a chair over a girl's head when she wanted to leave. Girls who were caught stealing had broom sticks shoved up their arses ... the scare tactics worked for years...

But what comes through in her interview in *The Glittering Mile* is her continuing sense of amazement at being able to perform as a woman at all. It's no wonder she thought of the Cross as the golden brick road. In the early seventies she had one of Australia's first sex-change operations. Carlotta remained the face of Les Girls as it became a right of passage for suburban mums and dads to experience Kings Cross. It would have seemed a ridiculous idea when the venture started out that it would end up being a show that ran for twenty-five years and ended up playing to RSL audiences in the suburbs and being the inspiration for the movie *Priscilla, Queen of the Desert*.

Away from the razzle dazzle of Les Girls and the neon lights of the main drag was a subterranean back-street space, El Rocco, a small pokey cellar in Brougham Street which could, at a squeeze, seat up seventy patrons. Originally a plumber's shop, it became a jazz club in 1957, founded by Arthur James and developed by the drummer John Pochee. It was the first club in Australia that existed only to play modern jazz.

After the war Australian jazz diverged into two major strands: Dixieland (or traditional jazz) and modern styles like be-bop and 'cool' jazz played by the likes of Charlie Parker, Miles Davis and Thelonious Monk. Modern jazz was cerebral. Rock 'n' roll stirred your loins, cool jazz wanted to make you think and dream. Reporters frequently commented on how soberly, even sombrely dressed the musicians were, far from the sartorial excesses of rock 'n' rollers. The *Australian Women's Weekly*'s Ainslie Baker wrote in 1960, with a sense of wonderment, that the musicians had 'a priestly air of dedication' about them and they appeared 'lost in meditation' when they were playing. The music was intelligent, forceful and complex. This sense of dedication to the music was compounded by the fact that alcohol wasn't allowed. The strongest drink was coffee – always described as 'wretched' – in tandem with cigarettes, which gave the cellar its memorable smoky ambience. Both Frank Sinatra and Sarah Vaughan sang on the minute stage. Some of Australia's greatest jazz musicians started out or played at El Rocco, including John Sangster, the brilliant pianist Mike Nock, alto saxophonist Bernie McGann, and Don Burrows.

El Rocco's influence was profound and any jazz aficionado from interstate or overseas made their pilgrimage to the tiny cellar. Its seminal importance in Australia's jazz history was confirmed in the 1990s documentary *Beyond El Rocco*. Clive James once said that the most daring thing you could do in the late 1950s, early 1960s was to go to the El Rocco. The music played was just as revolutionary and shocking as the drag scene or striptease.

The Cross still seemed like a village where everyone knew each other and writers found themselves in like-minded company. Nancy Phelan, a novelist, memoirist and travel writer, came from a comfortable life in the North Shore but immediately fell for the gentler charms of Kings Cross, liking 'the vitality, the contrasts and the characters, the feeling of life going on'. She had a flat a few doors from Norma Chapman's Clay's Bookshop in Macleay Street and met regularly with women writer friends like Jessica Anderson, who lived in the same street in Cahors, and Betty Roland, a two-minute walk away in Ward Avenue.

'We were all busy but at times it was pleasant after work to drop in on each other for a cup of tea or a glass of wine or to go for a walk.'

The Glittering Mile made the Cross seem a more exciting, more brazen, more inclusive community than anywhere else in the country. It was a relief valve for people who felt suffocated by the stultifying conservative morality and cultural shallowness of mainstream Australia. It existed because it was needed.

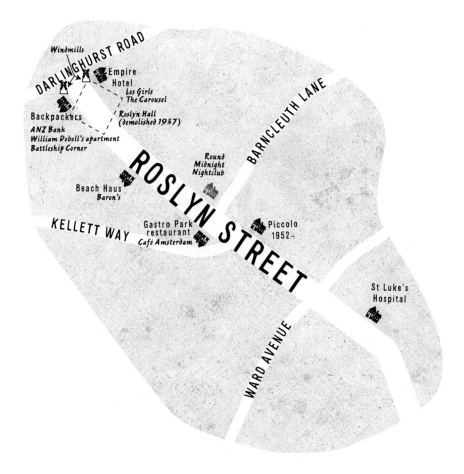

Windmills

DARLINGHURST ROAD

Empire
Hotel
Les Girls
The Carousel

Backpackers

Roslyn Hall
(demolished 1937)

ANZ Bank
William Dobell's apartment
Battleship Corner

BARNCLEUTH LANE

Round
Midnight
Nightclub

ROSLYN STREET

Beach Haus
Baron's

KELLETT WAY

Gastro Park
restaurant
Café Amsterdam

Piccolo
1952–

St Luke's
Hospital

WARD AVENUE

SOMETIMES OF A MORNING I take an alternate route to the post office in Fitzroy Gardens and walk down Kellett Way and, as I cross Roslyn Street into Barncleuth Lane, where soiled ibises forage in the smelly garbage, I hear a man shouting out *'Silvana! Silvana!'* and I know it's Vittorio calling to me from outside the Piccolo Bar where he is serving his customers at the outdoor tables. It's his mocking nickname for me because we both adore the ethereally beautiful Italian actress Silvana Mangano. I wave or stop to talk to him but occasionally he'll yell out to me in front of customers and passers-by, *Hey, Silvana, I loathed your latest novel.* It's hard to get upset by his critical mauling because if he liked something he'll be equally vociferous in his opinion, crying out in his high-pitched Italian inflected accent, *It was beautiful!*

Vittorio Bianchi is small, almost impish, and not shy about voicing his opinions. He never holds back what he thinks of you, although his mercurial attitude can change daily. When happy his tongue flickers in and out of his mouth like that of a lascivious lizard. Exceptionally well-read, with a deep and abiding passion for theatre, he runs the minute Piccolo Bar like a showman, as if the customers are his audience.

For decades its walls were a visual cacophony of images of singers, performers and film stars (his favourite, James Dean, had twenty-nine photographs devoted to him). There were benches along the walls, a few chairs, six tables, a jukebox forever playing jazz in the corner and a minuscule kitchen at the back. As Vittorio said, *There is no room for people to be strangers.* And it was this ethos that drove him and made the tiny Piccolo such an essential part of the folklore of the Cross.

His journey to Kings Cross began in Seiano, a small village near Napoli. He was born in 1934 and had two sisters and a brother. His father, who had served in the First World War, was blind and prone to violent rages. When Vittorio was eight he was raped by an American soldier. He was too young to know what the American had done to him and afterwards he took the man home and introduced him to his family; in return the rapist thanked the family by giving them chocolates. When Vittorio turned fourteen his father sent him and his sisters, Rosa and Rose, to Sydney by ship. They arrived without knowing a word of English. Vittorio had to pay back the fares to Australia by working in his uncle's box factory in distant Homebush. Later, working in a grocery store near Chinatown, he met a huge bear of a man, half Italian, half Egyptian, called Ossie (short for Osvaldo) who owned the Piccolo Bar. Ossie offered Vittorio full-time work at the café. It was a close and tempestuous relationship. Ossie was a gambler and when he lost, which was often, he would take out his anger on Vittorio. Ossie's love for jazz, filling the jukebox with it, brainwashed Vittorio into a jazz fan.

Vittorio worked five nights from six to six. His theatrical, camp manner became a drawcard, as did his ability to put disparate people together at tables and force them to talk to one another. During the 1960s and 1970s visiting the Piccolo was a prerequisite for saying that you had experienced the Cross. It was an intimate sanctuary for bohemians, actors, artists, authors, writers manqué, visiting celebrities (Liv Ullmann, Marianne Faithfull) and even politicians like the former Prime Minister Gough Whitlam. Vittorio knew the witch Rosaleen Norton, who had shifted from Brougham Street and lived a few doors down, and the painter Brett Whiteley would slip in to the Piccolo, sometimes sober, most times dazed and mentally adrift in a narcotic trance. Singers like Wendy Saddington, Rene Geyer and Peter Allen were often there, as were actors, poets and filmmakers.

One of his closest friends was Elizabeth Burton. The only strip show Vittorio ever saw was when Burton performed at the Pink Pussycat, saying of her act, 'The first time I watched her it was so beautiful tears came to my eyes.' In the early 1980s he and Burton helped formed the Sideshow Company, producing cabaret shows every Sunday night. He was the white-faced master of ceremonies and sometimes he'd sing. In fact, Vittorio was so stage-struck that he went to acting classes at the Ensemble Theatre and ran the coffee lounge there for seven years. His favourite visitor to the Piccolo was Lindsay Kemp, the dancer and director whose Jean Genet influences were obvious in the exaggerated theatricality and excesses of both his performances and costumes. Vittorio was so in awe of Kemp that he found 'It was embarrassing to take money from him because he was a genius.' Vittorio became such a well-known Cross figure that he was given a radio show on Triple J called 'Voice of the Piccolo', where he chatted about his friends, the books he was reading, recent films he had seen, and the music he liked.

He knew from the age of ten, when he fell in love with a man, that he was homosexual. He described his love life as a disaster. He was deeply in love with a man for fifteen years without ever having sex. But then Vittorio always had a very romantic view: 'My idea of true love is to love somebody without having sex – real unselfish love. Sex changes everything.' Part of the problem, as Vittorio often said – and he was completely honest about his faults when he wanted to be (rather than listing the faults of others) – was that love brought out aspects of himself that he hated: jealousy, suspicions and meanness.

When Ossie died in the early 1990s Vittorio cried for a week. Seven days later his beloved sister, Rosa, died of a heart attack ('I had no more tears left for her'). He bought the Piccolo and continued to run it into the new millennium. In the delightful book *People of the Cross* (1993) he reflected that:

> *Twenty-five years ago the Cross was a beautiful wonderful place. It was like a village where everybody knew everybody, everybody was kind, with lots of ideas and always doing things – artists, writers, actors, musicians, people who didn't have much money.*

He distinguished two sorts of people. 'Night people are different from Day people. As the hours go from night to morning, people get more desperate, or lost, more full of booze, or pills ... they're looking for friendship, love, a fuck in the night, especially between the hours of one and four ... there's a lot of lonely people around and they congregate in places like the Piccolo.' Drunks are the worst because they always want to fight and as for heroin addicts he thought them sick, and sick people are very cunning. But he had his own drug problems, or to be more specific, the Piccolo did.

The café was in the news at the turn of the millennium. The *Daily Telegraph* produced a series of sensational front page exposés of what was happening in the Piccolo. In June 2000 a reporter wrote that he had sat inside the café for six hours over two days and watched a barista hand over press-sealed bags of marijuana to an average of nine customers an hour. The police, reacting to the stories, raided the Piccolo. An employee, a married father of three who had arrived from Vietnam in 1982, was charged with supplying marijuana.

The café continued but it seemed scruffy and out of step with the gentrification of the area. The Piccolo was Vittorio's whole life but he was growing older and found ghosts were becoming more real to him than people: 'The trouble is dead people are more alive when they're dead than when they're alive. They're always with me. I talk to them and they visit me.'

The place was still inextricably bound up with the history of the Cross and was frequently photographed for magazine and newspaper articles as a typical Kings Cross slice of bohemia. The ABC series *Rake*, about a louche barrister who used it as the café of choice, added to its aura, but then in 2011 it suddenly closed for business. There was a handwritten sign in the window, *We will be back*, but that seemed unlikely, as there were rumours about unresolved financial and tax problems. Residents were also worried about Vittorio himself – just how would he exist without his beloved Piccolo?

Just across the street another famous Kings Cross institution, Baron's, closed on Halloween 2007. It once was part of a gentleman's residence known as the Praxo, built in 1882. Thirty years later there were further additions to the façade in the 'Arts and Crafts' style. Over time the 5–9 Roslyn Street address was home to hairdressers, cafés, a laundromat and even a shop that sold shells and stuffed birds. There was a take-away, the Salad Bowl, which in turn became a French restaurant, La Cafeteria, and in September 1979 it re-opened as Baron's. The name became as recognisable as the Piccolo in its status as a Kings Cross institution and its location in 'the heart of the seediest part of the Cross'.

When it opened the owners could only afford second-hand furniture and cheap carpet. Originally most of its customers were waiters, barmen and chefs who came to wind down after their night shifts. When the licence was extended from midnight to 3 am in the early 1980s, it became popular with actors and musicians. Soon it became a raffish place to drink; even the whole English cricket team, when Bob Willis was captain, used to frequent it.

Baron's became one of the first clubs in Sydney to secure a 24-hour licence to trade. The 'nefarious late-night nook' began to attract a huge diversity of customers: police prosecutors, students, doctors, lawyers, MPs, young clubbers and musicians like Bono of U2, who thought it the best bar in the world. Though, to the squeamish, its murky interior could not hide the sticky cherry red Chesterfield sofas, nicotine-stained brown walls, chocolate ceilings, and suspiciously moist red carpet with its dull gold pattern dotted with cigarette burns like hundreds of bird droppings. You could play backgammon in the small rooms out back or sprawl over the sofas. In its penumbral rooms lovers, drunkards, celebrities drank, sniffed cocaine in the toilets or broke the toilet seats in sordid trysts. It was the most inclusive bar in the Cross. It didn't matter who you were, you mixed and did so with a spirit of good will, helped by the most popular cocktail, margaritas.

You could drink, smoke and, after the jukebox played 'My Way' at 4 am to remind patrons just how late it was, you could stay on and see the sunrise, though few did, no doubt not wanting to be horrified by how dilapidated and tawdry Baron's looked in forensic light of day.

The third owner, Michael Cherote, bought the club in 2004, declaring 'The best thing about Baron's is that it's a place where 20-year-olds to 60-year-olds can meet and relax in comfort. It doesn't matter if you're a barrister or a street sweeper'. He knew he was buying a slice of history, because by that time the Sebel, Chevron, Gazebo, Les Girls and the Bourbon and Beefsteak had gone. For Cherote, Baron's was the last of the old landmarks that defined the Cross. But in late 2007 the whole building was sold in order to be razed. Many locals and habitués of the venue protested against the closure and a thousand people signed a petition, but the new owners promised that they would reinstall Baron's once the renovations were completed. Of course that didn't happen. Instead the space reopened with minimalist surrounds and gorgeous staff. The inclusive Baron's had been replaced by the exclusive Beach Haus, described as a playground for 'holidaying Euro kids'.

The fish bowl front of the building itself was retained and the new structure was based on Gaudi's architecture, with white tiles lining the outside walls which resemble frozen waves about to break on the shore. The bow shaped front, with its floor to ceiling windows, gazes down Roslyn Street past Ward Avenue to the gates of St Luke's hospital, which was once the home of Patrick White's parents. Its fashionable luxuriant garden was the basis for Laura Trevelyan's home and garden in *Voss*:

> *On that side of [Potts] Point there were several great houses similar to the Bonner's, from which the human eye could have taken aim through the shutters. Barricades of laurels blinded with insolent mirrors.*

St Luke's is a luxurious and costly nursing home. The novelist Jessica Anderson, who used to live in Franconia, spent her last months there, and Labor leaders Gough Whitlam and the former Premier of New South Wales, Neville Wran, are spending their last years in the rest home in a crepuscular mental fog.

The restaurant on the Roslyn Street site, Gastro Park, has become one of Sydney's important gastronomic venues. Its most celebrated dish is the snapper fillet cooked with scales lifted and crisped to resemble a fish with risen hackles, accompanied by squid ink and squid crackle. One restaurant reviewer called it 'probably the most beautiful dish to have graced a Sydney restaurant in some time'.

Also undergoing transformation was the second-hand bookstore that had a curtained-off section devoted to 1970s and 80s porn. The manager told me that the high price of the porn magazines was because the girls still had pubic hair and therefore were collector's items. After it closed it became a swish men's clothing store and the green neon sign 'Books' that once flickered and buzzed for years outside the adult bookshop was bought by the Sydney City Council as a heritage souvenir of the old Cross.

Roslyn Street is a perfect example of the demise of celebrated Kings Cross names. By the end of 2011, Barons, Les Girls and the Piccolo had closed or gone, with Vittorio's empty café a forlorn reminder of these vanished institutions. There was talk that it would become a convenience store when suddenly, in February 2012, the Piccolo re-opened. Family members helped renovate it. Most of the chaotic memorabilia was not replaced and the few photographs, now pinned neatly to the freshly white painted walls, only hint at the former anarchistic college of images. The official launch was 17 February with Ayesha, the guest of honour, coming dressed as Marilyn Monroe. Her elegance and theatrical presence was a glamorous reminder of another era.

Vittorio is in his seventies yet he still works there every day. He is happy to be back, surrounded by people he loves. His voice is older and carries less, but if he sees me on the way to the post office, he can still be heard calling out, *Silvana! Silvana!*

'IT WAS LIKE A HORROR
MOVIE IN SLOW MOTION'

IN 1964 A METHODIST MINISTER, Ted Noffs, had just started up an audacious experiment in the Kings Cross community – the Wayside Chapel – when he was woken one night at his flat in Hughes Street to find a young woman dead at his front door. She had been dropped off by her panic-stricken friends after she overdosed on Methedrine. The chapel had been open for only a few months and it was Noffs's first time dealing with an overdose. Knowing next to nothing about drugs he thought it was an aberration. Soon he was to realise that this dead girl was not unique at all.

As he remarked later, 'Watching the escalation of the drug problem from 1964 to 1970 was like watching a horror movie in slow motion.'

In 1955 the *Sun-Herald* warned its readers that rock 'n' roll music with its primitive beat and hysterical female audiences would soon be coming to Australia. But the warning was unheeded; Australian youths took to the music as eagerly as the Americans, despite their horrified parents. It was not all American rock 'n' roll – an Australian rock 'n' roll culture quickly developed. In 1963 the dishevelled Kings Cross cinema was converted into a venue for surf music, a reaction of sun-loving surfers against the pale, skinny rockers and their blues-based music. This music was optimistic, inane and fuelled by basic, insistent beats. Named Surf

City, the venue attracted up to 5000 people of a weekend, where the teenagers listened to bands and did their trademark dance 'the Stomp' (the hands held behind the back and the dance itself merely simple steps sideways from foot to foot). The singer Little Pattie had a double-sided hit with 'Stomping at Maroubra' and 'He's My Blond Headed Stompie Wompie, Real Gone Surfer Boy'.

Local surf bands such as the Atlantics and American acts the Beach Boys played there. After the short-lived but influential surf music died out the following year, the 'beat boom' became popular, with bands like Ray Brown and the Whispers, the Missing Links and Billy Thorpe and the Aztecs playing regular gigs at Surf City before it closed down at the end of the decade. It was an alcohol-free venue but drugs began to appear, especially Drinamyl (an amphetamine nicknamed Purple Hearts), Mandrax (a sedative, colloquially referred to as Mandies), and Seconal (a barbiturate).

The rift between the generations became impossible to bridge. Teenagers left home, or were sent packing by their parents, and headed for the bright lights of Kings Cross and its music, drugs and social scene. Many turned up at the Wayside Chapel.

There were no churches in area when the Methodist church bought two two-storey flats at 27-29 Hughes Street, and in January 1964 a mission was established in the ramshackle buildings. Appointed to run it was 38-year-old Reverend Ted Noffs, a chubby man with unkempt hair and a mild, inoffensive manner that belied his inner toughness. He had worked in the slums of Chicago so he was not naïve; still, what he found horrified him. His aim was a non-denominational church, open twenty-four hours every day, that targeted the 'Beatles, beatniks and bohemians'. It was clear to Noffs that many of the young who were populating the streets were troubled, had no social support and had a disturbing attraction to drugs.

What the Methodist hierarchy didn't expect was that Noffs had no intention of duplicating a regular church. Soon his complex had a closed circuit television system, a coffee shop, disco, a theatre, poetry readings, music nights and debates. It published an ideas journal and a poetry magazine (Noffs's own attempts at poetry have a peculiar adolescent angst). He began to question the church's teachings and drifted away from organised religion, which he thought had isolated itself from the realities of the world. The chapel encompassed every faith. He held mass baptisms and officiated at more than 30,000 weddings, many for people who never went to church, including the stripper Sandra Nelson when she married the Paradise Strip Club manager Les Ramsay. By the 1970s he was one of Australia's best-known religious leaders and its most outspoken. His own church branded him a heretic on three occasions.

Because damaged, drugged, mad youths frequented the chapel, Noffs knew more than anyone else just what a problem drugs were becoming. The police refused to believe him, regarding him as a well-meaning fool. That was the problem with the adults – they really had no clue what was happening in the younger generation. Throughout 1965 hardly a night went by without Wayside ministering to drug casualties, while the government and the law refused to acknowledge any problem existed. These attitudes infuriated Noffs and in the same year he set up a crisis centre to deal with the escalating numbers of drug overdoses, potential suicides and other related problems.

By early 1967 the chapel was receiving 400 calls a week from people with drug problems, and the exhausted staff had to deal with fifty to sixty drug casualties every week. His next step was to open the Drug Referral Centre the same year, the first in Australia. Of course it caused an outcry; the public, police and government were against it, but Noffs knew the centre was needed, even more so when the psychedelic drug LSD became a ubiquitous presence. The gruesome emotional effects on some users, who sometimes descended into madness, only added to the centre's necessity. Assailed by these problems, it seemed to Noffs that 'the Cross was getting crazier and crazier'. It began to act as a host for a lost generation of young people who came from all parts of Australia, escaping from dysfunctional homes or authoritarian parents. What they found was the quick relief of pills, LSD and heroin, and they descended rapidly into addiction and prostitution as a way of paying for the drugs.

By 1975 Noffs had buried more than 150 people who had died of drug overdoses. Even middle-class families were not immune to the epidemic. The writer Kylie Tennant had written a novel, *The Joyful Condemned*, about young, vulnerable girls in the Cross during the Second World War, but she found herself personally caught up in the sordid reality of hard drugs when her mentally unstable son, Bim, who started his drug-taking with Mandrax and Seconal, quickly graduated to heroin. He left Kings Cross and attempted to give up drugs in the Blue Mountains. He seemed to be cured and happy. One day he borrowed $500 from his mother to pay for his enrolment at Sydney University. Instead of enrolling he ventured into the Cross to buy drugs. He was found dead in an abandoned house after he had been bashed and robbed.

Kings Cross became the visible and outrageous symptom of the sexual revolution of the late 1960s. Sandra Nelson's audacious public exhibition of herself in topless dresses was, in a brief couple of years, drained of its daring. Even the Hasty Tasty restaurant had topless waitresses (including my wife's mother who, as a single parent with no qualifications, had the beauty and assets required). But the event which began the cynical commercialisation of the sexual revolution was the arrival of the first Americans on R&R from Vietnam in 1967. At its peak, a plane load of GIs landed every day for six days of rest and recreation. By the time of the last flight in 1972, 280,000 American servicemen had descended upon Sydney, spending close to $80 million ($763 million today). They brought with them the latest craze from the United States, go-go dancing. The Cross became go-go land, particularly clubs like the Whisky-A-Go-Go on William Street, where scantily clad girls danced in cages. Some of the servicemen arrived with drug habits picked up in Vietnam, especially the insidious heroin. Most of the Americans, however, were spending their R&R picking up willing girls and paying for sex. Prostitutes hadn't been seen in the area in such numbers since the Second World War.

The young American men weren't interested in fancy nightclubs or restaurants but in the seedy striptease joints, which were nothing more than brothels and cheap food outlets. The legendary Bourbon and Beefsteak opened in 1967 to cater to the GIs. It was owned by a Texan, Bernie Houghton, who had spent three years in Vietnam, supposedly as a construction material boss, although rumours had him working for the CIA. The Bourbon and Beefsteak, on the site of the former strip club the Diamond Horseshoe (and before that the swanky Tabou), was cluttered with so many examples of bric-a-brac, Stars and Stripes flags and American memorabilia that it had the appearance of being created by a hoarder of kitsch. It didn't have the rarefied cuisine of the posh Chelsea across the road; instead it had steaks, lobsters and Mexican food. Tortillas and enchiladas were especially flown in and it was probably the first place in Australia to serve guacamole. Houghton built up the restaurant to more than twice its original size to fit in the enormous crowds of both locals and GIs. Americans, celebrities, servicemen and tourists made it a thriving pick-up joint, helped by the big bands and a spacious dance floor. Houghton also owned the Texas Tavern just down in Macleay

Street, which had a restaurant and 130 rooms. It was next to 44 Macleay where Abe Saffron rented an office. Polite and reserved with strangers and reporters, Houghton's closest friends considered him a loudmouth. An enigma to the public, he so successfully avoided the spotlight that many newspapers never had his photograph on file.

The American influence extended to drugs. The number of Australians addicted to heroin escalated over the next decade. Heroin seizures by Customs increased almost twenty-fold between 1981 and 1983, from 3.9 kilograms to 72 kilograms. Drug addiction also changed sexual tastes. During the 1950s and 60s heterosexual men would come to the Cross for oral sex with drag queens, something they didn't get at home. From the 1970s the clients of brothels and street walkers began to demand oral and anal sex which their wives and girlfriends wouldn't give them. The increasing volume of pornography coming into the country, most if it available in Kings Cross sex shops, stimulated the demand for sexual variety, but it was drug addiction that made it possible. Junkie prostitutes were, unlike previous generations of hookers, more likely to cater to these formerly distasteful sexual acts because they needed money to pay for their habits.

The physical assault on the Cross was even more remarkable in its brutal indifference to the locals. Ninety per cent of Kings Cross Road houses, terraces and the charming Belvedere boutique hotel had been demolished to make way for a tunnel which opened in 1975. The evisceration was also occurring elsewhere in Kings Cross.

Once the most charming boulevard in Australia, by the late 1960s and early 70s Victoria Street had degenerated into rows of deteriorating terraces that barely hinted at the splendour of its fashionable past. It was now housing for working-class families, pensioners, single mums, Kings Cross identities, and a constantly shifting population of young people and students. By June 1971, Frank Theeman, a would-be developer, had acquired all properties between numbers 55 and 115 Victoria Street in the expectation of building three 45-storey towers, a 15-storey office block with sixty-four stepped terrace apartments and, of course, an enormous eyesore of a carpark.

Theeman was a Viennese Jew born in 1913. After a brief incarceration in a concentration camp in 1938, he managed to immigrate to Australia in 1939. He founded Osti Holdings, which became one of the top lingerie makers in Australia, making him a multi-millionaire. A squirt like his friend Abe Saffron, he wore expensive gaudy suits; a coarse toupee sat on his bald head like a furry doormat and he had spectacles with such strong lenses his eyes seemed huge like a grasshopper's. Although married, he had an insatiable need for sex with other women. He was vain enough to think his looks appealed to women rather than the contents of his wallet and so, to stave off the ageing process, he had undergone monkey gland treatment.

When he sold his Osti empire he was highly cashed up, and looked for other business opportunities. In 1970 and 1971 he spent nearly $7 million buying up properties in Victoria Street and several more in Brougham Street. He wanted to spend $70 million on redevelopment. He had connections to criminals, the police and politicians, so he saw no threat to his plans. Eviction notices were given to 300 tenants in early April 1973 ordering them to vacate as soon as possible. All but twelve were evicted in one week. To make sure none of them returned, Theeman's thugs threw bricks through the windows, vandalised the buildings and set fire to them, making them uninhabitable. Those who remained had their gas and electricity cut off.

The Victoria Street Action Group was set up on 8 April to draw public attention to the need for low-income housing in the inner-city, hoping that squatting in the buildings would protect them from further malicious vandalism. The squatters who moved in were a motley bunch of students, intellectuals, feminists, communists, anarchists and working-class people, a unique and combustible mix that somehow cohered.

In order to stop this movement and force the squatters to stop their campaign, Arthur King, a highly vocal member of the Victoria Street Action Group, was kidnapped by a couple of thugs on 14 April. He was tied up and gagged, shoved in a car boot and driven around the city for two and a half days, his abductors forcing him to take Mandrax and threatening to kill him. The two ruffians had been hired by Jim Anderson, Saffron's business partner, to scare King. They succeeded all too well: after the traumatised King was released, he returned to his house, had a quick shower and fled, never to return. He refused to tell anyone what had happened.

The New South Wales Builders Labourers Federation (BLF), led by the charismatic Jack Mundey, declared a union green ban on Victoria Street. The Green Ban was to protect buildings of architectural importance, to preserve the homes of low-income earners and to protest against the relocation of evicted residents who were shipped out from the Cross, where many had spent their whole lives, to public housing in far western Sydney. Despite the Green Ban, the vandalism and threats continued.

Returning from a voyage in late April 1973, merchant seaman, musician and communist Mick Fowler was greeted by his distraught mother sitting on the front step of their terrace at 115A surrounded by their belongings. She had been given $50 by Theeman's dogsbodies and told to leave. Fowler, a solid powerfully built man, was furious and decided to fight back. But while breaking into his own house, Theeman's stand-over man Joe Meissner, a former world karate champion, blockhead and sadist, had him arrested by the police, who made it perfectly clear whose side they were on. But Fowler wouldn't be put off and a few days later, with the help of about fifty members of the BLF and members of the Seamen's Union, he stormed his own terrace and kicked out Meissner and three of his goons. Fowler now had his home back plus the promise of protection by the BLF.

Fowler represented the brave and public face of the tenacious struggle to survive what became known as the siege of Victoria Street. Bulky but solid, with an impressive moustache, he'd often sit outside playing his ukulele or guitar, singing protest songs in his rasping voice. Sometimes he slept or played on the roof to gain media attention. He recorded his own songs, like 'Green Bans Forever'. His fanatical resolve drove Theeman to distraction. Mandy was nine at the time and lived with her parents and brother and sister under Fowler's house in a cramped basement. She remembers him playing music at all hours, and his heroic consumption of marijuana and alcohol as he kept watch over his house, protecting it with his life. Mandy's father was a drummer, so he got on very well with Fowler the musician. Her family of five split up and left the tiny basement before the violence escalated. Because they were renting, their bond was paid and they were given the equivalent of two weeks' rent to vacate.

During the struggle, thugs set fire to the houses used by squatters. In the spring of 1973 a 24-year-old Aboriginal woman, Esther Marion Blaszkows, returned to an abandoned house in Victoria Street where she was squatting. Sometime after she went to bed a fellow squatter in the derelict house woke her, shouting that the staircase was ablaze. He tried to get her to jump out the window but she panicked and refused. Trapped, she died of asphyxiation. There was no electricity or gas connected so it's certain the fire was deliberately lit.

Theeman was becoming increasingly agitated by how much

the Green Bans and the squatters were costing him. He pestered his 'good friend' Police Commissioner Fred Hanson until the Commissioner agreed to rid the street of the squatters, who quickly discovered they were going to be evicted. They erected barricades and set up a siren to warn each other of the expected police raids. Early in the morning of 3 January 1974 a menacing pack of 250 police blocked off both ends of the street. With them were about thirty eager pupils of Meissner's karate school, carrying axes, sledgehammers and crowbars. For $50 each they set out to demolish the terraces and frighten the squatters into leaving. They smashed through doors and wrecked as much as they possibly could. People were threatened with guns and fists. The violence was watched by the police, who did nothing to stop it. Protesters and squatters barricaded themselves inside the houses. The merciless attacks lasted two days and were so successful that the only tenant remaining was Fowler, who would remain a defiant lone presence in his condemned terrace for the next three years. Fifty-three people were arrested including journalists, feminists like Anne Summers, writers, cartoonists and members of the BLF.

Theeman was becoming desperate. He was bleeding money but was still unable to get his hands on the derelict houses because the New South Wales BLF had banned its members from working on the project. There were ideological divisions between the New South Wales BLF and the union's federal body, which was based in Melbourne, and known for its corruption and criminal activities. Led by Norm Gallagher, a bloated, coarse man with a face resembling a blight-ridden potato, the federal body hated the New South Wales BLF's leadership and policies and, backed by developers, Gallagher took over the New South Wales branch. Gallagher was easily bribed and, once he had control of the New South Wales organisation in October 1974 his first decision was to lift the green ban on Victoria Street.

Theeman was jubilant, but he didn't count on an heiress in her mid-thirties who lived at the southern end of Victoria Street. Juanita Nielsen was a journalist who owned her own local newspaper called *NOW*. She lived on the eastern side of the street, near the mess of construction work for the Kings Cross railway station (which would not open until 1979). An only child of the wealthy Mark Foy family, well-known for their eponymous department store, she was married for ten years to a Danish sailor. After the marriage broke up in 1973 she left Denmark and returned to Sydney. Soon she was living in 202 Victoria Street, from where she published the fortnightly newspaper which produced innocuous puff stories about local businesses and restaurants in contra deals for advertising.

Nielsen was a tall, striking-looking woman. She was never seen without her make-up, which took an hour to put on, especially her false eyelashes. As a close friend said, 'There was a lot of work in putting these on each morning and getting the glue on was a trauma each day.' She was equally meticulous about her hair, wearing wigs in a high beehive style. To some there was the arch touch of the drag queen about her, but she was feminine and attractive enough to grace the covers of several detective novels as a femme fatale and she had a narcissistic certainty of her own beauty, frequently publishing her photograph in her newspaper.

At first she was not that interested in the war between the squatters and the developer, but as the violence increased, including the death of a woman in a suspicious fire, she became concerned not only about the brutality but the fact that the new development would push out the working class. Her alternative vision was of a 'slowly evolving social mix' of commercial and low to high-income residentals.

NOW became a paper of protest against Theeman and the project. Nielsen used her sexuality to gain what she wanted. She had a calculated affair with Jack Mundey so she could get closer to the decision-making about the green bans. When Gallagher took control and lifted them she was devastated. Her solution lay in her attractiveness and she deliberately set out to have an affair with John Glebe, Secretary of the Water and Sewerage Employees' Union. Glebe banned the necessary connection of water services to Theeman's project in the hope of 'stopping the final destruction' of Victoria Street. Glebe fell for Nielsen, who was in some respects using him. Her biographer Peter Rees defends Nielsen because of the larger issues at stake: 'She had become a woman obsessed – not with someone in her life but with her street.'

Theeman was incredulous; he had been outfoxed. By the middle of July 1975 his debts were $7.46 million, with more than $2 million interest owing. He was being charged ten per cent interest on his loan and shelling out $3000 a day in holding costs and all he had to show for it were rows of abandoned and derelict terraces. His agitation grew as Nielsen continued her vocal campaign against him and his project in her newspaper. On 26 May 1975 Theeman had a meeting with Jim Anderson and handed him a cheque for $25,000. What exactly the money was for was never discovered (but perhaps in hindsight can be guessed at).

On American Independence Day 1975, Nielsen was invited to the Carousel by Eddie Trigg, a dim sidekick of Anderson's, to discuss the nightclub advertising in *NOW*. Just after 10 am Nielsen walked up Earl Place, behind her home, passed through Springfield Avenue, and then across Darlinghurst Road to the entrance of the Carousel Club at the corner of Roslyn Street. She went inside and was never seen alive again.

No-one was ever charged with her murder and her body has never been found. There was talk that her death had been an accident, and speculation about the places where her body was disposed of have ranged from it being carved up and put in rubbish bins to being buried under a new runway at Sydney Airport. After several years three people were charged with conspiracy to abduct Nielsen on an earlier occasion. Edward Trigg was sentenced to three years jail; Lloyd Marshall, public relations officer for the Carousel, was acquitted; and Shayne Martin-Simmonds, a dogsbody at the squalid Venus Room, was jailed for two years. He allegedly told police he was asked to abduct Nielsen 'because some people wanted to talk to her because she was making waves'. He also told them of a plan to 'grab her by the arms and maybe put a hand over her mouth or pillow slip over her head'.

Her mysterious disappearance was not officially called a death until 1983, when a coroner and jury of six declared that Nielsen had died 'on or shortly after 4 July 1975'. The place and manner of death was unknown but there was evidence of police corruption and links between her murder, property developers and Kings Cross criminals. There can be no funeral for Juanita Nielsen.

By the time Mick Fowler left his terrace in May 1976, a deal had been agreed that twenty-two of the thirty-two houses on the building site would be restored, and a ten-storey apartment block complex built behind them. Done in the worst possible 1970s taste, its ugliness and cheapness is always remarked upon, especially when you see them from a train heading to the Cross from the city or the Domain; they seem to visually contaminate the whole ridge. The redevelopment also spelled the end of the 'roomers' of Victoria Street. The working class couldn't afford the restored terrace houses and they are now owned by the wealthy. Mick Fowler died in 1979. His funeral cortège of 700 people stopped outside his house in Victoria Street accompanied by a band playing his beloved jazz. The siege had cost the lives of two women, the dislocation and relocation of a community, hideous destruction and the further corruption of the police and the judicial system. The street was partially saved by bravery and a special combination of protestors and agitators. Without them Victoria Street would now be a strip of huge apartment blocks resembling the brutal hideousness of Soviet architecture.

La Croix

Post office

Maggie's restaurant

Wine bar

Bernie Houghton bust

Playground

Maramanah (demolished 1954)

MACLEAY STREET

BARODA STREET

FITZROY GARDENS

Gazebo
Cheverells

El Alamein Fountain 1961

No. 1–13 Elizabeth Bay Road demolished in 1972

Police station 1987

Kingsley Hall 1931

WARD AVENUE

BARNCLEUTH LANE

FITZROY GARDENS ARE THE SOCIAL lungs of Kings Cross. It is one of the few places where residents can escape their cramped apartments and relax in a lush oasis of tranquillity, breathing in the delicious scents of flowers and shrubs. It's where friends catch up, the lonely can watch the world go by and the mad can talk to themselves without been given a second glance.

What's noticeable now are the many dramatic changes around the perimeter of the park. The Rex Hotel was converted to apartments in 2002. The windows are shuttered and French doors open onto minuscule Juliet balconies. The interior is described as 'clubby but edgy'. The owners sought to appeal to the 'urban professional investor' and 'empty nester'. On the southern side of the Rex is the Potts Point Post Office, which also includes the Kings Cross Post Office which was once a separate entity in the shopping complex at the top of William Street, but is now incorporated in the one building. On the same strip is an intimate, gloomy grey bar called Valluto with a mainly gay clientele. A café-restaurant, La Croix, is on the site of a greengrocer's that closed when the more comprehensively stocked Harris Farm grocery opened in Springfield Avenue and took all its customers. La Croix calls itself a tartine café where almost everything is served on toasted Sonoma miche bread. The café's pretentious French name for the Cross, matched by furniture that borders on kitsch and expensive 'especially sourced' knick-knacks for sale, makes it difficult to imagine such a place operating ten years before, let alone being successful. It's a ladies-who-lunch space with flattering lighting that softens wrinkles and bad plastic surgery. Its customer demographic graphically illustrates just how gentrified the area has become.

There is also a restaurant on the ground floor of the Gazebo apartments. The outside area has bare tables, cushioned slatted garden chairs and at night glowing table candles. The interior has studded leather timber bar stools and communal tables with the quirky touch of a stuffed fox wearing sunglasses fixed upside-down to the ceiling. It attracts a younger set than La Croix and is often featured in gossip columns because it's a place frequented by models, actors and media personalities; few of the locals are regulars. It's a spot for those in their twenties and thirties who come to dine in order to be seen and gossiped about. Many of the women model themselves on vapid celebrities like Paris Hilton or the Kardashians and show off spray-on tans, porcelain smooth Botox foreheads, faux blonde hair and heels so high they approach the absurdity of the shoes worn by Venetian courtesans, whose heels were so vertiginous they were only able to walk in them supported by servants.

In between La Croix and the Gazebo is Maggie's, an Austrian restaurant which doesn't have their swish clientele. Maggie the owner is not to be confused with the other Maggie who runs a brothel of the same name in Kellett Street, although there have been occasions when couples arrived for a feed at the bordello and horny men fronted up to the restaurant. Maggie, an attractive white-haired woman in her late fifties, runs it with Teutonic efficiency and a remarkable memory for her customers' names and food preferences. The restaurant doesn't accept credit cards because in saving money she can give her diners bigger portions, including the enormous Bangalow pork dish, which I can testify is almost impossible to finish. Most of her customers are locals who want to re-experience the comfort food of their youth, especially the ever-popular Wiener schnitzel. It's not unusual to see plump tattooed middle-aged gay guys eating at a table next to solitary widows, young families and, on occasion, the former Prime Minister Paul Keating.

This is a place where older women who have lived in the Cross for years come to eat and gossip. Mandy and I have heard some of these women's stories, including the woman who survived an air crash in the mountains of New Guinea, and that of Margo Thatcher, the ice skater who came to Australia from England in the late 1950s and reinvented herself as the official photographer for Les Girls. There was also a woman in her late seventies who always wore tight white leather trousers, vivid scarlet lipstick and jet black dyed hair. Her one claim to fame – which she liked to boast about – was that she had been Abe Saffron's mistress way back in the days of the Roosevelt nightclub.

The Gardens are their most attractive and enticing during late spring and summer. The central tree is an enormous Hill's Fig, some hundred years old. Its branches arc across a third of the park, creating a calm and consoling dark green canopy. Nearby is a tall delicate Chinese elm, surrounded by clumps of palms, tree ferns and gorgeous, brightly coloured flowerbeds. Placed strategically around the gardens are raised hexagonal planter beds built from 5000 convict bricks. It's only after you've sat contemplating the park that you begin to realise how subtle the landscape design is. There are lawns, terracotta paving stones, hard sand spaces but no direct paths. You can enter the park anywhere – at ground level, up half a dozen stairs or drift in from the main road. The gentle rise and fall of its various levels provides a lyrical, even feminine sensuousness to its layout.

The gardens were created in 1973 by the Lithuanian immigrant Ilmar Berzins, the first qualified landscape architect in Australia. He also designed the exquisite McElhone Gardens down the road in Elizabeth Bay, with their tranquil lawns, pond full of goldfish, backdrop of Elizabeth Bay House and impressive spectacle of the harbour. One of his influences was the Canadian landscape designer Christopher Tunnard, author of the seminal work *Gardens in the Modern Landscape* (1938). The book emphasised parks as outdoor 'rooms', comprising contemplative elements, diverse plant species, flowerbeds and intricate walling or paving. All these fundamental concepts can be seen in Berzins's design of Fitzroy Gardens. For landscape architectural critic Tempe McGowan, Berzins's work was 'small scale interventions in the public domain ... he held a passionate belief that all people need to enjoy nature and that nature, in turn, can ameliorate the human temperament'. After thirty-five years of service for the Sydney City Council, Berzins resigned as head of the Parks and Recreation Division in 1986.

In 2008 the Sydney City Council began consultations and submissions for what they termed an upgrade of the Gardens. By 2010 the Council proposed not so much an upgrade as a drastic demolition and replacement. Residents were alarmed. On the plans Berzins's Gardens were pictured as a bleak conceptual mess and coloured a murky green; the paving stones, which are actually a warm ochre colour, were rendered metal grey. The new design was presented in warm, vibrant colours under a bright sunny sky. Berzins's original designs showed young and old people, the poor, and sailors enjoying Fitzroy Gardens. The new design concept was peopled with young middle-class professionals wearing groovy sunglasses striding down two severe pathways that bisected the gardens. More prominence was given to the pathways than the trees and gardens. This was not a contemplative, peaceful space to enjoy and breathe in the natural world; this was a denuded park to pass through on the way to somewhere else rather than resting in or taking pleasure in the location. There would be no more eccentrics, sailors, artists, bohemians, the old or children; instead the Cross would become a bland and generic thoroughfare for cashed-up professionals.

Residents wanted the Gardens 'refreshed' and 'revitalised' not demolished and redeveloped into a yuppie pathway. A committee called Friends of Fitzroy Gardens and Lawrence Hargrave Nature Reserve was formed. It was an unusual mixture of friends and enemies who bonded in an attempt to defeat the City of Sydney Council and its leader, Lord Mayor Clover Moore. In late October Mandy and I attended a meeting with twenty or so others at the Rex Centre that overlooked the Gardens. There was the familiar dormouse figure of a local who had an AVO out on him; Michael Gormley, a journalist, an inveterate and articulate letter writer and severe critic of the new design; a Greens Councillor (with a gaunt pale vegan face); the owner of a small art gallery; Malcolm Duncan, a plump, whisky-marinated, kilt-wearing barrister, a defender of lost causes in court and a former fellow student of his *bête noir*, the Liberal politician Malcolm Turnbull; Roz Sharp, whose photographs of the Cross and its denizens are a splendid documentary record of our area; Robyn Greaves, who does a sterling job of providing services in the area for the old and disabled; and, among others, Tony, a thin, intense postman. We were an odd bunch of residents to construct the community's defence. The postman suggested that the Lawrence Hargrave Reserve be untouched because of the presence of the hover fly. No-one knew exactly what was so special about the insect but the postman explained that unlike the mosquito and common fly, when it hovers 'it doesn't make a noise'. Someone asked if the fly were endangered.

'Well,' said the postman, 'you can find them in Surry Hills and Newtown but only in the Lawrence Hargrave Reserve in the Cross.'

As a defence it left something to be desired, but as the evening wore on we developed a strategy of public meetings, posters and petitions. When Mandy said we should also use Facebook and Twitter she was met with incomprehension, which gives an idea of the age of most of us.

Petitions gathered 3000 signatures, posters were distributed and letters of protest sent to the Lord Mayor. The first major rally was held on a sunny Saturday morning in early November. The crowd filled the gardens. Speakers included Malcolm Turnbull, the Federal Liberal MP. I gave a short talk on how tacky and desolate the gardens would look if the new design were followed. The pressure kept on growing. Clover Moore was up for re-election as a State MP and, judging by the mood of Kings Cross, she would lose crucial votes. In the middle of November she put aside the plans in what newspapers called 'a backflip'. The abandoned design work had cost $355,000 and public consultations about $260,000. The alternative scheme would restore the fountain and undertake maintenance work on the Gardens. It was a proud moment. The community had bonded in order to defeat a design that was ugly and destructive of one of the few places where locals can relax and enjoy nature; and it stopped the drive to glorify gentrification rather than social cohesion.

If we thought we had won the battle for the protection of the Gardens then we didn't count on Clover Moore's anger at having lost. She turned to the young mothers who had begun arriving in the Cross.

The sight and sounds of children in the Cross are still a relatively recent phenomenon. They were a rare presence in the 1990s and those were generally the kids of drug addicts. I remember a pair of exhausted junkies sitting down outside the scruffy Goldfish Bowl, a two-year-old on the mother's lap, when a middle-aged man offered the couple a hundred dollars for the child. *'Fuck off!'* shouted the father. Instead of scuttling away, the pedophile offered an extra hundred dollars. He only stopped pestering the couple when the mother threatened to call the police. It used to be that once a couple had a child and it began to walk, they'd shift to the suburbs for a bigger house and a backyard for the children to play in. Nowadays Australian parents' attitudes are more open to the European practice of children being brought up in apartments.

By 2011 it was estimated there were about 120 toddlers in the area. A parents' association wanted the existing small playground to be redeveloped so that it would not only be an area for toddlers but for children up to the age of twelve. A proposal was put forward by the Lord Mayor which argued for more space, percussive and water installations and equipment for toddlers up to teenagers. These ideas were written in the usual verbal gibberish the Council communicated in: 'Opportunity exists to embellish the space to enhance the alfresco experience for the whole community', 'Constructed, interactive and art elements allowing for non-prescribed outcomes and visual clues across site' and the mothers wanted 'a less open layout which can create a slow reveal of play options'.

There was no doubt that this would be a battle between those who saw the extension of the playground as an invasion of middle-class values, and families – the very families that many of us fled in order to live in the Cross, free of the suffocating bonds of suburbia. Locals thought the solution was simple – the playground should be built on adjoining Lawrence Hargrave Park, which had the space to furnish all they needed. Local historians like Warren Fahey and Delia Falconer, a mother of young twins herself and author of the superlative book *Sydney*, spoke out against the proposal.

Mandy and I and a couple of other residents turned up at the Sydney Town Hall to argue for the Hargrave Park idea. The cavernous chambers where the proposal would be voted on was stacked with dozens of prams, mothers and babies. The microphones mysteriously failed so that people who were arguing against the proposal like myself had to literally holler across the huge chamber and compete with noisy babies and bad acoustics. As I was shouting above the din, trying to be heard, a house husband behind me kept on hissing, *'Fitzroy Gardens are ugly!'* It was then I realised that few, if any, new residents liked the Berzins design – it was too cluttered, too subtle, and most importantly, too old; they would prefer the Gardens be obliterated and replaced with a minimalist plot that matched their brand-new neat functional flats.

The vote was passed enabling an extension of the playground. It meant that it would eat into the concept of the Gardens and, really, it was the equivalent of someone punching a hole in a beautiful painting. When the vote passed the mums cheered, with one loopy woman hysterically pumping the air as if she had won the lottery. Then Moore triumphantly invited in a waiting *Daily Telegraph* photographer who took pictures of the scene. It was further proof that from the beginning of this circus the result had been preordained. At that moment I knew this was the beginning of the destruction of the Gardens by stealth.

To sit on a bench in the Gardens of a summer weekday and relax in the sun-dappled light is one of the delights of the Cross, although it's sometimes hard to filter out the incessant honking and croaking of the omnipresent Australian white ibises with their scimitar beaks, black faces and necks and wings stained brown or grey, who forage in garbage bins and noisily fight over discarded food. At night they squabble on top of the palm trees and in the fig tree, keeping residents awake. In the morning the areas where they have perched during the night are evidenced by the grubby white splashes of their shit staining the pavement tiles below.

It's rarely mentioned but the Cross has a vibrant bird life, in addition to the putrid ibises. There are the familiar aggressive mynahs, rock doves, vociferous crows, noisy miners, feral pigeons (presently there is a man who sits on a bench in the Fitzroy Gardens and feeds a flock who, in their desire to get as much seed as possible, perch all over him so that he soon resembles a feathered coat), cockatiels with their Elvis quiffs, chattering green lorikeets, screeching sulphur-crested cockatoos happily leaving a trail of destruction in their paths, yellow-faced honey-eaters, magpies, fantails, butcher birds with their melodious piping, pied currawongs (one still sits on my fire escape railing of an evening chortling its double call of 'curra-wong'), sparrows and, in summer, the swifts, trilling fairy wrens and wattlebirds.

A common sight over the decades in the neighbourhood are exotic bird owners strolling down the glittering mile or sitting outside a pub with a parrot on their shoulder. The most popular breeds seem to be the black palm cockatoo with its distinctive red facial skin, and pale yellow lorikeets. The most ubiquitous birds, especially in the hours just after dawn, are the seagulls squabbling over rubbish and discarded junk food before the street cleaners arrive.

The book collector David Mitchell had a large black cockatoo for a long time. The hard-drinking cartoonist Lance Driffield who worked at *Smith's Weekly* with Kenneth Slessor could not bear to think of his parrot cooped up all day in his tiny Kings Cross flat, so he used to take it everywhere in an enormous birdcage. Other residents, like some still do today, strolled around the Cross with a parrot or cockatiel on their shoulders. There was a well-known 'Bird Man' who entertained tourists in the Fitzroy Gardens. His actual name was Owen Rutherford Lloyd, a plumpish fellow with a black suit, thick glasses and a debonair moustache. His act was playing a homemade phonofiddle, a single-stringed violin with a saxophone-like funnel held between his knees. The sound, according to the writer Delia Falconer, was like a horrifying whine, 'somewhere between a theremin and a musical saw'. What set his act apart was that he had budgerigars lined up along the horn's mouth and on the bow itself. To top everything off a cockatiel stood on his head.

Lloyd started performing in 1965, very aware that his act was 'quite unique, having no counterpart in any part of the world'. There's plenty of evidence that the tourists liked his show, but for residents in nearby apartments the Bird Man's act was musical torture. Twenty-seven residents of Franconia complained to the Council that the sound was 'repetitive dirges' and a man in Baroda Hall grumbled about the 'irritating and very penetrating noise created by an elderly man who plays a peculiar instrument'.

For the next few years, right into the 1970s, Lloyd continued to perform despite complaints from locals, the Council trying to stop him, and the mysterious incident when lead pellets were fired at him. In 1972 the Town Clerk was assured that the Bird Man had stopped playing in the Cross, but Lloyd wasn't that easy to get rid of and, according to Falconer, there were reports that he was still playing his phonofiddle with the dancing budgies into the 1980s, providing tourists with one of the most memorable attractions of the Cross.

The range of animals and birds is extraordinary. Over the years I've seen rabbits in apartments, pet rats, ferrets being taken for a walk, a tame rooster on a leash pecking at a bowl of water, a Shetland pony waiting patiently outside the New York restaurant for its owner, two goats (one leashed, the other not) ambling along Darlinghurst Road, and a python wrapped gently around a woman's neck like a shiny scarf.

But it's the dogs that grab your attention. There seem so many. In the morning when I walk to the post office there are dozens of them being taken for a walk before their master or mistress heads off to work, leaving them alone in their apartments. And what a mind-boggling range of breeds they are: tremulous whippets, snuffling bulldogs, dribbling boxers, querulous pugs, fluffy Maltese terriers and Pomeranians, happy labradors, mixed breed cattle dogs, poodles, shih tzus, cocker spaniels, a Siberian husky, clever Boston terriers, German Shepherds, chihuahuas, fox terriers, dachshunds, hyper Jack Russells, two Japanese Akita dogs that are never let off their leashes as they can be ferocious, a great Dane and two Mexican hairless that look as if they've been shaved by a blind hairdresser using a shearer's comb.

The spectre of loneliness and childlessness draws residents towards the companionship of animals, but lately there has been a pernicious trend of junkies breeding dogs to sell to pay for their habits. Local vets try to stop the addicts forcing the bitches to breed twice a year. The most popular breed is the chihuahua. Cute, small, with big eyes, as pups they are easy to sell, but hard to part with, especially for the women addicts and dealers who decide to keep them, wheeling them around in prams, dragging them along with them as they stagger through the streets, dazed out of their minds on drugs, the dog, trembling with nerves, afraid of being stood on. The chihuahuas are badly trained, generally hungry and react viciously to anyone other than their owner; they have a nasty habit of attacking the drug-sniffing dogs, which amuses their owners no end.

The local dogs like to urinate on the plinth of a bronze statue of Bernie Houghton erected in his honour on 31 July 2002. On top of the plinth is a sculpture of his head created by local artist Tony Johansen, known in the wider artistic community for his failed court action to have an Archibald Prize rescinded. The idea for the statue came from Les Girls' stalwart Carlotta, who met Bernie, as he was known to all, when she was seventeen. She thought he should be acknowledged, 'to commemorate all his kindness over the years', especially for giving more than $1.5 million to charities. The venture was approved by South Sydney Council. Said its mayor, John Fowler; 'It's because of Bernie that the Kings Cross community is vibrant, alive and so diverse.'

The statue is a reasonable likeness to Houghton, although it is more benign and avuncular than the man himself. Even if he had been involved in dubious CIA operations and had shady dealings with criminals, money laundering and the police, he did make the Bourbon and Beefsteak internationally famous and created an inimitable Kings Cross institution. If you follow his gaze across the gardens, you will see the police station, like a portable classroom slowly sinking into the earth. There is a nice irony in that the spot used to be an illegal casino run by the sartorially elegant Perc 'The Prince' Galea. It was stylish with a sultry Hollywood glamour. Baccarat, roulette, blackjack and craps were on offer as were free food and alcohol. Hostesses in sexy evening frocks doubled as escorts at the end of the night. Politicians, lawyers, sportsmen and entertainers went there, as did Frank Sinatra when he toured Australia.

The present car park was once the site of the swanky restaurant Kinneil, which had been a part of Barncleuth, once owned by David Jones but bought and extensively renovated in 1891. It was part of a long row of magnificent Italianate three-storey terrace houses that stretched from numbers 1 to 13. The houses were eradicated in 1972 as was the beginning section of Elizabeth Bay Road. One only has to see photographs of the terraces to regret they were ever demolished. They gave a grandeur and a sense of pride to the space which is now prosaic and undistinguished. It's a reminder of just how much Kings Cross is a place of disappearances. Streets, houses and communities have vanished as if they never existed. What becomes unsettling is just how much of this damage was done in the rapacious 1970s, truly a barbarian decade. But there's another curious aspect to this culling, in that in the stretches of houses razed, including William Street in 1916, right up to the destruction of Kings Cross Road, Victoria Street and Elizabeth Bay Road, it was always the people who lived in the buildings and houses of uneven numbers who were the victims of redevelopment. Lucky owners and renters lived in the even numbers.

Across from the police station is the El Alamein fountain. It looks like a dandelion head on a steel stalk, spraying water that, when affected by wind, scatters wildly like watery spores. It's a common backdrop for photographs, the ultimate visual proof that one has been to Kings Cross. Someone commenced a new tradition by jumping into the fountain one hot New Year's Eve in 1964. Police barely made any attempt to stop it that first time but for years afterwards a battle would rage every New Year between police trying to protect the fountain and the crowd trying to jump in.

It's sometimes forgotten that the fountain is a sacred war memorial, as a law student recently found out. In a story headlined 'Vile Insult to Fallen Heroes', the *Daily Telegraph* thundered that Alexander Mathews, twenty-nine, 'desecrated the memory of our fallen soldiers' by urinating into the fountain early one morning after a heavy drinking session. After a local spotted Mathews with his pants down urinating into the fountain at 6.40 am, she hurried to the nearby police station and reported him. The appalled Magistrate, Hugh Dillon, said, 'The public is entitled to be outraged.'

Through the haze of the fountain's spray one can make out the Bourbon and Beefsteak. It was closed for two years after severe rain damage. The shuttered building had an abject loneliness about it and when it re-opened as the Bourbon, it was in stark contrast to the bustling raucousness of the original Bourbon and Beefsteak, whose name it traded on. The interior that faces the street is a white-tiled front bar and about as inviting as a lavatory. It's a split-level space that leads into the main dining room area with a more discreet back dining room featuring brown leather banquettes and blue velvet dining chairs. The food is Creole based, including jambalaya, deep fried oysters, and clam and corn chowders, most of the dishes two to three times the price food used to be at the Beefsteak. The inclusive world of the Bourbon and Beefsteak has gone, replaced by a clinical space which has disconnected itself from the past, attracting young professionals, lawyers, property developers and politicians. Those who remember the original Bourbon don't go there. The food and alcohol are expensive and the ambience lacks the informal conviviality of Bernie's club.

The older blocks of apartments are generally child-free. Across from Fitzroy Gardens on Macleay Street is a row of 1930s art deco buildings. Franconia is probably the most striking. The flats are highly sought-after. There are residents who have lived there for decades, some now so infirm that they have professional companions, generally Asian, to help them through their day. Mandy and I got to know an Italian gigolo in his late sixties who was kept by a woman in her eighties whom he had to 'entertain' as well as walk her ancient dog. There seemed to be only one exception to the aged population and that was a striking blonde girl about eight or nine years old. She would emerge from the august façade dressed in tiny dresses that emphasised her sexuality. Confident and disturbingly attractive, the girl spent countless hours in the gardens alone, talking to whoever took her fancy, especially men. The locals nicknamed her 'Lolita'. One time two middle-aged women had to rescue her when a man started to walk away with her to his car.

Another time 'Lolita', dressed in a tight blouse and tiny shorts, focused her attention on two rough characters who were dismantling their stall at the Sunday markets. One of the guys asked if she wanted to come with them. She was weighing up their offer when I went up to the grinning men and said, 'Don't you dare.' They started to argue their innocence, but stopped when they realised other suspicious locals were also eyeing them.

There are many women – married and single – who lived in Franconia. One of the youngest was Leanne Edelsten, who had once been famous for being married to Dr Geoffrey Edelsten, a flamboyant and controversial owner of medical centres. He became so wealthy that he bought the Sydney Swans football team during the 1980s and married Leanne, who was half his age, showering her with presents, including a pink car and a pink helicopter. She was just out of her teens, thin, blonde and with the attractively vacuous face of someone who hadn't experienced much of life. In 1990 Edelsten was jailed for soliciting a hitman to assault a patient and for perverting the course of justice.

After divorcing Edelsten, Leanne married again but the marriage didn't last. She became an intensive care nurse at St Vincent's and developed a reputation as a socialite, an easy position to attain in the superficial, vulgar world of Sydney society. In 2004 she was having lunch at a city restaurant when a plump man of about sixty-five with beady eyes approached her table and, with a leer, purred: 'In my opinion all intelligent women talk with their hands.' Later, he whisked her off to his room at the Four Seasons Hotel and, in her own delighted words, 'ravished' her.

The man was Clive James, an expatriate Australian who had made his name in Britain as a television critic, light versifier, celebrated TV host, tango enthusiast and brilliant essayist. Leanne was a quarter of a century his junior but she adored him and he was smitten by her. Despite the fact that James was married with two children, Leanne became his mistress, coldly saying of the wife, 'She's not a woman to feel sorry for. She's beautiful, intelligent, her own person.'

For a period of eight years James and his Kings Cross lover maintained a global affair via emails, photographs and role-playing. One email from the polymath James panted, 'All I need is a few hours in a sun-flooded room with a certain naked nurse.' He referred to her as 'Ms Hood' (after Little Red Riding Hood – the 'Ms' is a delightful feminist touch). She nicknamed him 'Mr Wolf' because he had 'devoured' her when they first met.

'If there's a poster boy for Senior's Week, he's it,' she trilled about his potency, 'I don't know whether it's got to do with experience, intelligence ... but he'd leave men half his age for dead.' They would get together whenever he was in Australia.

The affair was suddenly broken off by James when his wife of forty years, the academic Prue Shaw, not only found the incriminating emails but also the revealing photographs Edelsten had sent to Mr Wolf. What James didn't count on was that Edelsten, who had thoroughly embraced the new mistress code of publicising affairs, especially if the married man was famous and/or wealthy, went on a television current affairs show to brag about their relationship, including excruciatingly embarrassing details about how they would have a cup of tea and a Cherry Ripe before and after sex.

Edelsten's public revelations added further to Mr Wolf's dark days. He had been diagnosed with leukaemia in 2010 and now his wife had kicked her philandering husband out of the family home. He ended up living in a dismal basement in Cambridge. Further indignity was to come courtesy of his mistress. In order to prove the affair, a camera crew followed Leanne to England where she was filmed confronting a gaunt and frail James. Not content to speak to her former lover, she showed him copies of the sexy photographs she had sent him and, to add to his discomfort, handed him a Cherry Ripe. The expression of horror and embarrassment on his face was probably only matched by

Eugene Goossens when Sydney customs officials found his stash of pornographic material. Like Goossens before him, and then Lim Yew Hock, the Malaysian High Commissioner whose fling with a stripper ruined his career, James was to discover that a relationship with a woman from Kings Cross was to wreck his life.

As he trooped off after the media ambush, he looked a shrunken, befuddled old man. As to Edelsten's motives in going public, she may have wanted revenge on her famous lover because of the cowardly way he ended the relationship by email. She succeeded all too well in humiliating James and she achieved a brief moment of the media attention which she seemed to crave. It proved that men's lust will bring them undone and, once again, that the Cross could dramatically change lives forever.

One woman who didn't care about the scandal was Rose, the beggar. She had been homeless for a year when she was offered a public housing flat. Before she shifted in she told me how excited she was because it would be the first home of her own. She only lasted a few months when neighbours complained about the noise and chaos her guests caused. Tossed out, she returned to her previous way of life and, as I write this, she has set up camp outside the Potts Point Post Office, near the swish La Croix café. She has a sleeping bag, a pillow and a plastic bag of books. She wakes up around the time the post office opens, flips open her mobile phone to see if there are any messages, and weighs up her options for the day. She is greeted by long-term locals and avoided by the newer residents. If she's unlucky a lithe, suntanned woman whose days are spent in restless wanderings with her two mangy dogs turns up and circles her, calling her crazy and loudly ordering her dogs to stay away from Rose, whom she thinks is mad and evil.

After emerging from her sleeping bag – unruly greying hair, watchful eyes, and wearing the same clothes whatever the season – she thrashes her bed against the low brick wall of a flowerbed, folds it up and puts it back against the post office wall, before she heads off for something to eat and to prepare herself for an evening of begging. In a way her lifestyle has made her a flâneuse – although she doesn't know it – and one whose understanding of Kings Cross is different from mine because her territory and its landmarks are determined by the dealers she buys drugs from when she's using smack, where she can shoot up and sleep undisturbed, and, of course, her intimate knowledge of the turf where she begs.

KITCHEN OF HELL

WHEN ABE SAFFRON'S VENUS ROOM opened in 1968 it was an attempt to recapture the stylish ambience of the Roosevelt at its height. The new nightclub had a stunning cocktail bar, the finest food, luxurious tables and chairs and intimate padded booths. The waitresses wore the latest fashion in mini-skirts and the customers turned up in tuxedoes and gowns. Even though it was one of the most spectacular venues in the Cross, it failed to make money. The times were against it; there was a move away from 1950s glamour. American servicemen on R&R wanted sex and cheap food. Saffron came to the conclusion that he had to transform the venue and he turned to a Scottish-born hoodlum, Jim Anderson, to do it.

The bulky, mop-haired Anderson gave himself the title 'Big Jim'. Born in a rough area of Glasgow, he eventually ended up in New Zealand as a traffic cop and the manager of a Maori show band, which played in Australia. In 1957 Anderson opted to stay in Sydney, becoming a recognisable figure in the nightclub scene, booking acts and working as entertainment director with the Rex Hotel, where he said he had his first contact with corruption and prostitution: 'The Rex Hotel was a place for working ladies of a high standard and quality, with complete police protection ... I studied the system pretty closely...'

With a sociopath's duplicity and a cultivated cheery disposition that belied his capricious acts of violence – the more frightening because of their unpredictability – Anderson relished his reputation as man to be afraid of. For someone like Virginia Perger, a stripper at the Bunny Club and a prostitute, he was a 'ruthless ... pompous ... SOB'. He had a passion for expensive jewellery, gold-digging mistresses (one of whom was a drag queen), and drove around the Cross in a white Rolls Royce Silver Shadow. He always carried a nickel-plated revolver and was generally escorted by two bodyguards as he toured the Cross collecting money from the various venues he ran in collaboration with Saffron. He was an informant for the police, an arsonist and a much travelled overseas courier for the purpose of laundering money. And a killer.

These qualifications made him the perfect choice to run the Venus Room at 6–8 Orwell Street, once the Staccato strip club. Anderson, as the licensee, would take forty per cent, Saffron sixty per cent of the profits. The high standards plummeted. The exquisite parquet floors were covered in cheap carpet that became beer soaked and foul smelling with cigarette burns so numerous it looked like a holocaust of dead cockroaches. The kitchen which once created magnificent three-course meals now only offered warmed-up pies and sausage rolls. It ignored its liquor licence and sold booze twenty-four hours a day. It had a tiny dance floor, a juke-box instead of a jazz band, a metal framed bar along the left wall, basic tables and chairs and dim lighting to hide the tackiness. Go-go dancers gyrated on the bar top while strippers worked the small stage.

It soon became a spot for drug deals, pick-pockets, criminals and kickbacks to a growing number of bent police. By the middle 1970s, even Anderson agreed 'it was nothing more than a brothel'. Up to fifteen girls worked every night, including a disturbing number of child prostitutes and, as a bonus for those who wanted something different, Anderson also supplied drag queens. Most of the hookers had heroin habits and would take ten to fifteen men a night at $30 a client. The squalid Venus Room seemed to encapsulate the sordid nightlife that was becoming pervasive in the Cross.

Anderson added to his notoriety on 22 June 1970. A police source rang and told him that Donny Smith, a stand-over man for a brothel madam, was coming to kill him. Smith had wanted to run prostitutes out of the Venus Room but Anderson, who had his own stable of whores, refused. Anderson always had a revolver, so he was prepared. He was balancing the account books – which meant the two sets of books, one for the tax inspectors and the second with the real figures that tabulated the actual money coming in – when Smith loomed up in front of him and snarled a greeting: 'Hello, cunt.' After a few expletives and bragging he was going to kill Anderson, Smith threw himself at Big Jim, hitting him with a gloved fist. The leather glove hid a hand wrapped in plaster of Paris and lead. Smith's sudden attack took Anderson by surprise and he fell onto the floor, his mouth smashed, several teeth littering the carpet and his nose a bloody pulp. A stunned Anderson slowly got up off the floor, thinking to himself, 'Fuck you, cunt. It's me or you.' Once on his feet he pulled out his gun and shot Smith through the heart. Smith fell to the floor but then sprang up again, thoroughly scaring Anderson with his miraculous recovery. Anderson fired again and hit his assailant in the leg, but like the android killer in *The Terminator* movie, Smith seemed impervious to the bullets, and he turned towards the front door that led out to Orwell Street, preparing to leave, when Anderson shot him in the back. Smith trotted a few unsteady steps to the front door and collapsed onto the footpath, one foot still in the doorway of the Venus Room, his face in the gutter.

Anderson was charged with murder and for discharging a gun in a public street. This was reduced to manslaughter and not long afterwards the Askin government granted a 'no bill', which meant all charges were dropped. It was rumoured that Big Jim had paid $15,000 to avoid prison. The killing made him even more feared. He had shot someone and got away with it. He and Saffron became known as 'The Invincibles'. It seemed they were above the law and indeed they were, much of it due to Saffron, who had corrupted the police force and politicians.

David Hickie writes in his book *The Prince and the Premier* that 1965 'was the turning point in the development of organised crime in Australia, and especially New South Wales'. The reason for this was the election of Robin 'Bob' Askin as Liberal Premier in 1965. During the war Askin was the SP bookie for his battalion, a loan shark, and ran the two-up games. Even when he was Premier he had an account with one of the largest SP bookie rings in the state. Saffron found the greedy politician easy to corrupt. Soon the Premier was on Saffron's payroll and was given tips on fixed horse races as 'a courtesy to Premier Askin'. Saffron also ran illegal casinos and to keep them from being raided he was paying the Premier and the corrupt Police Commissioner Norm 'the Mushroom' Allan $5000 to $10,000 per week each. Askin often met Saffron at restaurants and phoned him regularly. The Police Commissioner was an even more frequent visitor and would lunch at Saffron's home. The result was that during the ten years from 1965 to 1975, as Alfred McCoy, author of *Drug Traffic,* points out, with 'the Liberal-Country parties in power, the State endured a period of political and police corruption unparalleled in its modern history'.

Above the law, Saffron's empire expanded outside Kings Cross and soon he controlled much of the vice trade, including illegal gambling and prostitution, in other states as well, bribing dozens of politicians and police to ensure he was protected. He made so much money that he took to loan sharking, providing short-term loans at exceptionally high interest rates. As Saffron's son, Alan, writes in his biography of his father, *Gentle Satan*, these were given to some of Australia's most prominent businessmen, including Sir Peter Abeles (the amoral transport mogul allowed his trucks to be used for delivering marijuana), Frank Theeman during the Green Bans on Victoria Street, and to Kerry Packer to pay off enormous gambling debts.

Saffron's relationship with Askin and Allan made him one of the most influential men in Australia. As Saffron's son, Alan, says:

> *There have been many accounts of my father's relationship with these two men but none realised the depth of his association and influence. Both were totally corrupt and my father's excellent business brain and complete integrity in his dealings with them allowed him to exploit their greed to the fullest.*

But it was more than that. There have been apologists for the softly spoken Saffron over the years, saying he gave to charity and always paid his musicians on time, and in cash, and that he merely positioned himself to take advantage of what people wanted – gambling, sex and grog – but he was worse than that; he allowed drug dealing on his premises which destroyed lives, he used his thugs to violently intimidate anyone he didn't like, and he corrupted the law and politics. His son rightly describes him as 'a sinful man'.

Sex provided Saffron with considerable cash flow and by 1974 he ran eight sex shops in the Cross. He also owned or part-owned strip clubs and budget cafés and restaurants where the food was unreliable but you could always get a drink after-hours. He ran a brothel in the Kingsdore Hotel in Darlinghurst Road and the orgy rooms in the Appin private hotel in Springfield Avenue.

His malign morality was contagious. At the Darlinghurst

Police Station, which oversaw Kings Cross, most of the police accepted bribes, worked as little as possible and made few arrests. At the station the police drank on duty and even converted one of the cells into a bar. It was estimated that during the 1970s the police were being paid bribes of upwards of $500,000 a year in total. The gangsters used the corrupt police to warn off competitors. Gaston, the owner of the Tabou nightclub and restaurant, was kidnapped for a day by Frank 'Bumper' Farrell and a few other cops on the orders of Saffron because the crime boss coveted the Tabou site.

During the day there were still signs of the old Cross. 'Meals on Wheels' found itself in the curious position of having to deliver food to rich old ladies who dined off silver in elegant apartments filled with antiques. As the volunteers discovered, these women had always had servants and had never cooked a meal in their lives and now they were too old to learn.

It may have been becoming an increasingly dangerous place but the Cross still attracted bohemians and artists like Don Walker, a songwriter with Cold Chisel. He arrived in 1976 and stayed for two years in the shabby Plaza Hotel in Darlinghurst Road ($20 a week for a room), a couple of doors down from Springfield Mall. The hotel's regular clientele was an unholy mix of hookers, dealers, junkies, trannies, crims and artists. Walker lived in a room off the first floor landing that was:

> ... *triangular and about as high as it is long, one single bed, one*
> *washbasin, eighteen inches of hanging space, all of it facing*
> *not out but in at a tiny exercise yard strangled by a fire escape*
> *going to a locked gate and a three-foot fill of garbage bags ...*
> *The bathroom round the corridor's got a pebbled floor with crud*
> *gummed in it and three showers and a bathtub no-one will ever*
> *be stupid enough to use.*

There were still cheap eateries around and he'd occasionally lash out on eggs and toast or a three-course watery roast at the Astoria 'with the dumb waitress with the cross eyes and the old girls leaving pools of piss on the café seats all for $2.70' as his evocative memoir *Shots* recalls. His friend, the lead singer of Cold Chisel Jimmy Barnes, liked to take his breakfast near the Manzil Room (where they had a regular gig) at a Turkish café where the owners would add hash oil to his short black.

It was a time when those who stayed at the Plaza had, as Walker writes, 'no philosophy or cause beyond cock and drugs'. His preferred drug was Mandrax, which he thought great for sex, 'that's if you can get through the door into the other room without walking into the wall five times first'. Because his room was so small and basic Walker spent time reading and writing in a café he regarded as *his*. One of Cold Chisel's most popular numbers, 'Breakfast at Sweethearts', is a paean to the importance that café played in his life, not only for the breakfast ('the best in town'), but because it gave him a view out onto Darlinghurst Road where he could enjoy the passing parade of drunks and streetsweepers as his hangover slowly dissipated, and fantasise about Anne-Maria, the mini-skirted waitress.

The contrast between the Cross of the day and night began to blur. Prostitutes became more aggressive in their importuning, men and women high on alcohol or drugs were everywhere of a day and the language of the streets grew louder, more obscene and profane. It was hard to avoid the sight of youngsters shooting up in lanes and doorways and homeless kids drifting through the streets. The number of runaway teenagers making for Kings Cross grew alarmingly. At the start of the 1970s there were 650 homeless children wandering the streets; the youngest was nine-years-old, the average age fourteen. Many had severe drug and alcohol addictions. More than a third were so disturbed they required full-time therapy and counselling. Up to eighty-five per cent came from broken homes, with a bewildering array of stepbrothers, stepsisters and step-parents. A quarter of the boys worked as prostitutes, compared with fourteen per cent of the girls. Drug and alcohol problems affected nearly half of the girls, more than twice the rate of the boys.

Criminals deliberately sought out these homeless kids, slipping packets of heroin and barbiturates under the front door of a Kings Cross refuge in an attempt to get them hooked; addicted children were more than likely to become prostitutes. Girls as young as thirteen sold themselves on the street or in brothels. In one bordello, publicised as Sydney's first sex supermarket, the girls stripped to disco music and offered their bodies for men to fondle, other girls and women prostituted themselves, while in the background television screens showed endless loops of pornographic movies featuring sexy schoolgirls. The cost of fondling a girl was $10. The life span of many of these children was short. A typical case reported in a newspaper was an anonymous fourteen-year-old girl who fled her unhappy home to find a new life in Kings Cross. She quickly became hooked on heroin, LSD, Mandrax and cocaine, then found work as a prostitute to pay for her drug habit. Four years later she was found on the floor of a sleazy room, dead from an overdose. If workers from the Wayside Chapel tried to protect these vulnerable girls they were threatened and, on one occasion, a staffer was stabbed in a bar trying to help one of them.

By the end of the 1970s child prostitution was overt and seldom policed. Children worked from the El Alamein fountain for $30 a client. The signal for paedophiles wanting to have sex was to show 'a keen interest in the fountain'. Another spot for young men to prostitute themselves was Costello's in Kellett Street, a two-storey dive where men paid for sex with boys. There were flimsy cubicles upstairs where the boys would have their encounters. One boy, who was recruited into a sex ring run by former Wollongong Lord Mayor Tony Bevan, was repeatedly drugged and forced to have sex in the cubicles and in some cases anally raped. The manager of Costello's, Johnny McLean, invariably got a tip-off when the police were going to raid and the boys, sometimes up to twenty of them, would be bundled through a door and forced to remain in a tiny space for an hour or more.

As the 1980s arrived, Noffs was in despair, trying to warn the public and police that child prostitution had reached 'contagious proportions'. There was an epidemic of drug taking amongst the children. Even concerned policemen were disturbed by what was happening. One Vice Squad member was quoted as saying they were 'frustrated, losing faith and giving up hope over it all'.

Experienced adult prostitutes noticed that the scene was changing dramatically – they now had to compete with transvestites and transsexuals as well as children. A hooker who went by the name of Loretta had worked her pitch for years near the Bourbon and Beefsteak and was disgusted by the new sex scene. One of her competitors was Karla, a hefty Maori who worked as a male prostitute. What amazed Loretta was that Karla made no attempt to disguise that she was a male wearing women's clothes.

'Lord knows, I'm not a paragon of virtue,' she complained, 'but how can anyone go off with that?'

The prostitution market was so lucrative that by the late 1970s there were more girls working the streets than during the R&R days. By this time the Wran government had de-criminalised prostitution and hookers literally fought for their pitches with knives and razors. Prostitutes came up from Melbourne to battle for a slice of the market which was now legal. Pimps were renting out rooms for $80 a shift, there were four shifts a day, seven days a week. Madams could make a considerable amount of money.

One such madam was Gabriella Sloss, whose husband, Albert, was the morally slippery Labor MP for Kings Cross. She had half a dozen bordellos (the most well known was Gabriel's Hideaway in Bayswater Road) and wrote a weekly column for *Ribald* magazine called 'Listen to me! By Mistress Gabriel'. The problem for the madams was the pervasive drug use. Of twelve girls one madam employed in her brothel, eight of them had $100-a-day habits. She despaired that her girls were 'on a merry-go-round of death. They are only working to pay for their habit, which is becoming greater day by day.' There was becoming a clear distinction between the drug-addled street walkers and those who serviced clients in a brothel. One prostitute, Ami, who worked in the luxurious 157 Pleasure Spa in Victoria Street, had come from Los Angeles and was proud to be working in a place that had a swimming pool and jacuzzi. She was particularly critical of the street girls: 'If they're going to be out there they should dress a little better. They look like whores.' But so many of the girls on the street were zonked out on drugs they just didn't care what they looked like or what bizarre sexual tastes they had to accommodate.

The night-time was a cacophony of car horns and loud music pouring out of the strip clubs and sex shops. Spruikers, brash and aggressive, only added to the noise. They began at around 7 pm and kept up their loud patter until dawn, verbally duelling with spruikers from different clubs across the main drag, and buttonholing passers-by with such enticements as, 'C'mon fellas, if you don't see it here they haven't got it', 'Shannin, the lady with more movements than a Swiss watch' and 'The Duchess of Peel from South Africa'. The Paradise Club spruiker would cajole men with, 'It's a filthy, dirty show downstairs. Come in and enjoy yourselves.' Police couldn't stop the racket because they claimed the barkers operated from private property.

At the Pussy Galore Club, the best of the strippers, dressed as a schoolgirl, would perform live in the shop window, flashing her backside for the crowds. Frank 'Tubby' Black ran the club for twenty years, even after it changed its name to the Kitten Strip Club (known around the traps as the only club in the Cross with a sprinkler system installed). Its glass door entrance was between a jewellery shop run by a gay couple and the Steve Brothers' deli. On the way in were screens showing pornographic movies. Men paid a $3 entrance fee. Upstairs they could ogle the strippers, drink sly grog and visit prostitutes on the top floor. Strip nights alternated with nude and mud wrestling. One act featured a naked girl who would swing suspended from the ceiling over the audience's up-turned heads, the men agog with lust at the fleeting sight of a real vagina orbiting above them. The acts must have been arousing because, as Black relates in his memoir *Kings Cross, Double Cross*:

> *Some fellows would put on condoms as they would get horny in the show and play with themselves. It got so bad we had to install special tins in the gents to put the used ones in, to stop the toilets from getting blocked.*

Many of the women were married with children and stripping paid the bills; others were just plain bored or drug users. The addicts were trouble. One of Black's favourite strippers, Gail, was found dead in a restaurant toilet in the Cross after injecting heroin. One girl died while performing. Sixteen-year-old Sonya Glendenning was dancing naked when she slumped onto the stage in a fit, overdosing on Dormel and Mandrax. The smart-alec headline in one of the tabloids was: YOUNG STRIPPER DIES OF DRUG OVERDOSE ON STAGE, COMMUNION ON SUNDAY, STRIPPING ON MONDAY. She had set her sights on becoming a stripper and at the age of fourteen she achieved her dream under the alias of Liza after lying about her age. She was Catholic, fit, a vegetarian and lived with her grand-mother in a housing commission house in Daceyville (the model suburb of the 1920s, which had been built with such high hopes to counter the squalor of inner-city places like Darlinghurst and Surry Hills, had become a blighted housing commission estate peopled with blue collar workers and the unemployed). Her fa-ther and mother tried to talk her out of working as a stripper but she was adamant. The parents gave up their opposition, realising she was happy at what she was doing and even saw her act on oc-casion. Because women caused him such problems, Black began to employ female impersonators and transvestites. He lost customers 'but they [the men] had better bodies and looked after themselves. The men were ten times better strippers than the women.'

The strip clubs continued to go down market. How could they compete with pornography? As the renowned American strip-per, Blaze Starr, lamented, 'Porn killed stripping … in my day nudity was so rare – *so special*.' The art of stripping had always been the art of the tease, but the sacrosanct pact between audience and strippers – thou shall not touch – seemed quaint given the imagery of pornography. In order to compete strippers now had to do what the business called 'Hot Shows'. Girls were expected to sit on men's laps and allow themselves to be fondled or even taken upstairs for sex. One of the few places where that wasn't happen-ing was the Pink Panther Strip Club.

The girls and drag queens who worked there thought the oth-er venues were low rent. Customers at the Panther sat on vinyl chairs. The acts were choreographed by Judd Lane and petting was not allowed. The women were paid $10 for their ten-minute acts, sometimes performing two or three times a night. Most would strip in other clubs as well. They hadn't had a pay rise for years and had to make or buy their own costumes. For a French performer like Danielle, the attitude towards stripping in Australia was very different to Europe. They were paid much less and didn't have the respect that European audiences gave them as professional entertainers. Australian men liked to heckle the girls. Sometimes the relationship between the strippers and audience was such a hostile one that they'd swap abuse and hurl obscenities at each other, both sides caught up in a verbal dance of mutual self-loathing.

Experienced strippers viewed their male audience as mugs. The cynicism wasn't helped by the bitchiness between performers, especially the drag queens teasing the real women. The exotic snake dancer Roberta Sykes, her black skin the result of an African-American father, grew weary of the petty jealousies, costumes shredded with a razor, cigarettes dropped into her drinks and once the word *Nigger* written in lipstick on her make-up mirror. There was also a growing chasm between those who saw stripping as an art and those who, as Danielle said, 'make no effort with their costumes and don't know any dance steps … they go on stage because it's easy money and easy work. No wonder the audience don't applaud.'

It was agreed by fellow strippers that Elizabeth Burton was probably the best of them all. Eldest of eight children, five boys and three girls, she was born in 1947 and brought up on a housing commission estate. Molested by a priest when she was eight, she left school at fourteen and took up a hairdressing apprenticeship. At the age of seventeen she became a dancer in the cages at the Whisky-A-Go-Go on William Street. Like many go-go dancers it was a natural progression into striptease. Off stage Burton thought of herself as an ugly duckling but when she was performing she felt wonderful because of 'the power I have over an audience'.

In 1968, at the age of twenty-one, she went to Vietnam as a go-go dancer performing outdoor shows for thousands of troops. One evening six drunken American soldiers dragged her into a hut on a beach and put a machine gun against her head and the

barrel of a German Lugar in her mouth and raped her in a violent sexual frenzy, masturbating on her and fucking her. After
discussing whether they would kill her, they suddenly left. She
dragged herself to the ocean and washed herself, pleading with
God to forgive her.

Back in Australia she worked at the Bunny Club as a waitress,
then travelled to the United States where she was employed as
a maid for two black women, and worked cutting and bagging
heroin and cocaine. She went on to be a hostess in Japan before
returning to Australia and stripping.

When she started out striptease was more burlesque; the girls
would have a character and a gimmick. There was less emphasis
on nudity and more on tease. For a fifteen to twenty minute show
she would have to remove twenty to thirty garments. By the mid-
1970s she was Australia's highest paid stripper, working at the
Pink Panther with a supporting cast of seven women and three
male nude artists. She pioneered a modern style of striptease that
moved beyond the traditional bumps and grinds, adding graceful gymnastic twists and turns, pushing her performance towards
acrobatics before finishing her routine nude.

Her signature act was 'Miss Modesty', where, to prolong the
show, she wore hat, gloves and shoes, stockings, suspender belt,
underwear and several g-strings. At the end of her routine she'd
do the splits to the *Love Story* theme and make her vagina pop
to the music. When shocked people said she'd gone too far she'd
reply: 'I mean, how many other ladies have a singing vagina? I
don't pop anything out of my vagina, I don't smoke a cigarette. I
just make her sing.'

To feminists and puritans she'd argue that stripping was a way
for women to be unashamed about their sexuality.

'People have not been educated to be comfortable with their
own bodies and their own sexuality. When I started out I always

made it a point to present my body as an object of beauty, not just a sex symbol. I felt that as long as I was going to remove my clothes I was going to do it with as much aesthetic appeal as possible'. In the 1970s wives and girlfriends sometimes accompanied their men to strip shows. She appreciated the applause of the women. 'I really feel thrilled when the women clap. I think their reaction is more important to me.'

To keep fit she practised the Four Ms: Mastication, Masturbation, Meditation and Mobility. She believed that if everybody chewed their food and looked after their digestive system, masturbated to relieve their tension, meditated to get in touch with their spiritual self and kept every part of their body moving, then 'they're on the right track'.

The worst audience she ever performed for was made up of drunken and obnoxious policemen. But the growing problem for her was to try and not look at the porno movies that were constantly playing in the strip joints. That was not how women wanted to be treated: 'It's the men that love violence ... They want to get tied up, whipped and smacked.' By the early 1980s she thought that stripping had deteriorated; no-one was willing to spend money on costumes or learn routines. For Burton there was also an important distinction between pornography and eroticism, and she came to the conclusion she was too old-fashioned. Believing that the days of true strip clubs were finished, she gradually moved away from the clubs and gave private performances in lounge rooms and theatres. She continues to perform, but only to women audiences, in workshops called 'Learn to Love Your Body'.

When she was stripping in the Cross, Burton lived at the Astra Hotel, on Darlinghurst Road, opposite Les Girls. She felt safe there and liked watching the goings-on:

'If you're a local people are warm and friendly – it's like family. It didn't matter who you were; a whore, a stripper, a waitress.'

But it was hard to ignore the ugly side. Now that criminals and corrupt police controlled Kings Cross it became a law unto itself. At the Texas Bar and Grill barmen spiked drinks and raped the comatose women. This was practised more frequently at Les Girls, where couples had their drinks spiked and were taken out the back where the woman was raped while she and her partner were unconscious. After the deed they were cleaned up and returned to their table, now stacked with empty beer bottles. A couple would be in such a chemical daze that they paid the bill and staggered out into the night, little realising what had happened to them.

At the grungy Manzil Room in Earl Place, a live rock 'n' roll venue, you could get any of the drugs you liked and if you were a member of a band – and it didn't matter what band – teenage girls offered you a free blow job in the men's toilets. If you wanted kink, then there were places to find it. Brothels began to specialise in S&M.

One man who pushed the boundaries of taste was an opportunist called Hollywood Jack. When he'd go to parties he would strip naked and tuck his exceptionally long penis between his legs, making it into a tail, put his hands up in the paws position and, pretending to be a kangaroo, would hop around the party guests making Skippy noises. Hollywood Jack realised that men wanted to see more extreme sex so he trained his dog to perform sex with girls for $10 a look. Another spectacle he came up with was a woman copulating with a donkey. A hydraulic jack, the sort used to jack up a car, was set up under a narrow bed with a naked woman on top of it. The donkey was tied above the bed so that it couldn't move its legs or body. The bed was pumped up until the donkey's penis could reach and penetrate the woman.

Even lawmen were capable of the most sordid acts. The owner of the Pussy Galore once found a Kings Cross detective in an upstairs bedroom of the strip joint, sodomising a naked under-age boy handcuffed to the bed.

Violence was palpable at night. The Charing Cross Gang, teenagers from Woolloomooloo and the suburbs, roamed the streets Friday and Saturday nights armed with studded belts, flick knives and knuckledusters in search of men with long hair. They would pounce on the poor boy or man and give him a brutal thrashing. One night forty boys outside the Wayside Chapel set upon a frightened long-haired sixteen year-old boy and beat him unconscious.

A visit to the Cross could be dangerous. A 19-year-old girl, Margaret Woolley, was killed when she was viciously thrown down the stairs of Les Girls by a doorman. She had been there with her friend Denise, a bus conductor. After watching the show they decided to take their beers up to the cocktail bar. They were stopped by a doorman who told them it wasn't allowed. When they pushed past him he became furious. He chased after them, grabbed Woolley by the shoulders and threw her down the stairs. With the help of another man the furious doorman then chucked the unconscious woman out onto the footpath. She died of multiple skull fractures.

Don Walker had been in the Cross for about five years when one of his friends, Graham Gaskill, a promising artist, was murdered. It was 1981 and the 29-year-old Gaskill had just sold his fishing boat. With the money he went to the Cross where he got drunk and, at about five in the morning, found himself in a restaurant. Carefully watching him were a woman and two teenage girls who had seen that he had a wallet full of cash. When he left the restaurant he wandered down a lane near the Wayside Chapel, the three women following him. They demanded money, and when he refused they smashed a bottle over his head and stabbed him several times with a knife. One of the girls was only sixteen and lived in the Cross with her de facto and their two-year-old daughter.

Night-time in Kings Cross became so hazardous that Sammy Lee, who managed Les Girls, wouldn't allow his three sisters, who were visiting him from America, to walk there alone at night. A policeman, new to the beat, told a reporter: 'There's no way I'd walk through here at night.' Marien Dryer, who had lived in the area for thirty-six years, said she had never been afraid of walking through the Cross even during the R&R years, but now she only did her shopping of a day. As far as she was concerned it was 'going to hell'. She wasn't the only one who thought that. One headline aptly summed up Kings Cross at the beginning of the 1980s: 'KITCHEN OF HELL'.

Simpsons heritage hotel 1892

The Yellow House

Vadim's
Benny's

Macleay
Regis

CHALLIS AVE

Terraces

ROCKWELL CRES

Rockwell
House
1835

Elizabeth Bay
House
1839

MACLEAY STREET

Ikon
Apartments
The Chevron
1960–85

Sheraton Hotel
1960

Manar
1921

MANNING STREET

No. 44a
Devere Hotel

Tusculum
1835

Wychbury

Apollo Restaurant
Texas Tavern

Warrington

CRICK

Former post office

HUGHES ST

GREENKNOWE

Tara

Wayside
Chapel

Byron
Hall
1929

Kingsclere 1912

No. 105
Kashmir Café

ORWELL ST

Gowie Gate

The Rex
Apartments
The Rex Hotel

Cahors 1940
Cahors 1840
Chelsea Restaurant

Franconia

Fitzroy
Gardens

NEAR THE CORNER OF CHALLIS Avenue and Macleay Street was once Vadim's, one of the most celebrated restaurants in the 1960s. It is recalled with an almost feverish nostalgia by those who went there, including the poet Les Murray, who reminisces about Vadim's in his poem 'Tanka: the Coffee Shops'. Don Whitington writes in his *In Search of an Australian* that one had never been to Sydney unless he or she had been to Vadim's. The restaurant had a limited menu of beef stroganoff, spaghetti bolognaise, Steak Diane and borsch. Because alcohol was not allowed to be served after 10.30, the wine was poured into coffee cups. It stayed open until three or four o'clock in the morning, serving a heady mix of people: the young art critic Robert Hughes, Vivien Leigh, Rudolf Nureyev and Margot Fonteyn, poets, novelists, painters and students. There was one table reserved and that was for the *Sydney Morning Herald* theatre critic Harry Kippax, where he wrote reviews of the shows he had just seen.

The attractions of Vadim's were 'the atmosphere, the food, the liquor, but mostly for the conversation: bawdy, brilliant, uninhibited, slightly crazy'. As Richard Neville said, it was the first place to give permission to the 'chattering classes' to chatter. All that talk, all that inspired conversation, has evaporated into the ether of time but to those who frequented the restaurant it must have seemed as if Vadim's was a fizzy cauldron of the best minds and talents in all of Sydney.

It abruptly closed in the early 1970s when Vadim's gambling debts became oppressively large and he hadn't the money to continue. It re-opened as Bennie's (sometimes spelt Benny's), a blacked-out bar which attracted a very different crowd: groupies, rock apes, roadies, band molls, A&R guys and the occasional band like Fleetwood Mac. It wasn't decorated – actually there just wasn't any décor at all, which gave the bar an unintentional minimalism. The walls were white, the threadbare carpet was the colour of dried blood, incandescent neon strip lighting pierced the retina and the chairs were uncomfortable. Vadim's may have been about conversation and ideas, but Bennies was about getting drunk, getting laid, and snorting coke.

If you arrive at the corner of Macleay Street in the afternoon, the first thing that will strike the flâneur is not visual but olfactory; the briny breeze coming up from the harbour only a short distance away, a reminder of just how close the harbour is. Across the road from Challis Avenue is the art deco masterpiece the Macleay Regis, one of the largest and most beautiful blocks erected in Sydney during the late 1930s. It was designed to maximise the daylight in every one of its eighty-seven flats and the five-bedroom penthouse. The entry porch and ground floor foyers are among the most spectacular of any of the apartment blocks in the area. Unlike the younger tenants, the owner-occupiers are a conservative and aged group (for decades only Liberal voters could buy an apartment), whose exits and entrances at times involve an arduous manoeuvring of walking frames or laborious and exhausting struggles to direct their bodies to do what they are increasingly unable to.

Just around the corner from Challis Avenue, on the western side of Macleay Street, is the site of the former Yellow House art gallery. During the 1950s and 60s, it had been the Clune Galleries, where Russell Drysdale, John Passmore and John Olsen exhibited. Run by the writer Frank Clune's son, Vince, with his wife Thelma, it became a bohemian drop-in centre for the young abstract expressionists like Robert Klippel, Stan Rapotec and the painter turned critic Robert Hughes.

But in 1970 the pop artist Martin Sharp held what was going to be the last exhibition before the building was to be demolished to make way for tower blocks. Sharp and his helpers painted the walls orange, red, black and blue. The opening in May was described as 'the wildest, most way-out scene of the week ... where guests wore really wild gear and many looked as if they had come from a performance of *Hair*'.

The venue did not close and was bought by a new owner, who allowed Sharp and his growing band of artists to continue to use the twenty-room building as a community art centre. Young musicians, poets and artists came to work and live at the 'artistic Luna Park', including Brett Whiteley and George Gittoes, drawn to Sharp's pop art imagination. Sharp thought that the Yellow House (a fantasy homage to Vincent Van Gogh, Magritte and the surrealists) was 'Probably one of the greatest pieces of conceptual art ever achieved.' The sherry and red wine of the Clune Galleries had given way to acid, mushrooms, marijuana and cask wine. Personal tensions began to undermine the community but, as art critic Joanna Mendlessohn wrote, 'Even before its demise, it had taken on a legendary quality, and its stature grew in the telling.' The building itself was never demolished but recently it was restored as the Yellow House restaurant, trading on the legend.

Strolling up Macleay Street it's not uncommon to see the former Prime Minister, Paul Keating. He has an imposing 1888 terrace in Challis Avenue which took a decade to restore. The interior decorator referred to it as the 'millimetre' house, due to Keating's penchant for perfection. The front terrace was retiled, new sandstone paving laid and period detail meticulously carved to look like new. The former Prime Minister likes to wear Italian black suits. With his alabaster skin and lugubrious expression he looks like a funeral director trying to flog a second-hand coffin.

His terrace is part of a majestic row which has no equivalent in Macleay Street. Instead, on the eastern side is a series of apartment buildings leading up to Greenknowe Avenue and on the other side are cafés, restaurants, delicatessens, video stores, banks, Woolworths and gift shops. The first cross street off Macleay, after Challis, is Rockwell Crescent, a stumpy cul-de-sac that ends with the entrance to St Vincent's College. On the northern side is a row of simple but impressively restored Victorian terraces, plus two small red brick terraces adjoining the school, one named Tarmons in honour of the original mansion long since gone. It's suspected that there is an entrance to an underground passage in Rockwell Crescent. No-one seems to know its exact location but there is a story that there was a tunnel under three old terraces in Macleay Street, opposite Rockwell Crescent. This underground passage connected these houses with Elizabeth Bay House and continued down to exit at the harbour. For some locals a confirmation of its existence was the discovery of two skeletons, each with manacles on their wrists and manacled to one another. There was the tantalising possibility that the men were convicts who had escaped into the passage, and either became trapped accidentally or were overcome by foul air. Back in 1945 Brewster could find no trace of the tunnel. So whether it actually existed remains speculation or a local myth.

Just off Macleay Street, on the western side, is the modern apartment block Rockwell. It was built in 1997 and many real estate agents believe that it was the beginning of the stampede of yuppies and empty nesters buying into Potts Point. Twenty years ago new buildings attracted about ninety per cent investors and the rest were owner-occupiers, but the Rockwell reversed the trend dramatically; it's eighty per cent owner-occupied, a phenomenon that has been duplicated in most of the new apartment blocks built since.

Here one can look across Macleay Street at three very different buildings. Number 40, a tall, narrow steel and glass building, is one of the few examples of 1960s architecture in the area. Now converted into apartments, it was formerly the Sheraton Hotel and was where the Beatles stayed when they came to Australia, bringing pandemonium to the normally sedate street. Next to it is Manar apartments. To the passer-by it looks like one big white art deco structure, but a closer inspection reveals that Manar is actually three buildings, the first one completed in 1919, the second erected in 1928 and the final one completed ten years later.

This apartment block has always been highly sought after and many famous and wealthy people have lived there, including politicians, lawyers, writers and film and TV producers. Warren Fahey, the performer and cultural historian, has a flat there and is the author of a book entirely devoted to the building, *Manar: A History of a Unique Slice of Potts Point*. As Fahey mentions, Lucy Turnbull, who was to become Lord Mayor (2003–4), and was partly responsible for the rejuvenation of the Cross, was born in Apartment 3 and lived there for a brief time, recalling 'crawling out of the front of the garden, down Macleay Street, where there was a fruit barrow near Crick Avenue'. To some the fact that the Chief Justice of the High Court, Sir Garfield Barwick, once resided there is interesting enough, given it was his advice to the Governor-General Kerr to sack Prime Minister Whitlam, but what makes him significant to the story of the Cross is that he willed two paintings to the National Gallery: *Early view of a bushfire at Potts Point, Sydney* and another *Bush Fire, Potts Point, 1840*. Both views reveal just how rural the area once was, despite the mansions, with rough tracks, scrubby paddocks, and gum trees.

Next to Manar is the budget hotel De Vere, once a Spanish Mission-style hotel prosaically called 44 Macleay. During the Second World War it became the Allied Soldiers' Club and it was claimed that 'over 264,000 soldiers were accommodated in the hotel at one pound a night plus one shilling for breakfast'. The figures are a startling illustration of just how many soldiers passed through the Cross during the war years. In the 1970s Bernie Houghton opened up the sleazy Texas Tavern next door, naming it after his home state.

The three-star De Vere has had its share of scandals, including being the hotel where author and political speechwriter Bob Ellis had an afternoon rendezvous with the screenwriter Alexandra Long. Both were married to others and when Long announced she was pregnant, Ellis went on radio, revealing in graphic and toe-curling detail how he was incapable of full penetrative sex that day and therefore wasn't the father, so there was no necessity for him to pay maintenance for the child. The DNA test revealed he was the progenitor.

What is striking is how different these three buildings look: the former Sheraton Hotel with its clean, stark lines; the serene gardens and dignified buildings of Manar; and the glum facade of De Vere. The three represent a huge spectrum of wealth and class and age. It may be Potts Point but this sort of juxtaposition is a feature of the area, where at its most extreme, say in Darlinghurst Road, a sex shop can adjoin a library.

Across the street from Manar are the Ikon and Rockwell apartments. Originally it was the site of the magnificent mansion Prestonville, built in 1876. Later in 1911 it was converted into the plush Cairo private hotel and guest house, with a function centre, spacious gardens and tennis courts. Right up until the 1940s, the Cairo was regarded as one of the most beautiful and chic buildings and grounds in the whole precinct. Like 44 Macleay it was converted into a boarding house to accommodate American troops. It was demolished to make way for the Chevron Hilton, erected in 1959, which was the first Australian hotel designed in the international style. The property developer Stanley Korman, a mixture of visionary and con-man, envisaged an 800-room building of thirty-five storeys, but this was never achieved because the second part of the project stalled due to a recession and in 1962 the hotel went into receivership. The site for stage two remained a gigantic hole for years and provided a fertile breeding ground for mosquitoes of plague proportions. The shady Korman (not helped by the ink blot of a moustache which gave him the appearance of a spiv), always one step away from bankruptcy and dubious dealings, was jailed in 1968 for improper business practices. The Chevron continued, with famous performers, comedians and singers playing its Silver Spade Room, and its Quarterdeck bar served as a cosy hub for homosexuals. The Chevron was pulled down to make way for the Hotel Nikko and it, in turn, like a relay race run by hyperactive property developers, was rebuilt as the bland, generic Ikon.

The next street on the western side has a strange, even unique meteorological feature. When the rest of the Cross is bathed in warm light and has little or no wind, Manning Street has a constant vortex of chilly winds as if it creates its own weather patterns. Next to a snug coffee bar is a gift shop selling an expensive mixed bag of objects from furniture to perfumed candles. It's an example of the number of gift shops that have sprung up in the last decade.

If Manning is a humdrum street, Tusculum, which runs off it, is a dramatic example of one of the remaining original mansions, a two-storey Italianate construction. The opulent garden was bulldozed when developers bought most of the land. The mansion had ended up a shabby boarding house but was saved from destruction. It's been restored and another building erected in its grounds for the Centre of Architecture. There could be no greater contrast between Verge's delicate design and the modern structure, a hideous looking building with an enormous dirty pink concrete wall facing the street, as if confirming the blank imaginations of modern architects. Tusculum House itself is not quite the architectural achievement one wants it to be. It has a beautiful sober ground floor, but the first floor with its stumpy columns looks as if it has been squashed on top of it and is sinking into it.

Next door are two eight-storey apartment blocks, Werrington, built in 1930, and Wychbury, four years later, both on land that had been part of the Tusculum estate. The two buildings represent the evolving style of the brilliant architect Emil Sodersten. Werrington shows the influence of Tudor Gothic whereas Wychbury is a striking example of the art deco style. The front of the building is a vivid demonstration of just how Sodersten utilised the common brick in his designs. The facade slews outwards and upwards with vertical recesses that lead to fanned brickwork above the top storey windows. As you lift your head heavenwards towards the pinnacle you see that the brickwork protrudes and is arranged in patterns, like radiant bursts of sunlight. It makes the neighbouring Centre for Architecture look brutal and unsociable.

Returning to continue along Macleay Street, opposite the Fitzroy Gardens is a German *konditorei* with a French name, the Croissant D'Or. It has had only three owners – the first two were German and the latest is Austrian – since it opened in 1953. In the beginning the only way to get hold of crucial ingredients like vanilla beans, marzipan and schnapps was to buy them from the chefs on cruise liners that anchored in Woolloomooloo Bay. There are old women who have been buying cakes there since it opened. The big sellers are danishes, croissants, crème caramel and cheesecake, but there are also brioches, strudel, esterhazy (a traditional layer slice of hazelnut wafers) and petits fours in the shape of strawberries decorated with musical notes.

Of all the streets I roam around in the Cross, I seldom venture far down Macleay Street. It may be charming, with luxury shops and sumptuous restaurants, but its main purpose seems to act as a costly conduit for shopping and eating. It doesn't have the potency of the social diversity and sense of the illicit found in Darlinghurst Road or Kellett Street. It's a delightful place of a day but it is at its best of a night. The variety of upmarket restaurants, small wine bars and cafés, the dolled-up women and smartly dressed men strolling down the leafy viaduct of the plane trees, window shopping or sipping wine or drinking coffee at outdoor seating, confirm why so many people call it Parisian. As the old ditty 'Billo' goes:

> *Can anyone point, to a better old sight, than Macleay Street on a Saturday night?*

HALFWAY BETWEEN
A CIRCUS AND A SEWER

WHEN THE POLICE CAME TO arrest him, Abe Saffron shat himself in fear. He was going to jail for three years, not for any of his crimes but for tax evasion. Like Al Capone, he had been brought down by the tax authorities ... and Jim Anderson.

For some years Anderson had been secretly skimming money from the venues he ran with Saffron. He was dissatisfied with his secondary position and wanted to usurp the King of the Cross. He mused about hiring a hit man to murder his business partner but then thought of a better plan. He had been Saffron's book-keeper for years and would tell the authorities about the two sets of account books the venues used, one containing the real earnings and the other a fictional creation to hoodwink the taxation department.

During the court case (or cases – there were several appeals) it was revealed that Saffron had himself skimmed $202,000 from Les Girls alone between 1976 and 1980. Other payments were bribes for bent cops and even health and building inspectors to overlook kitchen and fire safety infringements. The evidence was clear; Saffron had evaded paying the required amount of tax and was laundering vast amounts of cash. The size of his tax evasion meant he owed the Tax Department $1.5 million. He was given the maximum sentence and on 27 October 1988, at the age of sixty-eight, he was sentenced to three years in Long Bay Jail (although he ended up only serving seventeen months).

Looking after Saffron's property portfolio while he was incarcerated was one of his closest friends, Peter Farrugia, who had helped his boss run the empire for twenty years. And what a huge portfolio it was, containing such Kings Cross premises as the Persian Room Restaurant, the Laramie, the Barrel Inn Restaurant, the Raft Restaurant (aka the Venus Room), La Bastille Restaurant (aka Café de la Paix), Patches Restaurant, the Pink Panther Strip Club, the Pink Pussycat, Les Girls, the Paradise Restaurant and Showgirls.

Known as 'the Black Prince', Farrugia was a multi-millionaire with an obsession with horse racing. He was a spiffy dresser and wore Italian suits and crocodile-skin shoes, more than likely from De Ferrari Moda, the William Street shop that clothed Premier Neville Wran, horse trainers, racing identities, criminals and advertising men. He looked mild and unthreatening and, most importantly, was a loyal lieutenant to his boss.

Saffron was released from jail just before he turned seventy. He was shamed and shunned. Then in 1992 his trusted friend Farrugia was shot dead on a remote Queensland farm when he tried to finalise buying a property. The murder affected Saffron greatly and he began to distance himself from his ventures and to worry about his reputation.

His nemesis, Jim Anderson, who had been given indemnity for his evidence against his former partner, kept a low profile, but a heart attack in 1995 was a sign that he should seek a quieter life. He retired to the Blue Mountains only to be infected by avian flu after feeding rosellas. In hospital he was found to be riddled with cancer and he died in July 2003.

By that time Anderson and Saffron were old news. Younger criminals now ran the Cross. The most prominent were of

Lebanese background. The Romanian underworld had tried to take control of the area but wisely faded into the background to concentrate on importing narcotics, especially cocaine, and selling them on to dealers. During the middle 1980s through the 1990s, the Kings Cross crime scene was ruled by Lebanese crooks and gangsters. Two of the most prominent were the brothers Louis and Bill Bayeh.

Louis was the eldest of three brothers. He migrated to Australia from Lebanon with his family when he was fourteen years old. Not very bright, with a tendency towards obesity, he gravitated to the Cross to work for the mobster Leonard 'Lennie' McPherson. Born into working-class Balmain, McPherson's crime file started in the 1950s and over the years he was known for street crime, bashings, shootings, theft, extortion and as a paid informant for the police.

To his criminal mates Lennie 'was a bloke in a girl's skirt' and, behind his back, they called him 'Mr Little' after he sent Christmas cards to his mates signed 'Mr Big'. He was afraid of horses because one had bitten him when he was a boy, and terrified of needles. Always big-noting himself, his vanity led him to have a facelift that did little to improve his doughy blob of a face. Like most mobsters he was paranoid and had reason to be. His Gladesville house was a fortress and he wouldn't get out of the car until the garage door had closed and his Alsatians were let out of the house. When he was driving his car he wore an army helmet and bullet proof vest. He'd secretly record conversations on a big reel to reel tape and pass them on to the police who, in turn, protected him from arrest.

He may have been ridiculed by fellow criminals but he was cunning, ruthless and extorted protection money from night clubs and strip joints such as the Pussy Galore. This bovine and callous thug mixed with Chicago mobsters and Manila gangsters, ran prostitutes, imported drugs, and was a stand-over man. He was sentenced to jail in 1991 for ordering the bashing of a business-man. Afraid of jail, he feigned mental illness, but the ploy didn't work and he was jailed for four years. There was no remorse, just maudlin self pity: 'I'm going to die in jail. My heart's enlarged since I've been in jail ... I can't walk upstairs. They want to give me a bloody plastic knee. Fancy getting a plastic knee in bloody jail. I'll probably come out a bloody cripple.' In 1996 the ailing 75-year-old gangster collapsed and died in Cessnock Jail.

Bayeh hero-worshipped McPherson and trailed him around like an adoring puppy. He did not drink, could not read or write, but McPherson made him co-partner in the Love Machine on Darlinghurst Road. As a former detective said of Louis, 'He wasn't muscle. Lennie had the best muscle. Lennie treated Louis like a dill. Lennie didn't want to get his hands dirty with brothels and strip clubs, so he let [Louis] run the Love Machine. Without Lennie, Louis would have been a nobody.'

Louis eventually had forty-six aliases, including Big Louie, Louis the Fly, Lebanese Louis, Lois, and Big Bayeh. Three dec-ades of charges against him included violence, bribes, supplying heroin, and attempting to pervert the course of justice. He was a featured player in the 1995 Wood Royal Commission into the New South Wales Police Force. It spent 451 hearing days, heard from 902 witnesses, and revealed to the nation the extent of cor-ruption in Kings Cross, including bribery, money laundering, drug dealing, fake evidence, and the police protection of pedo-philes. Police Commissioner Tony Lauer resigned, his position untenable given the level of police corruption. Policemen rushed to resign and others were arrested. Twelve people committed suicide.

At the Royal Commission Louis claimed he had paid po-lice hundreds of thousands of dollars to leave his nightclubs and brothels alone. Donald Stewart, chairman of the National Crime Authority (and resident of Kings Cross), described him as obese, illiterate, unable to find gainful employment, a hypochondriac, anxious, panic-stricken, of questionable morals and the 'author of his own misfortune'.

Unlike his brother, Bill Bayeh wanted nothing to do with Lennie, and ran his own empire out of the shabby, murkily lit Cosmopolitan Café in Darlinghurst Road. Addicts helped Bayeh cut and pack heroin and cocaine in a flat in MacDonald Street before the drugs were sold at the café. He employed as many as forty dealers who were sacked if they didn't refer to him as 'the Boss'. He was a spendthrift and lived an opulent lifestyle. He believed he was invincible, not such an unreasonable idea given he spent $5000 a week bribing officials and paying protection money to the police.

Over a six-month period he would typically deal around 2.55 kilograms of cocaine and 340 g of heroin. The misery his drugs caused was immense. Virginia Perger, a drug dealer and prostitute in the Cross, had a daughter, Denise. In 1992 Denise bought bad cocaine from one of Bill Bayeh's dealers. She injected it in her ankle and was blinded and lost her leg. At the time of writing she is blind, brain damaged, the mitral valve in her heart has been replaced by an artificial valve, and she's confined to a wheelchair.

At the Wood Royal Commission there was video evidence of Bill Bayeh and two of his dealers manufacturing 1500 caps of illegal drugs. In 1999 he was sentenced to fifteen years in jail after pleading guilty to conspiring to supply a large commercial quantity of heroin and cocaine. His brother Louis ended up serving time in jail too.

By the 1990s hard drugs had made Kings Cross an epicentre of degradation, wretchedness and cruelty. A decade before, it had seemed the heroin epidemic couldn't get worse. New South Wales

Premier Barrie Unsworth's son died of a drug overdose in 1977 and in 1984 it was revealed that the Prime Minister Bob Hawke's daughter Rosslyn and her husband were heroin addicts. A legend of rugby league, Jack Gibson, would wander through the Cross talking to anyone who could tell him just how his son ended up an addict, dying of an overdose. Drugs had crossed all barriers of background, education and class.

If one person personified the toxic influence of drugs it was Pandelis Karipis, also known as 'Fat George'. He owned a number of brothels and shooting galleries and ran the Kellett Street brothel Pink Flamingo, which was less a bordello and more a drug dealing emporium. He imported heroin and cocaine from Thailand, paying off crooked Customs officials, and shelled out a fortune for police protection. An obese, physically repulsive man, he kept his prostitutes almost as prisoners. Two hefty guards made sure the women couldn't leave the premises and, in order to control them, he got them hooked on heroin until they were totally dependent on the drug and accepted it in lieu of money. The girls were as young as fifteen. In one incident, which tells us everything we want to know about Fat George and his ghastly world, he caught a 17-year-old girl stealing a bag of heroin and cocaine. She was gagged and beaten continuously for three days. Despite the gag the other girls in the Pink Flamingo could hear her screams throughout the building. On the third day Fat George made her kneel naked on all fours 'like a dog', and anally raped her with a Coca-Cola bottle. Then she was handcuffed to a fridge and forced to give her morbidly obese tormentor oral sex. There were rumours that when girls became too wasted and harder to control, he and his cohorts would kill them with hotshots and deliberate overdoses. His savagery and depravity ended in 1995 when he was charged with supplying and possessing heroin, offering to supply heroin, and common assault.

Heroin seemed everywhere. Father Steve Sinn, the parish priest at St Canice's in Roslyn Street, would help feed up to three hundred people who turned up for a midday meal. He reckoned that eighty per cent of them were heroin addicts. By the end of the decade the number of people shooting up in its church grounds was so great that the parish decided to close down its five-days-a-week kitchen and put the word out that shooting up around the church was to stop. As Father Sinn said, 'They were shooting up in the toilets because that is one of the few places you can get water and you need that to mix the drugs. But there were so many syringes being disposed of they were blocking the toilets.' The kitchen re-opened after a month but the old problems returned. He had to deal with spaced out and violent people, one of them stabbing him in the hand with a flick knife.

The shooting galleries began operating in the early 1990s and by the millennium they were big earners. They were in dingy hotel rooms, strip tease joints, sex shops and clubs like Porky's. The addicts paid between $5 to $10 to use a room for ten minutes. Clean needles were available at a price. Some of these galleries were filthy beyond belief with needles scattered on the floor, rubbish, vomit, and sprays of blood on the sheets and walls. Cocaine was more profitable because coke addicts shot up to a dozen times a day, while the average heroin junkie managed up to three shots. These grim shooting galleries operated with the knowledge of the police and the encouragement of health officials who felt it was better to have injecting done off the street.

Heroin was not only sold by people like Fat George. One of the largest heroin supply networks operated out of the exclusive Elan apartments, newly opened in 1997. They used five 'safe houses' in the Cross as distribution centres. Marijuana was sold openly along with heroin. The 'Smoko' dealers who worked from a site off Roslyn Street near Kellett Way were in their teens. They hid balloons of heroin under their tongues and sold them for $80 each. Coffee houses in Roslyn Street like Café Amsterdam, Café Bliss and the Piccolo sold marijuana, and Springfield Avenue was a spot where heroin dealers operated with impunity.

The baseness of the Cross became palpable; there always seemed to be violence in the air. In 1997 even locals were afraid when a deranged man with a hatchet went berserk over several months. The attacks were originally thought to be random but it became clear that the madman was targeting young foreigners. He befriended his potential victims with idle chatter or asked for a cigarette. He bludgeoned a Czech tourist to death in William Street. A month later he attacked an Irish tourist in Roslyn Street and two weeks later he tried to kill a 46-year-old local man at the same spot. Both victims managed to fight him off before fleeing. He waited for a few days and then attacked a Dutch backpacker who also managed to escape. Restaurants and backpacker hostels were near empty while the killer was on the loose. He was caught but the tense, shrill atmosphere seemed a reflection of what the Cross had become.

Up to twenty Aborigines took control of Fitzroy Gardens, drinking and fighting through the day and night when not aggressively begging or dealing marijuana and heroin in Springfield Avenue. The screams of the Aboriginal women being bashed in the Gardens by their men became a familiar sound in the night. When drunk, the Aborigines abused passers-by and threatened them. Locals were too afraid to venture into the Gardens after dark. Next to the Gardens, the hugely popular Bourbon and Beefsteak was no oasis of peace either. Between 1998 and 2000 it had the most reported assaults of any hotel in Sydney.

John Birmingham, on assignment for *Rolling Stone*, spent a few weeks living rough in the Cross. He saw a 13-year-old smack addict slapped around by her 15-year-old pimp, strung-out user-dealers and a homeless man who was 'quite good company when he wasn't suffering from some sort of psychotic episode'. The stayers, Birmingham wrote, had 'cut some sort of Faustian deal to survive on the edge of the abyss. The younger faces … just disappeared or grew so old so fast it was like watching a special effects movie.'

His depressing portrait was all too true. Half the prostitutes were under sixteen years old. They may have started out fresh-faced, but to the locals it was an all-too-familiar story as the young faces became haggard and splotchy within weeks because of drug use. They were transformed into wraiths, with rake-thin bodies, greasy hair, their voices nasal and harsh. The need for drugs meant that some would work through the night, finishing in the early morning giving oral sex to garbage men in the front seat of their trucks.

The sense of lawlessness wasn't a figment of the imagination. There seemed to be no law up in the Cross because the police were more interested in taking bribes than helping residents.

Their greed and immorality were blatant. Michael Duffy, a publisher and writer, lived in the area in the early 1990s and like other locals came to the realisation that 'If you were burgled or otherwise placed in need of the New South Wales Police Service's finest, good luck to you. Complaints to the station by the El Alamein Fountain drew the response that the detectives were too busy fighting serious crime.'

Bribing the Kings Cross police became necessary if you wanted to break the law. During this time I had an office in Minton House on the corner of Darlinghurst and Bayswater Roads. Every Friday up to a dozen policemen would troop up to the top floor where drug dealers would hand out the bribes. It was a much shorter walk from the new police station in Fitzroy Gardens than the former police station in Darlinghurst.

Prostitutes had to pay protection money to the police if they wanted to work. Kings Cross was the most lucrative drug market in Australia and the police spent much of their time keeping track of where the sales were being made and demanding money from the dealers. The rest of the time they spent drinking or embarking on long boozy lunches at places like the Bourbon and Beefsteak where it was not uncommon to have criminals, drug dealers and the police at the same table thoroughly enjoying each other's drunken company. A rare honest cop, Glen McNamara, reported how the detectives filled in their day:

> *The hours of duty for a detective on the day shift were between 8.30 am and 5 pm. Morning coffee commenced about 9 am and continued until about 11.30 am, whereupon there was a discussion about a suitable luncheon venue, which lasted until about 12.15, then lunch commenced and usually concluded about 3.30 pm. It was followed by an ale or dozen at the infamous drinking establishment, the Bourbon and Beefsteak.*

It was no wonder, as McNamara noted in his book *Dirty Work*, that street-level crime was out of control with junkies assaulting and robbing each other, locals and tourists, with little fear of being arrested. There were vicious attacks on gay men in Rushcutters Bay which the police did nothing about. The system worked because even honest police were prepared to protect those who were corrupt. The moral values of the Kings Cross police were so debased that they sheltered pedophiles from the law. Detective Senior Sergeant Graham 'Chook' Fowler and his deputy Detective Sergeant Larry Churchill protected the notorious Dolly Dunn, a former Catholic school science teacher who manufactured amphetamines in his kitchen which he sold in order to make money to pay off the police and buy narcotic drugs for the young boys he filmed while he raped them. Churchill's luck ran out and he was jailed for protecting drug dealers and involvement with a $4 million importation of amphetamines. Dunn went to jail for supplying drugs. Another policeman, Ricky Hazel, also confessed to extorting money from Dunn.

The term used by the police for the bribes was 'the joke' or 'the laugh'. They forced dealers to hand over protection money, and drug money stolen during raids would be divided up amongst those 'in on the joke'; even shoplifters were let off if they paid bribes. The police fabricated evidence and perjury was common. One member of the Police Drug Unit was secretly filmed taking drugs, having sex with a prostitute and then asking if she could supply child pornography. It was hard to differentiate between the law and the criminals. The Wood Royal Commission would put a stop to 'the joke'. One of the worst offenders, Detective Sergeant Trevor Haken, 'rolled over' and became a witness for the commission. His evidence and that of others resulted in eight police being dismissed from the police force, including Haken. Others were jailed while dozens resigned before they could be investigated.

The Kings Cross police force may have been purged of many of their corrupt officers but nothing much changed on the streets. As 2000 loomed, the area seemed defeated and exhausted.

It may seem a strange thing to write but I had a marvellous time in Kings Cross during this period. I had an office at Minton House overlooking Darlinghurst Road and I spent more time than I should have watching the passing spectacle below my second storey window. Across from me was a long hotel balcony where tourists and flabby suburban voyeurs looked down, both literally and metaphorically, on those locals they thought were a rung below them on the evolutionary ladder. The grubbiness and unkempt appearance of the street had an alluring squalor to it, as if confirmation of Slessor's 'You find this ugly, I find it lovely'.

Later I rented an office down in William Street. After I had finished writing for the day I'd put my feet up on my desk and work my way through a bottle of gin. Nicely sozzled I'd walk up William Street as day became night and turn left into the main drag, entranced by the pulsating technicolour neon signs, bemused by the zonked-out hookers, the agitated pimps, the barking spruikers reciting the same come-on as always, the tourists astonished by the blatant whores and drug taking, the smell of food fried in old fat insidiously seeping out from junk food shops and old ladies in tatty dressing gowns buying their fags and milk.

If I wanted a refuge from the noisy street I'd slip into Mrs Chapman's tiny bookstore, a chaotic mess of tottering towers of books and stuffed shelves. It was impossible to find the book you were after, but all you had to do was ask for the title and Mrs Chapman would point it out, generally at the bottom of a column of books and woe betide you if you caused the stack to fall over in your quest to pluck it out.

I'd take my chihuahua, Ren, to the Sebel Bar where I'd knock back several martinis, or I'd go to the Bottoms Up bar at the Rex and be amazed by the worn, debauched, ageing faces and think to myself how desperate and ugly people looked, only to glance in a mirror and be shocked by my own similar appearance. Wandering past Porky's you could always be assured that there would be fierce fights between drunks on a stag night and the bouncers, or a pissed and pissed off man being physically thrown down the stairs and out onto the street. Occasionally I'd pop into the Bourbon and Beefsteak and spot drunken plainclothes cops drinking with known criminals, middle-aged women on the prowl for men, hungry locals downing the free snack food, gays looking for rough trade, garrulous Americans and dazed Japanese sailors staring at sozzled girls in skimpy dresses gyrating on the dance floor to the live band.

Yes, there was a menace and sense of threat, but as I was a local, I thought myself immune. The spruikers recognised me, as did the prostitutes, who, if they tried to pick me up out of the sheer habit of approaching every man they saw, would apologise on recognising me with, '*Sorry, luv.*' I was intrigued at how immorality and human degradation could exist unapologetically, and out in the open. It may seem odd but I was captivated by the obvious signs of decline. There was a palpable sense that no-one outside Kings Cross, let alone inside it, cared that much about its future.

One afternoon I stopped to talk to the playwright Alma de Groen at a local bus stop. She was planning to live in the Blue Mountains and when I asked her why, she told me she couldn't take the sleaze and dirt of the Cross any more. I could understand her distaste, but I felt differently. There was a dark manic energy pulsating through the streets, but at least it was an energy, and it invigorated me, as did the sense of danger. It was so much better than living in a nice bourgeois suburb. And it's amazing how attractive decay can be, especially when bathed in incandescent neon lights promising sex, junk food, liquor and a good time. The Cross had a luminous and eerie glow, like phosphorescence created from rotting vegetable matter.

The locals I knew developed a macabre sense of humour; perhaps the only way to deal with what was happening was to laugh. One night at the Mansions I witnessed two bouncers escort an obnoxious drunk who had abused them into a corner of the bar. They laid into him while the other drinkers casually watched as if it were something on television. Two drag queens near me laughed as if it were a piece of theatre and I found myself laughing too. The line from Lou Reed's 'Street Hassle' sprang up in my gin-soaked brain: 'halfway between a circus and a sewer'. It was an apt description of the Cross.

The performing self

THE ECCENTRIC, THE MAD, THE strange and the exotic have been drawn to the Cross. For one writer in 1946, these men and women were a vital and fundamental element of the area's mystique:

> *The Cross and the Loo have more than their quota of queer characters, for they abound in all the absurdity and tragedy of weird costumes, ruined lives and sick brains. The Dickens like atmosphere they impart is really a portion of the charm of the district, for, unlike the majority, they appear year after year, as timeless as are most landmarks.*

As one reporter observed, 'The whole area has the air of a big theatre front.' It was a place where larger-than-life personalities could be accepted and thrive, as though acting out their lives on a stage. People created their lives as a performance piece, where they could enact a character who would not be accepted elsewhere. For young people the Cross was a place of personal transformation. The precinct nurtured the kinds of people they wished to become. By mixing in bohemian circles, one learned how to talk, behave and dress like one and so become a bohemian. Then there were those who totally reinvented themselves, like the drag queen Carlotta who underwent surgery in order to become a woman.

Because it is a small area, it was and is a daily occurrence to see or run into local identities and eccentrics. One was the Duke of Darlo, a spectral figure who wore a long black coat in summer and winter and patrolled the streets dangling an enormous bunch of keys. He imagined he was the area's 'honorary watchman'. There was the gay dandy, Hector Bolitho, who achieved fame as the biographer of the English royal family. Slessor recalled he was:

> One of the most dashing figures of Sydney's newspaper world in the early 1920s ... Small, dapper, chubby, daintily dressed, with lemon yellow gloves and a bowler hat.

Other locals remember Bolitho strolling up Macleay Street wearing a bowler hat and lavender gloves.

Getrud Bodenwieser, a dancer and choreographer and artistic director born in Vienna, came to Sydney in 1939 and founded one of the most significant dance companies ever in Australia. She lived in the Cross and staged many of her dance pieces in the Minerva. A fastidious dresser, with dark hair and piercing eyes, she walked the streets of the Cross and, according to *Memories, Kings Cross 1936–1946*, was 'usually in a bit of a trance, in fact quite often a road safety risk. She was very short-sighted, moved along slightly hunched, usually dressed in black, her face hidden behind a veil.'

Other singular characters may have lived outside of Kings Cross but they came into it because it allowed them to perform, like Sister Ada Green, who preached a fire and brimstone gospel in Springfield Avenue in the 1940s and 50s. A small woman with a flowered hat in the shape of a sponge cake, she would joyously shout out *'Praise Jesus'*, to which the cynical crowd would cry in unison, *'And pass the ammunition'*. Paying no need to the mockery, she'd cry out *'I can save you!'* to which the inevitable response would be, '*Can yer save me a pretty one?*' Whenever she called out '*Christ Jesus*' the audience responded with an equally loud '*Kraft Cheeses*'. She was serious in her desire to save souls and the interjections were nearly always boisterous and good-natured. Whenever one of her 'flock' spoke, the audience would groan in mock agony until Sister Ada started thumping her ever-ready tambourine. The noise of her sermons and the crowd resulted in her many arrests, often witnessed by an amused George Sprod:

> *To the mingled cheers and boos of the mob, she'd mount the steps*
> *to the paddy wagon like an aristocrat going to the guillotine, still*
> *preaching defiantly until the steel door clanged shut.*

In the 1950s perhaps two of the wildest characters were Luba Shishova and Bea Miles. Luba, as she was known to everybody, was in her late twenties when she arrived in Sydney from China in 1952. A moon-faced brunette dancer with a voluptuous body, she first went to court in 1953 – in a fit of anger she had trashed the kitchen where she worked as a short-order cook and been fired. From then on she was uncontrollable. A heavy drinker, she had a foul mouth and even worse temper.

She thought of nothing of performing an impromptu strip-tease act on the streets or dancing semi-nude in restaurants and on Kings Cross balconies. One of her favourite antics was lifting her skirt in public revealing she had no underwear. One night in February 1957 she went berserk at the Hasty Tasty. When the manager ordered her from the premises she started to throw knives, forks, spoons, chairs, tables, and bottles. She was finally subdued and faced disorderly conduct charges. When the magistrate asked if she had any questions, she snarled, 'Yes, is that manager bastard still alive?'

She blackmailed restaurant and café staff with the threat to take off her clothes. One Saturday she performed two impromptu strips after the owners refused to pay. The first occasion was on the footpath outside the Moka coffee lounge. The following day she stripped outside the Hasty Tasty. According to a *Truth* reporter:

> *Luba started blistering the paint-work with her language, and then, standing athwart the main entrance, she repeated her striptease as at the Moka with the same words, same music.*

In one three-month period she found herself in court twenty times for her outrageous behaviour. One time she turned up drunk, smoking and wearing a polka dot two-piece swimsuit. She explained, in her deep Russian accented voice, why she was wearing the bikini: 'This is how the bloody coppers pinched me, so this is how I come to court.' She abused police, was condescending towards magistrates and threatened witnesses. She was thrilled by the controversies and the press coverage. Sometimes she would enter a restaurant and dance on tables, lifting her dress higher and higher (revealing she wore no underwear) and then she'd grab a beer belonging to a stunned patron and down it in a gulp. For a decade she kept up this 'one-woman Russian Revolution' and then, just as suddenly as she appeared, she vanished.

In the 1950s and 60s Bea Miles lived in a storm water drain in Rushcutters Bay Park. Born Beatrice Miles in 1902, she was mercurial, a brilliant student who had begun an arts degree but gave up after a year. Not long afterwards she contracted encephalitis – inflammation of the brain – which added to her instability. Her bohemian lifestyle and advocacy of sexual freedom were, as far as her father was concerned, further signs of mental illness and he had her committed to an asylum for two years.

Miles was known for her ornery habits of regularly travelling by taxi or tram, invariably refusing to pay the fares. If she thought someone was not giving her the respect she thought she deserved, she could become violent. Any taxi driver who forced her out of their vehicle copped her anger. A hefty, blubbery woman, she jumped on car bonnets, ripped off doors and kicked in the side panelling. At times she could rustle up money and pay for a taxi ride. In 1955 she took a return taxi trip to Kalgoorlie and back, paying £600 for the journey. Her stubbornness and refusal to obey rules had her banned from the Library of New South Wales. One of her mischievous acts was to turn up at a Sydney bank where she would sit and smoke under a sign saying: *Gentlemen will refrain from smoking*.

She knew all of Shakespeare by heart and quoted him for a fee of sixpence or a shilling. Her portly face had a cascade of chins, she was smelly, wore grubby coats and a bank teller's visor protected her eyes. She described herself as 'a true thinker and speaker. I cannot stand or endure the priggery, caddery, snobbery, smuggery, hypocrisy, lies, flattery, compliments, praise, jealousy, envy, pretence, conventional speech and affected artificial behaviour upon which society is based.' Her erratic demeanour and her unsociability made her one of the most recognised characters in the Cross and beyond. As far as the locals were concerned the laughs her stunts generated far outweighed the irritation she caused. A contemporary of hers remarked, 'She was a character at the Cross, about the only part of Sydney which could absorb her.'

On one occasion when both Luba and Bea ended up in court the police thought it would be a lark to put both women in a cell together. It was thought that once Miles started spouting Shakespeare Luba would 'go off like a firecracker'. But all was calm in the cell. They were seen sitting opposite one another, staring at each other, not saying a word, two performers unwilling to share the spotlight with the other.

Then there are those who come from the suburbs and never leave the Cross, experiencing it as a place where they are accepted for who they are or who they have become. Ayesha was one of the most beautiful performers at Les Girls. Her Eurasian features, lithe body and chic style made her one of the most memorable of the acts. She was a boy from Hurstville, a talented student and a piano teacher who discovered that dressing as a female was totally natural and comfortable. He reinvented himself as Ayesha and in 1966, at the age of twenty-one, started performing at Les Girls.

She has been plagued by long-term illness and has to take an extensive range of pills daily, which sometimes make her grumpy and ill. She has the imperious manner of a diva, a voice that sounds as if it's been cured in tobacco smoke and a cutting wit, especially when talking about her fellow drag queens. Every day she rises around dawn and visits her favourite coffee shops, accompanied by Youhoo, her small scruffy white dog who patiently trails behind her, staying longest at the Piccolo sharing memories and gossip with one of her closest friends, Vittorio, the owner. She rarely has the same clothes on twice, wearing everything from Marilyn Monroe-style dresses to slinky 1930s numbers. Once it was against the law for her to walk the streets dressed as a woman but times have changed and she pays no attention to those tourists and visitors who do a double take, puzzled as to her gender. Around midday there is her usual lunch at a hotel – she does not drink alcohol – and then, in the early evening, she slowly walks home to her small public housing apartment, stopping to have a soft drink and natter with the tradies, oddballs and determined drinkers at the Old Fitzroy Hotel.

The transvestism was not all one way. In the 1930s and 1940s it was also against the law for women to dress as men. The black Australian singer Nellie Smith performed as a man and off stage wore men's clothes. It was probably only in the Cross that she could get away with it.

The raffish air and tolerance of the Cross allowed people to explore the more erotic aspects of their psyche. John Coutts had grown up in England and at the age of twenty-one he went to Sandhurst where he was commissioned a Second Lieutenant in the Royal Scots. He was forced to resign in 1925 after marrying a nightclub hostess without the permission of his regiment. After divorcing her, he migrated to Australia in 1930 and lived in Kings Cross, working as an illustrator and photographer in the underground fetish clubs.

Sometime in 1936 he discovered his muse, Holly Faram. Ten years younger, she had started out as an artist's model, posing nude from the age of sixteen. Later on she modelled for such painters as William Dobell and Norman Lindsay. She became Coutts's favourite model and it didn't take much persuasion for her to be photographed in fetish wear. She had dark hair, was very attractive and had an undeniable sexiness. High heels, knee high boots, erotic underwear and leather dresses suited her. In her photographs she has the bemused air of a dominatrix who enjoys her work. It was not only her smouldering beauty that appealed but her obvious enjoyment of the fetish wear and poses. Her casual acceptance of outré sexual desires was, for its times, outrageous. Now it is fashion.

They married in 1942 and Coutts's nude photographs of her made her a favourite pin-up of servicemen during the war. Their marriage didn't survive the war and Coutts migrated to America where, under the naughty wink-wink non-de-plume of John Willie, he published, wrote and illustrated an infamous S&M magazine, *Bizarre*. Some of the early issues featured his ex-wife looking as glamorous and sexy as any of his American models.

Holly occasionally modelled part time, including posing for

the cover of People magazine, while she worked as a waitress at the Arabian. Despite smoking ninety cigarettes a day she lived until 1983 when she died at seventy years of age in her McElhone Street home. The photographs in the fetish magazines didn't bother her; in fact, she was amused, and as she aged, flattered by them, saying, 'I enjoyed life. I'd just like to live it over again, in the same way.'

There were others who came to Kings Cross and found themselves self-destructing because of drugs or alcohol. Some succumbed to momentary and expensive gratifications. An excess of pleasures gave a few the sense that such a debauched lifestyle would last forever, then they discovered when it was too late that the Cross had corrupted their moral values and fastened on to their weaknesses of character like a blood-sucking lamprey, leaving them to wander through the Cross broke and defeated, lost souls. Even a short stay in the Cross could bend, corrode or break you. In W.A. Harbinson's *Running Man* (1967), an alcoholic writer comes to the Cross expecting it to be 'fabulous', but he finds no such thing. It's his Aboriginal mate, Collins, who tells him a few home truths:

> *Behind every neon light in the Cross there's a fella like you – a small, scared, defeated thing crying that he doesn't belong, that he's just passing through. Believe me, if the tourists knew they'd shiver. Well, in a sense it's true. They often do just pass through – but they come in like half baked humans and they leave like wet spaghetti.*

The Cross lured people who hoped the exciting lifestyle would wear off on them, but they couldn't compete with the more flamboyant characters or live a bohemian life, no matter how much they wanted to. In 1962's *The Kings Cross Caper*, George Smidmore, a forty year old, lives in the Cross having consciously worked at 'being crazy and unconventional for too long'. An accountant during the week, he lives alone in a tiny flat trying to emulate what the beautiful Carmen and most of her friends were – 'characters'. He realises he doesn't have the temperament to fit in and that his Kings Cross experiment has been a failure; he should have left the Cross long ago for a quiet and respectable life with a wife and two kids in the suburbs.

It's this mixed richness of people, damaged or not, which still disturbs visitors and attracts yahoos. Sightseers often came to the Cross just to stare at Rosaleen Norton, the self-proclaimed Witch of the Cross. The attention amused her and she created a persona that frightened visitors. Even today, packs of drunks from the suburbs sit at the front windows or outside tables of hotels laughing, sniggering and jeering at trannies, the mentally disturbed, Aborigines and oddly dressed locals.

One summer's evening I was sitting outside the Bourbon and Beefsteak, having a drink, when an inebriated Aboriginal woman fell down in the middle of Macleay Street. A car narrowly missed running over her. The driver jumped out of his car and rushed to her aid. A crowd of blow-ins from the suburbs behind me laughed at the woman's plight and several shouted out, 'Get a look at that drunken Abo!' Their condescension, racism, vulgarity and intolerance was a reminder of just why young men and women escape these dreadful people to come and live in the Cross.

It still remains a place to perform. Aziz Shaversian, known as Zyzz, was a thin boy who reinvented himself as a body builder. His transformation was quick and dramatic, enhanced by steroids. He became a social media celebrity and a model for the online bodybuilding community, where he'd post thousands of photos and videos of his body. One commentator observed, 'Zyzz was in fact a character; almost an actor, within a vibrant subculture.' On weekend nights he liked to show off his new body on Darling-hurst Road. Wearing only a thin singlet and trousers, he'd adopt poses for the thousands of people watching and photographing him. He had a small head and bulging arm muscles that reminded me of Popeye. He travelled to Thailand to buy cheap steroids on a 'roid holiday but suffered a cardiac arrest in a sauna, dying at the age of twenty-two. There are more than 100 videos dedicated to him on YouTube, viewed by millions.

Perhaps Ayesha best sums up the transformational power of the Cross: '…had it not been for Kings Cross, everything that happened in my life would not have been possible. The Cross is still a kaleidoscope of outcasts and mainstreamers, and attachments form between the oddest of bedfellows.'

REJUVENATION

THE DESTRUCTION OF THE TWIN towers in New York by Muslim terrorists on 11 September 2001 was a catalyst for the metamorphosis of Kings Cross. One effect of the terrorist attack was people's fear of flying. Tourism declined steeply. The downturn was particularly noticeable in Kings Cross where hotels, running at twenty-five per cent lower occupancy than usual, faced an uncertain future. There were up to 5000 hotel rooms or 'dorms' available at the many backpacker hostels, but few were filled. The tourists preferred to stay at the new hotels around Darling Harbour rather than the old-fashioned ones on the ridge. The solution was to convert the hotels into apartments.

In the space of only a few years one hotel after another closed – the Manhattan, the Gazebo, the Landmark, the Rex, Hampton Court, the Sebel and others – making a total of twelve hotels gone. All told 2000 hotel rooms were converted into 1400 apartments. From the beginning of the decade up to 2006 more than 2500 people moved into the area. This was a huge demographic shift in more ways than one. These newcomers were cashed-up professionals, both straight and gay, young couples and empty nesters. It was a transformation as dramatic as the boom in apartment living during the 1930s.

The changes to the area became evident in Macleay Street as

delicatessens, butchers, restaurants, pricey gift shops and hair-dressers opened. The Sydney City Council, lead by Lord Mayor Lucy Turnbull, used this economic momentum to rejuvenate Kings Cross itself. One of her targets was the sex industry. In order to stop further development she legislated that new brothels, strip clubs and adult shops be separated by at least seventy metres. She failed to see, like many others, that the sex business in the area was in terminal decline. Porky's, which opened in the late 1980s, had lost half of its customers; once 600 people a night used to come through its doors, now it had barely 300 on a Saturday. From the 1980s onwards the sex industry began its drift into the suburbs. Once the majority of Sydney's brothels and prostitutes were in the Cross but Australian society was, in general, becoming more tolerant, even of commercial sex. The popularity of pornography on the internet had a colossal impact, and it was estimated that around sixty per cent of the sex industry had been driven by tourists who now stayed elsewhere.

In 2003 a $20 million public works program (which eventually cost $30 million) was announced, aimed at 'civilising the Kings Cross red-light district'. The project was driven by the new Lord Mayor of Sydney, Clover Moore, who wanted the nightclubs, the brothels and the spruikers to be replaced by 'services' for locals and a friendlier atmosphere. Her aim was to transform the area into an urban village like Woollahra or Paddington. One of her councillors even wanted the Council to buy the sex clubs, striptease venues and adult bookshops 'and convert them into more family-friendly businesses'. Moore also wanted to get rid of the neon signs and replace them with identical steel boxes to hang from the awnings. She wanted spruikers banned, saying in defence of the sensitive new residents, 'They have to get past spruikers, and then they have to get past the drug dealers, and then they have to get past the sex workers, and they can find it quite exhausting to get home and cook their dinner.'

There was something pathetic about her objections, as if walking down Darlinghurst Road was like running a brutal gauntlet. First Turnbull and now Moore, the new Lord Mayor, wanted to feminise the space and valued homogeneity over diversity, and conformity over eccentricity and difference.

The early months of the redevelopment were chaotic and badly planned. What infuriated the locals was that the Council allowed the developer of the Rex Hotel to avoid housing the library and community centre even though they were part of the original plans. In May 2003 I chaired a meeting at the Reg Murphy Centre, just around the corner from the Rex. It was packed with locals and some from the eastern suburbs, many having to stand. The City of Sydney Councillors didn't turn up, which was sensible as they would have been heckled. The meeting started off as could only could happen in the Cross: a guy in his late thirties, high on drugs and drunk, burst in, shouting and screaming and threatening everyone with a six-inch nail. The reason for his fury seemed vague. Nick Farr-Jones, a former rugby player, theatrically took off his jacket ready to 'handle' the fellow. Eventually the madman left, waving his nail in front of him, frightened people parting before him like the Red Sea. Most of those sitting down didn't react at all; it was then I knew that they were locals.

The meeting didn't achieve much. There was a feeling amongst residents that we weren't being listened to and that the Council had its own secret agenda. The rejuvenation of the area took two long years. During that time the Council's maladroit administration of the works program meant that the Cross resembled a war zone. There were deep water-filled holes, barriers, temporary wooden pathways, the constant sound of jackhammers, mud, and inept planning meant that the workers – and there were never enough of them – seldom finished a section of paving or digging in one go, but were shunted off to other unfin-ished sites. Shops reported a fifty per cent drop in earnings and many businesses went broke. In and around Darlinghurst Road itself there were sixty shops for lease, empty or boarded up. Three banks left for the less raffish Macleay Street; even Hungry Jacks closed. The prolonged and inchoate public works made residents despair and nearly destroyed the spirit of the Cross.

Finally the works finished and we were left with wide granite stone footpaths, 'smart' poles, and conformist signage, especially in Macleay Street. The Council bought the Woolworths building for ten million and installed the library in it, plus City of Syd-ney bureaucrats. The streets were cleaner, the new apartments stylish and expensive and even more people shifted into the area. The Council was determined to shut down the adult shops and a number of them had to close after police raids confiscated their merchandise. The striptease joints began to close down for lack of customers. The Pink Pussycat, probably the most famous of them all, closed in 2003. I had only been in it once, when Mandy and I went to it after her father's wake (Eros defying Thanatos). From the road there was a long narrow stairway up to a ticket booth. The rooms were painted black, a stage or catwalk jutted out into the room and televisions played pornography. On the night we were there only a couple of the girls stripped, most pole-danced, some clumsily in almost a caricature of sexual come-on, though one was so good she seemed a professional making money on the side. Donald Horne, author of *The Lucky Country*, wanted it pre-served: 'I'd keep the Pink Pussycat in situ, as a heritage site, at least its façade.' To pay for its preservation Horne suggested that it could be turned into a History of the Cross museum. It's now a dingy internet café.

The redevelopment of the Cross also meant a reappraisal of its purpose. Now that the sex industry was fading and the hotels had become apartments it was decided to transform the area into a 24-hour, seven-days-a-week entertainment district. This excited the liquor industry especially. The former site of the National Bank became the gigantic swill barn the Sugarmill. The Carousel became the Empire, another beer barn catering to footballers, their scraggy groupies and bogans. Nightclubs and restaurants opened, trying to attract an affluent young crowd or sophisticated diners. The optimism was catching. The Bourbon and Beefsteak was a case in point. In the late 1980s it was awarded the city's first seven-days 24-hour licence. It was so successful that 12 million people passed through its doors over twenty-five years. It was also a magnet for drunken violence. Between 1988 and 1996 the Kings Cross police had been called to the venue no fewer than 550 times. It was a place where lives could go wrong.

One of the best-known incidents occurred just before owner Bernie Houghton's death in 2000 when the Australian test batsman, 24-year-old Ricky Ponting, went on a bender. In the early hours of the morning, after flirting with Carlotta and not realising she wasn't a woman, he set his sights on a brunette, who rejected his advances. He chased her around the dance floor, grabbed her in a wrestling headlock and pushed her to the floor where he pinned her down by his arms. When he wrapped his hands around her neck an off-duty security guard, who was drinking at the bar, had had enough. The 130-kilogram Islander stood up, went over to Ponting and knocked him out. The Test cricketer was unconscious for over a minute. Morning newspapers had front page pictures of Ponting standing unsteadily outside the Bourbon and Beefsteak with a hideous black eye. The cricket board suspended him, though after public acts of contrition he went on to become captain. For commentators and columnists this was just another example – and there were many – of how the Cross could bring out the worst aspects of your personality and ruin your reputation, even your whole life. So concerned were the rugby league authorities that they suggested a blanket ban on players entering Kings Cross, hoping it might stem the growing number of late-night incidents of bashings and players being shot at that were tarnishing the sport.

When Houghton died he left his estate to seven close friends and set aside money for the staff. They sold the Bourbon and Beefsteak in 2005 for the astonishing sum of $53 million, and it proved the most obvious example of just how sanguine people were about the revitalisation of the Cross. The staff hoped that the new owners would keep the bar as it was.

Instead it underwent an $8 million 'major overhaul'. The cluttered memorabilia and objects disappeared: the Indian chief wooden statue, movie star posters, signed shirts and football jumpers, neon signs, the red telephone box and the Vietnam detritus of uniformed mannequins, helmets, flags and a battered M16. It was gutted, the word 'Beefsteak' was dropped from its name, and the designers created a mirrored, timber, limestone and chrome interior described as 'A 1960s LA and Palm Springs vibe'. The warm New Orleans French Quarter feel was replaced with a series of neat sanitised rooms that lacked atmosphere. The owners wanted to attract cashed-up young professionals, which was fine during the weekend, but by alienating the locals, the Bourbon was near empty of a week night. As the Friday and Saturday night crowds waned, it dawned on the management that one of the main reasons people came to the Bourbon was because of its history; it was an icon of Kings Cross, but the renovated hotel had few reminders its fabled past. A year after the Bourbon opened the management launched an upstairs party spot, pointedly called 'the Cross' and stuck on the walls as much Kings Cross memorabilia, especially photographs, as they could rustle up. But, as the historian Paul Ham said of the new Bourbon, 'Money can't buy authenticity. Rather it is acquired gradually, absorbing local stories, lives and pasts.' The soulless venue was losing extravagant amounts of money and by 2009 its clientele had become backpackers and tourists who had come to see the famous B&B, and instead found an imposter that depended on trivia nights and $10 steaks (favourite of disgraced Judge Marcus Einfeld who, before he was jailed for perjury, devoured them with a canine ferocity that seared itself into my memory). In early 2010 a hail storm caused the collapse of the roof and that of the adjoining Club Swans. The hotel remained closed until another publican bought it and Club Swans for $22 million – much less than the excessive price paid for the properties just a couple of years before.

A further sign that the area was becoming trendy was the spectacular renovation of the Goldfish Bowl. On the corner of Darlinghurst Road and Victoria Street, it had been a soiled, clammy bar with unparalleled views of the passing parade. It was a bar of last resort of a night where anyone could get a drink. It had short-tempered bouncers and gaunt staff, many of them with the mottled face of alcoholics. Middle class people, unless slumming, avoided it, which was why residents were fond of it. It may have been a rough venue but it was *ours*. It was sold and became a chic bar with DJs, a strongly enforced dress code allowing in only a certain hip crowd, and obese bouncers kept out hoi polloi. You couldn't even look into the club because its large bay windows, which had given it the name the Goldfish Bowl, were now hidden behind what looked like a steel spider web which meant those inside could stare out while the excluded couldn't peer in. The new Goldfish Bowl was symbolic of how gentrification was changing the very nature of the Cross itself.

Yet this process didn't stop the drug trade. Residents were used to seeing needles in the streets, doorways and lanes. It was not unusual to come upon someone or a group shooting up. Pastor

Graham Long of the Wayside Chapel and his staff would find up to 130 needles per day around Hughes Street. Paramedics spent most of their time responding to overdoses; in a twelve-month period in 1999–2000 there were 677 call-outs to drug overdoses and it was reckoned there were 800 heroin deals a day in the area. The public phones in Bayswater Road were some of the most profitable in the country, taking $25,000 a month in coins from junkies making calls to their dealers. Deaths were common, with a disturbing number of fatal overdoses happening in the Tudor Hotel.

A proposed solution to these deaths was to have Australia's first legally sanctioned medically supervised injection centre. This proved a contentious idea for both the locals and Australians at large. At first it seemed that the Sisters of Charity would operate the centre at St Vincent's Hospital, but Australia's Cardinal Pell, a dogmatic man of stunning intolerance, rejected the plan and it wasn't long before the Vatican forbade the nuns to have anything to do with it. When the Uniting Church stepped in there was fierce opposition from politicians, including Prime Minister John Howard. Shock jocks and tabloid columnists opposed it in a hysterical campaign that only revealed their ignorance of the problem of drugs in the Cross. The local Chamber of Commerce was appalled, especially as the centre would be on the main strip, at number 66. The members were certain that the location would put off 'normal people' coming to the Cross and that it would have a 'honey-pot' effect, drawing drug dealers to the area. The eccentric, kilt-wearing solicitor, Malcolm Duncan, took legal action to shut it down. He lost, as he usually did, and the injection centre opened in May 2001 for a trial period.

The prediction that there would be a honey-pot effect proved to be prescient, though short-lived. Not long after the injecting centre opened, a drug syndicate based itself next door in the dingy Tudor Hotel, selling cocaine and heroin. It was a larger operation than the usual sporadic dealing. Five people operated out of Room 15. Heroin was referred to as 'hot chocolate' and cocaine 'cappuccino'. On an average day the group's runners made thirty to fifty street deals, with the syndicate netting up to $3500 a day before it was busted.

This blatant drug dealing near the centre ceased. Between the time it opened in 2001 and April 2010, there were 12,050 registered injecting drug users. In that time the staff managed 3426 overdoses without one fatality. The centre also tracked the changing patterns of drug use. In the beginning heroin was the most widely used drug, but during a drought the painkiller oxycodone became the user's favourite. Nicknamed 'Hillybilly Heroin' it's a morphine derivative, and the word 'oxy' began to be heard more often on the street as agitated addicts sought it out. In the end most locals found the centre was a relief; no more stepping on needles, walking around addicts shooting up or watching paramedics trying to revive someone who had overdosed. Deaths on the street fell from 120 to twelve a year and ambulance calls were down nearly ninety per cent. The government agreed that the trial over ten years had accomplished what it set out to do and in 2012 both sides of New South Wales Parliament made the injection centre a permanent facility.

By the time Pastor Graham Long took over the Wayside Chapel from Ted Noffs in 2004, it had been operating for forty years; the building was falling down, with almost half of it being condemned. Long, in his fifties, an ordained minister of the Uniting Church, set about finding money to construct a new building. After an $8 million development the new buildings were opened in May 2012. The complex has a prayer room and a new café, linked by a wall and 'inspirational' graffiti, which Long believes articulates the delicate balancing act between the sacred and the profane, the essence of the Wayside philosophy. The community hall is used for yoga classes, concerts and live theatre. There are extensive shower and bathroom facilities, a youth area, a rooftop garden and op shop, which has included Governor Marie Bashir's cast-off clothes. Perhaps it's a sign of having more money, or the necessity of needing more people to deal with an increasing number of those wanting help, but there are now thirty-one full-time employees, when ten years before there was only one.

The patient and inspiring Long used the occasion of the new building to strengthen the Wayside's bond with the community. Despite some of the visitors not wanting to share the place with others, Long has made sure that residents can eat and mingle with the visitors, a mix that perhaps could happen only in the Cross.

There are always people milling about the front, shooting the breeze, coming down from drugs, waiting for a meal or news of a source of drugs. One surprising statistic is that twenty per cent of those seeking help are Aboriginal, a sign that there is something hideously wrong in their communities. These troubled souls who come to the Wayside are the drug addicted, the homeless, the mentally ill, victims of incest, and the lonely. Most are physically and mentally damaged. There are the toothless junkies, the twitchy meth drinkers and the methadone dependent. One former junkie now on the 'done has been in and out of jail all her life, her four children farmed out to foster parents, creating yet another generation that the Wayside will have to care for. There are meth drinkers of both sexes and ice users. One alcoholic, an ex-Vietnam vet, believes that ASIO has put a chip in his head to follow his every move. On one occasion a naked ice addict turned up on the doorstep, plucking fiercely at his flesh trying to remove the demons that were inside him. At one stage he had his whole hand up his rectum trying to remove them. Another time a naked girl appeared at the Wayside and was put in the observation room; when they checked her later she had earphones in her ears and the iPod itself was secreted in her vagina. Many of the visitors have a dysfunctional background. There was a man who, when he was three, was called into the bedroom by his father who was sitting at the dressing table with a rifle between his legs aimed at his head. 'I love you,' he said to his son before pulling the trigger and blowing his head off. He and his siblings ended up being sent to foster homes and, to totally mess up his life, his mother killed herself.

The Wayside is a refuge for the damned, the desperate and the disturbed. These are people who have lost their way because of drugs or are products of several generations of welfare dependency and the breakdown of family life. The policy of pushing madmen out of the asylums and into the streets has meant that Kings Cross has became a haven for these deluded crazies whose personal issues are so horrific that there is no chance of them being cured of their affliction. There have been criticisms of the Wayside becoming a 'honey pot' for those people who wouldn't ordinarily come to the Cross. There's no denying this does happen. When the new centre opened there was an increase in visitors unable or unwilling to work or look after themselves, keen to test the limits of Wayside charity. It's also common to hear many of them talking aloud about how they're going to the Wayside to conduct drug deals or find out where they can buy some.

Given the large number of registered addicts, it was still extremely profitable to deal in drugs. Many brothels sold drugs or got the girls hooked on them. When police raided one bordello on Darlinghurst Road they found heroin, drug paraphernalia and an estimated $1 million in cash. But heroin was not the only drug available in the Cross. Cocaine and ecstasy were extremely popular in the nightclubs, and a bikie gang war over their distribution in the Cross was behind killings and beatings. The turf war grew worse from 2006 to 2009 with violence breaking out in sixteen nightclubs, bars and hotels. The Hells Angels, Comancheros,

Nomads, Rebels, Bandidos, Gypsy Jokers and Notorious gangs fought each other, brawling and shooting, kidnapping, sexually assaulting women and holding rival gang members to ransom, gangs – of up to thirty men – attacked each other in the streets and demanded clubs pay them up to $5000 per week for protection.

Abe Saffron had nothing to do with the bikers. By this time he was considered redundant and, besides, he was becoming preoccupied with his reputation. The nickname 'Mr Sin' particularly annoyed him and he sued the *Gold Coast Bulletin* for its crossword clue: *Who is the Sydney underworld figure nicknamed Mr Sin?* The answer, printed the next day, was Abe Saffron. He also took the authors of *Tough: 101 Australian Gangsters* to court for calling him Mr Sin. There was something delusional about this; after all, Saffron had a criminal record and had been adversely mentioned in Royal Commissions. He had been a major player in pornography, prostitution, fire bombings, drugs, violence and bribes. His malignant influence was like an ever-expanding mycelium of dank rot that corrupted law enforcement and the government. The old hypocrite refused to acknowledge, even to himself, just what a sleazy, heinous man he really was. When he looked in the mirror he saw a businessman and philanthropist, not a gangster.

He continued to work from an office in Crown Street, always immaculately groomed, with a religious silver neck chain and chunky gold rings. Photographs on his walls included the gangster 'Bugsy' Siegel, who founded the casino city of Las Vegas for the Mafia, and New York mobster Meyer Lansky. In 2006 Saffron died peacefully at the age of eighty-six, his latest mistress at his bedside. His funeral was attended by arthritic gangsters, senile criminals, relatives, ageing friends and the drag queens Carmen and Ayesha. A rabbi delivered a eulogy, calling him 'a great Australian icon', but the *Age* crime reporter John Silvester was closer to the truth when he said, 'He was scum. He will not be missed.'

By the time Saffron died the sobriquet King of the Cross was being worn by John Ibrahim, who was in his middle thirties. He was the second child born to Lebanese Muslim immigrants. When John was young, his father returned to Lebanon and disappeared from his life. His pious Muslim mother couldn't control her wayward sons. Ibrahim grew up in the western suburbs, a cocky boy with no interest in school. He drifted into the Cross and became a gofer for Bill Bayeh, then at the height of his drug dealing. One evening the 15-year-old Ibrahim saw Bayeh being jostled by two men and went to his rescue, only to be stabbed with a kitchen knife. The blade pierced his lungs and damaged his liver and intestines. He was in hospital for six months. When he came out, a grateful Bayeh gave his young apprentice 'opportunities'.

It wasn't enough for Ibrahim to be an errand boy for Bayeh, so, at the age of nineteen he borrowed $70,000 and bought a slice of the Tunnel nightclub in Earl Place. What followed was a meteoric rise through the malevolent and unscrupulous world of Kings Cross's nightlife. By the age of twenty-two his club was very successful and he remained highly ambitious. He was cocky about his fighting prowess ('I've never lost a fight') and had by that age seen 'violence beyond belief'. He didn't drink, take drugs or gamble. His time in the Cross had convinced him that there was 'no such thing as Women's Lib.' He knew from experience that in the Cross women were a way for men to make money and 'a way for men to get off'. His religious and Lebanese background troubled him. He thought of himself as 'the worst Muslim ever made'. Unable to read more than a couple of pages of the Koran he was the only one in his family who had never been to a mosque. In an interview he confessed he hated family get togethers and yet there was a sense that he had assumed the role of his absent father and was attempting to control and protect his unreliable and unpredictable brothers.

A couple of years later the Wood Royal Commission accused Ibrahim of being 'the new lifeblood of the drug industry at Kings Cross'. He denied it, but the stain remained. At a trial ten years later he was said to be 'a major organised-crime figure, the subject of 546 police intelligence reports in relation to his involvement in outlaw motorcycle gangs'. Yet his only crime conviction was for hitting another teenager when he was fifteen. He has been charged with manslaughter and witness tampering but both charges never came to trial. His ability to avoid convictions earned him the nickname Teflon John.

This talent doesn't extend to his family or inner circle, many of whom by 2011 were either in jail, dead or before the courts. His brothers are particularly clumsy in their criminal endeavours; younger brother Fadi was shot five times in 2009 and was alleged to have conspired to murder a man. Michael, the youngest of the brothers, was alleged to have organised a murder. The eldest brother, Sam, was a former bikie boss who was on trial for the kidnapping of a teenage boy. Semi Ngata, Ibrahim's close friend and bodyguard, a hulk of a man known as Tongan Sam, was arrested on weapons and drugs charges. Ibrahim's son allegedly assaulted a man, and Maha Sayour, Ibrahim's sister, was arrested when nearly $3 million in notes was found hidden in the ceiling of her house. Even Ibrahim bemoans the fact that he can't control his brothers, calling them 'fucking idiots'. As one police report had it, 'The persons Ibrahim associates with have been charged with murder, bribery, supply drugs, possess prohibited weapons and can be considered extremely dangerous and well-connected within the criminal milieu.'

How does he account for his rise to wealth and influence? 'I didn't shoot my way to the top, I charmed my way there,' he has said on more than one occasion. He describes himself as a nightclub promoter and consultant, who 'works with' or has part of up to twenty clubs in the Cross. He lives in a $3 million house over-looking the water at Dover Heights and owns two townhouses in the same street. He drives a Bentley and wears designer clothes. Short like Saffron, he has, as I can attest, blinding whitened teeth, a swarthy complexion, languorous eyes, plump lips, and a beaming smile that segues into a smirk. Like the former King of the Cross he drinks little and says he takes no drugs; he needs his mind and reflexes to be sharp and clear – at every moment he has to be on top of his game. The world he operates in is dangerous and there are plenty of enemies, some of them created by his feck-less brothers and others who want to usurp him as 'King of the Cross'. Paranoia is a sensible survival mechanism in the jungles of the Cross.

When he walks through the streets of a night he has a body-guard or sometimes two, but I've seen him of a day strolling down Darlinghurst Road by himself with the insouciance of a flâneur, taking in his businesses and properties and enjoying the admiring glances and gushing of dozens of well-wishers.

But when the occasion demands it, he has an innate theat-ricality, especially at the funerals of gangster mates. He and his companions wear black suits, thin black ties and practised scowls, their true emotion hidden behind sunglasses as they present a united front for the media. These funerals are not about grief but a subtle rearranging of the new hierarchy. He's at the top of his game now, untouched by the law, with the press reduced to call-ing him a 'Kings Cross identity', knowing that if they insinuated he had anything to do with criminal activities then they'd be sued.

On Saturday nights he likes to present himself as an actor on the neon stage outside *Porky's* with Frank 'Ashtray' Amante, or he strolls up and down the Glittering Mile with the aplomb of a godfather, shaking hands, checking up on the latest gossip and revelling in being in the spotlight. He likes to say he doesn't appreciate media attention, but, according to the *Daily Telegraph*, his favourite newspaper, he secretly sends it new pictures and stories about himself. He adores being in the company of celebrities and thinks of himself as a ladies' man, with an especial fascination for Anglo blondes.

Violence and allegations of drug dealing have dogged him over the years. He changed the name of the Tunnel three times, the first after it was sprayed with fifty bullets, when it became EP1; then, after police alleged that the club was part of a well-organised drug trade in the Cross, it metamorphosed into the Dragonfly. After it was changed back to the Tunnel, the nightclub was named one of Sydney's most dangerous clubs, with drunken assaults, drink spiking, sexual assault, shootings and kidnapping linked to the premises.

In 2006 the New South Wales Crime Commission seized Ibrahim's assets, including his luxurious home, on the balance of probabilities that he had engaged in criminal activity. It was eventually resolved, with the Supreme Court ordering him to pay the State $150,000 without an admission of guilt. Every time he is quizzed about how he earned his money and influence he says, or gets his lawyer to say, 'Either I'm the smartest criminal out there, or I just run a legitimate business and people just want to fantasise.'

And that was the quandary for the creators of *Underbelly, the Golden Mile,* the 2010 television mini-series about crime in Kings Cross during the time of the Wood Royal Commission. Much of it concerned police corruption and the drug wars between rival gangs in the 1990s. It was bookended by the John Ibrahim story, beginning with him arriving in Kings Cross with dreams of making it big in the nightclub scene, and the final episodes focusing on his rise to become King of the Cross. The trouble with his episodes is that nothing much happens. Just how he rose to the top and became a multi-millionaire was never explained. Ibrahim had been asked to be a consultant on the series and it was never made clear whether he was or not. And, as happens in other controversial series based on living people, his lawyers would have examined the scripts very closely. The result was that his character drifted through events, a handsome but mysterious cipher. The actor who played Ibrahim, Firass Dirani, was in a series I created, *The Straits* (set in the Torres Straits, my original pitch was 'The Sopranos with thongs'). One day when I was on the set I asked him how difficult it had been, given the producers had to make sure they didn't defame Ibrahim. He shook his head, bemused.

'Sometimes,' he said, 'it seemed as if the lawyers had written the scripts.'

The success of the mini-series *Underbelly* meant that Ibrahim's fame spread beyond the Cross to the rest of the country. His enigmatic role in the nightlife of the Cross further endeared him to viewers, and bedazzled fans still line up to shake his hand or be photographed with him.

Gentrification hadn't made much difference to criminal activities. What made it distinct from the 1990s was that the blurring of day and night, which once made that decade menacing and distinctive, had now sharpened into the separation of day and night, like the former Cross. During the day the locals own the area and the night-time belongs to the hordes of visitors and the criminals.

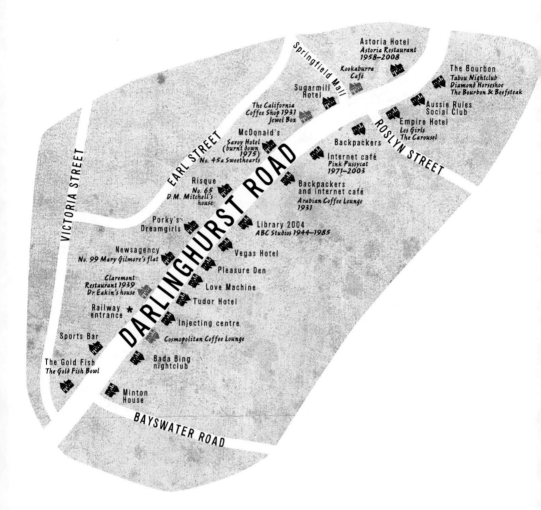

DARLINGHURST ROAD

VICTORIA STREET

EARL STREET

Springfield Mall

ROSLYN STREET

BAYSWATER ROAD

Astoria Hotel
*Astoria Restaurant
1958–2008*

Kookaburra
Café

The Bourbon
*Tabou Nightclub
Diamond Horseshoe
The Bourbon & Beefsteak*

Sugarmill
Hotel

Aussie Rules
Social Club

*The California
Coffee Shop 1931
Jewel Box*

Empire Hotel
*Les Girls
The Carousel*

McDonald's
*Savoy Hotel
(burnt down
1975)
No. 45a Sweethearts*

Backpackers

Internet café
*Pink Pussycat
1971–2003*

Risque
*No. 65
D.M. Mitchell's
house*

Backpackers
and internet café
*Arabian Coffee Lounge
1931*

Porky's
Dreamgirls

Library 2004
ABC Studios 1944–1985

Newsagency
No. 99 Mary Gilmore's flat

Vegas Hotel

Pleasure Den

*Claremont
Restaurant 1939
Dr. Eakin's house*

Love Machine

Railway
entrance

Tudor Hotel

Injecting centre

Sports Bar

Cosmopolitan Coffee Lounge

Bada Bing
nightclub

The Gold Fish
The Gold Fish Bowl

Minton
House

THE FIRST THING THAT STRIKES you as you turn the bend from elegant Macleay Street into Darlinghurst Road is the sickly sweet smell of an ice cream parlour. Then suddenly the visual muddle of Darlinghurst Road greets you like a slap in the face. If the Macleay Street signage discreetly whispers, in Darlinghurst Road it shouts at you in reds, blacks and yellows, the writing, sizes and fonts all alarmingly different. Clover Moore's 2003 plan for discreet signage failed. It's more than apparent that the flâneur has left salubrious Potts Point behind. If Macleay Street appeals to the higher instincts, Darlinghurst Road proudly flaunts its appeal to baser desires.

In 2013 there are three hotels in a row on the eastern side, the newly renovated Bourbon with its '1930s New York vibe' and Creole food; Club Swans, closed and derelict; and the former Les Girls site, now the pedestrian Empire Hotel. Though it has to be said that the expensively revamped Bourbon is no longer the visual clue for people coming into the main drag from the north end that you are unmistakeably entering the salacious heart of the Cross, because this new incarnation had dissociated itself from Darlinghurst Road and obviously wants to be seen as a continuation of respectable Macleay Street

The Vegas is a few doors down from the library. Famous for its 'underwater pole dancers', who gyrated in giant fish tanks wearing only strategically placed crystals, and go-go dancers in cages, it makes most of its cash from thirty pokie machines. They're popular with Kings Cross locals, many of whom work the night shift and like to play the pokies in the pre-dawn hours. The Vegas opens early and its smoking area, which overlooks the street, quickly fills with men and women nursing hangovers, those on a bender, a determined minority of alcoholics, with flushed faces, bluish noses, red eyes, sagging lower eyelids and racking coughs. The hideous faces, some worn like ancient driftwood, others blubbery with booze, resemble those in a painting by Hieronymus Bosch.

The road is a higgledy-piggledy mess of convenience stores, tobacconists, backpackers, cheap hotels, travel bureaux, tattoo parlours, chemists, massage parlours, kebab takeaways, empty shops, hairdressers, liquor outlets, McDonalds, adult stores and striptease joints. There is something transitory in their tackiness, like a movie set left out in the elements for years, lit up with neons in the evenings to hide their ugliness and impermanence.

The junction with Springfield Avenue has changed from the drug-dealing square it was a decade ago. One of the plans after 2000 was to return it to being a road again, but reason prevailed and it remained a square, repaved and widened. In the middle of it is a row of benches, which locals nickname 'the Zoo'. Drugged trannies, the homeless, agitated ice users, Aborigines and the stark raving mad sit or squat there, the sight so offending the Sugarmill management that they wanted the council to get rid of the benches and their unsightly guests who, apparently, repulse the patrons.

What you witness in the mall can jolt you. One of the few times I was drinking at the Sugarmill I saw two Aboriginal men collapsed against the opposite wall. There was something limp about one of them. I went over to offer assistance. Both had shot up, one was overdosing. The ambulance was called and while waiting I learned from the older one that it was the first time they had tried the drug. They had been down from the country for two days, intending to return that day, but had spent all their money on heroin.

It was when I saw a junkie I knew in the mall that I was reminded of how used I had become to the excesses of the denizens of the Cross. She had just shot up and was standing still as a statue, staring at the pavement, but caught in mid-stride, as if frozen. She kept the pose for some minutes, like one of those buskers pretending to be a statue down at Circular Quay. A family of tourists passed by and the father glanced at her said to his wife and son, 'Hey, get a load of this.' The astonished trio gawked openly, no doubt the junkie confirming what they'd been told about horrors of Kings Cross.

Across the road from 'the Zoo', on the corner of Darlinghurst Road and Roslyn Avenue, a plaque inlaid in the footpath tells the tourist that this location was nicknamed Battleship Corner, where the prostitutes plied their trade in the Second World War. It continued to be a highly sought-after pitch. When Mandy was tap-dancing in the Cross during the 1980s the prostitute who worked the site made it clear in no uncertain terms that Mandy was not to encroach on it.

Pitches were important and I've witnessed brawls between the hookers over them. When I was first in the Cross there were many more prostitutes in Darlinghurst Road. Walking along it I would hear the constant seductive mantra of 'Would you like to see a lady?' The word lady had a lower-class sense of propriety about it that was at odds with the flimsy dresses, towering heels, embalmer's make-up and pinned eyes. Their pimps would supervise their girls from the hotel bars. One lunch-time I was musing on something while looking out the window of my office in Minton House when I saw a zonked-out hooker stagger onto the road. She took no notice of the traffic. A car braked hard but couldn't avoid hitting her. She fell onto the road in slow motion and lay there. She didn't seem to be that hurt but her pimp rushed out of the Crest Hotel, jumped over her supine body and tried to pull the frightened driver out of his car, angry at him for harming his meal ticket, screaming at him, 'The fucking bitch won't be working for fucking weeks, man!' By this stage she had got to her feet and limped to the footpath, where she slumped on the side of the gutter, not so much in pain, but wide-eyed with incredulity, as if she hadn't been hit by a car but by reality itself.

By the late 1990s there were fewer girls working the Glittering Mile, though they returned in numbers if the American Navy was in town. One of the stayers was a woman in her fifties, who had dry strawberry blonde hair that hadn't seen a comb in some time and wore a mucky cardigan and dowdy skirt. Her customers were men about her age or older. One regular stood her up and the next day she spotted him outside the newsagent where she had her pitch. She grabbed hold of him and abused him loudly.

'I thought you were supposed to fucking turn up yesterday!'

He looked like a cowed husband and meekly apologised, 'Sorry, love.' She was not mollified.

'Well, that's not fucking good enough,' she said, jabbing his chest with a finger, demanding he make good his missed appointment. She must have put up with a lot over the years. One time I overheard her telling another hooker that she'd had a drunken old bloke the night before who, as he was fucking her, shat himself.

'Oh,' she grimaced, 'what a bloody mess and stink.' Another time she had just picked up a regular from outside the newsagent when she said to him, 'Look at that, will you? Those two lesbians kissing.' Indeed two women were kissing each other passionately on the lips nearby. 'Disgusting. Totally disgusting,' she said, before escorting her stooped white-haired client to the KX hotel.

Some hookers vanished only to reappear months or years later. Two I knew were a plump, attractive Chinese woman and a brunette; the brunette wore tight denim shorts showing off her pert arse and a blouse unbuttoned sufficiently to reveal impressive breasts. Unlike many girls who work to pay for drugs, these two women earned a fortune but wasted it on gambling. It always amazed me that men would pay junkies for sex, given just how damaged they looked with their ravaged, splotchy faces, anorexic limbs and dazed eyes. But then, some men like to feel superior to the women they buy. A frequent sight is drug-addled prostitutes attempting to put on their make-up using reflective surfaces, especially in the doorways of the strip joints. I once saw a gaunt, confused hooker standing in the doorway of Porky's rubbing her face and cheeks with imaginary powder and rouge. The bouncer had enough and, snarling 'Get out of here,' pushed her out onto the footpath where she tottered upright for a moment and then, like air slowly being let out of a balloon, collapsed onto the ground at my feet.

One intriguing prostitute was a woman in her early twenties. She had blonde hair, luscious red lips and the clear white skin of someone not using drugs. Her pimp was a tall, solid fellow with a black beard, black clothes and always wore a black overcoat in any weather. He seemed more an aspiring bohemian than a bludger. His girl wore cowgirl costumes and was often seen on her pitch reading, sometimes the *New Yorker* or *Macbeth*. I once asked her why she liked *Macbeth* of all Shakespeare's plays.

'Because that's the way the world is,' she purred.

Hookers used to work out of the strip clubs after they were legalised to be brothels, but that is rare now. Joints like Dreamgirls are trying to go upmarket, which means they no longer show live sex or have women giving blow jobs to patrons on stage. The strip clubs and nightclubs lose money of a week night. Frank 'Ashtray' Amante, who runs Dreamgirls and Porky's Gentlemen's Club next to it, predicts that within a few years there will be no prostitutes and no strip joints. He might be right. The Pink Pussycat has closed down and the others seem scruffy and sad. The Love Machine has a permanent sign out the front, *Waitress wanted.* Sitting in the doorway is a morose spruiker who seems to reflect the reality of what's inside up the frayed carpeted stairs.

There are adult shops where men can go and have sex. A friend works three nights a week in such a shop on the main strip. Men don't go to buy porno magazines or movies but to visit the Suckatorium. Here like-minded men have oral sex. The curious thing is that although it's a gay venue, my friend believes that most of the men who visit are married.

At night you don't see just how ramshackle the buildings are. Of a day time, if you lift your gaze above the awnings, the facades are a shocking sight. Ferns and grasses sprout from the mortar, concrete is crumbling, window frames are rotting and sheets or T-shirts cover the dirty windows, reminding me more of a frontier town than Montmartre. Perhaps the most beautiful building on the main drag is the former four-storey Woolworths. It's classic late 1930s art deco facade of grey-green tiles is where the library is now located. It's up on the first floor and is a calm oasis from the constant movement of people and noise below. The building is next to the coarse Vegas, which is in turn next to the injecting room. If I stand on the library's balcony, straight across the road the first floor window of the Risqué sex shop greets me with voluptuous store dummies dressed in kinky nurse's outfits or schoolgirl uniforms. If anything sums up the Cross it's this sort of striking juxtaposition.

Risqué Boutique Adult Shop is a classy joint compared to the other adult shops on the strip. Previously called Ricco's, it was renovated in 2003 and since then has become one of the few upmarket sex shops in the area. It pitches itself as an adult sex toys specialist, selling leather and BDSM products, sex lotions, sexual enhancers, latex and rubber underwear. They have adult toys for couples, including a mind-boggling selection of anal sex toys. Risqué advertises itself as the only supplier in Australia of the luxury silicone love dolls, the Candy Girl series. The store carries vibrators, as well as an impressive selection of bondage whips, floggers, leather paddles and slappers, love sex swings, hand cuffs, ankle cuffs, ball gags and other bondage toys. They can also supply specialised fucking machines. It's proud of its reputation as a first stop for strippers and dancers to find accessories such as shoes, lingerie and costumes.

The ground floor and first floor windows have store dummies totally at odds with the slim waisted, small-breasted dummies used in normal shop windows. The Risqué mannequins have exaggerated curves and are arranged to emphasis the sexual assets of a woman. The assistants are enthusiastic and change the costumes on the dummies practically every day, showing imaginative flair for provocative costumes and poses. Their customers are an eclectic bunch: silent Japanese tourists, young unembarrassed couples fondling dildos and vibrators, giggling groups of women, lonely male masturbators buying artificial vaginas, single women searching for the perfect vibrator and middle-aged couples trying on fetish wear and fur covered handcuffs.

The sexual display of Risqué is testimony to the old libertarian values of the Cross. The shop is in the Browley building, built on the site of David Scott Mitchell's old house. Mitchell was an avid collector of both visual and written erotica and it is somehow appropriate that a century later in the same spot Risqué is a profane shrine to the pleasures of the flesh. I am yet to see anyone other than happy people inside or leaving the store.

A few doors down is McDonald's. The fast food joint can see the worst of human behaviour of weekend nights with fights, shouting matches, people too drunk or drugged to order and even an alleged incident where the night manager protected himself from an irate customer by throwing hot cooking oil over him. On its site once stood the Savoy Hotel, which was burnt down by an arsonist, Sweethearts coffee lounge, and the entrance to my agent's office which first drew me to the Cross. It's proof again of the bewilderedly quick transformations the area undergoes.

In the morning I sometimes come back from the post office on the eastern side of Darlinghurst Road and have to make a slight detour around a group of half a dozen to a dozen people huddling outside the front door of the injection centre, desperate for it to open. The addicts are the usual underclass junkies, but there are middle-class and middle-aged men and women using the centre, a confronting illustration of just how drugs have affected all levels of society. Ice has become so prevalent that tobacconists sell glass pipes to smoke it in, even though it is illegal. One owner was recently fined for having 504 glass pipes and 114 bongs.

Locals rarely shop in the main drag because Macleay Street has the products and upmarket cafés they like, whereas Darlinghurst Road is for tourists and visitors. Thousands of residents use it as a conduit to the railway station or a way of getting to William Street for the walk into the CBD. Those who use it of a daytime are the druggies, junkies, maddies and the desperate, who hang out around the station.

The junkies have only two topics of conversation: scoring drugs and money. They wear the same dirty frayed clothes day after day, their hair is greasy and their runners filthy. Their arguments are a nasal cacophony of angry voices: 'I gave you half, you fucker', 'Where's the money, cunt?', 'Hey, you didn't pay me back that dollar!', 'You fucking ripped me off, you dog', 'You cunt of a bitch, where's me fucking oxy?' They blithely yell out their intimate feelings across the street: 'If you won't look after me, I won't look after you, fuck face.' And 'I love you, Kas!' They neither notice nor care what passers-by think.

They are what I call the Wraiths, an ever-changing collection of the damned. They spend much of their time sitting on their haunches against the wall, their world narrowed to their addictions. On wet and windy days they look their worst: clothes damp, shit and urine stained; hair matted, body odour foul, anxious eyes focused on the next fix; their pinched faces and rotten teeth a testimony to their habit. They bicker amongst themselves, beg for a cigarette from passers-by, sit against the wall twitching and shuddering from bad drugs or, after having hit up, try to stand on their rubbery legs, but their slight bodies are too heavy and they slump to the ground. Their sense of dignity has been replaced by a shameless acceptance of their addictions.

Next door to the newsagent is an entrance way to a former sex shop now boarded up with a giant blackboard. This is where the Wraiths sit, squat and sleep. It took a few months before the blackboard was used and this was due to Lawrence, a homeless man who lives in a cave opposite the Old Fitzroy Hotel. He has long straggly grey hair, a weathered face and a black coat covered in big white letters announcing the end of the world. He started writing his apocalyptic visions on the blackboard in terse aphorisms and slogans:

> *Climate Change – Last Days, the Day of the Lord will come like a Thief in the Night and the heavens will fly away in a GREAT NOISE. DNA: Everything created under the rule of the gods. The Day of the King Tides, rising of the Oceans.*

The trouble was that the Wraiths would rub off his warnings or change them into obscene messages. One day I was passing and saw Lawrence dipping a paintbrush into a can and wiping it over his words. I asked him what he was doing.

'It's varnish,' he said with some satisfaction. 'My warnings will remain here forever.'

The Wraiths are constant complainers, whether it be about the quality of drugs, their lack of money, the cops who search them, or the welfare system which they are dependent upon. They betray, steal and lie to each other. When there are no drugs available they become highly agitated and violent towards each other, men hitting women and women spitting on and hitting men, fighting in front of the warnings about Armageddon, while their hungry and lean chihuahuas yap furiously. It's as if they are permanently stuck in a ghastly purgatory destined never to rise to heaven or descend to hell.

Everyone is to blame for their condition except themselves. For the Wraiths, the real world is a hologram at best; at worst it doesn't exist, which is why they walk out into the traffic without noticing it; and swear at drivers who have the timidity to beep their horns as a warning. Their solipsism and selfishness means they're not interested in the Kings Cross community or contributing to it; instead they take from it as much as they can get away with.

Sometimes the Wraiths disappear, mostly to jail, and return, clear eyed and healthy but within a few days they are back on the junk or oxy or Xanax or ice; mostly they live in a parallel word that seldom infringes on the life of the residents. Tourists are appalled by them and locals think, *There but for the grace of God go I.*

But even the Wraiths don't stick around at night, especially Fridays and Saturdays, when they retreat to the Wayside Chapel. As night falls, Darlinghurst Road undergoes a startling transformation. The neons and the shop windows' coloured lights come on and their garish sheen hides the drab, dilapidated appearance of the street. It's around this time that the residents also retreat to their apartments. The hordes begin to arrive, first of all bucks' and hen's night parties. Affluent couples make their way down Bayswater Road or Macleay Street to eat at some of the most fashionable restaurants in Sydney.

The hip, beautiful people disappear into expensive, trendy nightclubs and restaurants while packs of girls and boys arrive from the western suburbs, many of them having drunk a sizeable amount of alcohol before coming, because drinks can be expensive in the clubs and bars. The boys wear the bland shirts and trousers while the girls wear tight minuscule mini-skirts with gravity defying high heels and thick make-up (there's no disguising the fact that there's an obesity pandemic in our society – some girls resemble Dumbo the Elephant wearing a tutu). They're as drunk as the boys and swear and vomit as the evening goes on. The sexes diss and slag each other off. There's nothing subtle or witty, it's just yobbo teasing and abuse.

The main drag is a constant traffic jam with impatient drivers beeping their horns, adding to the cacophony of loud music pouring out of the striptease joints and cars, spruikers yelling above the music, throttling motor bikes, musicians busking and people shouting, giggling, crying, threatening and singing. Groups bar hop and those who can't get into nightclubs or bars because of space restrictions or a lack of money drift aimlessly, many too drunk or stoned or pinned to think rationally.

On weekend nights some 20,000 people come to Kings Cross and of these there are about 6000 on Darlinghurst and Bayswater Roads around midnight. Four open-air urinals, each designed for four men at a time, are set up in Springfield Avenue and are used by about 5500 men. Girls urinate and shit in doorways, in Fitzroy Gardens and Lawrence Hargrave Park. Back on the main drag the girls tease the boys by flashing their tits or pulling down their knickers. One of the rites of passage is to get a tattoo from one of the three parlours on Darlinghurst Road, including Max's Village Tattoo Shop, which has been going for several decades. The latest one is Kings Cross Ink, which cost a million dollars, some of it provided by John Ibrahim. To show off when you are actually getting a tattoo, there is a special black leather bed, like an operating table, in the front window where passers-by can see the tattooist at work.

As the night grinds on, the violence and tension in the air rises and angry drunk men try to take on the bouncers or each other, while girls fight other girls. Some leave on the last train while others stay in bars drinking until the early hours of the morning. Those wanting to get home plead with or bribe taxi drivers, others sit exhausted in the gutters or on benches waiting for dawn.

About five o'clock on Saturday or Sunday morning the changeover begins. The drunks and drug-addled stagger out of venues, couples and groups on ecstasy laugh inanely and hug and kiss one another, the women wobble on their high heels, their make-up smudged and groups of drunken and slurring blokes brag about their adventures, imaginary or not. Residents who are up early try to avoid passing the nightclub Bada Bing, because of its reputation for violence and the aggressive Lebanese men, bristling with testosterone, who congregate outside, deciding what to do next, their drugged minds perched precariously on the edge of happiness or violence. Other potential threats to avoid are the packs of young men, barely out of their teens, wandering drunkenly along the streets, spoiling for a fight to make their night memorable.

By 6 am Darlinghurst Road is slowly being restored to the locals. Cleaners, most of them Asian and in teams, vacuum hotel carpets, clean windows, scrub bathrooms, sweep floors and collect rubbish. Residents come out to buy newspapers and items for breakfast. Street cleaners arrive to clear the rubbish-strewn footpaths. Seagulls and pigeons fight over crusts and junk food at the corner of Bayswater and Darlinghurst Roads. Waif-like hookers shiver in doorways waiting for their drug dealers. Tired bouncers recount their night to other bouncers, each trying to outdo each other's stories of the bad behaviour of the visitors. Exhausted bar staff flop down on couches and relax. Solitary drinkers watch English soccer in the Sports Bar. A skinny hooker, licking an ice cream and crying violently, tells her indifferent fellow workers, 'I didn't know him. He chased me down the street. No-one would help me.' Drunks sleep in doorways and the binge drinkers head for the Vegas.

The morning sun coming in through the Heads shines directly onto the Sydney CBD office blocks, thousands of windows reflect the sun like golden eyes staring blankly up at the Cross. As the sun rises higher it pours down onto Darlinghurst Road, the neon magic of the night gone, the drabness and tackiness revealed once again. The circadian rhythm continues and the Wraiths set up their headquarters next to the railway entrance again as thousands of office workers hurry down into the bowels of the station to catch their trains. Yawning brothel workers and hotel staff head home to sleep.

Kings Cross now belongs to the residents before the human tide arrives in the evening searching for fun, drugs, drink, romance, sex and hard partying. Where else would these hordes go? Cities need places like Kings Cross – it exists, and has existed for decades, as a necessary relief valve for society. Some of the behaviour of these visitors can be obnoxious, violent and repulsive, but then, the Cross allows them to behave in ways that wouldn't be tolerated in the communities where they live.

WE ♥ KINGS CROSS

ABOUT 4 AM ONE SATURDAY morning in 2012, a stolen silver Honda sedan was in Darlinghurst Road caught in dense, slow moving traffic. The footpaths were still filled with people. The police presence was greater than usual in an attempt to stop a rumoured bikie war breaking out. Two policemen noticed the young driver and the car crammed with people. They yelled out for it to stop but it didn't and so they chased the Honda on foot.

Inside the car were five teenagers and a man who had been on a six-hour joyride across Sydney. The driver was a 14-year-old boy; a seventeen year old, Troy Taylor, was in the front passenger seat; in the back was a thirteen year old with two other youths aged fourteen and sixteen, and a man, twenty-four, who had smoked cannabis and had more than twenty alcoholic drinks.

When he saw the police running through the traffic after the car, the teenage driver panicked. Realising he wasn't able to escape the gridlock of vehicles, he sought an escape route. He spun his wheel and mounted the footpath, scattering screaming and terrified pedestrians in his way. In the chaos two women were hit by the car. Both rolled off it, but one, Tanya Donaldson, twenty-nine, fell under the vehicle, which seemed to have no intention of halting. In order to stop the car, the two constables opened fire, aiming at the driver and hitting him in the chest and arm. Six bullets were fired, one lodging in Troy's neck. The officers dragged the wounded and bloodied front passenger out of the car and, not content with having shot him, punched him in the head and handcuffed him before dragging his limp body across the street, the bullet still embedded in his neck. A taxi driver who witnessed the skirmish with hundreds of others said, 'I thought they must be bad guys, then I saw it was kids … His face looked like a baby.'

The incident was recorded on CCTV and by dozens of horrified bystanders on mobile phones. The woman and the two wounded car thieves were rushed to St Vincent's. The fourteen year old's heart stopped twice, once at the scene and then during surgery. The next day both teenagers were said to be in a serious but stable condition, a few beds from one another. Donaldson, who had suffered chest injuries, was released next morning.

Troy's father said that although his son 'was no angel', and had been in trouble with the law from the age of eight, his behaviour didn't justify the beating given to his wounded son. What disturbed many people was that the two wounded boys were Aboriginal. Police feared that Aborigines in Kings Cross may cause trouble. Memories of the 2004 riots in Redfern following the death of 17-year-old Thomas 'T.J.' Hickey who, in attempting to escape from police on a bicycle, accidentally impaled himself on a fence, were still fresh.

But far from Aborigines taking to the streets, the local elder Mick Mundine said there shouldn't be any trouble following the incident:

'This happened in the Cross and I think we'll just leave it at that. This has nothing to do with race.'

The boy's lawyer, barrister Christine Nash made it just as plain: 'This has nothing to do with Redfern, the family do not want any more troubles stirred in Redfern, this happened at Kings Cross, it's totally unrelated.'

What the bloody incident reminded people was that the Cross is a singular space apart from the rest of Sydney, where incidents that might not be accepted elsewhere are seen as part of Kings Cross's fatal attraction. There's a comparison to be made with the end of the movie *Chinatown* where private detective Gittes, played by Jack Nicholson, tries to seek justice for a cold-blooded murder. But as a police officer says in the last line of the film, 'Forget it, Jake – it's Chinatown.' Just as the rule of law and social values didn't apply in LA's Chinatown, so it remains with Kings Cross.

A telling example of just how the Cross could be morally separate from the rest of Australia was one judge's remarks in the 2010 District Court trial of the Safi brothers. The two 'physically imposing' brothers pleaded not guilty to kidnapping but guilty to intimidating the manager of Stripperama on Darlinghurst Road. Judge Norrish, in sentencing the Safi brothers, said that standover tactics were 'commonplace' in the nightlife of Kings Cross and such 'morally repugnant' behaviour could not be judged in the same light as in the wider community.

A few months after the shooting of the Aboriginal teenagers, on Saturday 7 July, the reputation of Kings Cross would be trashed even more, this time throughout Australia in a moral panic of the sort not seen for years. That balmy evening, around 10 pm, a young man, Thomas Kelly, aged eighteen, came to the Cross with his new girlfriend and a female colleague from work. The trio were on their way to celebrate the eighteenth birthday of one of their workmates. It was his first time in Kings Cross. The group had been in the Cross for only two minutes and were walking down Victoria Street, Kelly holding his girlfriend's hand and clutching his mobile as he talked to a friend, when he was king-hit by a stranger. He fell to the footpath, seriously injuring his head, and never regained consciousness.

It took twelve days to find and arrest his alleged assailant who, before hitting Kelly, was said to have attacked four others. It was front-page news. Day after day the headlines verged on the hysterical: 'Kings Cross's streets of shame', 'Taming the Cross', 'How Kings Cross went from hedonism to hell', 'Chilling allure of city's underbelly', 'The Cross crisis', 'Late night war zone', 'Crackdown on red light club scene'.

What provoked this community anxiety and outrage was more than just Kelly's death. It seemed confirmation of the growing level of violence, especially on Friday and Saturday nights when 20,000 people make the area party central. Kings Cross may have been designated a 24/7 entertainment district, but the so-called late night economy is really an alcohol-fuelled economy. At the time of the attack on Kelly, there were 193 licensed premises in the area and fifty-eight of those could trade after midnight. The result had been glassings, brawls, shootings and king-hits; the perpetrators, both men and women. Those who cannot get into the hotels or bars drift around the streets in drunken mobs, a volatile mix of aggression whose binge drinking results in the streets becoming, as the local *Wentworth Courier* aptly put it, 'a vomitorium'.

The Assistant Police Commissioner, obviously appalled by what was happening, said of Kelly, 'He was in one of the city's most dangerous locations on the most dangerous night of the week.' It's not as if this reputation was anything new. Kelly's parents had been worried that their son was even visiting the Cross at all. Their last words to him before he set off were, 'Please be careful, please take care.' If anything confirmed its status as a perilous space, then the deadly king-hit was it.

Even the broadsheets were horrified and demanded something be done about the alcohol-fuelled violence. The *Sydney Morning Herald* held a packed forum, 'Action on the Cross', to debate how to tackle the violence. MPs, the Lord Mayor, a crime statistics expert, the chief executive of the Australian Hotels

Association and the Assistant Police Commissioner were on the panel. It was explained that on weekend nights there were generally forty police officers on patrol, and on an average night there were eighty assaults, fights or examples of anti-social behaviour, 200 less serious incidents of anti-social behaviour like urination, vomiting and street drinking. There were more assaults on the police than there were officers on patrol and of all assaults eighty-six per cent of them were alcohol related.

A campaign called *Real Heroes Walk Away* was launched and Carlene York, the New South Wales Assistant Commissioner, saw that a solution lay in women, saying they had 'a strong influence over their boyfriend to talk some sense into him and to lead him away from violent situations'. York didn't seem to understand that times had changed; the number of women committing assaults had jumped by fifty per cent since the mid-1990s, compared to an increase of just under twenty per cent for men. Doctors at the emergency wards at St Vincent's had noticed a huge rise in the number of women affected by alcohol: 'We used to talk about the girlfriends waiting dutifully for their boyfriends to sober up, but … now it's the boyfriend waiting.' I can confirm this, having stayed overnight in the emergency ward and noticing that of six aggressive drunks, five were women. The idea of a young woman being able to talk sense to her boyfriend was nonsense.

The media hysteria faded while the police and government tried to find ways of curbing the violence by recommending early hotel lock-outs, plastic glasses after midnight, ID checks, more bouncers, additional CCTV cameras, non-service to drunks and extra trains and taxis. Slowly it dawned on people that Kings Cross was not so much a depraved exception to the rest of Australia as a microcosm. It was much more convenient, given its reputation, to blame the Cross for Kelly's death, but the fact was that there were many examples from across the country of people being killed by king-hits. As Doctor Gordian Fulde, head of St Vincent's Emergency knew, the issue went way beyond Kings Cross:

'We're becoming an angrier and more violent society.'

Added to this volatile mix was the growing culture of youth binge drinking across the country. These nasty social trends poured into the Cross of a weekend and the combination was bound to cause trouble.

Locals began to resist the constant media bashing of the Cross, the tightening of restrictions on hotels and even the innocuous small wine bars. Many felt the precinct was being unfairly picked on, given that the government had redeveloped the Cross as a 24-hour entertainment district. The truth was that robberies and car thefts were down in the area and there was only a slight increase in assaults. What was self-evident was that the people causing these problems were visitors. A coalition of businesses and locals held a number of rallies under the slogan of *We ❤ Kings Cross.*

The coalition of locals and businesses didn't stop the introduction of tighter restrictions, which included a limit of four alcoholic drinks per customer and a ban on selling shots after midnight. After six months hotels and clubs noticed a huge dip in sales. The older, cashed-up drinkers began to abandon the area in favour of the city and other nightspots, leaving behind a younger cheaper crowd who 'pre-fuel' before heading up to the Cross. Revenue for many spots fell by up to thirty per cent and venues had to let staff go or close, as happened to the Bank nightclub on Darlinghurst Road.

Kings Cross has always undergone changes, some traumatic; the area itself has been gouged to make way for new roads and a railway tunnel. Streets and lanes have been erased and thousands of people forced to leave their homes and relocate. It has gone through a series of transformations, from the exclusive era of the mansions, to the Golden Age of apartment living from the 1920s to the 1950s, to the sexual revolution which disintegrated into the 1990s moral malaise of rampant crime, drug use, police corruption and sexual decadence.

Every incarnation becomes the real Cross. It has always retained a durable sense of its identity, despite drastic changes, and it has been a stunning example of Jane Jacobs's theory, in her seminal *The Death and Life of Great American Cities* (1961), that the most vibrant urban cultures thrive where there is 'a most intricate and close-grained diversity of uses that give each other constant mutual support, both economically and socially.' For her these places balance eccentricity and consent and contain the elements of mutuality, self-government, neighbourliness, diversity, intimacy, convenience, content and safety. Ideally the area has two or more primary functions that generate activity with different rhythms throughout the day and night, and there are short street blocks with buildings mingled in a loose weave that includes both new and old structures and adequate residential density to make things exciting.

With the massive influx of new residents to the Cross, it has become an expensive place to live, and the very people who helped make the Cross famous, the bohemians and young artists, have been priced out and have drifted off to Surry Hills and Newtown. Linda Jaivin, a local author, relates the story of performance artist Penny Arcade, a former Andy Warhol superstar, who lived for two years in Kings Cross, declaring it 'the last intact bohemia in the world'. She believed it was only a matter of time before it became an anaemic version of the original; with gentrification the area is cleaned up, rents rise and bohemians are forced out. For Arcade the bourgeois and bohemian cannot exist together because they're 'two entirely separate value systems.'

This process is reinforced by the way Kings Cross has become a historical village. There are a hundred plaques laid in the pavement lining Darlinghurst Road, relating the history of the area. Visitors like them but locals, like the writers Delia Falconer and Peter Robb, call them 'gravestones'. Robb believes the plaques 'make it seem like it's over'. A few restaurants and nightspots are realising that people come to the Cross because of its reputation and exciting, raffish past and so, like the Roosevelt bar, try to incorporate its history into their venues. Elizabeth Bay House is a telling example of transformations over the years from posh mansion to artists' rooms to boarding house and near demolition before becoming a museum.

When the hugely successful *Underbelly* was being filmed around the area, with its crews often blocking off streets, I realised that the Cross had become not only a giant film set but its disreputable reputation was being transformed into something glamorous and exciting. The Kings Cross myth is being burnished by films, television series, novels, non-fiction, poetry and even a reality TV program set in the emergency room of St Vincent's Hospital. There are art deco tours, walking tours, music tours and curious stickybeaks still come to see the notorious Cross for themselves. Several times a day a sightseeing bus lumbers up William Street, extolling the history of 'the red-light district'. It seems one can't escape from the sense that glories of the past are more important that what's happening now. All the familiar landmarks have gone. Once a place that revelled in the present and the promise of the future, it is now looking backwards and has become a site of memories, rather than possibilities.

If anything confirmed the massive changes in Kings Cross it was the 2013 *Time Out* guide to Sydney. It rarely mentions the area, except for a condescending reference to visiting the tired strip clubs as almost an historical necessity, calling Kings Cross 'Sydney's legendary seedy entertainment district' and recommending

*... sticking your head into a strip club for at least a single
(admittedly overpriced) drink. We're not saying you're going
to necessarily feel better about yourself, but it's a Sydney rite of
passage.*

What's unmistakable is that the Cross matters little creatively or
as a place of significance. The magazine has detailed maps of the
Sydney CBD, Surry Hills, Bondi, Darlinghurst, Newtown, Manly, and even Parramatta, but where a map of Kings Cross should
be is a blank section, as if it has become a Terra Nullius. One of
the main reasons is that the young creative people who came to
the Cross in successive waves over the decades and helped determine its identity can no longer afford to live in the area and have
spread out to places in the inner west, like Marrickville.

In an area of 1.4 kilometres, where over 20,000 people live,
with over 2.5 million visitors a year, Kings Cross has a proud tradition of tolerance and diversity. Residents have always understood that the Cross stood for values different from mainstream
Australia, but now people from suburbia are shifting in, this tolerance and sense of diversity is withering as the newcomers aim
to rid the area of its danger, edginess and difference, remaking
Kings Cross in their own bourgeois image.

The new arrivals have been attracted to the area because of the
name and its extraordinary history. But the irony is that it's those
authentic parts of Kings Cross, the striptease joints, neon lights,
spruikers and prostitutes, that the Lord Mayor, Clover Moore,
representing her new constituents, wants to get rid of. There is
no doubt that the Cross has been revitalised by the new residents
and it has a vitality and swish ambience reminiscent of the golden
decades from the 1930s to the 50s. But these newcomers also bring
a middle-class sense of homogeneity. Cheap cafés are supplanted
by soigné restaurants; shoe stores and boutiques appear and push

out the discount stores and sex shops. Inclusiveness is replaced by exclusivity and there is a narrowing of diversity. The geographer Neil Smith, the American author of *The New Urban Frontier*, is even more blunt: 'the gentrification and redevelopment of the inner city represents a clear continuation of the forces and relations that led to suburbanisation'.

It is evitable that the gentrification will tame the area. It was once a dangerous place, not so much for its criminal activity, but because it was the id of Australia, and that's why it was feared. The Cross constantly undermined the myth of the upstanding Australian, a person of strong moral values, a paragon of normality and suburban rectitude. The Cross offered instant gratification, sexual immorality, neon-lit temptations and illicit pleasures. It appealed to the unruly desires of the id. What made moralists furious was that the Cross excited passions and loosened self-control. Moral lines were crossed as one slipped from the unambiguous morality of mainstream society into a vague immoral zone, where few things were forbidden and temptations were everywhere. The Cross unlocked secret desires and allowed them to flourish, even if that meant sometimes experiencing a hideous dark night of the soul.

People came for what they couldn't elsewhere. It is a natural human impulse to want to experience the forbidden, whether it be drugs, illegal alcohol or sexual excess. The Cross once stood out as a beacon of proud difference and as an entry point for those things that were morally abhorrent to the rest of society. But the values of Kings Cross are not so different any more from the rest of Australia. The decline in sex shops and strip joints is a sign that stripping is no longer shocking and that the internet and suburban sex shops have made this aspect of Kings Cross redundant. Drugs can be purchased just as easily in the outer suburbs and large country towns as they can in the Cross.

Its name still has a potent drawing power. The lure of its history brings people in and even its racy reputation still entices. Not so long ago students from Grafton High School's senior rugby league team played a finals match in Sydney. After the game three of the Year 11 students sneaked out of their hotel room in the Rocks and headed for the Cross. They gathered all their money together and found they had $150, enough for one of the boys to have sex. They approached a pimp who arranged a prostitute for them. Once the school found out all three were banned for a year from the team.

It must not be forgotten that the Cross is a place where young people want to experience what they can't elsewhere. Recently an 18-year-old woman from the Blue Mountains explained why she had wanted to see it:

'I'd never seen a hooker in my life. It's like a whole new world, especially coming from the Blue Mountains, we don't have that totally crazy world, it feels like you're in America.'

Quite simply Kings Cross fulfils young people's needs. They want to enjoy long nights in bars and clubs. They want to go to a place where they can let go – after all, that's one of the great pleasures of being young and living in a great city. And that's why, from Dulcie Deamer onwards, long-term or former residents constantly complain how the Cross has changed for the worse. They forget that they conflate the exciting times of when they were young in the Cross with their mature selves and the nostalgia for the past that is really nostalgia for their youth.

Kings Cross is like a piece of urban DNA where the two spirals interweave the safe and the dangerous, the Australian and the foreign, the old-fashioned glamour and trashy sexual exploitation, the underworld and city professionals, the seedy and glamorous, the hetero and gay, sexual freedom and commercial sex, the underclass and the rich, the beautiful and tawdry. Once those two helical chains are separated, the true Cross will become a homogenous social and cultural landscape at odds with its own history.

I'm aware of this happening in my own building. Since beginning to write this book in earnest three years ago, Doncaster Hall's demographics have changed greatly. The old ladies are dead, the two crack whores are gone, as has the French DJ next door and many others. The loud noises of constant renovations reverberate through the building as more young professionals, both gay and straight, shift in. Make no mistake, there are still tenants and transients in the building whose personal stories one can only guess at. The other night when I came in the front door, a wiry white-haired man snuck in with me. He rushed past me on the stairs, only for a malevolent man of about thirty with pinned, excited eyes to come down to greet him. A woman in a scanty outfit, obviously a hooker, also came down the stairs. The old man's first words to her were, 'Someone has stolen her, Cressie.' With that the woman sat down on a step and wept. The two men glanced up at me, grabbed her by the arms and hurried into the foyer and outside.

I am constantly amazed at just how well this teeming mass of humanity, living on such a small hilltop, can tolerate and respect each other, whatever station in life we happen to be from. It's a place where you can see human folly lit up in neon light, where the extremes of behaviour can occur, where dozens of locals turn up for a funeral of a dissolute beggar. It's a place of excess and crime, but also of extraordinary acts of kindness and compassion, a site where there is a sense of being unbound by convention and conformity.

On my walks around the Cross, whether it be going to the Post Office, shopping or just taking in the day, I run into and greet many locals, as one would in a village; friends, shopkeepers, beggars, restaurant owners, tradies, sparkies, the mad – both medicated and unmedicated – writers, film stars, barristers and baristas. It becomes obvious that an essential part of the myth of Kings Cross is the people and characters that have so defined its allure for a century or more. They seem more alive to the pulse of urban living than those anywhere else.

Perhaps the cruel reality is that Kings Cross has served its purpose. For decades it was the vanguard of modernism, sexual mores, music, design and nightlife and an escape from a parochial and puritan Australia. But now all that has changed. The rest of Australia has caught up and Kings Cross is no longer needed as it once was.

But there's also something else. In writing this book, my sense of the Cross has expanded to include all the phantoms of those long dead who made it special and whose lives enriched and made the Cross what it is. For me Kings Cross has become a sentient presence; every building, every apartment, peels off layer by layer, in a series of pentimenti that reveal innumerable personal stories of love, crime, drugs, terror, loneliness, and riotous good times. I cannot separate myself from these echoes of the past and how they resonate in my mind, so that the streetscape and its people are made up from the reality of what I observe and my imagination. Like many others who have lived here I am so possessive of it that I regard it as mine. This is my Kings Cross.

NOTES

DURING THE GESTATION OF THIS book I began to move away from a strictly chronological and neutral account of Kings Cross. I became fascinated by Georges Perec and how his novels, especially *Life A User's Manual*, based on the occupants of a block of flats in the XVIIth arrondissement of Paris, and his non-fiction examined with a forensic yet poetical gaze the banal things we take for granted in our lives.

Psychogeography may be a pretentious word, but it is based on the concept of the flâneur, or urban wanderer, whose study and quirky appreciation of our city surroundings transform the familiar streets and buildings into something new and personal. Merlin Coverley's *Psychogeography* (2006) was my guide to trying to incorporate my own psychological appreciation of the Cross into a history.

Another book that had a profound effect on me as I was writing was *The Death and Life of Great American Cities* (1961) by Jane Jacobs. Its mixture of the personal and polemical is utterly engrossing as Jacobs analyses what constitutes a neighbourhood and the insidious threats of too much gentrification and development at the cost of diversity.

Prologue

At that time my agent was Hilary Linstead. The address is now McDonalds. All the adjectives like 'notorious', 'sleazy', 'sinful', etc. are common shorthand ways of referring to Kings Cross. The old woman's name

'Shirley' is fabricated. I forget what name the policeman called her; my brain was addled at the time. I bought an apartment at Oceana, at the end of the cul-de-sac in Elizabeth Bay Road. Built in the late 1950s, it was an example of minimalist architecture. The block it stood on had once been part of Elizabeth Town, an area Macquarie had reserved for Aborigines. I sold the apartment when my relationship broke up and before concrete cancer was discovered. The cost to cure the building was astronomical.

They've come to stay

Much of the information comes from many books and articles including: D. Collins *An Account of the English Colony in New South Wales* (1975); J. Connor *The Australian Frontier Wars* (2002); G. Karskens *The Colony: A History of Early Sydney* (2009); K.V. Smith *King Bungaree: A Sydney Aborigine Meets the Great South Pacific Explorers, 1799–1830* (2001); K.V. Smith *Bennelong* (2001); K.V. Smith *Eora: Mapping Aboriginal Sydney 1770–1850* (2006); W. Tench *Sydney's First Four Years* (1961); P. Turbet *The Aborigines of the Sydney District Before 1788* (1989); and P. Turbet *The First Frontier: The Occupation of the Sydney Region 1788 to 1816* (2011). Also the City of Sydney's website Barani: Indigenous History of Sydney City: www.sydneybarani.com.au/

In *Sydney's Little World of Woolloomooloo* by Isadore Brodsky (1966) there is a long discussion about the genesis of the word Woolloomooloo.

TROVE, the National Library of Australia's online digital archive of Australian newspapers, includes the *Sydney Gazette*.

There is an 1828 sketch by Edward Mason of the Elizabeth Bay Aboriginal settlement. As regards Aboriginal protests to stop the injecting centre, see Daniel Dasey 'Aboriginal bid to stop drug room in Cross', *Sun-Herald*, 6 May 2000.

Doncaster Hall

The number of renters in the building seems to have increased, with investors buying up the apartments as they come onto the market. The previous owner of my apartment was Tony, a tubby Englishman with a round face as shiny and smooth as a baby's, which gave him an uncanny likeness to the bawdy comedian Benny Hill. He once confessed to me that when Mandy was living in the flat below me he used to look at her through the spyhole in his door as she walked up the stairs to my apartment in her nightgown. He also told me he was writing a 20,000-word essay about his adventures with women, comparing them to different cars, from a Rolls Royce to a battered old Holden. He was not attractive to women and so resorted to paying for sex. One evening he brought back to Doncaster Hall a skinny blonde hooker who was a familiar face on Darlinghurst Road. Her pale blotchy skin and dull eyes were a testament to her large drug intake, which her whoring subsidised. Mandy and I hardly knew Tony but after we had bought his apartment he invited us, plus several other locals he had met in bars throughout the Cross, to have a goodbye dinner with him at the Mansions hotel. He was going to the tropics for a holiday before returning to England permanently. Near the end of the dinner I realised that the attractive brunette who was accompanying him on his holiday barely knew him either. The money from the sale of his apartment had paid for a more swanky prostitute than his usual scrawny street walkers.

Kings Cross has always been a place of transformation and constant reinvention. There are few times in its history where it has remained static because it has always tried to accommodate contemporary desires or predict them, whether this be in food, retail, drugs or sex. So there are places I have mentioned that simply do not exist any more. For instance, the shop downstairs which sold Aboriginal art and boomerangs for forty years closed in February 2013 and is now a forlorn, empty shell next door to the even more forsaken and derelict De Ferrari menswear shop.

Guiseppe Simonella's obituary was in the *Sydney Morning Herald*

(2006). Kelsey Munro, 'Beak hour traffic destroying heritage buildings', *Sydney Morning Herald*, 3–4 September 2011 (re cockatoos damaging property). Old people being driven out of the area because of rising rents in Erin O'Dwyer's 'At the crossroads', *Sun-Herald*, 30 September 2007.

George Sprod's books include *Sprod's Views of Sydney* (1981), *Life on a Square-Wheeled Bike: The Saga of a Cartoonist* (1983), *When I Survey the Wondrous Cross: Sydney's King's Cross Ancient and Modern* (1989). An exhibition catalogue was published in 2009 titled *That Odd Mr Sprod* (text by Dan Sprod).

The quarrel

The essential book on the early history of the area is Freda MacDonnell's *Before Kings Cross* (1967). Avryl Whitnall's *Villas of Darlinghurst* (2002) gives a comprehensive account of the mansions. Elizabeth Butel and Tom Thompson's *Kings Cross Album* (1984) and Anne-Maree Whitaker's *Pictorial History Kings Cross* (2012) have some delightful images of the villas and grounds.

D. Cherry *Alexander Macleay, from Scotland to Sydney* (2012); B.H. Fletcher *Ralph Darling: A Governor Maligned* (1984); J.H.L. Cumpston *Thomas Mitchell, Surveyor General & Explorer* (Melbourne, 1955). Alexander Berry re Mitchell: 'boatswain whistle', page 272 in *Frederick Robert D'Arcy: Colonial Surveyor and Explorer and Artist* by Andy Macqueen (2010).

Governor Darling despaired of quality workmanship in the colony. As he wrote at the end of 1827: 'There are no Master Builders in the Colony of any respectability. The Mechanics are for the most part independent Journeymen, profligate in their habits, without character and without means; and, when Contracts have been entered into the Government has generally been obliged to advance Money to supply a portion of the Materials and the Mechanics, and not withstanding this has been disappointed.' He obviously changed his mind.

Mitchell's exact words regarding his plan for William Street were:

'I have the honour to transmit a plan of the ground adjoining the Race Course on the east ... I have the honour to state, for the consideration of His Excellency the Governor, that the hollow and lowest part of this ground is nearly in the prolongation of Park Street, across the Race Course; thus admitting of the easiest ascent to the Woolloomooloo Estate, which is likely to become, at no remote period, a part of the town. Such a street prolonged would also ascend between Judge Dowling's and Mr Laidley's allotments ... to the new road [New South Head Road] on the opposite side; this great street, at right angles to George Street would form a very important line in the plan of the town. I would therefore honour it with the name of his present majesty.'

The officials and property owners were lucky to escape just with Mitchell's abuse. Years later in 1851 the prickly Mitchell believed he was a victim of a slight by the wealthy merchant Stuart Donaldson, who was running for political office at the time. Only a duel would satisfy him. It was acted out in what is now Centennial Park. They each exchanged three shots. Mitchell put a bullet through the merchant's belltopper grazing his scalp while the man Mitchell sneeringly called 'The Grocer' put a bullet in Mitchell's neck which did little harm. The seconds then interfered and the combatants left the ground. It was thought to be the last duel fought in Australia.

The biographies of many major participants in the story of Kings Cross are in the *Australian Dictionary of Biography* or *ADB* as I will refer to it in the rest of the end notes.

Falling

'Woman falls through skylight', *Sydney Morning Herald*, 17 May 1927; 'Sydney deaths', *Townsville Daily Bulletin*, 26 September 1936 (husband and wife killed by cyanide fumes from a flat opposite seeping into their flat); 'Crashed to death', *Canberra Times*, 28 December 1936; 'Suicide finding: Miss Tempest's death. Veronal poisoning', *Sydney Morning Herald*, 12 November 1938; 'Wife of baronet: suicide in residential', *Sydney*

Morning Herald, 1 April 1939; 'Sydney soldier's death. Mysterious fall from enclosed balcony', *Advocate*, 2 September 1940 ('Police are puzzled as to how Wyatt fell from the balcony, which is enclosed by lattice work and canvas blinds'); 'R.A.A.F. member killed by fall', *Canberra Times*, 22 January 1943 (K.E. Hughes had been in ill health for some time); 'Girl jumps from window', *Sydney Morning Herald*, 24 July 1943 (she lived and said she jumped because 'she feared the attitude of two Negroes'); 'Two boys found dead in bathroom', *Barrier Miner*, 12 April 1945; 'Child falls to death', *Sydney Morning Herald*, 26 October 1946 ('Coralie Janet Gollan, 8, was killed instantly last night when she fell down the light well of a block of flats'); 'Woman falls 100 feet. Death in city', *Sydney Morning Herald*, 13 November 1947 (Mrs Ideal Horrell Greenwood, 56); 'Seaman slipped from parapet', *Canberra Times*, 1 June 1948 (Clive Norman Geddes, 20, accidentally killed when he fell from the third floor of the Goderich Private Hotel, Bayswater Road); 'Jumped to his death', *Barrier Miner*, 25 January 1949 (Harold Duff (26) was said to be suffering from acute neurosis); 'Two suicides in Sydney', *Townsville Daily Bulletin*, 26 January 1949; 'Professor found dead in locked room', *Mercury*, 20 April 1949 (gassed himself, police found his diary from which several pages were torn); 'Migrant dies in plunge from window', *Sydney Morning Herald*, 19 May 1951 ('Police believe despondency caused by memories of labour camps in Russia led a Czechoslovakian migrant to plunge 50 ft to his death from a King's Cross window last night'); 'Fall kills ex-trainer', *West Australian*, 27 February 1953 ('Fred Williams (73) a well-known racing man fell 50ft to his death from a King's Cross hotel today'); 'Wealthy turf man falls to death', *Canberra Times*, 27 February 1953 (Williams's pyjama-clad body was found in a parking lot in the hotel grounds of Hampton Court); 'Fell from ninth-storey window', *Canberra Times*, 23 March 1953 (Norman Burt died after overbalancing and falling); and 'Lover in car park plunge', *Daily Mirror*, 30 December 1986 (a young woman fell five storeys from the roof of a Kings Cross car park after making love with her boyfriend).

The above list is as frightening as the headlines and items in Michael Lesy's quirky masterpiece of nightmarish human behaviour, *Wisconsin Death Trip* (1973), a book that not only influenced this one but my book *The Cheated*, which also dealt in dark newspaper items and photographs.

William Street

The definitive account of pre-1916 William Street is Max Kelly's *Faces of the Street: William Street, Sydney 1916* (1982). Trolling through TROVE regarding William Street, many stories refer to it as a potential Champs Élysées and to its failure to become one. A typical headline: 'City boulevard a broken dream', *Sydney Morning Herald,* 1 June, 2006.

The swells of Woolloomooloo Hill

'Swells of Woolloomooloo', 1 May 1834, *Sydney Morning Herald*; also in the *Sydney Morning Herald*: 'Furious driving', 1 March 1845 (the cabman Thomas Henry Baxter was fined £4 for furious driving; a cab man named Bussey was convicted for furious driving on 1 March 1848).

John O'Brien *On Darlinghurst Hill* (1952); Anne-Maree Whitaker *St Vincent's Hospital 1857–2007* (2007); and B. James *The Golden Decade of Australian Architecture* (1978).

The contents of Craigend, 9 March 1837 newspaper advertisement. Macquoid's suicide, *The Australian*, 28 August 1843, 'Papers in the case of the late Sheriff Macquoid d. 1841'.

Goderich Lodge is one of the earliest documented works of John Verge. W.E. Sparke lived in Orwell Street in the 1860s before he built a cottage and turned it into the villa Maramanah. He was a bachelor who would never receive lady visitors into his house. He was burnt in a bath at Maramanah and moved down to Elizabeth Bay where the hot water system again proved faulty and he died in the bath.

James Dowling had arrived in 1828 with his wife and six children. In 1828 Dowling wrote to his patron in England, Lord Henry Brougham, saying he couldn't keep out of debt, but he built Bougham Lodge in 1831.

John Verge completed the designs of it. Dowling became chief justice of
the colony in 1836. He was esteemed and a profound thinker. His reports
on nearly 500 cases he presided over are in *Dowling's Select Cases 1828 to
1844: Decisions of the Supreme Court of New South Wales* edited by T.D.
Castle and Bruce Kercher. He was knighted in 1838. After his death tenants rented the house and it was also used as a boys' school. Demolished
in 1882, it became Brougham terrace, which, in turn, was demolished
in 1971 to make way for Kings Cross station. Dowling named Victoria
Street after the Queen on 22 September 1849.

Drunkenness and jail, etc.: *Sydney Gazette*, 5 August 1837. 'Mr Rae's
first lecture on taste', *Sydney Morning Herald*, 27 July 1841.

Sydney Morning Herald, 2 June 1849, said of Peacock's work that it
was 'carefully painted, exhibiting extreme fidelity to nature, as well as
skill in miniature handling and high finish'. George Edwards Peacock in
The Picture Gallery: Guide, State Library of New South Wales, which has
more than forty of his paintings (2002). What happened to him after he
returned to the UK in 1856 is a mystery.

Brougham Street

Fights and drug deals still happen in Brougham Lane. One of the reasons for Brougham Street seeming so dull and banal is that it has no restaurants or cafés. 'Phantom of Holiday Inn room 357', *Daily Telegraph*,
14 October 2002. In 2012 a developer produced plans to demolish flats
around historic Telford Lodge (1831) and build a much larger apartment
block.

A tap on the window

Books consulted include *Rivkin Unauthorised: The Meteoric Rise and Tragic Fall of an Unorthodox Money Man* by Andrew Main (2005) and *The Killing of Caroline Byrne: A Journey to Justice* by Robert Wainwright (2009).

Paul Barry, 'Gordon, you lied to me and you lied to Australia', *Sunday Telegraph*, 6 May 2012. The article was Barry's reaction to Gordon

Wood's interview with Liz Hayes on Channel Nine's *60 Minutes*. After serving three-and-a-half years in prison, then released on appeal, Wood did a paid interview with Hayes where he seemed evasive at times. Barry called some of Wood's answers 'bullshit' and he insisted that Wood told 'new lies'.

Rene Rivkin's suicide resulted in headlines like 'Rivkin takes secrets to grave', *The Australian*, 2 May 2005. Most, if not all, of the obituaries called him 'a disgraced stockbroker'.

An article on Rivkin and the young men he surrounded himself with is 'The boys who ran with Rene Rivkin', *Daily Telegraph*, 15 April 2006. The piece was interesting enough but the photographs of the stockbroker holidaying with his male harem was an eye-opener. The boys wore togs and little else, seemingly proud to show off their hirsute tattooed bodies, all of them looking, as the saying goes, 'flash as a rat with a gold tooth'.

The revolutionary and the book collector

Eileen Chanin's 2011 biography *Book Life: The Life and Times of David Scott Mitchell* is exhaustive but dry. Of articles on Mitchell, one of the best is by Steve Meacham, 'The book collector: one man's giant quest', *Sydney Morning Herald*, 9 June 2007.

Visions of a Republic: The Work of Lucien Henry, edited by Ann Stephen (2001), is a history, biography and an art book, which published Lucien Henry's artwork for the first time. Henry also liked dogs. Just before he left for Paris in 1890 he painted one of the few portraits of an Australian terrier at that time (*Australian Terrier on a Packing Crate in Garden*). Henry was attracted to a local breed that was still in the process of evolving. Its long legs and floppy ears were to develop into short legs, a long head and pricked ears.

'Rambles though Sydney', *Sydney Morning Herald*, 30 May 1864, 'some future topographer may unravel the knotty question'.

Victoria Street

Important women writers lived in Orwell Street: Dymphna Cusack and Florence James wrote much of *Come in Spinner* at number 18, and number 22 was where the authors Marjorie Barnard and Flora Eldershaw once lived. James Fairfax, publisher of the *Sydney Morning Herald* lived at 112 Victoria Street.

The Melinda Gainsford-Taylor quote is from Anna Patty, 'Hard work tempered with a touch of larrikinism', *Sydney Morning Herald*, 25 May, 2008. Adam Bell wrote about Misty's in 'Students exposed to brothel', *Daily Telegraph*, 19 March 2006; also 'Judge orders brothel to shut', *Sydney Morning Herald,* 8 December 2006.

'The Golden Age'

Aunts Up the Cross by Robin Dalton (1965) is an evocative and delightful memoir about the 1920s and 1930s in the Cross.

Deamer's first flat cost a pound a week and was in a grey-stone, three-storey terrace at number 26 Bayswater Road. She had a room on the first floor out the back with a gas ring and a window overlooking a dismal back alley, the plus being that the sound of trams up and down Bayswater Road until 2 am was muffled.

The primary biography of Christopher Brennan is by Axel Clark (1980). Other references include Brennan's entry in *ADB*. Christopher Brennan is the subject matter of novelist Brian Castro's *Street to Street* (2013). The Historic Houses Trust of New South Wales held the exhibition *Kings Cross, Bohemian Sydney* at Elizabeth Bay House, 31 May–21 September 2003.

Jack Lindsay's *The Roaring Twenties* (1960) is a vivid mixture of truth, tall tales, and bibulous recollections, but wonderfully conveys the exuberance of the times, something that Dulcie Deamer's posthumously published memoir *Queen of Bohemia* (1998) fails to do. Two excellent surveys of this era and bohemian life are Peter Kirkpatrick's *The Sea Coast of Bohemia: Literary Life in Sydney's Roaring Twenties* (1992) and

Tony Moore's *Dancing with Empty Pockets: Australia's Bohemians* (2012).

Bill Hubble's obituary of Joan Lindsay Burke 1912–2004 'A steadying hand among the bohemians' was in the *Sydney Morning Herald*.

The Spectacular Modern Woman: Feminine Visibility in the 1920s by Liz Conor (2004); Elizabeth Wilson's *Adorned in Dreams: Fashion and Modernity* (1985) and *The Sphinx in the City: Urban Life, the Control of Disorder, and Women* (1991).

Neon

Muriel Feldwick 'The lights of King's Cross', *Sydney Morning Herald*, 12 March 1932; 'Bright neon sign: alleged nuisance', *Sydney Morning Herald*, 22 December 1938; 'Nightly brilliance of King's Cross', *Sydney Morning Herald*, 26 May 1939; Jean-Paul Severn, 1966 pulp fiction *Vice Trap, Kings Cross* ('something unwholesome'); 'Blackout faults. Many city lights. Big N.E.S. test', *Sydney Morning Herald*, 18 August 1941.

Angela Cuming, 'Switched on in 1974, now naughty sign is history', *Sun-Herald*, 17 October 2004. The City of Sydney bought the green-and-red sign that says 'Books' outside the Roslyn Bookshop. The City of Sydney also lifted its ban on neon, illuminated, animated and flashing signs for sex industry premises on Darlinghurst Road.

According to *Memories, Kings Cross 1936–1946,* an oral history published by the Kings Cross Community Aid and Information Service (1981), one of the first neon signs was for hairdresser Mavis Pearce at 133 Darlinghurst Road (she specialised in perms and advertised 'An Easter Special full head non-electric wave for 10/6 and a beautiful setting for 2/6'). Soon cafés and coffee shops like the Willow Café and the Arabian had their names up in neon.

The underbelly of Australia's Montmartre

Bad Characters: Sex, Crime, Mutiny, Murder and the Australian Imperial Force, Peter Stanley (2010).

The main source for this chapter is Larry Writer's admirable *Razor:*

A True Story of Slashers, Gangsters, Prostitutes and Sly Grog (2001). Other references include *Sin City* (2010) by Tim Girling-Butcher, a slim history of crime and corruption in twentieth-century Sydney. Kate Leigh's story, 'Kate, uncrowned queen of crime' was told in the *Sunday Telegraph*, 20 August 1995; the following Sunday it was Tilly Devine's turn in 'Rich and violent life of Sydney's vice queen' *Daily Telegraph*, 27 August 1995; also the 'Razor gang' Wikipedia entry.

'Razor used: man's throat cut', *Sydney Morning Herald*, 17 February 1928; 'A razor affray: two women arrested', *Mercury*, 22 June 1928 (two women coked out of their heads tried to slash one another); 'Razor attack: woman slashes young man', *Sydney Morning Herald*, 14 August 1929; 'Alleged razor slashing: man badly injured', *Barrier Miner*, 30 September 1930 (a young man walked up to an older man and after accusing him of stealing his girl, slashed the victim).

A vivid but sometimes factually incorrect contemporary description of the two gangs fighting it out in Kellett Street is in 'Sydney underworld: members of gangs fight fiercely in Darlinghurst flat', *Advertiser*, 10 August 1929 (Bendroit is called Bendrodt). Also, Max Presnell 'Jim Bendroit brought class to Harbour City's age of swing', *Sun-Herald*, 20 January 2013. When Presnell was young he met Bendroit (1896–1973), who was in his seventies, still an immaculate dresser and pugnacious when threatened.

'Fatal shooting in Sydney', *Courier-Mail*, 7 August 1939 (Calletti shot in a Brougham Street house). Calletti's fight with the Brougham Street gang is in Peter Doyle's superb *Crooks Like Us* (2009), which draws on the forensic photography archive at the Justice and Police Museum, Sydney.

'Attempted murder', *Examiner* 9 March 1931 (Patricia Kelly was savaged with a razor by her jealous boyfriend); 'Woman charged with razor slashing', *Canberra Times* 26 September 1932.

'Sly grog selling', *Sydney Morning Herald*, 11 June 1926 (Richard Moss was caught selling four bottles of beer to two men); 'Woman sold beer to constable', *Sydney Morning Herald*, 19 June 1929 (Marie Williams, 41, had already been caught and fined the year before for selling illegal liquor); 'Christmas Eve raid', *Sydney Morning Herald*, 29 December 1932 (Hudson selling beer from No. 9 flat, Acacia Flats); 'Sly grog sales', *Sydney Morning Herald* 2 July 1936; 'Sly grog selling', *Sydney Morning Herald*, 3 December 1937 (a raid on the Tabarin Cabaret).

John Rainford's *Consuming Pleasures: Australia and the International Drug Business* (2009) is one of the more comprehensive histories of drugs in Australia. 'Cocaine traffic: men sentenced to twelve months imprisonment', *Sydney Morning Herald*, 7 May 1930 (the dealer was caught selling cocaine to addicts in Kings Cross).

Last orders

Graeme Blundell, 'The last hurrah', *The Australian*, 21–22 October 2000; 'Stars' hotel bows out', *The Australian*, 21 October 2000.

Louis Nowra, 'And some peanuts for my chihuahua', *Sydney Morning Herald*, 4 November 2000.

'There was a disgraceful state of things going on there'

'Gambling den raid in Sydney', *Canberra Times*, 23 March 1932 (41 men arrested in Kings Cross); 'Gambling's big grip', *Cairns Post*, 11 April 1936; 'Thirty-five arrests in King's Cross flats: alleged gambling', *Sydney Morning Herald*, 24 September 1937.

One of the most comprehensive articles on Phil 'The Jew' Jeffs was 'King of the vice trade' a historical feature in the *Daily Mirror* (1992).

'Duck dances on tin: police search for showmen', *Courier-Mail*, 19 November 1934.

'Strip to the earrings', *Memories, Kings Cross*.

Fire

'Benzine explodes: man severely burned', *Sydney Morning Herald*, 16 November 1929; 'Woman fatally burnt in Sydney fire', *Courier-Mail*, 10 June 1940. (The article mentioned that four other young women had had narrow escapes. The firemen found Mrs Gillmer badly burnt, lying on the floor of her bedroom.)

Maramanah burning down in *Aunts Up the Cross* and *Memories, Kings Cross*.

Even as I compile these end notes, a man has been charged with attacking a woman at the Love Machine on Darlinghurst Road. A 67-year-old woman at the club alleged she had been strangled, punched and kicked by a man claiming he was going to set the place alight. 'I fought for my life for seven minutes.' The man went on to set fire to the building. Flames poured out of the top floor before firefighters put it out. Two hundred people who were at the strip club and in nearby residential units were evacuated. Nobody was harmed by the blaze. 'Bail denied to strip club fire suspect', *Sun-Herald*, 5 May 2013.

There were suspicions that Saffron may have been linked to the fire that killed seven people riding Luna Park's ghost train in June 1979. Kate McClymont 'They weren't meant to die', *Sydney Morning Herald*, 26–27 May 2007. The link was never conclusively proved.

Reaching for the sky

ADB and TROVE were used for information on the architects and buildings. 'Walking down art deco lane', *The Paper*, Issue No. 79, September–October 2006; *Art Deco in Australia: Sunrise over the Pacific*, edited by Mark Ferson and Mary Nilsson (2001) and *Homes in the Sky: Apartment Living in Australia* (2007). Each of these new buildings had an individual style that gave the skyline an eclectic but united feel. Wyldefel Gardens, a 20-apartment block built in 1936, was a faithful adaptation of a house near Adolf Hitler's in the hills of Oberammergau, Germany. As one critic enthused, it was 'a little bit of modern Germany transplanted to the shores of Sydney ... a scheme of modern building which is a triumphant *fait accompli* and a significant forecast'.

For the 1930s and early 1940s the most entertaining book about the locals and the atmosphere is H.C. Brewster and Virginia Luther's

Kings Cross Calling (1945).

One of the supposed dangers for women in the Cross was cocktail parties 'to which young, and very frequently inexperienced girls are invited. These parties develop into nothing less than drinking orgies, with all the resultant misery. Many a young girl has lived to regret the fact that she went to a seemingly innocent cocktail party': 'Night orgies', *Cairns Post*, 11 April 1936.

'Spacious days of long ago: new flats for old mansions', *Sydney Morning Herald*, 23 July 1938; 'Flats at King's Cross. New buildings for 2000 people', *Sydney Morning Herald*, 25 August 1938.

As one notices, most apartment blocks adjoin each other. The fact is that building by-laws were ignored. The blocks of flats should have been separated from one another by laneways some three to six feet wide to provide adequate ventilation: 'Flats in King's Cross. New by-laws', *Sydney Morning Herald*, 22 August 1939.

Ray Mathew *The Life of the Party,* Currency Press; his obituary was by Myfanwy Gollan, 'Literary wit with the wavy brown hair', *Sydney Morning Herald*, 25 June 2002.

'King's Cross, Sydney's Little Europe', *Advertiser*, 7 October 1939, by the novelist Ernestine Hill (1899–1972). 'It's a quiet life at King's Cross', *Mail*, 25 November 1939 (rules for tenants about noise: 'You must not play your radio after 10.30 pm or before 9 am …'); 'Suggested renaming of King's Cross', *Sydney Morning Herald,* 7 November 1939; R.A. Simpson 'King's Cross: Sydney's Bohemia', *Sydney Morning Herald*, 9 September 1939 (landladies and communists); 'Sydney communists: rowdy meetings', *Townsville Daily Bulletin*, 1 December 1931; 'Pepper-throwing communist', *Examiner*, 14 December 1931.

'Ghosts in crinolines: when King's Cross was dotted with stately homes', *Sydney Morning Herald*, 30 November 1937. (This long article has photographs of the various mansions, most in a state of decay, with Roslyn Hall in ruins.)

M.R. Pearson 'King's Cross as Australia's Bohemia', *Mail* (Adelaide),

18 February 1939. ('The population is 100,000 persons, and as many canines.' Sections on flowers and food: '…is it not a legend that no one at the Cross bothers to cook?')

No Names… No Pack Drill by Bob Herbert (1980). Landladies feature heavily in *Memories, Kings Cross*, including women like 'Irish Mary', as they do in other memoirs of the time. Jon Rose's *At the Cross* (1961) is one of the few books that features an adorable landlady who was fond of gays.

John Horbury Hunt was a Canadian who migrated to Australia in 1863. He underwent an apprenticeship with Sydney architect Edmund Blackett for seven years before starting his own practice. He designed cathedrals (Armidale's St Peter's Anglican Cathedral), churches, chapels, houses, homesteads and schools (Kincoppal, Rose Bay). His adventurous, distinctive architecture was considered to be twenty years in advance of his peers, according to the *Australian Dictionary of Biography*, 'some of it unequalled in the world at that time, and sowed the seeds of some aspects of modern architecture in Australia'.

Beggars

An early version of this chapter appeared in the *Griffith Review*, Number 22 .

Kings Cross is different

I have quoted from *Memories, Kings Cross 1936–1946,* cited above. Information about Peter Finch comes mainly from Trader Faulkner's biography (1979). Biographies of Errol Flynn, the *ABD* and 'Colourful Sydney Identity #93 Errol Flynn', *Time Out Sydney*, June 2012.

The newspaper file for Argus, 'the world's greatest mind reader and world famous telepathist' is extensive. He performed in Kings Cross of an afternoon at the Top Hat in 1937.

Betty Roland was a playwright and memoir writer. *The Devious Being* (1990) focuses on her time in Kings Cross where she lived for some years. Her most well-known play is *The Touch of Silk* (1942).

Trams: 'A girl injured', *Townsville Daily Bulletin*, 27 August 1932 (nine-year-old girl caught under tram, her left leg nearly severed); *Shooting Through: Sydney by Tram* by Caroline Butler-Bowden, Anne Campbell and Howard Clark (2009).

Kellett Street

John Newton 'Meat and greet', *Sydney Morning Herald*, 28–29 June 2003 (re the New York Restaurant). Noel Risby 'She who knows the score', *The Paper*, June 1998 (article on Maggie Krauser).

Alexander Male Escorts: 'From jail bird to brothel keeper', *Sydney Morning Herald,* 12 July 2003. The article is about Brian Roberts being jailed for four years in 1996 after he forged the will of his murdered client Ludwig Gertsch and stole $500,000. He was struck off as a solicitor, changed his surname to Mainwaring and opened up the brothel at number 52 Kellett Street.

One story that stays with me from the Mansions Hotel is that of a lonely woman called Emily Muriel Holland, who was a permanent resident. Just after the Second World War she was involved in a divorce from her appalling husband, John Holland, whom she had married in 1932. It didn't take her long to discover that he was often unfaithful to her. In 1937 he was a war correspondent in Asia when she joined him in Singapore. Things went badly and a few weeks later he told her he had grown so used to sex with Asian women he no longer wanted to be with European women. She managed to escape Singapore in 1942 but her husband was captured by the Japanese. He later broadcast propaganda for the enemy. I often thought of her sitting in her hotel room, devastated, and humiliated in court and in the newspapers, not just by the stigma of divorce from a compulsive philander but also a traitor.

Little Europe

Memories, Kings Cross, 1936–1946 has many anecdotes about the local attitudes to the Jews and other refugees.

There were countless articles published about Jews and refugees with people objecting to their growing presence in the Cross. In 'Alien refugees', a letter to the *Sydney Morning Herald*, 12 April 1944, George Berger, a refugee, denied that Kings Cross had become 'a mecca of thousands of refugees'.

Walter Magnus, *ADB*. The essay by Margaret Kartomi, Francis Dreyfus and John Whiteoak, 'Berlin to Bondi: the flight of the Weintraub Syncopators' was published in 2004 by Giramondo and later expanded into a book by Francis Dreyfus, *Silences and Secrets: The Australian Experience of the Weintraub Syncopators* (2013).

Ernestine Hill 'Sydney's Little Europe' (the ubiquitous 'Auf Wiedersehn' and 'Tell Hitler he can have Danzig if he'll give us back King's Cross'). The joke about 'someone spoke to me in English' comes from Frank Roberts 'Kings Cross today', *The Bulletin*, 3 February 1962.

In 1954 Isaac Kahn, well known for his charity, sold the Oriental Hotel to the Queensland Temperance Union for £250,000 even though the local breweries were offering up to £300,000.

The Devil is a woman

Main sources for this chapter include two books by Nevill Drury: *Pan's Daughter: The Strange World of Rosaleen Norton* (1988) and *The Witch of Kings Cross* (2002); also Marguerite Johnson 'The witching hour: sex magic in the 1950s Australia', *Journal for the Academic Study of Magic* Issue 5.

Norton's desire to have a penis is from *The Witch of Kings Cross* page 42 where it is said she 'often' expressed this fantasy. *The Art of Rosaleen Norton with Poems by Gavin Greenlees, with an Introduction by Nevill Drury* (1982 edition) has both colour and black and white reproductions of her art, which shows little evidence of good draughtsmanship and at times the drawings verge on kitsch.

Richard Moir self-published a book in 1994 about Norton, *Rosaleen Norton – Kings Cross Witch,* subtitled *Face to Face in the Elusive Years 1969–1979*. It was printed in Old Gothic script and only on one side of each page. Moir wrote about being kissed by Rowie who 'was a good tongue-kisser – at fifty-three she kissed like a sensual, experienced 20-year-old.' The book was a limited edition of 250 copies (mine is 76). There have been stage shows about Norton (*The Devil is a Woman*), documentaries, and Robert G. Barrett's novel *Rosa-Marie's Baby* (2003).

Newly released information about the Goossens and Norton scandal comes from David Salter's 'The conductor, the witch and the vice squad', *Good Weekend*, 3 July 1999. The youngest daughter of Goossens, Renee, wrote a memoir about her father called *Belonging*. She has kind words for her father, none for her wicked stepmother and only a pained response to her own mother's cold aloofness.

'Toulouse-Lautrec mural judged obscene', *Canberra Times*, 30 April 1954.

Kings Cross Road

TROVE supplied various reports including: 'Viciously attacked by eagle', *Burnie Advocate*, 12 January 1950; 'Eagles as pets "a scandal", says woman victim', *Argus*, 12 January 1950; 'Eagle swoops down on child in King's Cross yard', *Sydney Morning Herald*, 12 January 1950.

As Jack Lindsay writes in *The Roaring Twenties*, he and his brother Ray lived there for a time when it was Woolcott Street, and watched 'prostitutes dance with their bludgers ... and clients dancing in the moonlight'.

Georgina Safe 'Sticks and stones ... we'll break their bones, say art vigilantes', *The Australian*, 16 June 2003. The article relates how 'art vigilantes' were threatening to ruin the sculpture *Stones Against the Sky*, dubbed 'Poo on Stilts' by locals.

Helen Greenwood 'Full of beans' *Sydney Morning Herald*, 26 June 2007 (about Café Hernandez).

Gaby Naher's memoir *The Truth About My Fathers* has some delightful memories of and information about the sumptuous and legendary Belvedere Hotel.

Septic Tanks

The Diaries of Donald Friend, Volumes 2 and 3.

The best book on American servicemen in Australia is the thorough *Yanks Down Under 1941–45: The American Impact on Australia* by E. Daniel Potts and Annette Potts (1985). Probably the most extensive newspaper article on runaway girls in the war years was in the *Mail* (Adelaide), 7 October 1944.

'Vivid story of life in gaol and big city slums', a review of *The Joyful Condemned* in the *Australian Women's Weekly*, 20 May 1953. *No Names ... No Pack Drill*, Bob Herbert's play about an American soldier going AWOL during the Second World War was staged at the Sydney Opera House in 1980 with Mel Gibson as the American.

Memories, Kings Cross has vivid anecdotes about the impact of American servicemen. Betty Roland writes about them in *The Devious Being*.

'Underground streams: location by diviners', *Barrier Miner*, 22 April 1942.

'You find this ugly, I find it lovely'

Two biographies of Kenneth Slessor that I consulted were *A Man of Sydney: An Appreciation of Kenneth Slessor* (1997) and Geoffrey Dutton's *Kenneth Slessor* (1991). A generous selection of his poems, essays, letters and journalism is contained in *Kenneth Slessor* edited by Dennis Haskell (1991) and *Kenneth Slessor, Selected Poems* (1993) is the perfect introduction to his superb poetry.

Bayswater Road

TROVE proved an excellent source, as did *Across the Border: Kings Cross Blog*: 'Hensley Hall', 13 April 2012. *My Darlinghurst Blog* is also very informative.

Minton House on the corner of Bayswater and Darlinghurst Roads was home to Australia's independent film community for over twenty-five years. More than 100 documentaries and feature films were developed, written, produced or scored at Minton House. Filmmakers Jane Campion and Baz Luhrmann had offices there. Late in 2004 it was saved from being turned into a huge backpacker's hostel.

The neon lights are being turned on again

'Only one night club open', *Sydney Morning Herald*, 16 August 1945. (It was the Roosevelt.)

'Wife left home to be an escapologist', *Mail*, 19 August 1944.

Herbert Eisen, 'Sydney's Montmartre', *Argus*, 31 March 1945; Leslie F. Hannon 'A new day at "The Cross"', *Sydney Morning Herald*, 1 October 1946 ('Kings Cross has two faces ...'); 'There's really no King's Cross', *Worker* (Brisbane), 21 July 1947 ('The shops show the cosmopolitanism of the place ...'); 'Delicacies at "The Cross"', *Courier-Mail*, 15 July 1950 ('Kings Cross has become the mecca for people with a taste for Continental foods').

Marilyn Lake *Faith Bandler, Gentle Activist* (2002) and Faith Bandler's Wikipedia entry.

'Theft of cocaine: chemist on six charges', *Sydney Morning Herald*, 17 June 1948 (Henry Eyre, chemist); 'Vice squad make raid in Sydney', *Barrier Miner*, 13 September 1949 (a Maltese man charged with having marijuana in his possession); 'Sex drug charge', *Courier-Mail*, 13 September 1949; '12 months gaol for possession of marijuana', *Canberra Times*, 28 January 1950. (Eric Raymond Cook: 'Under its influence even children would commit crimes of violence.')

'Gambling dens open under eyes of the police', *Daily News*, 12 September 1949 ('While a reporter watched outside the King's Cross school, a uniformed policeman ...').

'Baccarat drama unfolds in court', *Mail*, 9 February 1952. (Baccarat school at Kings Cross run by 'The Pig' and 'The Greek'.)

'Police baccarat raid story', *Sydney Morning Herald*, 24 April 1953. (In the article it was reported that police raided a lavish baccarat school fitted with warning devices at Roslyn Gardens.) 'Jack Davey in gambling raid', *Barrier Miner*, 23 March 1953 (Roslyn Gardens).

An enterprising boy, Perc Galea started out part-owner of an illegal gambling joint in Elizabeth Bay. In 1953 police raided it and arrested 46 gamblers. From then on he bribed police so successfully that he was rarely raided. He opened the Victoria Club on the site of the present Kings Cross police station. It offered baccarat, roulette, blackjack and craps, free food and alcohol and 'a bevy of hostesses in skimpy evening frocks who doubled as escorts'. It became a fashionable place to be seen, attracting entertainment figures, politicians, lawyers and sportsmen. During R&R the demand was so great he opened up other premises. Sartorially elegant, he was nicknamed 'The Prince'. In 1985 it was alleged in a police intelligence report that the illegal casinos had 'provided colossal cash flows to the underworld and enabled organised crime to consolidate its power in Sydney'.

'Lonely Yanks Roam Sydney', *Argus*, 1 May 1954 ('... 3,000 American sailors from Admiral Halsey's "Goodwill Fleet" now in Sydney').

John Huxley 'Revealed: ASIO history at the Cross roads', *Sun-Herald*, 24 October 2010; 'Sydney Man Fears Assassination: Closely Resembles Petrov' *Cairns Post*, 5 July 1954.

William Dobell's painting *Kings Cross* was of smooching, talking couples seen from his apartment window. Also consulted was *William Dobell: An Artist's Life* by Elizabeth Donaldson (2010). Years later a local artist, Tony Johansen, faced more than $500,000 in legal costs after losing his attempt to have the 2004 Archibald Prize given to Craig Ruddy's portrait of David Gulpilil overturned. Johansen was penniless. He had asked to paint Mandy and me; the result was so awful that Mandy wanted to buy the picture and 'destroy it'.

Dorothy Drain wrote about the Cross many times. She arrived as a young journalist and stayed, becoming editor of the *Australian Women's Weekly*.

Women on the edge

TROVE proves the Shirley Beiger case took up an extraordinary amount of space in Australian newspapers during 1954. Some headlines at random include: '"Not guilty," pleads model: challenged jurors in a firm voice', *Courier-Mail*, 23 November 1954; 'Police claim model admitted firing gun', *Courier-Mail*, 7 September 1954. The long article on the moral ramifications of Beiger's de-facto relationship is in 'The Shirley Beiger case emphasises the research bureau finding that ... we condone the de facto union', *Western Mail*, 16 September 1954. There's also a chapter on Beiger and her trial in James Cockington's *Banned* (2005).

'Women in mêlée at King's Cross', *Canberra Times*, 25 February 1946 ('Four women, two of them wearing scanty midriff costumes, staged a "donnybrook" in Victoria Street, King's Cross, last night.').

Some of the reports include: 'Policeman's plucky action in Sydney shooting case', *Sydney Morning Herald*, 23 May 1951 (Dorothy Thompson and Patsy Day); 'Two women charged: sequel to gun fight in King's Cross flat', *Cairns Post*, 12 April 1951 (Dorothy Thompson and Patsy Day); 'Flat quarrel. Woman "Pulled gun from frock"', *West Australian*, 15 January 1948; 'Woman hurts taxi driver', *Barrier Miner*, 22 November 1948; 'Sydney shooting: King's Cross affray', *Cairns Post*, 24 August 1945 (Stanley Keith Birch); 'Man shot at Kings Cross', *Mercury,* 22 August 1945; 'Gun duel between two women in King's Cross flat. Revolver versus rifle', *Cairns Post*, 11 April 1951 (Policeman Cooper).

Duncan McNab's *The Usual Suspect: The Life of Abe Saffron* (2005) is a surprisingly circumspect, even defensive portrait of Saffron. *Mr Sin* by Tony Reeves (2007) seems more accurate and therefore damning. Alan Saffron's biography *Gentle Satan: My Father, Abe Saffron* (2008) is a personal interpretation of his notorious father but is undermined by a lack of research and a moral squeamishness. Mark Dapin's novel *King of the Cross* (2009) is obviously based on Saffron, though the eighty year old is called Mendoza.

Roberta Sykes writes of her Kings Cross experiences in *Snake Dancing* (1988).

When there were reports of striptease parties in 1940 police were horrified that girls would allow themselves to strip in front of a room full of men who paid 15 shillings for the privilege. Their act consisted of appearing in flimsy, flowing clothes and as they danced the girls removed garments one at a time until they were almost naked. The police couldn't understand how a girl would undress in front of 'a mob of men' and how could they protect them? Unable to control these strip parties, police feared that they would spread into the 'dives' of Kings Cross: 'Strip-tease parties growing in Sydney: 15/- for near nudity', *Sydney Morning Herald*, 1 August 1940.

Llankelly Place

Apparently the correct pronunciation is *Thlankethly*.

Philip Cornford, 'Men bowed heads before being beaten to death' *Sydney Morning Herald*, 20 February 1997.

Daniel Scott, 'Storrier with a happy ending', *Sun-Herald*, 30 March 2008; Susan Kurosawa, 'Art transplant', *The Australian*, 14–15 June 2008 (a mixed review of the newly opened Storrier Hotel). Storrier's comment about Kings Cross is in 'The art of inspiring a hotel', *Sydney Morning Herald*, 4 February 2008.

One Saturday I was having a late lunch outdoors with Mandy at LL Wine & Dine restaurant in Llankelly Place when I saw the familiar unkempt, shuffling figure of Rose working her way up the lane begging from customers sitting outside cafés and restaurants. By this stage in our relationship we had an unspoken agreement that she wouldn't ask us for money but that either Mandy or I would give her five or ten dollars, but on our instigation rather than hers. When she came to our restaurant diners were horrified and looked away when she held out her hand. I called her over and Mandy gave her five dollars. Much to the disgust of the other customers she stayed to talk to us. Homeless for years, she had finally been given a housing commission apartment. Part of the agreement was that she had to give up heroin.

'I'm on the 'done now,' she smiled, pleased to be surviving on methadone. 'Course I need the yandy,' she said, which was probably part of the reason she continued to beg, as she smoked a lot of marijuana. She was clutching a *Good News Bible* and was looking depressed. Her older sister had just died. I asked her how old her sister had been.

'Sixty,' she said. 'I'm ten years younger.' I couldn't believe Rose was fifty. She looked ancient and yet ageless. 'Her son is very upset,' she said, asking if we knew him. We did. The son was a regular face around the Cross. Small like a jockey, with a street tough chihuahua always at his side, he is always on the move, making deals and being a useful go-between. The funeral had been postponed because Moree, where the family had come from, was isolated by floods. She shuffled off down the strip to continue her begging, much to the relief of the diners around us who were, judging by their reactions, visitors to the Cross.

The Glittering Mile

The 1964 documentary *The Glittering Mile* is available on YouTube. The documentary *Beyond El Rocco*, directed by Kevin Lucas, was released 1990.

Marien Dreyer, who lived in Kings Cross Road, 'The Dirty-Half Mile', was a serial complainer, as one sees in *The Glittering Mile*. Her plays are forgotten today (one was set in a Kings Cross flat, *Bandicoot on a Burnt Ridge*). She kept a diary of activities she had witnessed as proof for the police whom she called over a hundred times. She complained about noisy parties, prostitution in doorways and a woman sitting on a ledge opposite her window wearing nothing but a hat.

Kenneth Slessor and Robert Walker, *Life at the Cross* (1965) is a gentle view of Kings Cross, whereas the photographic book *Kings Cross Sydney* (1971) by Rennie Ellis and Wesley Stacey is a much harder look at the drugs and sex culture starting to prevail in the Cross.

Frank Crook wrote about Lee Gordon in 'Flash Gordon made Sydney rock 'n' roll', *Daily Telegraph*, 1 October 2007. The documentary filmmaker Hugh Piper was a fund of information about Gordon. I also consulted *ADB*.

Sandra Nelson was 'a mad lay' in Frank Black's *Kings Cross Double Cross*. Lim Yew Hock's biography and infatuation with Nelson was sourced from Wikipedia and newspapers of the time.

Name Dropping: An Incomplete Memoir by Kate Fitzpatrick (2004).

In 1958 *Truth* noted an increase of 66 per cent in homosexual offences in New South Wales, from 286 in 1954 to 475 in 1957. The newspaper blamed English influences 'where, in some circles, homosexuality almost amounts to one of the social graces'. As Charles Higham relates in his memoir *In and Out of Hollywood* (2009), even Kings Cross was a dangerous place to be on 'the beat' because of police entrapment. But by the early 1960s gays became such an intrinsic part of the Cross that the 1966 edition of *Camp*, an American guide to 'interesting institutions', mentioned gay haunts like the Chevron hotel's Quarterdeck Bar, Les Girls, the Rex Hotel and 'The park around the public library and El Alamein Fountain' as pick-up sites and gay friendly.

Source material for gays and drag shows comes from: *Carmen: Having a Ball* (1988); *Carlotta, I'm Not That Kind of Girl* (2003); *Camp Nites: Sydney's Emerging Drag Scene in the '60s* by Pride History Group (2006); *Camp as a Row of Tents: The Life and Times of Sydney's Camp Social Clubs* by Pride History Group (2007); and *New Day Dawning: The Early Years of Sydney's Gay and Lesbian Mardi Gras* by Pride History Group.

Roslyn Street

An important reference for Vittorio's biography is the chapter on him in *People of the Cross: True Stories from People who Live and Work in Kings Cross* by Gina Lennox and Frances Rush (1993).

Chris Ruhle 'He's back: Vittorio returns with a revamped Piccolo Bar', *Sydney City News*, 16 February 2012. The Piccolo was in the tabloids when staff were caught selling marijuana. There were many front cover stories with hysterical headlines, like Adam Harvey's 'Coffee and pot', *Daily Telegraph*, 13 June 2000, which not only included the reporter witnessing dealing but had a photograph of 'a Piccolo Bar café assistant' ('Dealer') with a customer ('Buyer') who purchased a $20 bag of marijuana.

In two years Beach Haus was issued with more than sixteen breaches of compliance regulations. According to police, patrons exhibited 'a demeanour consistent with the use of party drugs'.

The new building erased any connection with the past. Few would know that the site of Gastro Park was frequently in the tabloids at the turn of the twenty-first century when it was a café known as the Café Amsterdam and after that the Café Karma. Both were equally infamous for selling marijuana. Undercover reporters chasing after a sensational and easy story would go to the café where they would be offered marijuana. The police were criticised for not closing the premises down but 'drug dens' like the Café Karma were difficult to prosecute; it could be done only under the 60-year-old *Disorderly Houses Act* and it took months to gather evidence for a conviction. There was no precise legislation which allowed the police to immediately close down premises which were selling drugs. A couple of years later, in 2002, the police raided Café Karma forty-eight hours after being granted new powers to close premises suspected of being used for drug trafficking. In October of that year the owner of Café Karma was charged with selling cannabis on the premises: 'Café owner charged', *Daily Telegraph*, 14 October 2002.

'It was like a horror movie in slow motion'

A romantic and not terribly accurate portrait of Surf City and the 1960s scene is in Billy Thorpe's *Sex and Thugs and Rock 'n' Roll* (1996). *Ted Noffs: Man of the Cross* by Phil Jarratt (1997) and TROVE. *Kylie Tennant: A Life* by Jane Grant (2006).

Peter Rees *Killing Juanita* (2004). Wendy Bacon, a journalist, was a fellow Victoria Street resident at the time of the Green Bans and knew Nielsen. She wrote about her when the New South Wales police reopened the investigation into Nielsen's disappearance twenty-two years before in 'Crusades of the Cross', *Sydney Morning Herald*, 5 March 1998. One of life's little ironies is that the feminist Anne Summers who protested against the destruction of the terraces at the time now lives in a restored one in Victoria Street.

Meredith Burgmann and Verity Burgmann, 'Green Bans Movement', *Dictionary of Sydney* website, www.dictionaryof sydney.org /entry/green_bans_movement. Also Meredith Burgmann and Verity Burgmann *Green Bans, Red Union* (1998).

Les Kennedy 'Lover pleads to let Juanita rest in peace', *Sydney Morning Herald*, 5 July 2005. On the thirtieth anniversary of her disappearance Neilsen's lover for seven years, David Farrell, pleaded for anyone who knew the truth about her death to 'come forward now'.

In 2013 Eddie Trigg died. There was a frantic search for a manuscript he had written in which he purported to reveal the true story of Nielsen's murder and claimed to know where her remains were: it wasn't found, of course (*The Australian*, 4 March 2013). Neil Mercer also wrote a story about Trigg: 'Trigg takes truth behind murder to the grave', *Sun-Herald*, 3 March 2013.

Ray Chesterton 'Remembering Juanita Nielsen', *Daily Telegraph*, 5 July 2000, was a piece about the twenty-fifth anniversary of the day she went missing and the annual get-together of her friends and relatives.

Toby Johnstone, 'Murdered activist's home on the market', *Sun-Herald*, 5 May 2013. Nielsen's former home at 202 Victoria Street was listed for sale as having mixed-use zoning with approval to add another level. The selling agent said it would make an ideal 'retail, commercial or light-industrial development'.

Juanita Nielsen's death has haunted our writers and filmmakers. Her life has been the subject of the semi-fictional films *Heatwave* and *The Killing of Angel Street;* there is a biography of her, *Killing Juanita*, by Peter Rees, and a fictionalised version in Mandy Sayer's novel *The Cross*. Every fourth of July a handful of mourners gather outside the former

Carousel nightclub to commemorate the anniversary of her murder. Victoria Street, which now looks like the splendid boulevard it once was, owes her and the BLF much.

Fitzroy Gardens

Elizabeth Meryment, 'La Croix', *Sunday Telegraph* review of 'a new Potts Point concept store and café that brings together French provincial furniture and a "tartine bar"'.

Delia Falconer, 'The Bird Man and Mrs Gluck', *The Monthly*, 31 March 2011.

Malcolm Brown's obituary of Malcolm Duncan: 'Outspoken barrister argued with passion', *Sydney Morning Herald*, 22 March 2011.

Maggie Hus sold Maggie's restaurant in 2012. As she said, during her time in the area she 'developed more compassion towards people'. She summed up the Cross as a place where you 'see the stars and the beggars. That's what life is all about.' Louis Nowra 'Crossing over', *Sydney Morning Herald*, 28 August 2008.

The Lord Mayor wouldn't have liked such headlines as 'Moore backdown on Fitzroy Gardens makeover pleases Cross locals', *Sydney Morning Herald*, 17 May 2011 and 'Moore backs down on Fitzroy Gardens', *Wentworth Courier*, 18 May 2011.

Tim Bristow took Sinatra to the illegal casino run by Eli Rose and Perc Galea described in Kevin Perkins *Bristow: Last of the Hard Men* (2003).

'Edelsten tells of torrid affair', *Daily Telegraph*, 24 April 2012 and Miranda Devine's 'Total turn-off', *Daily Telegraph*, 25 April, 2012. Other articles had such juicy headlines as 'Clive ripe for affair: Edelsten' and 'Edelsten says she had affair with Clive James'.

Kitchen of Hell

Laurie Smith, 'Kitchen of Hell', *Daily Mirror*, 25 October 1979 (Loretta: 'Lord knows I'm no paragon of virtue …')

Toni Eattes 'Girls staffing first sex "palace"', *Sunday Telegraph*, 14

December 1980; Graham Williams et al, 'Fears that child prostitutes will go to suburbs', *Sydney Morning Herald*, 20 March 1981 (in this piece Noffs described child prostitution as having 'reached contagious proportions').

Nancy Berryman, 'The new and old faces of Kings Cross', *Sun-Herald*, 20 December 1980 (Meals on Wheels and the 157 Pleasure Spa).

Nancy Berryman and Andrew Watson, *Sun-Herald*, 30 September 1979 (Costello's, young boys, child prostitutes; '250 boys make their living from prostitution in the Cross'); Louise West and John Hewitt 'Orphans of the night', *Sunday Telegraph*, 16 March 1980; Dennis Minogue 'The changing faces of the Cross', *The Age*, 8 February 1975 (gays, sex clubs and sleaze); David Halpin 'Vile teen trade in "cabarets"', *Sun-Herald*, 22 March 1981; John Murphy 'Kelly, 19, is already old', *Sunday Telegraph*, 22 March 1981; Graham Williams 'Kings Cross: home for 650 street children', *Sydney Morning Herald*, 17 July 1981.

Men wanted to have sex with men dressed as women. Transsexuals – trannies, that is, men who took hormones, developed breasts and did 'tape jobs' to hide their penises – worked the shadowy lanes off William Street. The act was generally in a client's car or if they wanted it in a room they had to pay an extra $5. On a good night a trannie could take home between $300 and $400. It was dangerous work, especially before midnight when groups of hoons passing by in their hotted up cars yelled abuse or threw stones. Then there were the cops demanding money; if they didn't get it they'd smash up the trannie. As one said of the cops, 'They are vile. They refer to you as a joke. They threaten you with sexual violence at the station. They humiliate you.'

Costello's gay club: Malcolm Brown, 'Boys in club were drugged, then ravaged', *Sydney Morning Herald*, 13 May 1996; transcript of ABC radio program *PM* of 1 February 2000, reporter Eleanor Hall; David Brearley 'Ward tells of rough sex with Marsden', *The Australian*, 2 February 2000 (Raymond Leary alleged he was raped by John Marsden, the former New South Wales Law Society president, in a Costello's cubicle when Leary was eleven in 1972).

Jim Anderson: Rachel Morris 'Farewell to king of the Cross', 16 July 2003. Virginia Perger's history, her comments about Jim Anderson, etc. are in Kate McClymont's 'The Virginia monologues', *Good Weekend*, 26 November 2005. Perger's drug dealing is in Haken's memoir, *Confessions of a Crooked Cop* by Sean Padraic as told by Trevor Haken (2005).

It was perilous being a woman prostitute. Marion Rooney was a 29-year-old hooker who worked out of room 21 at the Mayfair Hotel. She was a suburban mother of four children and neither her husband nor children knew she was a prostitute. Rooney was known at the Mayfair as Blonde Jan. She was described as a naturally happy person who was always laughing. By the early evening of 30 December 1971 she had had sex with one client on the carpet of her rented room and then with a soldier. It was at around 8 pm when she approached a 19-year-old soldier, Gary Porth. He had previously been discharged from the Army, suffered head injuries after being hit by a falling tree, undergone treatment at a psychiatric hospital and then rejoined the Army. He had only had one sexual experience with a girl before. Blonde Jan touched him on the groin area when they were in the lounge, which so disturbed him that he left, but she caught up with him near the elevator. He said he didn't want to go with her, but she was persistent and he eventually agreed, even though he said he was nervous and didn't want to have sex with her. In room 21 he started to undress and when he finally removed his shirt she laughed at him and his embarrassment. He told her to stop but she kept on laughing. Humiliated and upset at being taunted, he threw a Coke bottle at her. She fell to the floor and then got up and, as he said in court, 'screamed and screamed at me, calling me a rotten mongrel and things like that. What with the grog and her screaming, I lost my head I suppose, and I hit her to stop her screaming.' They wrestled and she scratched him. He picked up a handkerchief, a man's one that was not his, and wrapped it tightly around her neck. The next thing he remembered was kneeling beside her, she was unconscious and her panties were off, which he did not remember doing. He tried to stop the bleeding with a towel but he couldn't. Scared at what he had done, and not willing to check if she were dead or not, he ran down the stairs and out into the street where he calmed down sufficiently to return to the lounge, where he sat down and awaited arrest. The police found Rooney naked, except for a brassiere pulled down from her breasts, a towel wrapped around her throat, a blood stained pillow near her head and blood splattering the bed quilt and wash basin in the corner of the room. Porth's mental illness and inadequacy with women were taken into account and he was sentenced to ten years jail for manslaughter.

In the middle 1970s Saffron leased the building at number 107–109 Darlinghurst Road, near where the railway station is now. In the 1950s he had shown imported pornographic movies at stag nights, but twenty years on these were legal and not a little innocent compared to the stuff he was now allowed to sell openly. On the ground floor was a sex shop selling pornographic books, with coin-operated booths for masturbating to videos, and a range of fetish and rubber clothing. On the next floor was an illegal casino, and the top floor was a brothel. For five years it earned Saffron a fortune. In 1978 police alleged it was being used for 'improper purposes' and in January 1980 it closed down, but it didn't matter because his empire was flourishing. Practically every night he toured the Cross, dropping in unannounced at his strip shows, brothels, casinos, restaurants and nightclubs, making sure things were operating smoothly, enjoying the deference everyone gave him. As one of his favourite crooners, Edwin Duff, sang in his 'Heartbeat of Sydney', 'Abe is the Boss'.

One of the most thorough biographies of Elizabeth Burton is in *People of the Cross* (1993) by Gina Lennox and Frances Rush. Bianca O'Neill, 'Colourful Sydney Identity #29 Elizabeth Burton', *Time Out Sydney*, 28 May–3 June 2008.

'At 16, she stripped, tripped and died', *Daily Mirror*, 11 July 1975. Nancy Berryman, 'Danielle's dream: to be best stripper: For her sailor hubby's sake she wears a wig', *Sun-Herald*, 28 September 1980.

In Berryman's report, Danielle said she used an alias because she didn't want her husband, who was in the Navy, to know what she did. Danielle wanted to be a stripper since she first saw a performance back home in France. She was too shy to strip for an audience until she was twenty-three and she got a job in a German peep show where she posed in a small circular room while voyeurs paid to peer at her through portholes and play with themselves. 'There were so many eyes but it was good money, $350 a week.' When she came to Sydney with her Australian husband she grew bored and started stripping in a George Street cinema.

Doody Scott Pilkington was another Kings Cross stripper who viewed her act as art. In 1981 she performed her one-woman show at the Adelaide Festival. 'The Stripper's Progress' consisted of four dances and reminiscences about her life as a stripper. A critic in *Theatre Australia* was stirred enough to write about how Doody 'used classic Brechtian alienation devices combined with elements of contemporary performance art to create a gutsy and challenging piece that was funny and deeply moving'. Doody had been dancing since 1969 when she gave up her job as an art teacher at Bendigo Girls High and came to Sydney to work at the Pink Panther, the Paradise Club and the Pink Pussycat. Her show recalled her days at the Cross, some of the strippers she worked with and what they thought of 'the mugs' who made up their audiences: Richard Coleman, 'Doody bares her soul for culture', *Sydney Morning Herald*, 14 August 1981.

'Deaf mute stripper using sign language', *Pix,* 30 April 1972, a series of photographs of various poses of the stripper at the Pink Panther Strip Club (now in the State Library of New South Wales archives).

Re the Pussy Galore Strip Club: *Kings Cross Double Cross: From Boys' Home to Bagman* by Frank 'Tubby' Black with David Dunne. It includes anecdotes about Hollywood Jack.

Louis Benedetto ran Australia's first strip club the Pink Pussycat, for fifteen years at the top of William Street: James Oram, 'Last Card Louis shuffles off', *Sunday Telegraph*, 14 October 1990.

Re the murder of Graham Gaskill: 'Woman, girls charged with man's murder', *Sunday Telegraph*, 4 January 1981.

Don Walker's memoir *Shots* (2009).

Sammy Lee died in 1975. John Yeomans wrote about him the day after: 'King of the "girls"', *Daily Mirror*, 22 July 1975. (Sammy Lee 'refused to allow his three sisters to walk in Kings Cross after dark'.)

Macleay Street

Tony Stephens wrote an appreciation of the recently deceased Vadim. Born Vadim Kargopoloff in Shanghai, he lost both parents and came to Australia in 1948 with his Russian step-parents after fleeing the Chinese revolution: *Sydney Morning Herald*, 22 August 2003.

Paul Keating's terrace and his search for perfection: 'Perfect Paul's finishing touch', *Sunday Telegraph*, 20 May 2013.

Peter Finch was a frequent visitor to Manar for a couple of years in the late 1930s when he was pursing a relationship with Marian Morphy, who lived there with her mother. Finch was smelly, had a wandering eye and behaved badly when drunk. Morphy was older, attractive and sophisticated. She tried to smooth his rough edges and partly succeeded. It seems that the relationship lasted longer than it should have because Morphy's mother adored him.

There's an excellent essay about Stanley Korman in the anthology *In the Gutter ... Looking at the Stars* by Korman's nephew, Ivor Indyk: 'The Silver Spade'.

Tim Barlass and Naomi Toy 'Bob Ellis's lost days inside Room 412' and 'Little Miss "It": the baby girl Bob Ellis says isn't his', *Daily Telegraph*, 5 May 1999.

Caitlin O'Toole 'The village where posh meets spice', *Australian Financial Review*, 23–25 February 2007. In the same article the Rockwall apartment block is credited with 'bringing the area into a new "gentrified" era'.

Amy Harris 'Another shot of Bourbon', *Daily Telegraph*, 5 March 2013. There were many newspaper reports about Ricky Ponting's 'Night of Shame' in 1999. Paul Ham, 'A romantic B&B', *The Monthly*, April 2012.

Halfway between a circus and a sewer

Gary Hughes interview with Don Stewart on publication of his memoir, *Recollections of an Unreasonable Man: From Beat to Bench*. Stewart relates the story of how, when the police came to arrest Saffron, he opened the door wearing only red boxer shorts. When the cops handed him an arrest warrant he lost control of his bowels. 'His red shorts turned yellow and they had to take him to the bathroom to clean him up': *Weekend Australian*, 24–25 February 2007.

'Abe on the up and up and swearing by Viagra', *Sydney Morning Herald*, 23 June 2001. Saffron's photographs of the gangster 'Bugsy' Siegel and mobster Meyer Lansky are in Alex Mitchell's interview with Saffron: '"Mr Sin": The Cross I've had to bear', *Sun-Herald*, 6 November 2005.

Andrew Keenan 'Abe's mum wanted him to be a doctor', *Sydney Morning Herald*, 14 October 1987. Also by Andrew Keenan, 'Abe jailed – but we are none the wiser', *Sydney Morning Herald*, 29 November 1988. Alex Mitchell 'The Saffron dossier', *Sun-Herald*, 28 May 1989. Saffron's death was front page news, with editors and journalists thrilled to be able to call him 'Mr Sin': 'The Mr Sin of Sydney crime dead at 86', 'Saffron provides only colour at funeral of Mr Sin', 'Underworld or heaven, Mr Sin's gone', 'The wages of Mr Sin'.

Michael Duffy interviewed Clive Evatt, one of Sydney's best-known defamation lawyers, who had Saffron as a client. Evatt said of Mr Sin that he was 'Absolutely dedicated to defending his good reputation': *Sun-Herald* 15 April 2012. Hugh Piper made the documentary *Mr Sin: The Abe Saffron Story* in 2010. He thought 'Abe was like an old Testament emperor.'

Keith Gosman, 'Black Prince of the Cross', *Sun-Herald*, 5 July 1992. (An article on Saffron's murdered sidekick Peter Farrugia, 'the life and times of a remarkable mobster'.)

Lennie McPherson: Malcolm Brown 'A cut above a common criminal', *Sydney Morning Herald*, 29 August 1996; 'McPherson given 2½ years' jail', *Daily Telegraph*, 19 December 1994; 'Lennie McPherson dies in jail, aged 75', *Sydney Morning Herald*, 29 August 1996; Kate McClymont 'Number up for a colourful career', *Sydney Morning Herald*, 30 August 1996; Philip Cornford 'Lennie's pride and joy – a picture with Mafia big shots', *Sydney Morning Herald*, 30 August 1996; and Martin Warneminde 'Lennie's secrets revealed to son', *Sun-Herald*, 1 September 1996.

Detective Sergeant Trevor Haken became an informant for the Wood Royal Commission into corruption in the New South Wales Police Service. His 2005 memoir *Confessions of a Crooked Cop* (by Sean Padraic as told by Trevor Haken) is a riveting read about the frighteningly widespread vice and corruption in the New South Wales police force, especially in Kings Cross.

Bill Bayeh: Ray Chesterton 'Who's a silly Billy then?', *Daily Telegraph*, 29 May 1999; Letitia Rowlands 'Bye, bye Bill: Bayeh gets 15 years for drug offences', *Daily Telegraph,* 25 May 1999.

Louis Bayeh was shot three times in 2000. In 'Underworld shadow of little substance' by Candace Sutton, *Sunday Telegraph*, 9 July 2000, she interviewed a former associate of the Bayehs who said of the duo: 'Louis is the older brother. Bill Bayeh is smaller, smarter and better dressed, not that either of them is really smart.'

Martin Warneminde 'Inside Fat George's shooting gallery', *Sun-Herald*, 27 May 1995. Also by Warneminde: 'Too fat so George strips for a search', *Sun-Herald*, 4 June 1995. Karipis was so fat that Long Bay jail didn't have a pair of security overalls big enough to fit him.

The bust of a heroin distribution network operating out of the Elan apartments: Letitia Rowlands 'High rise "heroin ring" smashed', *Daily Telegraph*, 30 June 1999. Adam Harvey 'Dealing on easy street: drug sellers' thriving trade', *Daily Telegraph*, 28 June 1999 (drug dealing on Roslyn Street). Father Sinn and the drug problems at St Canice's in Malcolm Brown 'Drug war's front line is the grounds of a Kings Cross church', *Sydney Morning Herald*, 1 November 1999. The number of times junkies using heroin or cocaine shoot up in Greg Bearup's 'Dan, dirty – but safe', *Sydney Morning Herald*, 10 March 1999.

Charles Miranda articles: 'Copycat may be stalking streets with axe', 25 October 1997 and 'Kings Cross, where locals fear to tread', both in the *Daily Telegraph*. Les Kennedy followed a similar line with his 'Police fear axe killer copycats may be at large', in the *Sydney Morning Herald*, 25 October 1997.

Norma Chapman's obituary was published in the *Sydney Morning Herald*, 27 October 2004, under the heading 'Legendary bookseller of the Cross'.

John Silvester and Andrew Rule *Underbelly: The Golden Mile* (2010). Martin Warneminde, 'On the beat with Kings Cross cops', *Sun-Herald*, 30 April 1995.

The performing self

'Darling, I'm guilty', *Argus*, 11 February 1956 ('Luba Shishova, 34-year-old Russian bombshell made another sensational appearance in court today'); 'Raver: Hot Luba's cold war', *Daily Mirror*, 31 July 1981. Bea Miles, various newspaper articles, *Memories of Kings Cross* (only Kings Cross could absorb her). Kate Grenville's novel *Lilian's Story* (1986) and the film of the same name are based on her.

'Hector Bolitho here to write', *Sydney Morning Herald*, 11 July 1946 ('... the famous biographer of Royalty ... is working on his 35th book – a biography of Queen Victoria').

Ayesha's biography comes from *People of the Cross* and personal conversations.

Holly Farum's beauty and sexual allure are on display in some photographs in *The Complete Reprint of John Willie's Bizarre* (Taschen, 1995). She also appeared on the covers of magazines, including *People*. She is remembered fondly in *Memories, Kings Cross*.

Rejuvenation

Website Thewaysidechapel.com.au; Charles Waterstreet 'Fallen and the Wayside', *Sun-Herald*, 18 December 2011; 'Wayside's new lease of life',

Wentworth Courier, 23 May 2012; 'Crossing the road to help rebuild the Wayside Chapel', *Sun-Herald* 20 May 2012; Steve Meacham 'No falling by the wayside for this revamped institution', *Sydney Morning Herald*, 20 May 2012; plus the book *Stories from the Wayside* (2012) and Nick Dent, 'These people are part of the community, same as you and me. They have stories, interesting stories...', an interview with Reverend Graham Long, *Time Out Sydney*, April 2011.

Jodie Minus 'Lord Mayor throws books at sin strip' in the *Sydney Morning Herald,* concerns Lucy Turnbull's attempt to clean up the Cross. Scott Bolles 'At the Crossroads', *Sydney Morning Herald*, 24 June 2003 (the article describes how developers and planners want food to be the new sex in Kings Cross as the once-sleazy hub of Sydney is transformed into a fashionable playground).

The English newspaper *The Independent,* 22 March 2003, published a long article about Lord Mayor Frank Sartor's push to make the Cross 'safe and pleasant': Kathy Marks 'How Sydney's Lord Mayor plans to "civilise" the seedy, star-studded world of its red-light district'.

Larissa Cummings, 'The Cross stripped and dying', *Daily Telegraph*, 21 April 2006.

Anthony Dennis 'Neglected alley cat runs out of lives', *Sydney Morning Herald*, 31 May 2003 is about the closing down of the Pink Pussycat (the strippers were starting to outnumber the patrons). The piece also included Donald Horne's comment.

The interview with Frank Amante was in Nick Ralston and Lisa Davies 'The Red Light Goes Out', *Sun-Herald*, 1 April 2012.

Sean Nicholls 'You can't do that here: push to take the X out of the Cross', *Sydney Morning Herald*, 24 June 2003. (The new Lord Major of Sydney, Lucy Turnbull, sets out to 'discourage the continuation of the area as a red-light district'.)

Michelle Singer, 'How a romantic vision ignited a revival of the fittest', *Sun-Herald*, 2 April 2006. By 2006, 2500 people had moved into the area since the Olympics, boosting the population by eight per cent.

Bonnie Malkin 'City leaders want less of a blue hue in red-light district', *Sydney Morning Herald*, 28 December 2005. The article reported that the Lord Mayor Clover Moore wanted some of the Cross's infamous nightclubs and brothels, and the workers who spruik them, replaced by services for locals and a friendlier atmosphere. One Liberal councillor, Shayne Mallard wanted the council to buy the sex clubs, striptease venues, adults shops and convert them into 'more family-friendly businesses'.

Football players and the Cross: 'Footy in the firing line: the Kings Cross brawl that led to shooting', *Daily Telegraph*, 4 March 2008. Many other articles including: 'Eels face a curfew after shooting', 'Footballers plus alcohol and Kings Cross equals trouble', 'NFL star Hayne in Kings Cross Shooting', 'Players baited by idiots: provoked in Cross venue with a history of trouble' (re a shooting at the Sapphire Lounge in Kellett Street), and Peter FitzSimons writing about the Ponting incident and others featuring footballers in 'Looking for trouble? Try dipping into the Bourbon', *Sydney Morning Herald*, 1 January 1999.

John Ibrahim has tried to avoid talking about his background but as a 22-year-old he opened up in a chapter devoted to him in *People of the Cross* (1993) by Gina Lennox and Frances Rush. Wherever Ibrahim went he attracted trouble, even when overseas. Angela Kamper's front-page story, 'Cross King in Greek island punch-up: Ibrahim hits target of alleged murder plot', *Daily Telegraph*, 27 July 2010; Neil Mercer 'Untouchable? The law v John Ibrahim', *Sun-Herald*, 20 February 2011. There is a substantial Wikipedia entry on Ibrahim.

Andrew Horney 'Too fast to last', *Sun-Herald*, 27 January 2013 (Ibrahim crying for James Miller); Garry Linnell 'Farewelling a murdered mate: They came to lay a sinner to rest', *Daily Telegraph*, 16 October 2008. Miller died soon after the Santa Barbara opened in the former Piano Bar.

Katherine Danks 'I don't know how $3m in cash got in my roof', *Daily Telegraph*, 7 December 2011. Maha Sayour, sister of John Ibrahim, could not explain to the court how nearly $3 million in ninety-five heat-sealed plastic bags were found in a ceiling cavity during a police raid on her house. She pleaded not guilty.

Amy Dale 'Wife fears for her life', *Daily Telegraph*, 2 December 2011. (Sam Ibrahim's wife told the court that she would fear for her life if her husband, a former bikie boss, was sent to jail for kidnapping a teenage boy.)

Lisa Davies, 'Police see if bikie law can stop parlour', *Sydney Morning Herald*, 6 June 2012 ('New South Wales Police are considering invoking new anti-bikie laws to stop Kings Cross Ink, a new tattoo parlour with links to the nightclub boss John Ibrahim').

Yoni Bashan 'Bikie war over the Cross', *Sunday Telegraph*, 3 April 2012; Les Kennedy 'Exposed: the gruesome underbelly of a turf war', *Sun-Herald*, 5 December 2010; 'Kings Cross ban on bikie colours in bars', *Daily Telegraph*, 9 June 2011.

Neil Mercer, 'Why Kings Cross needs a quick fix', *Sunday Telegraph*, 13 November 2005. (About sixty shops in and around Darlinghurst Road are now for lease, boarded up or empty.)

John Kidman '800 deals a day and police can do nothing', *Sun-Herald*, 14 December 2003. The article concerned the worsening heroin crisis in Kings Cross. Most of the deals were done around the Bayswater Road public phone, a hop, skip and a jump from the injecting room.

Ingrid van Beek, the medical director of the injecting centre, wrote an account of the injecting centre, called *In the Eye of the Needle*. The book so incensed the Kings Cross barrister Malcolm Duncan that he spent $209.65 buying up all the copies in the local bookshop: 'Livid about a book launch', *Sydney Morning Herald*, 13 November 2004.

The conservative journalist Miranda Devine made her opposition to the injecting centre clear in her column titled 'Vale the old Kings Cross, victim of lethal injection', *Sun-Herald*, 28 September 2003; Janet Fife-Yeomans' report on Oxycontin use at the injecting room in 'Using cancer drug to make hillbilly heroin', *Daily Telegraph*, 27 October 2008.

Darlinghurst Road

Anne-Maree Whitaker insists in her *Pictorial History Kings Cross* that David Scott Mitchell's home, once 17 Darlinghurst Road, is the site of the present 'Browley' building, 65 Darlinghurst Road, which houses the Risqué adult shop.

Eamonn Duff 'Steroid vacation', *Sun-Herald*, 27 May 2012 (re Zyzz).

Ilya Gridneff 'John Ibrahim's bazooka-proof tattoo parlour', *Sun-Herald*, 20 May 2012.

'Man burned by oil at Macca's', *Wentworth Courier*, 15 February 2012 (a manager allegedly threw oil in a customer's face).

Some shootings showed a brazen contempt for the law. One gunman threw his victim to the ground and shot a man in the knee outside the Bada Bing strip club in Darlinghurst Road in view of dozens of night clubbers. The previous year, around the corner in Kellett Street, the owner of the Sapphire Bar was shot in the leg and on the same night another gunman tried to shoot a man in Ward Avenue. Asian gangs came to the Cross and in one incident at the Buddha Bar rival gang members had a shoot-out reminiscent of the wild west. One man died, another was shot in the back, another two were wounded in the legs.

'The trial of the Safi brothers', *Daily Telegraph*, 29 July 2010.

Lawrence's doom and gloom graffiti didn't last long. The board it was painted on was ripped down for an entrance to a backpackers. In early May 2013 the Housing Commission suddenly turfed harmless Lawrence out of his cave in the overgrown space opposite the Old Fitzroy Hotel. He gathered all his possessions together in a supermarket trolley and resorted to living on the streets.

We ♥ Kings Cross

The shooting of Troy Taylor and the young driver was in all the media, with headlines like 'Bloody ending to teen joyride', 'Anger grows over police shooting of joyriding juveniles', 'Cannabis and drink before a joy ride', 'I thought they must be bad guys, then I saw it was kids', 'Brutal

Kings Cross arrest sparks anger', 'Father of hit teen slams police' and 'Youth no stranger to police courts'.

The killing of Thomas Kelly: '"Please be careful": last words to a son killed in the Cross', *Sydney Morning Herald*, 11 July 2012; 'Violent city given pause as "good bloke" TK farewelled'; 'It's hard to believe he has been taken away'; 'King-hit killer identified'; 'Taming the Cross: Clover's plan to make the Strip safer'; 'Frightened girlfriend breaks her silence'; 'Dark Heart: how Kings Cross went from hedonism to hell'; 'Inside the Kings Cross cauldron'; 'Chilling allure of city's underbelly'; and 'Top cop's grim warning for Kings Cross'.

Richard Noone 'Violent young women are spiking the punch', *Daily Telegraph*, 9 August 2012 and 'Girls cheer as diggers bashed by Cross mob', *Daily Telegraph*, 1 June 2012.

Andrew Clennell 'Kings Cross club blitz: crackdown on venues in wake of violent killing', *Daily Telegraph*, 18 July 2012. Henry Budd 'Kings Cross crackdown "won't stop violence"', *Daily Telegraph*, 10 September 2012; this piece is about Kings Cross businesses launching a campaign in response to alcohol restrictions following the death of teenager Thomas Kelly. T-shirts were distributed, emblazoned with WE ❤ KINGS X.

Barclay Crawford 'A drunken teen crisis', *Sunday Telegraph*, 1 January 2013; Matthew Moore 'Streets get tough, laws get tougher', *Sydney Morning Herald*, 21–22 July 2012; 'Action on Kings Cross', *Sydney Morning Herald*, 18 July 2012; Andrew Clennell 'Tough Licensing laws to tame Kings Cross', *Daily Telegraph*, 16 August 2012.

The plaques project was overseen by the then City of Sydney historian Shirley Fitzgerald: 'Telling tales of the Cross', *Sunday Telegraph*, 19 December 2004. Linda Jaivin's response is in 'From BoHo to PoHo: plaques and decay. Can Kings Cross survive a $30 million facelift?', *The Monthly*, June 2005.

'Fulde saddened by death', *Wentworth Courier*, 25 July 2012 (a more violent society).

Tim Dick 'At the crossroads', *Sydney Morning Herald*, 18 September

2010 ('a new age of suburbanisation is dawning').

Eamonn Duff 'Boys on a sex romp out of their league', *Sun-Herald*, 11 September 2011 (the three school boys went to the Cross to hire a hooker).

Brad Newsome 'Medico team inspires a dose of wonder', one of the many reviews of *Kings Cross ER*, the reality program filmed in the emergency department of St Vincent's hospital.

The Music Tour in February 2013 included visits to the hotels, nightclubs and venues that were once part of the area's thriving music scene.

The amount written about Kings Cross, its characters and stories is extraordinary. Mandy and I edited an anthology, *In The Gutter ... Looking At The Stars, A Literary Adventure Through Kings Cross* (2000), which illustrates just how many important Australian authors wrote about the Cross. Over the years fiction has celebrated Kings Cross or used it as a shorthand for sleaze and corruption. Non-fiction works and biographies flourish as does nostalgia in such plays as Alex Harding's *Only Heaven Knows* or semi-autobiographical novels like *Angel Puss* by Colleen McCullough, set in Kings Cross in the 1960s, about X-ray technician Harriet who lives in a terrace peopled with bohemians, lesbians, painters, prostitutes and migrants. More common are the harsher views, like the 2004 play *Cross Sections*, a 24-hour snippet of life in Kings Cross about 'lost souls, rent boys, prostitutes and the homeless' or *Faith Singer* (2001) by Rosie Scott, a story about a washed-up rock star, Faith, a 14-year-old junkie and prostitute, Angel, and bent cops in the pay of a wealthy pedophile: in the Cross people are 'so smeared with evil I had to look away for safety'. Novelists like Richard Flanagan use the Cross as a site of debasement. In his *The Unknown Terrorist* the heroine, Gina Davies, who goes by the name 'the Doll', works as a pole dancer in a Kings Cross nightclub. The absurd story has the Doll become a prime suspect in the investigation into a foiled terrorist plot to blow up Sydney's Olympic Stadium.

In 1962 Frankie Davidson sang 'Have You Ever Been to See King's Cross?' which reached Number 8 on the hit parade. Since then Paul Kelly wrote 'Darling It Hurts' (1984), about seeing his girlfriend working as a prostitute on Darlinghurst Road ('I see you standing on the corner with your dress so high') but it is probably Don Walker's 'Breakfast at Sweethearts' which remains the most immediately identifiable song about the Cross. Then there are movies like *Angst* (2000), directed by Daniel Nettheim, about three self-obsessed flatmates in Kings Cross, and the crime drama *Two Hands* (1999). The TV series *Underbelly* proved immensely popular.

ACKNOWLEDGEMENTS

Phillipa McGuinness's enthusiasm for the project meant much to me. Linda Funnell's meticulous editing, despite the difficulty of the book's structure, was wonderful. I couldn't have asked for a better editor. All mistakes are mine.

Although the City of Sydney didn't fund this project, its historian, Lisa Murray, kindly read a draft and made some pertinent comments. John Moyle provided a story from his own life in 'Falling'. John Webber's photographs of the Cross were a great visual aid, as were Roz Sharp's. Ayesha is always fascinating to talk to as is Vittorio Bianchi of the Piccolo. Screensound has some interesting newsreels and amateur footage of Kings Cross. Michael Gormly's writings on the Cross were very informative. I worked with Hugh Piper on a film script about Lee Gordon and Lenny Bruce and the research was extremely valuable for the 1960s section. Warren Fahey shared his knowledge of the area with me and Murray Bail's choice of local restaurants gave me better insights into the importance of food to the local economy. Bill Harding bought me *At the Cross* and its affectionate portrait of Kings Cross in the early forties started me thinking about this book.

The Old Fitzroy Hotel reminds me of the old Cross, with its diverse clientele of heavy drinkers, tradies, sparkies, bohemians, gays, the mad and the dangerous, and it provided me with many characters who know Kings Cross well, including M.O., hard man and debt collector, who knew and worked for Saffron and the Bayehs. Graham Hill's recollections about cleaning and fixing a brothel spa still give me a shudder when I think about it. I also want to thank those sources who keep the illegal economy of the area going but, of course, cannot be named.

This book is dedicated to Mandy, who approached Phillipa and told her I wanted to write a book about Kings Cross. Her knowledge and experience of the Cross were a constant inspiration.